Colonial Origins
of the
American
Constitution

Colonial Origins

of the

American

Constitution

A DOCUMENTARY HISTORY

*Edited and with an
Introductory Essay by*
DONALD S. LUTZ

Liberty Fund

This book is published by Liberty Fund, Inc., a foundation established to encourage study of the ideal of a society of free and responsible individuals.

The cuneiform inscription that serves as our logo and as the design motif for our endpapers is the earliest-known written appearance of the word "freedom" (*amagi*), or "liberty." It is taken from a clay document written about 2300 B.C. in the Sumerian city-state of Lagash.

Library of Congress Cataloging-in-Publication Data

Colonial Origins of the American Constitution: a documentary history/
    edited by Donald S. Lutz
        p.   cm.
    Includes bibliographical references.
    ISBN 0-86597-156-0 (hc).—ISBN 0-86597-157-9 (pb)
        1. Constitutional history—United States—Sources.
    2. Constitutional history—United States—States—Sources.
    I. Lutz, Donald S.
    KF4502.C58   1998
    342.73'029—dc21   97-12481

Liberty Fund, Inc.
11301 North Meridian Street
Carmel, Indiana 46032

10 18 19 20 21 C 7 6 5 4 3
18 19 20 21 22 P 9 8 7 6 5

Contents

Preface xv

Introductory Essay xx

NEW HAMPSHIRE

1   Agreement of the Settlers at Exeter in New Hampshire,   3
    July 5, 1639
    The covenant that created Exeter's first town government.

2   General Laws and Liberties of New Hampshire,   5
    March 16, 1680
    *An apparent legal code for the province of New Hampshire that
    also lays out the government's institutions and powers.*

MASSACHUSETTS

3   Agreement Between the Settlers at New Plymouth   31
    (The Mayflower Compact), November 11, 1620
    The oldest and most famous colonial political covenant.

4   Plymouth Oath of Allegiance and Fidelity, 1625   33
    *The oldest surviving citizenship oath—designed to bring post-1620
    arrivals into the Mayflower Compact agreement.*

5   The Salem Covenant of 1629   35
    *Another citizenship oath, but one that functioned for several years
    as the only basis for town government.*

6   Agreement of the Massachusetts Bay Company at   36
    Cambridge, England, August 26, 1629
    *An equivalent to the Mayflower Compact but written by the
    colonists in England before they set sail.*

7 The Watertown Covenant of July 30, 1630 38
*Strictly speaking a church covenant, it is also a political covenant
because the settlers were establishing a theocracy.*

8 Massachusetts Election Agreement, May 18, 1631 40
The oldest colonial provision for a formal electoral process.

9 The Oath of a Freeman, or of a Man to Be 41
Made Free, 1631
*Until 1631 almost all freemen had been politically bound by the
church covenant. This oath covered nonchurch members.*

10 The Massachusetts Agreement on the Legislature, 43
May 9, 1632
*The first formal specification of Massachusetts political institutions
and, although brief, still a protoconstitution.*

11 Cambridge Agreement, December 24, 1632 45
*Town meetings predated this document, but it is the oldest
surviving agreement formally establishing the institution.*

12 Dorchester Agreement, October 8, 1633 46
*Establishes a town meeting and is the oldest document to create an
elected council to run government between meetings.*

13 Cambridge Agreement on a Town Council, 48
February 3, 1634
An ordinance passed by the town meeting creating a town council.

14 Massachusetts Agreement on the Legislature, 50
May 14, 1634
*A revision of, and enlargement upon, The Massachusetts
Agreement on the Legislature [10], which looked like a
constitution and essentially functioned as one.*

15 The Oath of a Freeman, May 14, 1634 52
*Replacement for The Oath of a Freeman [9], which reflects an
evolving sense of citizenship by not requiring church membership.*

16 Salem Oath for Residents, April 1, 1634 54
An oath for noncitizen residents.

17 Watertown Agreement on Civil Officers, August 23, 1634 56
Ordinance establishing the town's first civil offices.

18 The Enlarged Salem Covenant of 1636   57
*Much longer than the document it replaces, The Salem Covenant
of 1629 [5], this covenant dwells on the values and commitments
held in common.*

19 Plymouth Agreement, November 15, 1636   60
*A brief, powerful statement of popular sovereignty—inserted later
into the Pilgrim Code of Law [20].*

20 Pilgrim Code of Law, November 15, 1636   61
*Not really a code of law but a political covenant/compact that
looks like and serves as a true constitution.*

21 Dedham Covenant, 1636   68
The agreement that established Dedham's town government.

22 The Massachusetts Body of Liberties, December 1641   70
*Important code of law that contains most of the rights in the U.S.
Bill of Rights, at least eight of which originate here.*

23 The Combination of the Inhabitants upon the   88
    Piscataqua River for Government, October 22, 1641
*A political compact resting town government on popular
sovereignty.*

24 Massachusetts Bicameral Ordinance, March 7, 1644   90
The first explicit creation of a bicameral legislature.

25 Massachusetts Ordinance on the Legislature,   92
    November 13, 1644
An ordinance altering the size and mode of electing the legislature.

26 The Laws and Liberties of Massachusetts, 1647   95
*A codification of earlier laws, this organic act also functioned as a
constitution for the colony.*

27 Massachusetts Ordinance on Legislative Procedure,   136
    October 18, 1648
*The earliest formal specification of internal legislative procedures
in the colonies.*

28 Towns of Wells, Gorgiana, and Piscataqua Form an   139
    Independent Government, July 1649
*Three towns in an area claimed by Massachusetts later to become
Maine use a compact to create a joint government.*

29 The Cambridge Agreement of October 4, 1652   141
    The Cambridge town meeting lays out the basic values and
    principles that are to guide Cambridge's elected representatives.

30 Puritan Laws and Liberties, September 29, 1658   143
    A revision of the Pilgrim Code of Law [20] and thus, in effect, an
    amending of the constitution of the Plymouth Colony.

31 An Act of the General Court, June 10, 1661   158
    The basic principles of Massachusetts government and also an
    attempt to define the relationship between colony and king.

RHODE ISLAND

32 Providence Agreement, August 20, 1637   161
    A brief political compact resting on popular sovereignty, and the
    earliest colonial attempt to separate church and state.

33 Government of Pocasset, March 7, 1638   163
    The political covenant that established the Pocasset town
    government.

34 Newport Agreement, April 28, 1639   165
    A brief, general compact establishing town government on the
    basis of popular sovereignty.

35 The Government of Portsmouth, April 30, 1639   166
    An unusual foundation document in that town government is
    grounded on an implicit civil covenant.

36 Plantation Agreement at Providence, August 27, 1640   168
    A compact written and adopted by representatives specifically
    elected to design a system of government by arbitration.

37 Organization of the Government of Rhode Island,   172
    March 16–19, 1642
    A compact that explicitly establishes a "Democracie," or "Popular
    Government," for the combined towns of Rhode Island.

38 Warwick Agreement, August 8, 1647   176
    The representatives of Warwick establish town government on
    popular approval of a civil covenant sanctioned by the king.

39 Acts and Orders of 1647   178
    This code of law also contains the institutional description that
    allows it to function as a constitution for the colony.

40 Charter of Providence, March 14, 1649   204
    Providence is granted a charter for its government by the colony
    government at the request of the freemen.

41 General Assembly of Rhode Island Is Divided into   207
    Two Houses, March 27, 1666
    The colony's legislature amends the Acts and Orders of 1647 [39]
    to divide itself into two separate houses.

                                    CONNECTICUT

42 Plantation Covenant at Quinnipiack, April 1638   209
    An interim agreement which, after fourteen months, was replaced
    by the New Haven Fundamentals [50].

43 Fundamental Orders of Connecticut, January 14, 1639   210
    A constitution that defined Connecticut's political institutions as
    both a colony and a state until 1816.

44 Guilford Covenant, June 1, 1639   216
    Written aboard ship, this covenant forms a people who agree to
    later create a government (see The Government of Guilford [49]).

45 Structure of Town Governments, October 10, 1639   217
    A set of amendments that address the status of the Fundamental
    Orders of Connecticut [43] as a federal system.

46 Fundamental Articles of New Haven, June 4–14, 1639   221
    A summary of basic political principles, with the discussion
    surrounding its adoption that reveals underlying reasoning.

47 Connecticut Oath of Fidelity, 1640   227
    A citizenship oath that brought those who arrived after 1639 into
    the 1639 founding compact—the Fundamental Orders of
    Connecticut [43].

48 Capitall Lawes of Connecticut, Established by the   229
Generall Court the First of December, 1642
*An ordinance that greatly reduces the number of reasons,
compared with English common law, for using capital
punishment.*

49 The Government of Guilford, June 19, 1643   232
*The detailed political covenant these colonists had agreed to
establish in the Guilford Covenant [44].*

50 New Haven Fundamentals, October 27, 1643   235
*The Constitution of New Haven that guided the colony as a
federation of towns until it united with Connecticut in 1662.*

51 Majority Vote of Deputies and Magistrates Required for   239
the Passage of Laws in Connecticut, February 5, 1645
*An amendment to the Fundamental Orders of Connecticut [43]
clarifying the bicameral relationship.*

52 Connecticut Code of Laws, 1650   241
*This code serves as a bill of rights and as part of Connecticut's
colonial constitution.*

53 Preface to the General Laws and Liberties of Connecticut   250
Colony Revised and Published by Order of the General
Court Held at Hartford in October 1672
*Designed to replace the code of laws passed before New Haven
joined Connecticut (see Connecticut Code of Laws [52]), the
preface shows that the code is considered to be part of the
foundation covenant.*

54 Division of the Connecticut General Assembly into Two   253
Houses, October 13, 1698
*A constitutional ordinance that officially established the
bicameralism that had been implicit but imperfectly operative
since 1639.*

NEW YORK

55 A Letter from Governor Richard Nicolls to the   254
Inhabitants of Long Island, February 1665
*The order that established a representative legislature in
New York.*

Contents

56 Charter of Liberties and Privileges, October 30, 1683 256
A constitution and bill of rights adopted by the legislature.

NEW JERSEY

57 Fundamentals of West New Jersey, 1681 263
A constitution adopted by the New Jersey legislature.

PENNSYLVANIA

58 Concessions to the Province of Pennsylvania, 1681 266
*An agreement that established the terms of settlement for
Pennsylvania.*

59 Charter of Liberties and Frame of Government of the 271
Province of Pennsylvania in America, May 5, 1682
*The first Pennsylvania constitution, including a bill of rights,
with a preface laying out the principles underlying it.*

60 An Act for Freedom of Conscience, December 7, 1682 287
*Establishes freedom of conscience for all those who profess a
minimal belief in God.*

61 Pennsylvania Charter of Liberties, 1701 290
*The Frame of Government (constitution) that replaced the 1696
frame and defined Pennsylvania government until 1776.*

MARYLAND

62 Orders Devised and Published by the House of Assembly 297
to be Observed During the Assembly, February 25, 1638
*Procedural rules governing the deliberative process in the
legislature.*

63 Act for Establishing the House of Assembly and the 299
Laws to Be Made Therein, 1638
*Political compact that formally established the Maryland
legislature.*

64 An Act for Church Liberties, 1638 302
*One of the earliest statements on religious freedom, this compact
extended that freedom to Catholics in Maryland.*

65 An Act for Swearing Allegeance, 1638   303
A typical oath confirming English citizenship that together with
the oath of a local political covenant expresses a dual citizenship in
a de facto federal structure.

66 An Act What Persons Shall Be Called to Every   305
General Assembly and an Act Concerning the
Calling of General Assemblies, 1638
A temporary constitution that grounds political institutions on
popular sovereignty—proposed by the Lord Proprietary and
approved by the freemen gathered in a General Assembly.

67 An Act for the Liberties of the People, 1638   308
A brief, temporary bill of rights.

68 Maryland Toleration Act, April 21, 1649   309
Established the broadest definition of religious freedom in
seventeenth-century colonial America until the establishment of
Pennsylvania.

VIRGINIA

69 Articles, Laws, and Orders, Divine, Politic, and Martial   314
for the Colony in Virginia, 1610–1611
Based on martial law rather than on consent and not in any sense
covenantal, the first colonial code of law reflects the importance of
religion to Virginia political culture.

70 Laws Enacted by the First General Assembly of Virginia,   327
August 2–4, 1619
The first colonial political compact of any type, this code of law is
also the first passed by a representative body.

71 Constitution for the Council and Assembly in Virginia,   336
July 24, 1621
Formally establishes a bicameral legislature for Virginia.

72 Laws and Orders Concluded by the Virginia General   339
Assembly, March 5, 1624
A major amendment to, and update of, Laws Enacted by the First
General Assembly [70].

Contents

NORTH CAROLINA

73 Act Relating to the Biennial and Other Assemblies and   345
Regulating Elections and Members in North Carolina,
1715
*Formalizes the legislature and the electoral process for selecting
representatives.*

SOUTH CAROLINA

74 Act to Ascertain the Manner and Form of Electing   350
Members to Represent the Province, 1721
*A legislative act that defines the basis for representation in South
Carolina and lays out a fair electoral process.*

GEORGIA

75 Act to Ascertain the Manner and Form of Electing   359
Members to Represent the Inhabitants of This Province
in the Commons House of Assembly, June 9, 1761
*The first formal definition of the electoral process underlying
representative government in Georgia.*

CONFEDERATIONS

76 The New England Confederation, 1643   365
*A true confederation and the first attempt to unite several colonies
created by different charters.*

77 The Albany Plan of Union, 1754   370
*Although never ratified, the first serious attempt to unite all the
colonies under a common compact.*

78 The Articles of Confederation, November 15, 1777   376
*The first U.S. Constitution—a compact that created a
confederation.*

Appendix: Unadopted Colonial Plans of Union   387

79 William Penn's Plan of Union, February 8, 1697   389
*The first proposal for uniting all the colonies under a general
government.*

80 Joseph Galloway's Plan of Union, 1774   391
  The immediate precursor to the Articles of Confederation.

Bibliography 395

Preface

This volume is not just another collection of documents assembled in the hope of illuminating general historical trends or eras. Instead, the set of documents selected for reproduction results from decision rules based on a theory of politics. The theory of politics is drawn from the work of Eric Voegelin, although it was the work of Willmoore Kendall and George Carey that first pointed to the possibility of, and need for, a collection of American colonial documents based on Voegelin's ideas.[1]

Eric Voegelin argues that political analysis should begin with a careful examination of a people's attempt at self-interpretation—a self-interpretation that is most likely to be found in their political documents and writing. The crucial point occurs when, either before or after creating a political society, a people reach a shared psychological state wherein they recognize themselves as engaged in a common enterprise and bound together by values, interests, and goals. It is this sharing, this basis for their being a people rather than an aggregate of individuals, that constitutes the beginning point for political analysis.

Essentially what they share are symbols and myths that provide meaning to their existence as a people and link them to some transcendent order. The shared meaning and shared link to some transcendent order allow them to act as a people, to answer such basic political questions as How do we decide what to do? By what standards do we judge our actions? Through what procedures do we reach collective decisions? What qualities or characteristics do we strive to encourage among ourselves? What qualities or characteristics do we seek or require of those who lead us? Far from being the

1. Voegelin's basic theory can be found in the introductions to *Israel and Revelation* (Baton Rouge: Louisiana State University Press, 1956) and *The World of the Polis* (Baton Rouge: Louisiana State University Press, 1957), which are the first two volumes of his five-volume work, *Order and History*, published by Louisiana State University Press. The book by Willmoore Kendall and George Carey is *The Basic Symbols of the American Political Tradition* (Baton Rouge: Louisiana State University Press, 1970).

repository of irrationality, shared myths and symbols constitute the basis upon which collective, rational action is possible.

These myths and symbols become at the same time both the basis for action as a people and the means of their self-illumination as a people. Frequently expressed in political documents, the core political symbols tend to structure the documents and determine their content. Voegelin also says that these shared symbols can be found in embryonic form in the earliest political expressions made by a people and in "differentiated" form in later writings. Put another way, by studying the political documents of a people we can watch the gradual unfolding, elaboration, and alteration of the embryonic symbols that define a given people. Voegelin calls this process "differentiation" but also refers to it as "self-illumination" and "self-interpretation."

Finally, in a synopsis too brief to do credit to such a profound theory, Voegelin argues that in Western civilization basic symbolizations tend to be variants of the original symbolization of the Judeo-Christian religious tradition. Without getting into a discussion of where this argument leaves the Greeks and Romans, suffice it to say that Voegelin's analysis led Kendall and Carey to reexamine early American political documents, and what they found was a variant on the symbolization of the Judeo-Christian tradition.

Using only a few of these early documents of foundation, Kendall and Carey identified a number of basic symbols present in all of them as well as in documents of the 1770s and 1780s: a constitution as higher law, popular sovereignty, legislative supremacy, the deliberative process, and a virtuous people. The important points made by Kendall and Carey are that there are basic symbols, in embryonic form, found in the earliest documents of foundation written by colonial Americans and that these symbols are found in American political documents written 150 years later, after the colonial era, but now in a differentiated form. While provocative and convincing, the position taken by Kendall and Carey cannot be considered firmly established until the early American documents of foundation can be comprehensively analyzed and the symbols traced through succeeding documents.

Later research by others does indeed show the continuity in symbols running from the Mayflower Compact to the American state and national constitutions of the late eighteenth century and that the embryonic basis for this political tradition clearly evolves from basic symbols in the Judeo-

Christian tradition.[2] Later support for the Kendall and Carey application of Voegelin's theory thus leads to the need for a comprehensive collection of documents that illustrates the evolution of American constitutional symbols.

Because there are thousands of candidates for inclusion in a collection of American political documents based on Voegelin's approach, a brief discussion of the decision rules used to select among them is required. The first decision rule was to include only those documents written during the colonial era. Post-1776 documents are readily available in a number of good collections, but there has been no good collection of pre-1776 foundational documents. The one exception to this rule in the present collection is The Articles of Confederation, which has been included because it is the direct culmination of colonial constitutional evolution. The Articles and the Declaration of Independence not only embody the colonial covenantal/compactual symbols but also together are what moved the colonies into independent nationhood. The state constitutions should also be included but are easily available in any library and are too long for inclusion, whereas the Articles of Confederation is brief and makes the transition from colonial to postindependence documents of political foundation dramatically apparent. Juxtaposing the Articles of Confederation with its immediate predecessors is therefore useful for illustrating the connection between pre- and postindependence documents.

The second decision rule was to include only documents written and adopted by the colonists, which excludes those written in Britain. Some may see this rule as tending to minimize the impact of the Mother Country on the process of constitutional development in America. The purpose of the rule, however, is to produce a coherent book of manageable length and not to imply the absence of English common law influences. The extent to which there was appropriation of English common law and foundational ideas by the colonists will be apparent in the documents written on this side of the Atlantic.

The third decision rule was to include documents that were in fact foundational. Political systems are not founded by judicial decisions or execu-

2. For an analysis that uses Voegelin's approach and explicates systematically many of the documents found in this collection, see Donald S. Lutz, *The Origins of American Constitutionalism* (Baton Rouge: Louisiana State University Press, 1988).

tive actions, so colonial case law and executive directives were excluded. Too often constitutionalism is viewed merely legalistically, whereas legalism is the result of constitutionalism and not the other way around. Foundational documents by definition create institutions and decision processes that did not exist before; or else they establish fundamental laws that give direction to what legislatures, executives, and courts later do, although these fundamental laws do not determine the actual form or content of later political decisions.

Finally, a document was included only if it had been publicly adopted by the entire relevant community through the consent-giving process in use by that community. This decision rule thus excluded political essays and tracts no matter how important or influential they might have been at the time. Often adoption resulted from legislative action whereby the legislature was conscious of acting in a foundational capacity. Usually these legislative actions amounted to amending the existing constitutional order at a time when a formal amendment process that directly involved the people had not yet been invented.

Even with these decision rules to narrow the eligible documents, some further exclusions were necessary. Some documents were too long and largely redundant in their content. So, for example, Connecticut had multiple codes of law adopted during the 1600s, but they largely reiterated the first law with minor variations, and including them served no real purpose other than to lengthen the book. The result is a collection of foundation documents from the colonial era that provides the basic information needed by any reader to understand the process of differentiation described by Voegelin.

Having established, therefore, at least in a preliminary way, the common threads running among them, these documents are presented here so that others may become familiar with, and advance our understanding of, their contents. There is much for us to learn. The Pilgrim Code of Law (1636), for example, is probably the first true written constitution in the English language; and if it is not, the Fundamental Orders of Connecticut (1639) most certainly is. Covenants, compacts, and citizenship oaths are prominent among our earliest documents. Those writing on political obligation have been quite taken with John Locke; however, in this collection we have people solving the problem of political obligation in a modern context even before Locke was born. The concepts of equality, popular sovereignty, majority rule, representation, and constitutionalism are a few of those whose meaning and origins can be illuminated by reference to these documents. Until now most of the documents have been lost to public view, and the few studied in depth have been studied in isolation. It is hoped that the publication of this volume will help achieve at least two ends: first, that the early documents in our political tradition will become well known to students of American politics; and second, that we will learn to read these documents together rather than separately.

The careful and attentive reader should begin with the understanding that the collection of documents presented here is not a book of readings. It is the foundation story of a people, told by themselves.

This volume is an altered and corrected version of a book originally published in 1986 under the title *Documents of Political Foundation by Colonial Americans*. The author wishes to thank Transaction Press for permission to reproduce whatever may overlap in that earlier book. The introductory essay for that volume has been significantly shortened and revised for this version, the headnotes to each document are completely new as well as lengthier and more detailed with respect to constitutional precedence, and the ordering of the documents has been radically altered. Also, seven documents from that earlier book have been dropped, and twelve completely new documents have been added. Finally, the documents themselves are in the public domain and have been corrected for any errors that may have crept into the earlier volume. In each case, the documents in this book have been carefully compared with their respective earliest surviving versions.

Introductory Essay

Part 1

FROM COVENANT TO CONSTITUTION

Local government in colonial America was the seedbed of American constitutionalism—a simple fact insufficiently appreciated by those writing in American political theory. Evidence for neglect can be found simply by examining any book dealing with American constitutional history and noting the absence of references to colonial documents written by Americans. Rather, at best there will be brief references to Magna Carta, perhaps the English Constitution, and probably the Declaration of Independence. If the authors of these books discuss the source of American constitutional theory beyond these few documents, they will almost inevitably mention European thinkers, John Locke being prominent among them. It is the purpose of this volume to end such neglect and reverse such attitudes.

Work by historians during the Bicentennial has pointed us in the direction of reexamining the colonial roots of our political system, but the implications of this work have not been absorbed by political scientists.[1] Furthermore, historians are not inclined to put their questions in such a way as to lead to the comprehensive examination of colonial documents of political foundation. Intellectual historians almost immediately look to Europe and the broader Western tradition when seeking the roots of constitutionalism for the simple reason that a profound constitutional tradition is there to examine. There has also been a tendency to view the American Revolution as the fundamental watershed in American history, closely followed by the Civil War. This outlook introduces an unavoidable sense of discontinuity in American thinking and affairs. Rather than suggest that the perception of such discontinuities should be rejected, it is instead argued here that we should look for continuities as well. One fundamental continuity to be found runs from the earliest colonial documents of foundation to the

---

1. In fact, this is a recovery of the implications of earlier work by historians. Prominent among the earlier works is that of Andrew C. McLaughlin, *The Foundations of American Contitutionalism* (New York: New York University Press, 1932).

written constitutions of the 1770s and 1780s. We should look to our own shores as well when seeking a constitutional tradition for America.

One important caveat must be mentioned. This author has argued elsewhere that there are two constitutional traditions running through colonial documents.[2] The first tradition can be found in the charters, letters-patent, and instructions for the colonists written in England. In certain respects, the United States Constitution favors this tradition. The second tradition is found in the covenants, compacts, agreements, ordinances, codes, and oaths written by the colonists themselves. While the U.S. Constitution embodies aspects of this tradition as well, it is in the early state constitutions that we find the full flowering of this second tradition.

These traditions, while in certain respects distinct, also interpenetrate each other. Most of the early colonial charters allow the colonists to design their own political institutions and practice self-government, and most of those charters that did not so provide explicitly at least permitted the colonists to fill in the blanks themselves. Charter revisions and colonial document writing took each other into account, and often one was the result of the other. Nevertheless, it needs to be emphasized that the former set of documents was handed down to, or imposed on, the colonists, while the second set was written by the colonists themselves.

The two traditions were blended to produce a constitutional perspective uniquely American. The fact that American colonists were invariably here as the result of a written charter that could be amended led to their becoming used to having a written document defining the context of their politics and having a document that could be altered through some political process. The English had a written constitution, but it was composed of the vast corpus of common law and legislative ordinance. English colonists in America became familiar with the idea of a single document being the focus of their link with that vast corpus.

At the same time, English colonists in America became used to writing their own documents to flesh out the particulars of their governments. This was partly the result of necessity—time and distance between England and America did not permit close control from England. It was also the result of choice. The religious dissenters who were prominent in the first waves of

2. Donald S. Lutz, *The Origins of American Constitutionalism* (Baton Rouge: Louisiana State University Press, 1988).

migration came to America to establish their own communities where they could practice their religion free from outside interference. This desire plus the structure of their churches led them to use self-written covenants as part of their political definition. It is a very short step to move to a blending of these two traditions wherein Americans would find themselves writing single, amendable documents as the focus of their political systems and calling these documents constitutions. The Pilgrim Code of Law, for example, begins by referring to both the charter from the king and the Mayflower Compact as its legal basis.

We will, in this volume, be concentrating on what has been termed here the second tradition. We will be looking at those documents of political foundation written by the colonists themselves. The charters are already well known and easily accessible.[3] The documents written by the colonists are not well known and are generally not easily accessible, even where they are identified. Nevertheless, the reader should keep in mind that the documents presented in this volume are only part of the picture, although they are the most neglected part of the picture.

Nor should the reader conclude that every document of political foundation is here included. No doubt there are others that remain buried in obscure collections, and perhaps future researchers will argue that some that are known and not included in this category should be. All that is claimed for the present collection is that it probably represents most of such documents, and that those reproduced here are typical for, and representative of, American colonial documents of political foundation.

We have spoken of a "constitutional tradition." We have suggested that the Pilgrim Code of Law (1636) was one of the first constitutions in the English language. We also speak of the Massachusetts Constitution of 1780 and the Pennsylvania Constitution of 1776 as if such titles were not problematic. All three kinds of statements assume that we know what is meant by the term "constitution." From the outset it is best to consider this term something to be determined rather than something assumed; it is because we start off thinking we know what a constitution is that we have not given these colonial documents the close textual analysis they deserve.

To illustrate this point, consider the 1776 Virginia Constitution. It is al-

3. The charters and the early state constitutions can be found in Francis N. Thorpe, ed., *The Federal and State Constitutions, Colonial Charters, and Other Organic Laws of the United States*, 7 vols. (Washington, D.C.: Government Printing Office, 1907).

ways reproduced in our century with the title at the beginning as "The Constitution of Virginia." This is immediately followed by the first part of the document, which is entitled "Bill of Rights." Sixteen sections later we come to the second part, which is labeled "The Constitution or Form of Government, Agreed to and Resolved Upon by the Delegates and Representatives of the Several Counties and Corporations of Virginia." Here we have a puzzle. If the part after section sixteen of the Bill of Rights is the Constitution, then is the Bill of Rights properly part of the Constitution? And if not, why is the entire document called a constitution? If the Bill of Rights is part of the Constitution, then why is the second part labeled the way it is? The 1776 Maryland Constitution uses the same format, as do those of New Hampshire (1784) and North Carolina (1776). Pennsylvania (1776) and Vermont (1776) label the second part "The Plan of Government" or "The Frame of Government," as does Massachusetts (1780). Furthermore, this latter document, considered the most influential state constitution ever written, describes itself internally as a "compact" and not a "constitution." It is worth noting that the originals of these early state documents were not printed with the word "Constitution" in their respective titles. Are these early state documents that we habitually label "constitutions" really constitutions or something else?

It is neither feasible nor appropriate to answer this question here in detail, but many of the early state constitutions were considered by their authors to be compacts. This raises the question of what a compact is and in turn leads us to the early colonial documents, for many of them were compacts. At the same time, many of these colonial documents were not compacts. In order to understand these colonial documents, we must first define the terms commonly used internally to describe them. Second, we must provide categories that will allow us to distinguish the various types of documents.

Let us address the second task first because it is more fundamental. If these are foundation documents, it is reasonable to ask what it is that each document founds. There are four distinct foundation elements, and any document can contain one, all, or any combination of these elements: (1) the founding or creation of a people; (2) the founding or creation of a government; (3) the self-definition of the people in terms of shared values and goals so that the founded people may cross generations; and (4) the specification of a form of government through the creation of institutions for collective decision making. Let us consider each in turn.

Sometimes a document of foundation will create a people but not a government. It is as if those signing or agreeing to the document were saying, "Here we are, a new people, one distinct from all other peoples, declaring that we are ready to take our place on the stage of life." The individuals composing the people were, of course, already alive as individuals, but the document creates a new life—that held in common. One could also speak of their creating a society, but this term is not quite strong enough because it implies simply a pattern of social interaction, whereas to create a people is to imply the creation or affirmation of a culture as well. A society may have rules for interacting, but it is the common values, goals, and shared meaning for a life together that define a people. While some social scientists will point out that all known societies have required shared values and meaning in order to function, the crucial fact of a foundation document containing shared values is the celebration and conscious affirmation of that which is shared. There is the implication of a link with something transcendent that ties them together as a people. It is the difference between working together to build a wall to keep out enemies and creating a church in which to worship the god of the land enclosed by the wall.

Other documents will create a people and then establish a government in only the most general terms. The Providence Agreement (1637) [32] is a good example. A group of individuals unanimously agree to form themselves into a people, and then to be bound as a people by decisions reached by a majority among them—including the form of government. It is easy to discern the dead hand of John Locke in the distinction between the unanimous creation of a people and the majoritarian basis for their government, even though in 1637 Locke's *Second Treatise* was still more than half a century in the future. The Plymouth Combination (Mayflower Compact) of 1620 [3] has the same Lockean format, as do other documents in the collection.

Those documents that contain the element of self-definition are particularly interesting. It is unusual for a document to create a people without also outlining the kind of people they are or wish to become, although some documents do contain further illumination of a people that already exist. This self-description of a people is the foundation element usually overlooked, yet from this element what we later call bills of rights will evolve. Three Virginia documents [69, 70, and 72] contain this foundation element and are typical in that the values of the people are implicit in the prohibitions enumerated. Commitment to godliness, order, and cleanliness are obvious. Despite its name, the Massachusetts Body of Liberties (1641) [22] also implies commonly held values, largely through a set of explicit prohibitions. That it is called a "Body of Liberties" points toward what this element will become. In other documents the values and self-definition of a people will be spelled out explicitly with no need for inferences on the part of the reader. Whether explicit or implicit, this foundation element represents what Voegelin sometimes called a people's self-illumination, and later in our history we will be unable to exclude this element from what we will come to call a constitution.

The fourth foundation element, the specification of a form of government, present only embryonically in documents like the Plymouth Combination (1620), gradually comes to occupy a larger proportion of our foundation documents. The word used internally to identify this element is often "constitute." That is, within colonial documents the writers usually "agree" to form a people or a government but "constitute" a form of government. That this part of early state constitutions, the part describing specific forms and institutions, is usually termed "The Constitution or Form of Government" thus becomes quite understandable. It is the fourth foundation element grown to prominence in a foundation document, and it is still being introduced by the term used in early colonial documents of foundation. Some colonial documents contain only this fourth element, others combine it with additional foundation elements. In either case, we can watch the development of American political institutions found later in our constitutions—institutions like popular elections, majority rule, bicameralism, separation of powers, and checks and balances.

Because one or more elements may be present in a given document, if only in embryonic form, it is often arguable just how the document should be categorized with respect to these foundation elements. As a further aid to comparative analysis, it is both useful and interesting to consider the various terms used internally in the documents, a task to which we now turn.

Part 2

DEFINITION OF TERMS

It has been said that humans have a tendency to develop a multiplicity of terms for things that are prominent in their lives so as to distinguish subtle yet important variations. Thus, for example, Eskimos are said to have many words to identify types of snow, and in classical Athens there were many forms of community identified, each with its own descriptive term. If we follow this same logic, it is apparent that the English-speaking people of the seventeenth and eighteenth centuries considered political agreements to be of great importance because they regularly used over a dozen different terms, sometimes interchangeably, but more often to distinguish subtleties they considered noteworthy. We will need to examine some of these linguistic alternatives for two reasons: because we require an understanding of what the issues were and because the more general words we have inherited were not used to describe the document as written. For example, when we examine the documents in this volume, we discover that the word "covenant" is only occasionally used to describe a document by those writing it, even though many of the documents were understood to be covenants by their respective authors and had the covenant form internally. "Covenant" was too broad a term, and the authors often preferred a more restrictive, precise title.

The same is true for "compact." The term is not used in any of the titles of these colonial documents, at least not by those who wrote them. The Mayflower Compact was not so named until 1793 and was referred to by the inhabitants of the colony as the Plymouth Combination, or sometimes simply as The Combination. To make sense out of these documents, then, we will first need to define the broad categorical terms of covenant, compact, contract, and organic act, and then recover the understanding in use at the time for charter, constitution, patent, agreement, frame, combination, ordinance, and fundamentals.

A contract, on the one hand, usually implied an agreement with mutual responsibilities on a specific matter; that is, a contract implied a restricted commitment such as in a business matter and involved relatively small groups of people. The contract could be enforced by law but did not have the status of law.

A compact, on the other hand, was a mutual agreement or understanding that was more in the nature of a standing rule that, if it did not always have the status of a law, often had a similar effect. A compact implied an agreement that affected the entire community in some way, or relations between communities. The word had the root meaning of "knitting together" or "bringing the component parts closely and firmly into a whole." A compact, therefore, was an agreement creating something that we would today recognize as a community. Because a compact was not as precise as a contract and more like a settled rule than an agreement with specific, reciprocal responsibilities, we do not find talk of a Mayflower Contract.

A covenant could be viewed as having two distinct though related meanings. As a legal term in England, it referred to a formal agreement with legal validity made under the seal of the Crown. This denoted an agreement of a serious nature witnessed by the highest authority. The religious counterpart to this secular or civil covenant was any agreement established or secured by God. The formal agreement made and subscribed to by members of a congregational church in order to constitute themselves as a distinct religious community had God as the witness and securer of the agreement. A religious covenant thus was essentially an oath, and if it established a political community, political obligation was secured by the oath rather than by merely resting upon the fact of consent having been given. Note that both the civil and religious meanings of covenant were related in that each was characterized by being witnessed and therefore secured by the highest relevant authority. Presumably any compact with both God and the Crown as securer would be simultaneously a civil and religious covenant. A civil covenant would require the presence of the royal seal, while a religious covenant could be invoked merely through the internal use of an oath.

Even with this restricted discussion two things become apparent. First, calling John Locke a "contract theorist" would have been considered a misnomer by colonial Americans. He was more properly a "compact theorist," and in fact we find that his *Second Treatise* always uses the word "compact" and not "contract." Second, the relationship between a covenant and a compact was a direct one. Both were based on the consent of those taking part. Both created a new community. Both implied a relationship that was stronger, deeper, and more comprehensive than that established by a contract. A compact, however, required simply the consent of those taking part, while a covenant required sanction by the highest relevant authority as well. In this regard, compact is the more modern of the two concepts, while covenant was the more natural term to use in a religious or a medieval context where the authority hierarchy was well defined and had a clear apex. A compact could be turned into a covenant merely by calling upon

God to witness the agreement, which also turned consenting to the agreement into an oath. If a people found themselves in a situation where a mutual agreement had to be drawn up but it was not possible to obtain the royal seal in order to give the document legal status, the easiest solution for a religious people was to call upon God as a witness to bind those signing until the king's legal sanction could be obtained. If, for some reason, a people reached a mutual agreement that was covenant-like but chose to call upon neither God nor the king, they must, for some reason, have considered themselves completely competent to establish the document's legality. This last instance would be one in which legality was viewed as resting on the authority of the people, indicating an understanding of popular sovereignty. A compact was just such an agreement, one resting only on the consent of those participating. For this reason, Blackstone could say, "A compact is a promise proceeding from us, law is a command directed to us."[4] The fact that most of the early colonists were a religious people—a religious people primarily from Protestant religions who were experienced in forming their own communities and familiar with the covenant form for doing so—becomes an important part of the background to American constitutionalism. That these people were often thrown by circumstances into situations where they had to practice this skill of community building through covenants and that the charters under which they sailed often required that they provide for self-government, or at the very least permitted such activities, must be viewed as another historical circumstance of considerable importance for American constitutionalism.

An agreement between God and his chosen people, then, was a covenant. The judicious Hooker refers to "Christ's own compact solemnly made with his church."[5] While the covenant to which Hooker was referring was not the Jewish covenant, the Protestants writing the colonial documents in question viewed their work as equivalent to the Jewish biblical covenants. It was certainly equivalent in the sense that calling upon God to witness a civil union not only turned a compact into a covenant but also indicated an accord with the broader covenant in the Bible, between God and his chosen people. Giving one's consent to join a civil community with this kind of covenant was in part an act of religious commitment, and elections to iden-

---

4. William Blackstone, *Commentaries* 1 (1765), 45.
5. Richard Hooker, *Of the Laws of Ecclesiastical Polity,* bk. 5, sect. 15 (New York: Everyman's Library, 1954), lxii.

tify "the elect" among those in the civil community were also acts of consent with religious overtones.[6]

Consent becomes the instrument for establishing authority in the community and for expressing the sovereignty of God. God transmits his sovereignty to the people through the broader covenant, and they in turn convey his sovereignty to the rulers on the basis of the specific covenant creating the civil community. The people's consent is the instrument for linking God with those holding temporal authority, whose authority then is viewed as sanctioned by God. Because this temporal authority comes through the people, however, the rulers are beholden to God through the people and thus are immediately responsible to them. This, the original basis of popular sovereignty, had been independently developed by both Protestant and Catholic thinkers during the sixteenth and seventeenth centuries.[7]

Given these characterizations, it can be seen that a covenant is simultaneously a compact as it contains everything essential to a compact. A compact, however, is not simultaneously a covenant because it lacks the explicit link with the higher authority even though the idea and form for a compact are derived from covenants, and the kind of community established is similar enough so that one could call a compact a near-covenant. Furthermore, there are circumstances in which an apparent compact is really a covenant in the complete sense. For example, suppose a people form a society under a covenant in either or both God's and the king's name. They then later form a government for this society in a document that does not

6. For an excellent introduction to the role of covenants in the Jewish political tradition, see Daniel J. Elazar, "Covenant as the Basis of the Jewish Political Tradition," *Jewish Journal of Sociology* 20 (June 1978): 5–37; and Delbert R. Hillers, *Covenant: The History of a Biblical Idea* (Baltimore: The Johns Hopkins University Press, 1969). For the appropriation and development of the covenant idea by Protestants, see Champlin Burrage, *The Church Covenant Idea: Its Origin and Development* (Philadelphia, 1904); and E. Brooks Holifield, *The Covenant Sealed: The Development of Puritan Sacramental Theology in Old and New England, 1570–1720* (New Haven: Yale University Press, 1974). For the nature and development of covenants in America, one might consult any of a great number of volumes. Among the better volumes is Peter Ymen DeJong, *The Covenant Idea in New England Theology, 1620–1847* (Grand Rapids, Mich.: E. B. Erdmans, 1964).

7. For the Catholic tradition, see Otto Gierke, *Political Theories of the Middle Ages* (Cambridge: Cambridge University Press, 1900); and Gierke, *Natural Law and the Theory of Society: 1500 to 1800* (Cambridge: Cambridge University Press, 1934). For the Protestant tradition, see Sanford A. Lakoff, *Equality in Political Philosophy* (Boston: Beacon Press, 1964), especially chap. 3.

mention any authority other than themselves as a people. Because the first document that formed them as a people also automatically establishes them as expressing the higher authority whenever they act through their own popular sovereignty, all subsequent documents by that people could be considered covenants as well because the link with the higher authority is understood. Nor is this implied covenant status always left for the reader of the document to infer. The Pilgrim Code of Law (1636) [20] is a good example. After establishing, in the first paragraph, the legal basis for holding the assembly that will write the Code, the first sentence in the second paragraph says: "Now being assembled according to the said order, and having read the combination made at Cape Cod the 11th of November 1620 . . . as also our letters patents confirmed by the honorable council, his said Majesty established and granted the 13th of January 1629. . . ." The combination of November 11, 1620, referred to here is, of course, what we now call the Mayflower Compact. The letters-patent refers to the charter from the king that was then in effect. The former document is a religious covenant, and the latter is a civil covenant. This sentence in the Pilgrim Code of Law serves a double function: first, of establishing the legal basis for their having the power to write such a Code; and second, of bringing the Code under the umbrella of the earlier covenants thereby making it an implied covenant.

It is perfectly possible for a contract to be elevated to compact or covenant status. For example, the king could put his seal on a contract; perhaps charters come most easily to mind in this regard. Such a document, however, would imply quite a different kind of community from a simple covenant. Because all the details of the relationship would be spelled out, the result would be less a community in which the partners are required to go beyond the legally defined relationship to fully develop the relationship and more one in which the partners are minimally required to fulfill the obligations specifically mentioned. Such a contractually based compact, or covenant, would not be a true covenant as understood in the Jewish tradition and would become a target for legalistic wrangling over the meaning and intent of specific words and phrases. The emphasis on the letter rather than on the spirit of the agreement would destroy community as implied by covenant or compact and result in something less—an association for specific, limited ends. True covenants and compacts, without any contractual elements, are thus communitarian oriented, while contractual variants are inclined to be legalistic. One characteristic of contractual variants was the tendency for them to become longer and longer specifications that were more and more precise and limiting. This characteristic, however, should not be pushed too far as an identifying property of a contractual society because there is another, noncontractual, form of agreement that might resemble it superficially—an organic act.

An "organic act" is one that codifies and celebrates an agreement or set of agreements made through the years by a community. In this way, a "common law" comprising legislative and judicial decisions made over a number of years can be codified, simplified, and celebrated in dramatic form, thereby also renewing the consent-based oath upon which obligation to the community rests. The early state constitutions adopted in 1776 could be viewed as organic acts as well as compacts as they usually summarized and codified what the colonists of each state had evolved over the previous 150 years. In the case of Connecticut and Rhode Island the colonial charters were formally readopted as constitutions—charters that had in these two instances been essentially written by the colonists. Massachusetts did not adopt or readopt anything in 1776 but continued to live under the 1725 charter as a continuous community. Examples of an organic act include The Laws and Liberties of Massachusetts (1647) [26], the Puritan Laws and Liberties (1658) [30], and the Connecticut Code of Laws (1650) [52].

These organic acts are long and contain precise terms for limited categories of behavior. Various provisions, for example, might regulate behavior in church, activities after dark, or dealings with Indians. While highly legalistic, they are laws after all, they are not contracts for there are generally no provisions for reciprocal obligations. They are instead compacts because they are community-wide agreements on how to behave.

We now have the basic characterizations for the analytic categories of religious covenant, civil covenant, mixed religious-civil covenant, compact, contract, and organic act. As was noted earlier, these terms were generally not used to describe colonial foundation documents, at least not by those writing them. It is necessary, therefore, to provide a brief characterization for each of the terms that were prominently used—agreement, combination, frame, fundamentals, ordinance, patent, charter, and constitution.

An "agreement" in the formal, political sense referred to an arrangement between two or more persons as to a course of action, a mutual understanding, or a common goal. The term was usually used to describe a document that we would recognize as a covenant or compact. Indeed, documents frequently used the phrases "to agree," "to compact," and "to covenant" interchangeably in their internal wording. Treaties were sometimes termed agreements. While an agreement was legally binding on the parties making it, the term more properly implied a sense of harmony, or concord, that transcended a purely legal relationship. To refer to a treaty as an agreement meant at the very least there was no dissension, but it usually implied more—a level of mutual pleasure that approached atonement, whether in the sense of reconciliation or of propitiation. An agreement, then, at least during the period in question, was far more than a contract. It clearly suggested a relationship that moved beyond the letter of the agreement toward mutual support and pleasure, something close to the "knitting together" implied by a compact or the spirit of community carried by a covenant.

A "combination" was viewed as a bringing together of two or more entities into a whole. The banding together, or union, of persons was usually for the prosecution of some common, broad objective. The term was often used interchangeably with agreement and compact and sometimes with alliance and treaty. As a legal term it had neither consistent nor widespread use, but American colonists were quite consistent in using it as the equivalent for agreement as just outlined. The document later to be known as the Mayflower Compact, which was clearly a covenant in form, was known to those who wrote it as the Plymouth Combination.

During the era in question, a "frame" referred to an established order, plan, scheme, or system, especially of government. It strongly implied a definite form, regular procedure, order, and regularity. It also implied an adapted or adjusted condition in the sense of changing to take into account new factors or conditions affecting the older form, plan, or system, while not rejecting that older one. Thus, a frame tended not to be a document of initial founding as much as it was one of refounding and hence was similar to an organic act. Document 59 is one where "frame" is used in its title.

The use of "fundamentals," as in New Haven Fundamentals (1643) [50], implied the base upon which something is built. It was used primarily to refer to immaterial rather than physical things, and thus was used to describe leading principles, rules, laws, or articles that served as the groundwork for a political system. Such a statement of principles might be an addition to a covenant or compact, a preface to a frame or ordinance, or it might constitute the agreement itself.

An "ordinance" usually referred to an authoritative command, although in a more restricted sense, narrower scope, and less permanent nature than a law or statute. The term was sometimes used to refer to the founding or instituting of something, but in the sense of making conformable to order, rule, or custom—as in placing or arranging in proper sequence or proper relative position. It would not be improper to view an ordinance as sometimes attempting to establish "orders" of people according to class, merit, ranking, status, importance, duties, or rights. As with fundamentals, political ordinances could be covenantal, compactual, contractual, or something else depending on the content. The words "ordain" and "order" were used as operative words in documents that legally produced an ordinance.

A "patent," as in letters-patent, had the root meaning of a public letter or document as opposed to a private one, usually from a sovereign or person in authority. It had a variety of uses—for example, to put on public record some contract; to command or authorize something to be done; or to confer some right, privilege, title, property, or office. A patent usually implied a monopoly of some sort, as in exclusiveness of use. Obviously a patent was related to a contract, but it was also related to a law in that it was handed down by some authority. It was unlike a contract in that it did not necessarily imply reciprocal duties but often simply recorded a grant with no duties assigned the grantee.

The word "charter" is derived from the Latin word meaning a leaf of paper, a writing, a document. Often it was a legal document or deed written on a single piece of paper by which grants, cessions, contracts, and other transactions were confirmed or ratified. It was also used to refer to a written document delivered by the sovereign or legislature to grant privileges to, or recognize the rights of, an entire people, a certain class, or specific individuals. Magna Carta comes to mind here as an example because it recognized the rights of the nobility, vis à vis the king. In his *Leviathan*, Hobbes says that charters are not laws but exemptions from the laws, an idea that also fits in with the purpose of Magna Carta or other bills of rights. Charters were also used to grant pardon and to create or incorporate boroughs, universities, companies, or other corporations. They were a written instrument or contract applied especially to documents or deeds relating to the conveyance of property. The word "charter" was used as a linguistic alternative for privilege, immunity, or publicly conceded right. To say that something was "chartered" was to say that it was founded, privileged, or protected. Charters and letters-patent were similar, although the latter term was broader in that it could refer to any authoritative document. A charter was invariably a patent, while a patent was not necessarily a charter. "Charter" was also closely related to "contract" as a legal term because it effectively constituted a contract between the authority granting it and the person(s) to whom it was granted. Unlike a simple contract, however, a charter often included so many statements of a general nature that it transcended the notion of a contract. A contract, for example, would not be an appropriate description for a document that contains statements as broad and vague as "and the proprietors shall establish a government whereby differences among the planters may be settled."

Although rarely used to describe early colonial documents, the word "constitution" is worth discussing in order to compare its usage with some of the other terms we are examining. Related to the term "constituent," which refers to that which makes a thing what it is in the sense of being formative, essential, characteristic, or distinctive, "constitution" is more immediately drawn from "constitute," which means to establish, ordain, or appoint in the sense of providing legal form and status. The word "constitution," properly speaking, referred to the action of making, establishing, decreeing, or ordaining something, usually in the sense of its having been made by a superior civil or ecclesiastical authority.

Additionally, a constitution had been used historically to denote limitations. For example, the Constitutions of Clarendon in England, a set of propositions drawn up at the Council of Clarendon in 1164, defined the limits of civil and ecclesiastical jurisdiction. Used in this way it was similar to a charter as exemplified in Magna Carta. The term "constitution" had also been used to describe the mode in which a state was organized, especially as to the location of sovereign power as well as to describe the fundamental principles according to which a nation, state, or body politic was organized and governed. For example, there was the Declaration of the Estates of Scotland (1689): "Whereas King James the Seventh did by the advice of wicked and evil counsellors invade the fundamental constitution of the kingdom, and altered it from a limited monarchy to an arbitrary despotic power...."; or Lord Viscount Bolingbroke's definition, "By Constitution we mean, whenever we speak with propriety and exactness, that assemblage of laws, institutions, and customs, derived from certain fixed principles of reason... that compose the general system, according to which the community hath agreed to be governed." [8]

In summary, we find the word "constitution" associated with making or establishing something, giving it legal status, describing the mode of organization, locating sovereignty, establishing limits, and describing fundamental principles. Not surprisingly, it was often used in association with charter, law, statute, ordinance, frame, and fundamentals. In our usage today "constitution" implies and incorporates at least part of all these other terms plus some of what we associate with compact. Although the usage of the word during the seventeenth century sounds familiar to our ears, the various components had not yet been brought together in any complete fashion. Also the term "constitution" was not used to refer to a specific document as we are inclined to do today. The English had developed the concept of a written constitution, but the writing was scattered over thousands of documents and no one was quite sure which documents should be included. When Americans finally brought all the elements together in a single document in 1776, the term "constitution" was to include far more than had been outlined by Bolingbroke. Indeed, the early state constitutions would derive their elements from agreements, compacts, and covenants as well as from frames, charters, fundamentals, and ordinances. The word "constitution" is not used in any of the documents duplicated in this volume, although the word "constitute" is used in several.

Part 3

ANALYTIC OVERVIEW

Although one major purpose for publishing these foundation documents is to lead others to analyze them both individually and together, it is not inappropriate to initiate that analysis by presenting here some of the apparent developments that they embody. Let us briefly outline some of the things that a reading of these documents together leads us to conclude.

1. Political covenants were derived in form and content from religious covenants used to found religious communities.

2. A complete political covenant had the following elements: (a) an oath

8. Viscount Bolingbroke, *On Parties* (1735), 108.

calling on God as a witness or partner; (b) the creation of a people whose members are identified by those who signed the covenant; (c) the creation of a civil body politic, or government; (d) the specification of the shared goals and values, a shared meaning, that defined (self-defined) the basis for the people living together; and (e) the creation and description of institutions for collective decision making.

3. The political covenant form evolved rather quickly into the political compact form. A political compact is identical to a political covenant except for the absence of an oath in a compact. The elimination of the oath resulted in the force of the document, and therefore the basis of political obligation, resting entirely on the consent of those signing it. The move from political covenant to political compact is thus a shift to de facto popular sovereignty.

4. The political compact eventually evolved into what we now recognize as the American form of constitutionalism. In this evolution, the first two compact elements—the creation of a people and of a government—become part of the American Constitution's preamble or the first few provisions in the Bill of Rights; the self-definition element evolves into a bill of rights, although parts of the self-definition are often found as well in a preamble or introduction; and the description of institutions for collective decision making grows into the body of the constitution proper, which becomes the major part of the total political compact's length. The early state constitutions, which contained all of these foundation elements, described themselves internally as "compacts."

5. The oath did not cease to be politically relevant but became the basis for creating and identifying citizens outside of the formal documents of foundation and sometimes in place of them (documents 4, 5, 9, 15, 16, and 47 are examples). During the colonial era it was not unusual for an oath to be used as the entire founding document. Anyone taking the oath was effectively performing the same act as signing the end of a political covenant or compact. Beyond the promise to be a good citizen, however, these "founding" documents had little further specification. Many colonial foundational documents have oaths for citizens and elected officials internal to them in addition to other foundation elements. Today we still use an oath to produce citizens and to activate the formalities of citizenship (such as the oath-taking in court), so in a real sense we still view our Constitution as equivalent to a covenant because it rests on the actual or implied oaths of all citizens.

That is, because new citizens are required to take an oath to uphold the Constitution, it must be assumed that citizens born here did something that was equivalent to an explicit oath at some point in their life.

6. During the colonial era, the terms "agreement" and "combination" were used interchangeably with "covenant" and "compact," both internally and in the titles of documents, to describe what were in fact either political covenants or political compacts.

7. With few exceptions, when the covenant or compact forms were used it was the people who were acting.

8. During the colonial era, when the legislature acted in a founding or foundation amending capacity, the resulting documents were interchangeably termed an "ordinance," an "act," or a "code."

9. With few exceptions, the content of the ordinance form was limited to one or both of the last two foundation elements.

10. During the colonial and early national eras, the terms "frame," "plan," and "constitution" were used interchangeably to describe that part of a political compact that created the institutions of decision making.

11. In approximately two-thirds of the colonial foundation documents the last two founding elements are separated, i.e., one element is found in a document without the other. In approximately one-third of the documents these elements are found together in the same document. Thus, colonists were twice as likely to separate these two elements as they were to combine them, which later led to some confusion as to whether state constitutions should include bills of rights. Some combined these founding elements in the body of the document; many separated the two elements into two sections, calling only that section containing the last element the "constitution"; and some did not contain a bill of rights at all. It is interesting that when the elements were combined in the early state constitutions, the bill of rights was always at the front of the document immediately after or as part of the preamble.

12. The colonists were willing to let the legislatures speak for them in matters of self-definition and the creation of governmental institutions but not when it came to forming themselves into a people or founding a government. The exception to the latter is found in those documents founding a federation or confederation of existing towns or colonies. This distinction led to the natural expectation that legislatures could write state constitutions that addressed only the last two elements. When these documents were com-

plete compacts and therefore included the other elements as well, the expectation was that the documents should be approved by the people as well. When the first group of elements was not present, popular ratification was not always expected.

Part 4

EDITORIAL DECISIONS

Whenever one is faced with transcribing historical documents there are a number of decisions that need to be made. One is whether to use the original spelling and grammar. In the case of these documents it was decided to introduce as few emendations as possible and to identify the emendations that might have been introduced earlier by others. One emendation introduced by this transcriber involves the occasional deletion of lists of names at the end of a document. These instances are noted by comments in brackets. Anything else in brackets constitutes an alteration introduced by an earlier transcriber that this one cannot eliminate by reference to the actual text. In many instances this is because the original text no longer exists and we are limited to some transcription in its place. The use of a bracket sometimes indicates a blank or an indecipherable word or words in the original text. In some cases the text that was transcribed had been systematically altered by an earlier transcriber. For example, the oldest surviving text may have been printed during the eighteenth century using the printer's convention of substituting the German *u* for *v* or *i* for *j*. For a while it was common practice when transcribing to emend these printer's conventions, and where an earlier transcriber has done so and that is the text being here transcribed, such transpositions are noted in the introductory remarks to the document or in the footnote at the end.

In every instance the effort has been made to locate a facsimile or accurate transcription for each document. Because there are often competing versions, the texts that are being used for transcription here have been identified in a footnote at the end and then faithfully transcribed. The original text often does not have a formal title at the beginning. In these instances the title used is either the one by which the document has traditionally come to be known, or else a simple descriptive title has been attached. Such traditional or descriptive titles are placed in brackets; any title not in brackets is in the original document.

If one is going to engage in close textual analysis it is crucial that the complete text be made available. This is the practice followed in all but a few documents in this volume. Several of these, such as the Connecticut Code of Law, are so lengthy that to reproduce them completely would extend this volume by several hundred pages. In those limited instances where the complete text is not transcribed, that fact is noted, what is missing is identified, and the place where the complete text can be found is indicated. The editing of these few documents has been based on the presence of repetitive material or material in a given text that is judged at best marginal to the political content. In the occurrences where editing has been used, it was judged better to present a partial text of an important but little-known document rather than to make exclusions because of length.

The order of the documents in the book is based on the universal and essentially invariant practice in early American history to list the colonies (and later the states) in their geographical order from north to south and then to arrange the documents for each colony or state in the historical order of their adoption—from earliest to most recent. Reproducing the documents simply in historical order would result in mixing up those from different colonies, which would make an examination of developments in a given colony quite difficult. Also, because the central colonies were developed much later than those in New England or the South and the latter two areas did not develop at the same rate, a simple historical ordering would also juxtapose documents that had in common only the accident of date. Nor would ordering the colonies alphabetically serve any purpose because it would place, for example, Rhode Island just ahead of South Carolina—a juxtaposition that would lose the benefits of a direct geographical juxtaposition of Rhode Island with Connecticut and South Carolina with Virginia.

Finally, a note is in order concerning dates. The calendar in use through most of the seventeenth century began the new year on March 24—the spring equinox. This resulted in every day between January 1 and March 23 being a year earlier than on our current calendar. Historians frequently list a double date such as February 19, 1634/1635 to indicate that it is 1635 according to our system of reckoning but 1634 according to the system used by the colonists. In every instance in this volume the date given in the title of a document reflects our current calendar system. The date internal to the document may reflect one year earlier. Also, it was common to list a date as "the second day of the first month" or "the second day of the seventh month." Because the New Year fell in March, the second day of the first month translates as March 2, whereas the second day of the seventh month translates as September 2.

Colonial Origins
of the
American
Constitution

I

[Agreement of the Settlers
at Exeter in New Hampshire]

July 5, 1639

T he first document reproduced in this collection is a typical political covenant. A comparison with the Mayflower Compact [3] shows both the similarity with that earlier document as well as the more developed, detailed content of this one. It is quite certain that the people of Exeter had not read, or even heard of, the Mayflower Compact. The similarities between the two result instead from their common roots in the church covenant form. Many editors, including Francis N. Thorpe, reproduce the agreement only up to the thirty-five signatures. In this volume, however, the oaths immediately following in the town records are also reproduced because they are clearly part of the founding act. The words "doe in the name of Christ & in the sight of God" constitute the oath that makes this agreement a covenant, and the oaths of the elders and of the people following the signatures, to be administered later to everyone joining these categories, ensure that all future citizens and leaders are made parties to the original covenant.

W hereas it hath pleased the Lord to moue the heart of our Dread Soveraigne Charles, by the grace of God, King of England, Scotland, France & Ireland, to grant license & liberty to sundry of his subjects to plant themselves in the westerne partes of America: Wee, his loyall subjects, brethren of the church of Exeter, situate & lying upon Piscataquacke, wth other inhabitants there, considering wth ourselves the holy will of god and our owne necessity, that we should not live whout wholsome lawes & government amongst us, of wch we are altogether destitute; doe in the name of Christ & in the sight of God combine ourselves together, to erect & set up amongst us such government as shall be to our best discerning, agreeable to the will of god, professing ourselves subjects to our Sovereign Lord King Charles, according to the Libertys of our English Colony of the Massachusetts & binding ourselves solemnely by the grace & helpe of Christ & in his name & fear to submit ourselves to such godly & christian laws as are established in the realme of England to our best knowledge, & to all other such lawes wch shall upon good grounds, be made & inacted amongst us according to God, yt we may live quietly & peaceablely together, in all godliness and honesty.

Mon., 5th d., 4th, 1639.
[Signed by John Whelewright and thirty-four others.]

THE ELDERS OR RULERS OATH

You shall swear by the great and dreadful Name of the High God, Maker and Governor of Heaven and earth and by the Lord Jesus Christ, the Prince of the Kings and rulers of the earth, that in his Name and fear you will rule and govern his people according to the righteous will of God, ministering justice and judgment on the workers of iniquite, and ministering due incouragement and countenance to well doers, protecting of the people so far as in you lieth, by the help of God from foreigne annoyance and inward desturbance, that they may live a quiet and peacabble life in all godliness and honesty. So God be helpful and gracious to you and yours in Christ Jesus.

THE OATH OF THE PEOPLE

We do swear by the Great and dreadful Name of the High God, Maker and Governor of heaven and earth, and by the Lord Jesus Christ, the King and Saviour of his people, that in his Name and fear, we will submit ourselves to be ruled and governed according to the will and word of God, and such wholsome laws and ordinances as shall be derived therefrom by our honored Rulers and the lawful assistants, with the consent of the people, and that we will be ready to assist them by the help of God, in the administration of justice and preservation of the peace, with our bodies and goods and best endeavors according to God. So God protect and save us and ours in Jesus Christ.

Complete text and spelling taken from Isaac W. Hammond, ed., *Documents Relating to Towns in New Hampshire* (Concord, N.H.: Parsons B. Cogswell, 1882), 32–134. The spelling and grammar of the original are retained here.

2

General Laws and Liberties
of New Hampshire

March 16, 1680

Thisdocument can be compared with such similar documents as the Pilgrim Code of Law, 1636 [20]; the Massachusetts Body of Liberties, 1641 [22]; the Connecticut Code of Laws, 1650 [52]; the Pennsylvania Charter of Liberties, 1701 [61]; and the three Virginia codes [69, 70, and 72]; all of which functioned as codes of law. These early legal summaries, however, inevitably had a constitutional status as well. For one reason, they defined the basic laws of what amounted to new polities because colonial charters granted significant independence for the creation and operation of local government. For another reason, because they selectively appropriated and altered English common law in light of their own beliefs and local situation, these codes amounted to a conscious refounding of English constitutionalism. More than a simple code of law, then, this document, and others like it, contains the beginning of a bill of rights, as well as a description of the basic institutions, and served as a constitution.

PROVINCE LAWS.

The Generall Lawes and Liberties of the Province of New Hampshire, Made by the Generall Assembly in Portsmo the 16th of March 1679/80 and approved by the Presidt and Councill.

For as much as it hath pleased our Sovereigne Lord the King, out of his Princely Grace and favour, to take vs, the Inhabitants of New Hampshire, into his imediate Governmt and Protection, the wch, as we are ever bound to acknowledge wth great thankfulnesse, soe we have great reason to hope and believe yt his Majesty will still continue to countenance and incourage vs with ye Injoymt of such Libertyes, Imunities and ppties as belong to free borne Englishmen, and whereas his Majesty hath been pleased by his Letters Pattents, sent to vs, to confer such power upon ye Generall Assembly as to make such Lawes and ordinances as may best sute wth ye good Governmt and quiet settlemt of his Majesties subjects within this Province:

It is therefore ordered and inacted by this Generall Assembly and the authority thereof, that no Act, Imposition, Law or Ordinance be made or imposed upon us but such as shall be made by the said Assembly and approved by the Presidt and Councill from time to time. That Justice and Right be equally and imparshally administered vnto all: not sold, denied or causelessly deferred unto any. 9 Hen. 3, 29 Stat.; 2 Edw. 3, 8 State.; 5 Edw. 3, 9 Stat; 14 Edw. 28: Edw. 3, 3 Stat.; 11 R. 2, 10, 17; Caro. 1, 10,

CAPPITALL LAWS.

Idollitry.

1. It is enacted by ye Assembly and ye authority thereof, yt if any pson having had the knowledge of the true God, openly and manifestly have or worship any other God but the Lord God, he shall be put to death. Ex. 22:20; Deu. 13; 6 and 10.

Blasphemy.

2. If any pson wthin ye Province professing ye true God shall wittingly and willingly presume to blaspheme the wholly name of God, Father, Son or Holy Ghost, wth direct, express, presumptions or high-handed blasphemy, either by willful or obstinate denying ye true God or his creation or Governmt of ye world, or shall curse God, Father, Son, or Holy Ghost, such pson shall be put to death. Levit. 24: 15 and 16.

Treason.

3. Treason against ye pson of our Souereigne, ye King, the State, and Comon Wealth of England, shall be punished wth death.

Publique Rebellion.

4. If any man conspire and attempt any Invasion or insurrection or Publique Rebellion against this his Majesties Province, or shall endeavor to surprise any towne or townes, fort or forts therein, or shall treacherously or perfidiously attempt the alteration and subversion of the fundamental frame

of ye Government, according to his Majesties constitution by his Letters Pattents, every such pson shall be put to death, or otherwise greveously punished.

5. If any pson shall comitt wilfull murther by killing any man, woe; or child, upon premeditated malice, hatred or cruelty, not in a way of necessary and just defence, nor by casualty against his will, he shall be put to death.

6. If any pson slayeth another pson sudenly, in his anger and cruelty of passion, he shall be put to death.

7. If any pson shall slay another through guile, either by pysoning or other such devilish practice, he shall be put to death.

Witchcraft.

8. If any Christian, soe called, be a witch, yt is, hath or consulted wth a familiar spirit, he or they shall be put to death.

Beastiality.

9. If any man lie wth a beast or bruite creature by carnall copulation, they shall surely be put to death, and ye beast shall be slaine and buried, and not eaten.

Buggery.

10. If any man lieth with mankind as he lieth wth a woman, both of them hath committed abomination; they shall be surely put to death, unless the one pty were forced or be vnder 14 years of age; and all other sodomitical filthiness shall be sevearly punished according to the nature of it.

False Witness.

11. And if any pson rise up by false witness, and of purpose to take away a man's life, he shall be put to death.

Man Stealing.

12. If any man stealeth mankind, he shall be put to death or otherwise grieviously punished.

Cursing Parents.

13. If any child or children above 16 years old, of competent understanding, shall curse or smite their natural father or mother, he or they shall be

put to death, unless it can be sufficiently testified that the parents have been very unchristianly negligent of ye education of such children, or soe provoked them by extreme cruell correction yt they have been forced thereunto to preserve themselves from death or maiming.

A Rebellious Son.

14. If any man have a rebellious or stubborne son of sufficient years and vnderstanding, viz. 16 years of age or upwards, wch shall not obey ye voyce of his father or ye voyce of his mother, yt when they have chastened him will not hearken vnto them, then shall his father and mother, being his naturall parents, bring him before the Majestrates assembled in court, and testifie vnto them that theire son is rebelleous and stubborne, and will not obey theire voyce and chastizemt but lives in sundry notorious crimes, such son shall be put to death, or otherwise severely punished.

Raped.

15. If any man shall ravish a maid or woeman by committing carnal copulation wth her, that is above 10 years of age, or if she were vndr 10 years of age, though her will was gained by him, he shall be punished wth death, or some other greivous punishmt as the fact may be circumstanced.

Wilful Burning.

16. Whosoever shall wilfully or on purpose burn any house, ship, or barque, or any other vessell of considerable value, such pson shall be put to death, or otherwise greviously punished, as ye case may be circumstanced.

CRIMINALL LAWS.

1. It is ordered by the Assembly and the authority thereof that wt pson soever is to answer any criminal ofence, whether they be in prison or under baile, his case shall be heard and determined at the court yt hath cognizance therof.

Adultery.

2. It is Inacted by this Assembly that whosoever shal comitt Adultery wth a married woe: or one betrothed to another man, both of them shall be sevearly punished by whiping two severall times, not exceeding 40 lashes, vizt., once when ye Court is sitting at wch they were convicted of the fact,

and ye 2d time as the court shall order, and likewise shall ware 2 cappitall letter A.D. cut out in cloth and sowed on theire upermost garmts on theire arms or back, and if at any time they shall be found wthout the said letters so woren whilst in this Governmt, to be forthwth taken and publiquely whiped, and so from time to time as often they are found not to weare them.

Fornication.

3. It is ordered by this Assembly and the authority thereof that if any man comit Fornication with any single woe: they shall be punished, either by injoyning marriage, or fine or corporall punishmt, or all or any of these, as ye judges of ye court yt hath cognizance of ye case shall appoint, and if any comitt carnall copulation after contract before marriage, they shall be amerced each of them 50s. and be imprisoned, if the court see reason; and if any cannot and will not pay ye fine, then to be punished by whiping. And for ye more discountenancing this prevailing evill, the Assembly hath further determined yt such as transgress in any of these wayes, shall be convicted in publique court, theire fines shall be paid in money.

Burglary.

4. For as much as many psons of late years have been and are apt to be injurious to the Lives and Goods of others, notwithstanding all Laws and means to prevent the same, it is therefore ordered by this Assembly and ye authority thereof yt if any pson shall comitt Burglary by breaking vp any dwelling house or ware house, or shall foreceably robb any pson in ye field or high wayes, such offenders shall for the first offence be branded on the right hand wth ye letter B; and if he shall offend in the like kind a 2d time he shall be branded on the other and be severaly whiped, and if either were comitted on ye Lord's day his brand shall be sett on his forehad, and if he shall fall into the like offence the 3rd time he shall be put to death as being incoragable, or otherwise greviously punished, as ye court shall determine.

Fellony.

5. And whosoever shall steale or attempt to steale any ship, barque or vessell of burden, or any publique amunition, shall be severaly punished according to the nature of such a fact, provided it extends not to Life or Limb.

6. That if any strangers or inhabitants of this Province shall be legally convicted of stealing or purloyning any horses, chattels, money, or other goods of any kind, he shall be punished by restoring 3 fold to the ptie wronged, and a fine or corporall punishmt, as the court or 3 of the councell shall determine. Provided that such sentance, where not given by ye court, it shall be at the liberty of ye delinquent to appeale to ye next court, putting in due caution there to appeare and abide a Tryall.

Council's Power in Criminals.

7. That any one of ye Councill may heare and determine such small thefts and pilferings as exceeds not ye damage or fine of 40s., or penalty of stocking or whipping not exceeding 10 strypes, or only legall admonition, as he shall see cause, saveing liberty of appeale to the delinquent as aforesd.

Swearing.

8. It is ordered by this Assembly and the authority thereof yt if any pson wthin this province shall sweare rashly or vainly by the holy name of God, or other oathes, he shall forfeit to the common Treasury for every such offence 10s., and it shall be in the power of any member of the Councill by warrant to ye Constable to call such pson before him, and vpon suffissient profe, to sentence such offenders and to give orders to levy ye fine; if such pson be not able or shall refuse the said fine, he shall be comitted to the stocks, there to continue for a time not exceeding 3 hours, nor less than 1 houre; and if any pson shall sweare more oathes than one at a time before they remove out of the roome or company where hee soe sweared, he shall then pay 20s., the like penalty shall be inflicted for profane and wicked cursings of any pson or creature, and for multiplying the same as it is appoynted for profaine swearing; and in case any pson so offending by multiplying oathes or curses shall not pay his or theire fine forthwith, they shall be whipped or comitted to prison till they shall pay the same, at the discresion of ye Court or Judges that shall have cognisence thereof.

Profaning the Lord's Day.

9. Upon information of sundry abuses and misdemeanors comitted by divers persons on ye Lord's Day, It is therefore ordered and inacted by this Generall Assembly, That wt pson soever wthin this Governmt shall pfane ye Lord's Day, by doeing unnessary servell worke or travell, or by sports or

recreations, or by being at ordinarys in time of publique worship, such pson or psons shall forfeite 10s., or be whipt for every such offence, and if it appeares yt ye sin was proudly or presumptiously, and wth a high hand, comitted against the known comand and authority of ye Blessed God, such person therein dispising and reproaching ye Lord, shall be sevearly punished, at ye Judgmt of ye Court.

Contempt of God's Word, or Ministers.

10. It is inacted c., for as much as ye open contempt of God's word and ye messengers thereof, is ye desolating sin of sevell States and Churchs, It is therefore enacted, that if any Christian, so called, in this Province, shall speak contempteously of the Holy Scriptures, or of ye holy penmen thereof, such pson or psons shall be punished by fine or corporall punishmt, as ye Court shall see reason, so as it extend not to life or limbe, or shall behave himself contempteously toward the Word of God preached, or any minister thereof called and faithfully dispensing ye same in any congregation, either by manifest interrupting him in his ministeriall dispensations, or falsely or peremtorily charging him with teaching error, to ye disparagmt and hinderance of ye work of Christ in his hands; or manifestly or contempteously reproach ye wayes, churches or ordinances of Christ, being duely convicted thereof, he or they, for the first transgression, be amerced 20s. to the province use, or to sett in ye stocks not exceeding 4 hours; but if he or they go on to transgres in ye same kind, then to be amerced 40s., or to be whiped for every such trancegression.

Forcible Detaining Possession.

11. It is ordered c., yt where a judgement is given in any Court, for any pson, or house, or lands, upon ye tryal of the title thereof, or other just cause, if the pson against whome ye Judgmt is given doth either forceably detaine possesion thereof, either against the officer impowered to serve an execution thereon, or otherwise after execution served, enter upon it again, and soe retain possession by force, he shall be accounted a high offendr against ye Law, and breaker of the publique peace; therefore, speedily to redress such a criminall offence, every of the Councill is impowered, and by his place hath power to give warrant and comand to ye Marshall, officer and other men whome he thinks meet to be imployed in the case or business, the Marshall or other officers requiring aid greater or less as need require to sup-

press ye force and give possession to ye owner, and to imprission such as doe appear to be delinquents and their aiders and abettors, to be forth coming at ye next Court, yt did give ye Judgmt in the case, there to make their answer, and whom the court doth find guilty, to sett such fine or other punishmt upon them, as the merrit of their severall cases doth require.

Conspiricie Against This Province, Etc.

12. It is ordered &c., That whosoever shall disturb or undermine the peace of this Province or Inhabitants thereof, by plotting wth others, or by his own tumultuous and offenceive carrage, traducing, quarreling, challenging, or assaulting, or any other way tending to publicque disturbance, in wt place soever it be done, or shall defame any Court of Justice, or any of his Majesties councill, or Judges of any court in this Province, in respect of any act or sentence therein passed, every such offender upon due proof made shall be by ye Councill punished by fine, imprisonmt, binding to ye peace or good behaviour, according to the quality and measure of the offence or disturbance to them, seeming just and equall.

And that such as beate, hurt or strike an other person, shall be lyable to pay unto ye ptie hurt or stricken, together wth such fine to the Province, as, on consideration of the ptie smiting or being smitt, and wth wt instrument, danger more or less, time, place, provocation, c., shall be judged just and reasonable, according to the nature of the offence.

Forgery of Deeds.

13. It is ordered, &c., yt if any pson shall forge any deed or conveiance, testimt, bond, bill, release, acquittances, letters of attourney, or any writing, to the injury of another, to prevent equity and justice, he shall pay ye ptie agreived double damage, and be fined so much himself, to ye Province's vse, and if he cannot pay it, to be publiquely whiped and be branded with a Roman F in ye forehand.

Defacing Records.

14. Be it also enacted, yt if any notary, or keeper of publique records or writings, shall wilfully imbazle or make away any such records or writings of concernmt comitted to his keeping and trust, or shall on ppose falsefie

or deface them by raceing out, adding to them, or otherwise, such corrupt officer shall loose his office, be disfranceized and burned in the face, according to ye circumstances of the case.

None to Endeavor to Corrupt Ye Officers.

15. And if any person shall endeavour to corrupt any officer yt keepeth such publique records or paps of concernmt, to procure him to deface, corrupt, alter, imbazle any of them, he shall be sevearly punished by fine, imprisonmt or corporall punishmt, as ye matter may be circumstanced.

Lying.

16. It is inacted by this Assembly, c., That wt pson soever, being 16 yeares of age, or upward, shall wittingly or willingly make or publish any lie wch may be tending to ye damage or hurt of any pticular pson, or wth intent to deceive and abuse the people with false news or reports, shall be fined for every such defalt 10s., and if ye ptie cannot or will not pay ye fine, then he shall sit in ye stocks as long as the court shall think meete; and if the offenders shall come to any one of councill aforesd to execute ye law upon him where he liveth, and spare his appearance at ye Court, but in case when ye lie is greatly prnitious to ye comon weale, it shall be more severely punished according to the nature of it.

Burning Fences.

17. It is inacted by this Assembly, c., That if any pson shall willfully, and of sett purpose, burn any man's fence, he shall make good the damage to the ptie wronged, and be amerced 40s. and be bound to the good behavior, if the court so meets.

Breaking Down Fences.

18. It is further ordered, That if any pson shall wilfully and on purpose brake down an other man's fence, gate or bridge, to ye anoyance either of a pticular person or a neighborhood, he shall make up such fence, gate or bridge, at his own charge, pay ye damage thereby sustained, and be amersed according to the nature of the offence, sauing the right of him yt pulls up a fence sett on his land without his approbation.

Defacing Landmarks.

19. And whosoever shall willfully pluck up, remove or deface any Landmark or bound betweene ptie and ptie, yt hath been or shall be orderly set up by psons therunto appointed, he or they shall be fined from 20s. to 5 pounds, as the offence may be circumstanced.

Unlawful Gaming in Publique Houses.

20. Be it inacted by this Assembly, c., That noe Innhoulder or publique house keeper shall suffer any unlawful games, nor any kind of gaming, in or about his house, for money or moneys worth liquors, wine, beer or the like, on forfeit of 40s., to be paid by the master or keep of such house, and 10s. by each gamester for every such default.

Lottery.

21. Be it further inacted, yt no pson in this Province shall play at cards, dice, or any such unlawful games wherein there is Lottery, at any private house or elsewhere in the Province, on penalty of 10s. fine, to be paid by evry one yt soe playeth, and 20s by the master or head of a family yt shall know of and suffer any such gameing where he hath to command.

Drunkenness.

22. For as much as it is observed yt ye sin of drunkenness doth greatly abound, to the dishonor of God, improverishing of such as fall into it, and grief of such as are sober minded, for ye prevention of ye growing and prevailing evill, It is inacted by this Assembly, and ye authority thereof, yt wtsoever pson shall be found drunk at any time in any Taverne, ordinary, alehouse, or elsewhere in this Province, and be legally convicted thereof, he or they shall for ye first defalt be fined 5s. to ye use of the Province—for the 2d defalt 10s.; and if he or they will not or can not pay ye fine, then to be sett in ye Stocks not exceeding 2 houres, and for the 3d transgression to be bound to ye good behavior; and if he shall transgress a 4th time, to pay 5 pounds or be publickly whipt, and so from time to time as often as they shall be found trancegressors in that kind. By drunkenness is to be understood one yt lisps or falters in his speach by reason of over much drink, or yt staggers in his going, or yt vomits by reason of excessive drinking, or that cannot by reason thereof follow his calling.

Fireing Woods.

23. Whereas many have sustained great damage by indiscreet and untimely fireing of the woods, It is ordered, that none shall fire ye woods at any time but between ye 1st of March and ye latter end of April; and if any shall unnessesarily fire the woods, or not observe this order, damnifie any, he shall make good the damage and be fined 10s., or sett in the Stocks.

Councill's Power in Criminals.

24. It is hereby inacted, yt it shall be in ye power of any member of the councill to hear and determine all criminall cases where the fine doth not exceed 40s., or ye punishment 10 stripes or committing to stocks, always allowing liberty to the delinquent of appeale to ye next Court for tryalls of actions wthin ye Province; and further, in cases doubtful or difficult, it shall be in ye power of ye Judge before whom ye pson is convicted, to bind them over to the next Court in this Province, to comitt to prison as ye fact may deserve, allowing also for entering Judgmt and fileling evidences 2s. 6d.

Prison Keeper's Charge.

25. It is ordered by this Assembly and ye authority thereof, yt no Prison keeper wthin this Province shall suffer any pson to goe wthout the presinks of the prison, yt is delivered unto them for debt, by virtue of any execution, and it is further ordered the houses and yards of the said keepers shall be allowed & accounted the presinks of the sd prison, and yt it shall be lawful for any officer wthin this Province, if he have occation to carry any prisoner to the neerest Prison in the Province, and yt if any Prison keeper shall suffer any such prisoner to goe wthout the presinks of ye sd prison, they shall be liable to satisfie the whole debt for wch ye sd Prisoner was imprisoned, and the sd keeper's fees shall be 5s. for turning the key, to be paid by the person imprisoned, before he be set at liberty.

Marshalls.

26. It is ordered by this Assembly and the authority thereof, yt it shall be lawful for either of the marshalls in this Province to levy executions, attachmt and warrants in any pt of ye sd Province, and yt feese for serving attachmt

wthin theire owne towns shall be 2s. for every attachmts, to be paid by them yt imploy them before they shall be compelled to serve it, and 2 for a warrt: for warrts served upon criminal offenders.

Judgmt and Execution to Stand Good Yt
Were Before Ye Late Change.

27. It is ordered by this Generall Assembly and that authority thereof, yt all Judgmts and Executions granted on any civill or criminal cases by former Courts of Justice wthin this Province, or ye County Court of Norfolk to any of our Inhabitants within this Province, shall be held as good and vallued for and against any pson as when they were granted by the Court at the time of tryall.

GENERAL LAWES.
TOWNSHIPS, &C, CONFIRMED.

1. To prevent contention that may arise amongst vs by reason of the late change of Governmnt, it is ordered by this Assembly and the authority thereof yt all land, Townships, Town grants, wth all other grants lying wthin the limitts of this Province, and all other rights and prop'ties, shall stand good, and are hereby confirmed to ye townes and psons concerned, in the same state and condition as they did before this late alteration. 33 Ed: 1.

Controversies of Land to Be Tried by a Jury.

2. And it is further ordered, yt if any difference or controversy shall hereafter arise amongst us about the titles of land wthin this Province, it shall not be finally determined but by a Jury of 12 able men, chosen by the freemen of each towne according to law and custome, and sworne at ye Quarter Court wch shall take cognisance of the case.

Contracts to Be Paid in Specia.

3. For preventing deceite in trade, yt all men may be on a certainty in matters of contracts and bargains, It is ordered by this Generall Assembly and the authority thereof, that all contracts, agreemts or covenants for any specia whatsoever shall be paid in the same specia bargained for, any law, vseage or custome to the contrary notwithstanding.

Horses.

4. It is ordered by this Assembly and ye authority thereof, that ye brand markets mentioned in the Law, title horses, to brand horses wth, shall be as followeth: for the towne of Portsmouth P, for ye towne of Hampton H. for ye towne of Dover D, and for the towne of Exeter E.

For the preventing of damage being done by horses wthin this Province, by reason of ye goeing upon our lands and pastures wthout some fettering, it is ordered by this Assembly and ye authority thereof yt no horse or horse kind shall be suffered to goe vpon any of our lands and pastures wthout fence wthin this Province, from ye 1st day of May vnto ye 1st of 8ber, without a sufficient pr of iron fetters on his feete, or a clog equivelent, vpon ye penalty for evry owner of any such horse or horse kind yt shall be taken doeing damage, or wthin any man's corne field, meadowes or inclosures, paying 5s. in mo, besides all damage to yt ptie yt impounded them; and if they be found doing damage wthout ye towne brande to wch they belong, ye owners of them shall pay 20s. in mony; and it is likewise ordered yt every towne wthin this Province shall have a distant brand marke, wch they shall brand theire horses wth all yt goe in ye comons from time to time.

It is further ordered that no horse or horses shall be suffered to goe vpon any of our lands and pastures wthout fense wthin this Province yt is known to be vnruly, wthout the approbation of ye selectmen, or ye major pt of them of ye severall townes, vnder ye penalty of every owner of such horse paying 10s. in money to ye ptie yt soe find them contrary to this order, or loose his ye sd horse soe taken.

Time and Place for Keeping Courts.

5. For the better adminstration of justice, It is ordered by this Assembly and the authority thereof, yt these courts following shall be annually kept wthin this Province: A GENERALL ASSEMBLY, to meete at Portsmo ye 1st Tuesday in March, to make and constitute such Lawes and ordinances as may best conduce to ye good governmt of this his Majesties Province, as allso wth the Presidt and Counll, to heare and determine all actions of appeale from Inferior Court, whither of civill or criminall nature. Alsoe, there shall be 3 other courts held at time and place hereafter mentioned by ye Presidt and Councll, or any 6 of ye Councll, whereof ye Presidt or his Deputy be one, together wth a Jury of 12 honest men, chosen and called as ye law directs, for such as desire to be tried by a Jury; evry of wch Courts shall have full

power to heare and determine all cases, civill and criminall, allowing one liberty of appeale from such sentance or judgmt as shall be passed in sd Court or Courts, to ye residt and Councll, together with the Generall Assembly as above sd, provided such appellant give bond to prosecute according to law. The time and place for holding such shall be as followeth:

At Dover ye first Tuesday in June; at Hampton ye first Tuesday in 7ber; at Portsmo the first Tuesday in 1ober.

All Tryalls by Jury.

6. It is further enacted yt all tryalls, whether capitall, criminal, or between man and man, both respecting meritine affairs as well as others, be tryed by a Jury of 12 good and lawfull men, according to the good & commendable custome of England, except the ptie or pties concerned doe refer it to the bench, or some express law doth refer it to their judgmt and tryall, or the tryall of some other court where jury is not, in wch case any ptie agreived may appeale, and shall have tryall by a jury; and it shall be in ye liberty of both plant and defendt, or any delinquent yt is to be tryed by a jury, to challenge any of ye jury, and if ye challenge be found just and reasonable by ye bench, it shall be allowed him, and others wthout just exception shall be impanelled in theire roome; and if it be in case of life and death the prisoner shall have libertye to except against 6 or 8 of ye jury wthout giving any reason for his exceptions.

Constables to Clear Their Rate in the Year.

7. For the better clearing of ye arrears in the hands of the constables.

It is ordered yt if any Constable shall faile to clear vp his rates wthin his yeare, he shall be lyable to have his estate distrained by warrt from ye Treasr, directed to ye Marshall or Marshalls wthin this Province; and for all rates for ye ministry and other towne rates, ye selectmen shall direct their warrts to ye Constables next chosen, to distraine upon the estates of such Constables as shall faile of their duties therein.

Freemen.

8. It is ordered by this Assembly and the authority thereof, yt all Englishmen, being Protestants, yt are settled Inhabitants and freeholders in any towne of this Province, of ye age of 24 years, not viceous in life but of honest and good conversation, and such as have £20. Rateable estate wthout

heads of persons having also taken the oath of allegiance to his Majs, and no others shall be admitted to ye liberty of being freemen of this Province, and to give theire votes for the choic of Deputies for the Generall Assembly, Constables, Selectmen, Jurors and other officers and concernes in ye townes where they dwell; provided this order give no liberty to any pson or psons to vote in the dispossion or distribution of any lands, timber or other properties in ye Towne, but such as have reall right thereto; and if any difference arise about sd right of voting, it shall be judged and determined by ye Presidt and Councill wth the Genll Assembly of this Province.

Marriage.

9. As the ordinance of Marriage is Honrable amongst all, so should it be accordingly solemnized. It is therefore ordered by this Assembly and the authority thereof, that any member of ye Councill shall have liberty to joyne any persons together in marriage; and for prevention of unlawfull marriages it is ordered yt no pson shall be joyned in marriage before the intention of the pties pleeding therein have been 3 times published, at some publique meeting in ye townes, where ye pties, or either of them doe ordinarily reside, or be sett up in writing upon some post of theire meeting house door, in publique view, there to stand soe as it may be easily read, by ye space of 14 dayes.

Making Rates.

10. That thear may be a just and eaquall way of raising means for defraying ye publique charge, boath in church and civill affairs, whereof every pson doth or may receive ye benefit, their persons and estates shall be asseassed or rated as followeth, vizt: to a single rate of a penny in ye pound, every male person above the age of 16 yeares, is vallued at 18 l., and all land within fense, meddow or marsh, mowable, shall be at 5s. [per] acres; all pasture lands without fence, rate free; all oxen 4 yeares old and upward, 3 l.; steers, cows and heiffers of 3 yeare old, at 40s., steers and heiffers, of 2 yeares old, at 25s.; yearlings at 10s.; horses and mares of 3 yeares old and upward, at 20s., sheepe above 1 yeare old, at 5s.; swine above one yare old at 10s.; and all other estates whatsoever in ye hands of whome it is at ye time when it shall be taken, shall be rated by some equall proportion, by ye selectmen of each towne, wth grate care yt pticulars be not wronged; and all ships, ketches, barques,

boates, and all other vessells wchsoever, shall be rateable, as allso, all dwellings houses, ware houses, wharffs, mills, and all handy-crafts men, as carpenters, masons, joiners, shoemakers, taylors, tanners, curriers, butchers, bakers, or any other artificers, victuallers, merchts and inn keepers shall be rated by estymation. If any persons be greved at their being over-rated, they shall have liberty to complain to ye next quarr Court, who shall give them all just reliefe.

Selectmen Take Accounts.

11. For ye more eaquall and imparshall valluing of houses and ships and other estates of mrchts, traders, handycraft, wch must necessarily be rated by estymatyon—

Be it enacted by this Assembly and the authority thereof, yt ye selectmen of ye severall townes shall forthwth take an accot of all such estates, wth ye vallue thereof according to theire ordinary way of rating; a list of wch estates, so taken and vallued, shall be trancmitted to a committee of 4 men chosen by this Assembly out of Dover, Portsmo, Hampton and Exetor, together wth 2 of ye Counll, wch comitte shall examine and compare sd list and bring sd estates to an equall valluation, having respect to the places where they lie, yt no towne or psons be burthened beyond proportion; wch act of said committee in the vtion of sd estates shall stand as a rule, according to which rates and asseasmts shall be made for ye future; ye psons chosen for this Comittee are Richd Walderne, Esqr, Elias Stileman, Esqr, Mr. Ro: Elliott, Mr. Anthony Nutter, Mr. Ralph Hall, Mr. Edward Gove, and ye time of meeting ye 2d Tuesday in Aprill in Portsmoo.

A List of Males and Estates to Be Taken.

12. It is ordered by this Generall Assembly yt warrts be forthwith ishued out to ye Selectmen of ye severall townes wthin this Province, yt they doe forthwth take a list of all ye male psons of 16 yeares old and vpward in theire respective townes, wth ye valluation of all their estates, according to such rules as are past this court; and all psons yt are so rated are to be rated by estymatyon and make returns thereof to ye commitee appointed for yt affaire, at or before the 2d Tuesday in Aprill next.

Bounty for Killing Woolf.

13. It is ordered by this Assembly yt evry psons wthin this Province yt shall, after ye date hereof, kill any woolfe wthin this Province, they shall forthwth carry the head of every such woulfe unto ye constable of ye same towne, who shall bury or deface the same by cutting the eares off, and ye sd constable shall give ye sd ptie a sirtifficate, attested under his hand, of ye day and ye rect thereof; and ye sd ptie procuring such a surtificate shall be allowed by ye Treasurer of ye Province for every woulfe soe ·killed 40s. out of ye next rate made for the Province, but if the ptie be an Indian that killed ye woulfe, he shall be allowed but 10s., and the sd Indian shall make proof that he killed ye sd woulfe wthin this sd Province.

Former Laws to Stand.

14. For a presant settlemt of matters in civill and criminall proceedings, and directions to Courts, Judges and all other officers, it is ordered that those Lawes wch we have fformrly been directed and governed by, shall be a rule to vs in all Judiciall proceedings, soe far as they will sute our constitution and be not repugnante to ye Laws of England, vntill such acts and ordinances as have beene or shall be made by this assembly and approved by ye Hond Presdt and Council, may be drawned up and legally published. The like lawes shall be a rule to all the selectmen in each towne for ye managmt of all theire prudenciall affaires, according to the lawdable customs hitherto vsed.

Province Rate.

15. For defraying to ye publique charge of the Province, It is ordered by this Assembly and ye authority thereof, yt a rate be made of 1½d. in ye pound, upon all psons and estates (ye Presdt and Council, ministers and elders of churches excepted), in this Province, according to ye valuation made by this Assembly, and yt ye Selectmen in ye severall Towns doe forthwth pforme the duty of theire places in ye valuation made by this Assembly, and yt ye Selectmen in ye severall Towns doe forthwth pforme the duty of theire places, in ye making such rates and comitting them to the respective constables, to be imediately collected, and the same to be transmitted to the Treasr of the Province. This rate is to be paid in the speatiaes at ye prices following, vizt: M'ble boards at any mills in Piscataqua Rivr at ye vsiall place of delivery,

at 30s. p. M. M'ble wt oak pipestaves, at some convenient landing place, where yye constable shall apoint,

	at 3 l. p.M.
R: o:·P: 1 Staves p supra,	at 30s. p.M.
R: o: hhd: ditto p supra,	at 25s. p.M.
Indian Corne	at 2½s. p. bush
Wheate	at 5s. p. bush
Malt	at 4s.
Fish	at price currt.

And whosoever shall pay theire rates in shall be abated ⅓ pt.

Constables to Clear Their Rates Within the Year.

16. It is inacted by this Assembly and the authority thereof, That whereas ye Constables of the severall Townes are injoyned to cleare their rates, on penalty of making good ye same out of theire owne Estates—

Penalty for Refusing to Pay.

17. It is therefore ordered yt if any pson or psons wthin this Province, rateable, shall refuse to pay his rate or rates, or discover any estate to the Constable, yt the Constable shall have power to seize his person and carry him to the next prison, there to remaine till he pay his sd rates, or give good security soe to doe.

Marshalls to Levy Fines.

18. It is further ordered, yt every marshall in ye Province shall diligently and faithfully collect and levy all such fines and sums of money, of every person for wch he shall have arrt or execution signed by the Treasurer, or other authority constituted by his Majesty in ye Province, and sd sums soe leyed he shall wyth all convenient speed deliver to ye sd Treasurer or ptie, or attorney yt obtained ye Judgmt or executions wyth wt hee hath done by vertue thereof, vnder his hand, at the next Quart Court, or Sessions in ye Province, after ye receipt thereof vnto ye Treasurer, Secty or Clark yt granted ye same; to be by him kept, and if ye execution or warrt be not fully satisfied the sd Secty., Clark, or treasurer may grant execution for ye remainder.

Marshal's Fees.

19. And it is hereby ordered yt ye Marshall's fees shall be as followeth: For all executions and warrs levyed by them vnder five pound, five shillings; for all executions not exceeding tenn pounds, twelve pence in ye pound; for all executions above tenn pounds and not exceeding forty pound, 10s. for ye 10 l., and six pence in ye pound for evry pound above forty, and one penny in ye pound for every pound abouve 100 l., out of the estate of ye pson the execution is served upon, over and above, besides ye execution, and in all cases where ye above sd fees for levying executions or fines will not answer the Marshall's travell, & other necessary charge, he shall have power to demand 6d.p.mile, and vpon refusall or nonpayment to levy the same, togeather wyth his other fees.

Marshalls May Call for Assistance.

20. And whereas the sd Marshalls have oftentimes need of Assistance in the execution of ye office, it is therefore ordered yt ye Marshall or Constables wthin ye Province shall and have liberty to charge any pson to assist them in ye execution of yt office, if they see need; and whosoever shall neglect or refuse to assist them when thereunto required, the ptie soe refusing, complaint being made vnto any member or members of ye Councill or Court, he shall pay such a fine in money, vnto yye Treasurer of the Province, as Judge or Court yt hath cognisance thereof shall determine, according to the nature of the offence.

Where Marshals Shall Make Demands.

21. And in all cases of fines and assesmts to be levyed, and upon execution in civil actions, the Marshall or Constable shall make a demand at ye place of the pties vsiall abode, if it be knowne, and of the ptie if he be there to be found; if not, the marshall or Constable so employed shall leave at ye sd house his demand of ye same, and lyable to be paid by virtue of sd execution, rate or warrt, for fine attested under his hand; and upon refusal or nonpaymt accordingly, the officer or Marshall shall have power, calling assistance, if they see cause to break open the door of any house, chest or place, where he shall have notice yt any goods lyable to such levyes or execution shall be; and if he be to take ye pson, he may do ye like, if ypon demand he shall refuse to surrender himself. And wtsoever charge the officer shall nessessarily be put vnto upon any such occasion, he shall have power to levy the

same as he doth debt, rate, fine or execution, And where the officer shall levy any such goods vpon execution, yt cannot be conveyed to ye place where ye ptie dwells, for whome such execution shall be levyed (if they be to be there delivered), wthout considerable charge, shall levy ye sd charge also wth ye execution, and in no case shall any officer be put to seek out any man or estates, farther yn his place of abode; but if ye ptie will not discover his estate, the officer may take this pson, and if any officer shall doe injury to any by couller of this office, in this or any other case, he shall be lyable vpon complaint of the ptie wronged, by action or information, to make full resstitution, and no marshall or constable shall in any case make a deputy.

Fines to Be Paid Forthwith.

22. It is farther ordered yt whn any Delinquents are fined to ye Province, they shall forthwth pay their fines in money, or yt wch is equivalent, or give good security to the Treasurer for the same, or ye pson shall be secured till they do it.

Near Relations Not to Vote.

23. For preventing all occation of ptiallity in Courts of Justice, and avoiding of jellousies, It is ordered yt in all civill cases betweene ptie and ptie, where the judges or jurors are neerly related to either ptie, as ye relation of ffather and son, either by nature or marriage, brother and brothrs, vnkle and nephew, landlord and tennant, yt judge or juror soe related shall not vote or give sentence in any case wherein his relations are ye pties concerned.

No Imprisonment Before Sentence.

24. Be it farther enacted yt no man's pson shall be restrained or imprisoned by any authority wtsoever before the law hath sentenced him therevnto, if he can and will put in suffisient security, bail or maine price, for his appearance and good behavior in ye mean time, vnless it be in crimes captall, or contempt in open Court, but in such cases where some express act of court doth allow it.

Legal Notice in Case of Attachment.

25. And it is farther ordered, yt in all attachmts of goods and chattells, Land or Heredittem ts by ye officer, notice shall be given to the ptie against

whom the suite is comenced, either by reading ye attachmt to him, or leaving a sumons or a copie of ye attachmt, vnder ye hand of ye officer, at his house or place of vsiall abode, or else ye case shall not proceed; but if ye ptie be out of ye Province and not like to return before ye court, ye case shall proceed to triall, but judgmt shall not be entered, untill a month after, and execution shall not be granted vntil ye plaintife have given suffissient security to respond, if ye defendant shall reverse ye judgment wthin the space of one year.

Ye Freemen of Each Towne to Chuse Their Officers and Make Orders for Their Townes.—Penalty for Offences.

26. Whereas pticular Townes have many things wch concerne only themselves and ye ordering of yr owne affairs of disposing of business in their owne Towne, It is therefore ordered yt ye freemen of every towne shall have power to chuse yr owne pticular officers, as Consta: Grand Juror, and Jury of Tryalls, Surveyors for ye highways, and like, annually, or otherwais as need requires, and to make such laws and constitutions as may concerne ye well fare of ye towne; provided they be not of a criminall but of a prudenciall nature, and yt the penalty exceed not 20s. for one offence, and that they be not repugnante to ye publique laws and orders of this Province; and if any Inhabitant shall neglect or refuse to observe them, they shall have power to levy the appointed penalty by distress; and if any man shall behave himself offencively at any town meeting, ye rest yr present shall have power to sentence him for such offense, soe as ye penalty exceed not 20s.

Prudential Officers.

27. And ye freemen of every towne shall have power to chuse yearly, or for a less time, a convenient number of fitt men to order ye prudenciall affairs of ye Towne, provided nothing be done by them contrary to ye Lawes and orders of this Province, and yt ye number doe not exceed 7 for one towne; and ye selectmen in evry town shall take care from time to time to order and dispose all single psons and inmates wthin yr townes to service or otherwise; and if any pson be greived at any such order or disposall, they have liberty to appeale to the next court of this Province, yt by law hath prop. cognicence thereof.

None to Cast Ballast into the River.

28. It is ordered yt no ship or other vessell shall cast out any ballast in ye channel, or other place inconvenient, in any Harbor or River wthin this Province, upon ye penalty of tenn pounds.

Age to Make a Valid Act.

29. It is ordered by the Generall Assembly, &c, That no pson in this Province shall have power to pass away lands, Herridittamts, or any other estates, or make any legall or vallued act, or be capable of suing or being sued in any of our Courts, in his or her own pson, vntill they attaine vnto ye age of 21 years; but any orphan may choose yr Gardean, to act for them at ye age of 14 years, to secure or Defend yr estates During ye minority; also yt all parents and masters shall have power in all civill cases to prosecute and Defend ye Rights of yr children or sevants during the time of their nonage, and in all criminal cases every person, younger as well as elder, shall be Lyable to answer in yr owne person for any misdemeanures charged upon them, and may also Inform against any other person to any Court, member of ye Counll, or Grand Jury man wthin this Province.

Any Member of Ye Council or Clark to Grant Attachmts, and How Attachments Are to Be Served.

30. And it is further ordered, yt it shall be in ye Power of any member of ye Counll or any Clarke of ye writs allowed of by any of our gen. Courts, to grant sumons and attachmts in all civil proceedings.

It is ordered, yt all sumons or attachmts shall be served 6 days inclusively before ye court where ye case is to be tryed, and ye cause or ground of ye action shall in ye said process be briefly Declared, and wt capassity ye Plaintiffe sheweth, whither in his owne name, or as Attorney, assigne, gardian, executr, Adminr, Agent, or such like: or in Defect thereof, if exception be taken before ye pties Joyne Ishew, it shall be accoumpted a Legall barr, and ye Plaintiff shall be lyable to pay Cost, but no circumstantiall error in a sumons or attachmt where ye ptie and case intended may be Rationaly understood, shall be taken as a sufficeint ground for a nonsuit.

Plant. or Defendt Not Apearing, to Be Nonsuited.

31. And if either plaintif or Defendant doe make default of appearing, having been 3 times distinctly called by ye Marshall, or other office appointed by ye court to call, the plaintiff shall be nonsuited and Lyable to pay the Defendant Cost.

Ye Defendt Not Apearing, Ye Surety or Goods Attached to Stand.

32. It is enacted by ye General Assembly and authority yrof, yt if ye Defendant faile of his appearance, if it apears by ye process yt goods were attached or surety or sureteis bound for his apearance after ye surety hathe been 3 times called, ye action shall proceed to tryall, and if ye Judgmt be granted to ye plaintif, execution shall Ishew forthe against ye Defendant, and ye surety or goods attached shall stand good for 1 moth after Judgmt., but if the execution be not extended wthin one moth after judgment, ye goods attached or suretys bound shall be Released.

No Officer to Baile Any Wthout Good Surety.

33. And yt no pson may Loose or be Defrauded of his Just debt, it is ordered yt no Marshall, Constable or other officer shall baile any pson yt he hath attached, wthout sufficient surety; vizt, one or more yt is a settled inhabitant wthin this province, and yt hathe a visible Estate to be Responsible, according to ye bond Required.

Judgment to Be Acknowledged Before 2 of Ye Counll, &C.

34. It is further enacted, yt any pson yt is attached to our gen. Court, and desirous to prevent farther charge, shall have Liberty, upon notice given to ye plaintiff or his attorney, to appear before 2 of ye members of ye Counll and ye Clark or Recorder of any gen. Court wthin this province, and acknowledge a Judgment, wch shall stand good and valid in Law, provided yt ye goods attached or surety bound shall not be Released till a month after ye acknowledgmt of such Judgmt, unless ye Crr give under his hand yt he is satisfied, and yt such pson as Live out of ye Province, the acknowledgmt of a Judgmt shall not free ym. unless they shall produce a sufficient surety yt is a settled inhabitant wthin ye Judgmt, and ye Execution to stand good against ye surety for a full month after.

Persons Notified Not Apearing, Ye Penalty.

35. Be it farther enacted, that if any pson summoned to answer any presentmt, or for any fact or misdemeanor, do not appear at ye time appointed, he or they shall be proceeded aginst for contempt, except it appears they have been prevented by the hand of God.

Plaint. May Wthdraw His Action.

36. It is also enacted, yt it shall be at ye Liberty of the Plaintiff to wthdraw his action at any time before ye Judge or Jury have given in yr verdict in ye case, in wch case he shall pay full Cost to ye Defendant.

None to Pretend Great Damage to Vex His Adversary.

37. And yt no pson, in his suit or plaint against another, shall falsely pretend great damage or debts, to vex or discredit his adversary, and if it appears to ye Court yt any plaintife hath wittingly wronged ye Defendant in vexatious suits or complaints, he shall pay ye Defendant double cost, and be fined to ye province 40s. or more, according to the demerrit of his fact.

Actions May Be Reviewed.

38. It is further enacted, yt it shall be in ye liberty of any pson to review any suit or action wherein he hath been plaintife or Defendant in any Court wthin this province, but if any ptie be tweice Cast upon a Review, and shall still persist in a Course of Law, if he be Cast a 3d time his Case shall be Judged vexatious, and shall pay double Cost and such fine as ye Court shall award, not exceeding five pounds.

Innkeepers to Sell No Strong Drinks to Children or Servants.

39. Be it also enacted, yt no ordinary or Innkeeper suffer any Servants, or Children vnder family governmt, to buy (or to set drinking of) any Liquor, wine or other drink, in their houses or where they have to doe, or to spend their time there, wthout ye Leave of yr parents or Masters, unless it be in Case of necessity, on pain of 10s. forfeiture for every offence, ½ to ye informer and ye other to ye poore of ye towne.

A Person Being 3 Mos in Town Shall Be an Inhabitant, Except.

40. Likewise it is further orderrd, yt if any pson come into any town wthin this province, and be there reced & entertained 3 moths, if such person fall

sick or Lame, he shall be relieved by yt towne where he was so long enter-tained, but if ye Constable of yt Towne, or any of ye selectmen, have given warning to such psons wthin ye space of 3 moths yt ye towne will not admit of him, if such pson shall stand in need of Reliefe ye towne shall supply his necessity, until ye Prest and Counll can dispose of him, as to ym shall seem most just and Equall.

Persons Sent From Other Towns, Ye Towns They Are Sent From to Pay the Charge.

41. It is also ordered, yt if any Children or elder pson shall be sent or come from one towne to another, to school, or to nurse, or otherwise to be edu-cated, or to a phisition or Chirurgion, to be cured or healed, if such shall stand in need of Relief they shall be Relieved at the charge of ye towne from whence they came or doe belong, and not by ye towne to wch they are sent; and in case they be sent from any towne wthout ye Province, the taker, nurse, phisition or Chirurgion to whome they are sent, shall take good security to save ye town and Province chargless, or shall be Responcable themselves, for such as need Releife.

President or Deputy to Have Casting Vote.

42. It is further ordered, yt ye Presidt, or in his absence his Deputy, shall have a Casting vote, whensoever there shall be an Equivote, either in ye Gen-eral Assembly, genl Courts, or Councll.

None to Bring in or Entertain Strangers Wthout Leave.

43. Be it also enacted yt no pson, mstr of any vessell, or other, do bring into any of our townes wthin this Province, any pson or psons, wthout ye approbation of ye Prest or 3 of any pson or psons, wthout ye approbation of ye Prest or 3 of ye Counll, or ye, selectmen of each Towne, nor yt any In-habitant wthin this Province, doe entertaine in his family any pson yt is not soe allowed, for more than one weeke, wthout giving notice thereof to 1 of ye Counll or to ye Selectmen of ye towne to wch they belong, on penalty of forfeiting 5 l. to ye towne, and be lyable to be sued and give bond to free ye towne from Damage. Provided this ordr shall not hinder any man from taking of any apprentice or Cov'ent servant, for a year or yeares, yt is at

present sound and well; and if such servant shall fall sick or Lame he shall be maintained by his Master during ye Date of his Indentures or Covenant, and afterwards by ye towne, in case of necessity.

Constables to Warn Freemen's Meetings to Choose Deputies.

44. It is enacted by this assembly and the authority thereof, yt ye severall constables in each towne of ye province doe warne and call together the free men of theire Respective townes, on ye first Monday in february, annually, and from among themselves to make their election of Deputies for ye Genll Assembly, who are to meet at Portsmo on ye first Tuesday of March, by 10 of ye Clock in ye forenoone, and ye number of Deputies for each towne to be as followeth, vizt: 3 for ye towne of Portsmo, 3 for ye towne of Dover, 3 for ye towne of Hampton, and 2 for ye towne of Exeter, whose names, after their election and acceptance, ye severall Consas shall make Return of to ye Assembly, as above vnder their hands; and if any Constable neglect his Duty in calling the free men together, or making Returns of ye names of ye Deputies chosen as above, he shall pay ye sum of 5 l. to ye Treasurer, for ye use of ye Province, for every such neglect; and if any Deputy, after his Election and acceptance, shall neglect his attendance at ye time and place of meeting, or absent himself from ye said Assembly wthout Leave, he shall pay a fine of 20s. to the Province, for Every Dayes absence, and so proportionably for every pt. of a day, vnless some Enevatable providence or such other occation Hinder, as shall be judged by ye Majr pt of sd Assembly a sufficient excuse for sd absence.

Pay for Entry of Actions.

45. And it is ordered, that for ye entry of all actions of appeale from ye qrtr Courts, shall be paid 20s. in money.

The text is taken from N. Bouton et al., eds., *New Hampshire Provincial, Town, and State Papers: Vol. 1, 1623–1686* (Concord and Nashua, N.H., 1867), 386–409. The document is reproduced completely and with the original spelling.

3

[Agreement Between the Settlers at New Plymouth] (The Mayflower Compact)

November 11, 1620

*A*lso known as "The Plymouth Combination," the Compact *was usually referred to by Plymouth inhabitants as "The Combination" and not until 1793 was it termed the "Mayflower Compact," when it was reprinted for the first time outside of Massachusetts by a historian in New York. The historical context surrounding its writing, as well as an analysis of its contents, can be found in Harry M. Ward,* Statism in Plymouth Colony *(Port Washington, N.Y.: Kennikat Press, 1973); in Willmoore Kendall and George M. Carey,* The Basic Symbols of the American Political Tradition *(Baton Rouge: Louisiana State University Press, 1972); and in Donald S. Lutz,* The Origins of American Constitutionalism *(Baton Rouge: Louisiana State University Press, 1988). Unlike colonies further south such as Virginia, Maryland, Pennsylvania, and the Carolinas where the presence of some settlers of higher social rank produced a natural, legitimate governing class, New England was settled by men of "the middling sort." In place of a government composed of men of "standing and reputation," the Pilgrims and other New England settlers resorted to formal agreements, signed by all males, as the basis for legitimate government. For this reason, while southern colonies moved gradually in the same direction, New England settlements immediately formed under what we now recognize as constitutional government based on popular consent. The Mayflower Compact is the oldest surviving compact based on popular consent; but see also documents 5, 7, 11, 12, 19, 21, 23, and 32–38.*

[The Plymouth Combination, or The Mayflower Compact]

*I*N *the Name of God, Amen.* We whose Names are under-written, the Loyal Subjects of our dread Soveraign Lord King *James,* by the grace of God of *Great Britain, France* and *Ireland,* King, *Defendor of the Faith &c.* Having undertaken for the glory of God, and advancement of the Christian Faith, and the Honour of our K[i]ng and Countrey, a Voyage to plant the first Colony in the Northern parts of *Virginia;* Do by these Presents, solemnly and mutually, in the presence of God and one another, Covenant and Combine our selves together into a Civil Body Politick, for our better ordering and preservation, and furtherance of the ends aforesaid: and by virtue hereof do enact, constitute, and frame, such just and equal Laws, Ordinances, Acts, Constitutions and Officers, from time to time, as shall be thought most meet and convenient for the general good of the Colony; unto which we promise all due submission and obedience. In witness whereof we have hereunto subscribed our Names at *Cape Cod,* the eleventh of *November,* in the Reign of our Soveraign Lord King *James,* of *England, France* and *Ireland* the eighteenth, and of *Scotland* the fifty fourth, *Anno Dom.* 1620.

John Carver,	Samuel Fuller,	Edward Tilly,
William Bradford	Christopher Martin,	John Tilly,
Edward Winslow,	William Mullins,	Francis Cooke,
William Brewster,	William White,	Thomas Rogers,
Isaac Allerton,	Richard Warren,	Thomas Tinker,
Myles Standish,	John Howland,	John Ridgdale,
John Alden,	Steven Hopkins	Edward Fuller,
John Turner,	Digery Priest,	Richard Clark,
Francis Eaton,	Thomas Williams,	Richard Gardiner,
James Chilton,	Gilbert Winslow,	John Allerton,
John Craxton,	Edmund Margesson,	Thomas English,
John Billington,	Peter Brown	Edward Doten,
Joses Fletcher,	Richard Britteridge,	Edward Liester.
John Goodman,	George Soule,	

The complete text, with original spelling, is taken from the John Carter Brown Library copy of Nathaniel Morton's *New Englands Memoriall* (Cambridge [Mass.], 1669); the library has the oldest surviving reprinting of the document. The original document disappeared sometime during the seventeenth century.

4

[Plymouth Oath of Allegiance and Fidelity]

1625

*T*he Oath of Supremacy, begun by Henry VIII to break the power
of the Roman Catholic Church, and the Oath of Allegiance,
begun by James I in 1605, after the Gunpowder Plot, were both re-
quired by Charles I, who reigned from 1625 to 1649. The latter oath
did not refer to the king as the head of the church and thus was more
acceptable to the Puritans. The Charter of Massachusetts Bay gave the
company liberty to admit new members on its own terms. The colony
at Plymouth, however, was not, strictly speaking, a colony because it
was outside of Massachusetts Bay territory and lacked its own char-
ter. Plymouth took advantage of its position to avoid both the Oath
of Supremacy and the Oath of Allegiance by writing its own oath,
which did not mention the king but instead created allegiance pri-
marily to the colony. In the absence of a document that explicitly cre-
ated a polity, such as the Mayflower Compact, an oath such as this
one became the covenantal basis for a "civil body politick," as the Pil-
grims put it, and effectively served as both a founding document and
a means of naturalizing later arrivals to the colony. Here, as in other
similar documents (9, 15, and 16, for example), we find an efficient
use of a religious form to implicitly create a civil society, establish and
underwrite its legitimacy, define citizenship, provide a means for
adding new citizens later, and define a police power, while enunci-
ating a political theory based on popular consent, political equality,
and loyalty to the common good of the citizenry.

FORM OF OATH FOR ALL INHABITANTS

You shall sweare by the name of the great God . . . & earth & in his holy
fear, & presence that you shall not speake, or doe, devise, or advise, anything
or things, acte or acts, directly, or indirectly, By land, or water, that doth,

shall, or may, tend to the destruction or overthrowe of this present plantation, Colonie, or Corporation of this towne Plimouth in New England.

Neither shall you suffer the same to be spoken, or done, but shall hinder & opposse the same, by all due means you can.

You shall not enter into any league, treaty, Confederace or combination, with any, within the said Colonie or without the same that shall plote, or contrive any thing to the hurte & ruine of the growth, and good of the said plantation.

You shall not consente to any such confederation, nor conceale any known unto you certainly, or by conje but shall forthwith manifest & make knowne by same, to the Governours of this said towne for the time being.

And this you promise & swear, simply & truly, & faithfully to performe as a true christian [you hope for help from God, the God of truth & punisher of falshoode].[1]

FORM OF THE OATH GIVEN THE GOVERNOR AND COUNCIL AT EVERY ELECTION

You shall swear, according to that wisdom, and measure of discerning given unto you; faithfully, equally & indifrently without respect of persons; to administer Justice, in all causes coming before you. And shall labor, to advance, & furder the good of this Colony, & plantation, to the utmost of your power; and oppose any thing that may hinder the same. So help you God.

---

1. The words "a true christian" were later struck out and the phrase in brackets substituted so that the last sentence read: "to perform as you hope for help from God...."

Text taken from Charles Evans, "Oaths of Allegiance in Colonial New England," *Proceedings of the American Antiquarian Society,* n.s., 31 (April 13–October 19, 1921): 383. Text is complete except for the ellipsis inserted by Evans.

5
[The Salem Covenant of 1629]

Probably the briefest covenant in American history, the Salem document nevertheless presumed that whoever owned it was in total agreement with the Puritan-Calvinistic arm of the English established church. Salem, like many other New England settlements, was initially founded as a popular theocracy—government rested in the hands of church members. Those who did not belong to the settlement's approved church, originally a group few in number, did not have rights of citizenship. An oath such as this one made one who took it simultaneously a member of the church and a citizen of the polity. Prospective members were subjected to a careful examination as to their knowledge, experience of grace, and godly conversation. Within a few years, as the percentage of nonchurch members grew, conflict within the colony forced the Salem community to draw up the Enlarged Covenant of 1636, which included specific articles encouraging harmony and fellowship (see The Enlarged Salem Covenant [18]). As the number of churched citizens faded into a minority, the form of a church covenant was retained, but the substance of the covenant shifted to become purely political.

We Covenant with the Lord and one with an other; and doe bynd our selves in the presence of God, to walke together in all his waies, according as he is pleased to reveale himselfe unto us in his Blessed word of truth.

Complete text and spelling taken from Williston Walker, *The Creeds and Platforms of Congregationalism* (Boston: The Pilgrim Press, 1960), 197.

6

[Agreement of the Massachusetts Bay Company at Cambridge, England]

August 26, 1629

*A*lthough not written on American shores, the Agreement at Cambridge was written not by any English authorities but by the colonists themselves before embarking. It stands, therefore, in the same category as the Mayflower Compact, which some historians believe was also composed in England before departure and only brought out for signing before debarking in America. The signatures affixed to the following document were put there in England, however.

––––––––––––––

The true coppie of the Agreement of Cambridge, August 26. 1629.

Upon due consideracion of the state of the plantacion now in hand for New England, wherein wee (whose names are hereunto subscribed) have ingaged ourselves: and having weighed the greatnes of the worke in regard of the consequences, Gods glory and the churches good: As also in regard of the difficultyes and discourgements which in all probabilityes must be forcast upon the prosecucion of this businesse: Considering withall that this whole adventure growes upon the joynt confidence we have in each others fidelity and resolucion herein, so as no man of us would have adventured it without assurance of the rest: Now for the better encourragement of ourselves and others that shall joyne with us in this action, and to the end that every man may without scruple dispose of his estate and afayres as may best fitt his preparacion for this voyage, It is fully and faithfully agreed amongst us, and every of us doth hereby freely and sincerely promise and bynd himselfe in the word of a Christian and in the presence of God who is the searcher of all hearts, that we will so really endevour the prosecucion of his worke, as by Gods assistaunce we will be ready in our persons, and with such of our severall familyes as are to go with us and such provisions as we are able conveniently to furnish ourselves withall, to embarke for the said plantacion by the first of march next, at such port or ports of this land as shall be agreed upon by the Company, to the end to passe the Seas (under Gods protection) to inhabite and continue in New England. Provided always that before the last of September next the whole governement together with the Patent for the said plantacion bee first by an order of Court legally transferred and established to remayne with us and others which shall inhabite upon the said plantacion. And provided also that if any shall be hindered by such just and inevitable Lett[1] or other cause to be allowed by 3 parts of foure of these whose names are hereunto subscribed, then such persons for such tymes and during such letts to be dischardged of this bond. And we do further promise every one for himselfe that shall fayle to be ready through his owne default by the day appointed, to pay for every dayes defalt the summe of 3 li[2] to the use of the rest of the Company who shall be ready by the same day and tyme.

This was done by order of Court the 29th day of August. 1629.

RICH: SALTONSTALL

THO: DUDLEY

WILLIAM VASSALL

NICH: WEST

ISAACK JOHNSON

JOHN HUMFREY

THO: SHARP

INCREASE NOWELL

JOHN WINTHROP

WILL: PINCHON

KELLAM BROWNE

WILLIAM COLBRON

1. Hindrance, obstruction, or delay.
2. The archaic symbol for an English pound.

The complete text, with the original spelling, is taken from E. S. Morgan, ed., *The Founding of Massachusetts: The Historians and Their Sources* (Indianapolis: The Bobbs-Merrill Company, 1964), 183–84.

7

[The Watertown Covenant of July 30, 1630]

*S*trictly *speaking the Watertown Covenant is a church covenant
rather than a political one and was the first collective document made by the Watertown colonists. Those signing it understood
the document to be establishing a church-state. Comparison with the
Mayflower Compact illustrates how little difference was needed to
make a church covenant a true political compact, and, as later compacts illustrate, how the move from church covenant to true political
compact was both logical and straightforward.*

July 30, 1630

We whose Names are hereto subscribed, having through God's Mercy es-
caped out of Pollutions of the World, and been taken into the Society of
his People, with all Thankfulness do hereby both with Heart and Hand acknowledge, That his Gracious Goodness, and Fatherly Care, towards us: And
for further and more full Declaration thereof, to the present and future Ages,
have undertaken (for the promoting of his Glory and the Churches Good,
and the Honour of our Blessed Jesus, in our more full and free subjecting
of our selves and ours, under his Gracious Government, in the Practice of,
and Obedience unto all his Holy Ordinances and Orders, which he hath
pleased to prescribe and impose upon us) a long and hazardous Voyage from
East to West, from Old England in Europe, to New England in America that
we may walk before him, and serve him, without Fear in Holiness and Righteousness, all the Days of our Lives: And being safely arrived here, and thus
far onwards peaceably preserved by his special Providence, that we bring
forth our Intentions into Actions, and perfect our Resolutions, in the Beginnings of some Just and Meet Executions; We have separated the Day
above written from all other Services, and Dedicated it wholly to the Lord
in Divine Employments, for a Day of Afflicting our Souls, and humbling
our selves before the Lord, to seek him, and at his Hands, a Way to walk

in, by Fasting and Prayer, that we might know what was Good in his Sight: And the Lord was intreated of us.

For in the End of the Day, after the finishing of our Publick Duties, we do all, before we depart, solemnly and with all our Hearts, personally, Man by Man for our selves and others (charging them before Christ and his Elect Angels, even them that are not here with us this Day, or are yet unborn, That they keep the Promise unblameably and faithfully unto the coming of our Lord Jesus) Promise, and enter into a sure Covenant with the Lord our God, and before him with one another, by Oath and serious Protestation made, to Renounce all Idolatry and Superstition, Will-Worship, all Humane Traditions and Inventions whatsoever, in the Worship of God; and forsaking all Evil Ways, do give ourselves wholly unto the Lord Jesus, to do him faithful Service, observing and keeping all his Statutes, Commands, and Ordinances, in all Matters concerning our Reformation; his Worship, Administrations, Ministry, and Government; and in the Carriage of our selves among our selves, and one another towards another, as he hath prescribed in his Holy Word. Further swearing to cleave unto that alone, and the true Sense and meaning thereof to the utmost of our Power, as unto the most clear Light and infallible Rule, and All-sufficient Canon, in all things that concern us in this our Way. In Witness of all, we do ex Animo, and in the presence of God, hereto set our Names, or Marks, in the Day and Year above written.

Complete text, with original spelling, taken from Cotton Mather, *Magnalia Christi Americana*, bk. 3 (London, 1702), 83. For historical context one might consult Champlin Burrage, *The Church Covenant Idea: Its Origin and Development* (Philadelphia: American Baptist Publication Society, 1904).

8

[Massachusetts Election Agreement]

May 18, 1631

*A*lthough elections had been held in a number of colonies *prior to this date, the Massachusetts Election Agreement is probably the oldest formal colonial provision defining an election process. The "commons" referred to here included all freemen, as clarified by an agreement on May 9, 1632. A "freeman" was one who held town privileges, one of which was the right to live in that town. A "freeholder," on the other hand, was a freeman who owned a certain amount of land, usually forty or fifty acres. The use of "freeman," therefore, essentially included all adult males in elections, without any property holding requirement, and established popular sovereignty, representation, political equality, and majority rule.*

For explanation of an order made the last general court, held the 19th of October last, it was ordered now, with full consent of all the commons then present, that once in every year, at least, a general court shall be held, at which court it shall be lawful for the commons to propound any person or persons whom they shall desire to be chosen assistants, and if it be doubtful whether it be the greater part of the commons or not, it shall be put to the poll. The like course to be held when they, the said commons, shall see cause for any defect or misbehavior to remove any one or more of the assistants. And to the end the body of the commons may be preserved of honest and good men, it was likewise ordered and agreed that for time to come no man shall be admitted to the freedom of this body politic but such as are members of some of the churches within the limits of the same.

Taken from E. S. Morgan, ed., *The Founding of Massachusetts: The Historians and Their Sources* (Indianapolis: The Bobbs-Merrill Company, 1964), 406. The spelling is Morgan's.

9

The Oath of a Freeman,
or of a Man to Be Made Free

1631

*T*he law in the Massachusetts Bay Colony that all freemen must
be church members was modified in 1632 so that no civil magistrate could be an elder in the church. To give force to this new law
an Oath of Freeman was developed. Without the oath, those inhabitants not members of a church would not be bound by the church
covenants, and thus not be bound to the colony. In 1634 it was replaced by a newer oath, which took into account the creation of the
Massachusetts Legislature in May of 1634 [14]. The replacement oath
is reproduced as The Oath of a Freeman, 1634 [15].

The Oath of a Freeman, or a Man to be Made Free

I, A.B.&c. being, by the Almighties most wise disposicon, become a membr
of this body, consisting of the Gounr, Assistants, & a comnlty of the
Mattachusets in Newe England, doe, freely & sincerely acknowledge that I
am iustly and lawfully subject to the goumt of the same, & doe accordingly
submitt my pson & estate to be ptected, ordered, & gouned by the lawes
& constitucons thereof, & doe faithfully pmise to be from time to time obedient & conformeable thervnto, & to the authie of the said Gounr & Assistnts & their successrs, & to all such lawes, orders, sentences, & decrees
as shalbe lawfully made & published by them or their successors; and I will
alwaies indeavr (as in dutie I am bound) to advance the peace & wellfaire
of this bodie or comonwealth to my vtmost skill & abilitie; & will, to my
best power & meanes, seeke to devert & prevent whatsoeuer may tend to
the ruyne or damage thereof, or of any the said Gounr, Deputy Gounr, or
Assistants, or any of them, or their siccessrs, and will giue speedy notice to
them, or some of them, of any sedicon, violence, treachery, or other hurt or

ciuil which I shall knowe, heare, or vehemtly suspecte to be plotted or intended against the comonwealth, or the said goumt established; and I will not att any time suffer or giue consent to any counsell or attempt that shalbe offered giuen, or attempted for the impeachmt of the said goumt, or makeing any change or alteracon of the same, contrary to the lawes & ordinances thereof, but shall doe my vtmost endeavr to discover, oppose, & hinder, all & euy such counsell & attempts. Soe helpe me God.

The text is taken from Charles Evans, "Oaths of Allegiance in Colonial New England," *Proceedings of the American Antiquarian Society*, n.s., 31 (April 13–October 19, 1921): 389. The spelling is the original, and the text is complete.

10

[The Massachusetts Agreement on the Legislature]

May 9, 1632

*T*he first formal specification of Massachusetts political institutions, this ordinance, passed at a meeting of the General Court,
ratifies the existence of the body passing it. Although the document is
brief, a careful reading reveals that the basics of a government are established, which makes it a protoconstitution. Note, however, that
the colony already has a functioning legislature, which represents an
earlier assembly of the people. In this respect it is typical of many early
foundation documents in that the legal founding follows the de facto
operation of institutions.

A General Court, holden att Boston, May 9th, 1632

Present, The Governor,   Mr. Nowell,
Deputy Governor,   Mr. Pinchon,
Mr. Ludlowe,   S. Bradstreete

It was generally agreed upon by erection of hands, that the Governor,
Deputy Governor, & Assistants should be chosen by the whole Court of
Governor, Deputy Governor, Assistants, & freemen, and that the Governor
shall alwaies be chosen out of the Assistants.

John Winthrop, Esq, was chosen to the place of Governor (by the generall consent of the whole Court, manefested by erection of hands) for this
yeare nexte ensueing, & till a newe be chosen, & did, in presence of the
Court, take an oath to his said place belonging...

It was ordered, that there should be two of every plantation appointed to
conferre with the Court about raiseing of a publique stocke...

It was ordered, that the towne of Waterton shall have that priviledge and interest in the [fish] weir they have built upp the Charles Ryver, according as the Court hereafter shall thinke meete to confirme unto them.

Text taken from N. B. Shurtleff, ed., *Massachusetts Colonial Records: Vol. 1, Records of the Governor and Company of the Massachusetts Bay Colony in New England, 1628–1686* (Boston, 1853–54), 95–96. For an introductory discussion on this and other colonial documents concerning representation, see Michael Kammen, *Deputyes & Libertyes: The Origins of Representative Government in Colonial America* (New York: Alfred A. Knopf, 1969).

II
[Cambridge Agreement]

December 24, 1632

*A*lthough the institution of the town meeting predates this
document and had already been adopted in a number of
colonies, this is the oldest surviving agreement establishing the practice. In most instances the town meeting seems to have been adopted
without a formal declaration or even a conscious decision. Even here
it seems to be not so much a matter of establishing a new procedure
as it is a matter of reestablishing it in such a way that attendance
can be legally enforced. The present document is notable for two reasons. First, it indicates the deep commitment to democratic processes
prevalent in colonial New England. Second, it illustrates the difficulties inherent in democratic processes. A direct democracy that
makes popular sovereignty operative on a regular basis places a great
burden on citizens—a burden that citizens may tend to avoid without further "incentives." The inadequacy of such incentives explains
the rapid move to representation that the next document [12]
exemplifies.

Ann Agreement made by A Gennerall Conf for a mounthly meeting.

Impr that every person under subscribed shall meet Every second Monday in Every mounth within the meetinghouse In the Afternoone within
half an ouer after the ringing of the bell and that every one that make not
his personall apearannce there and continews ther without leave from
[   ] untill the meeting bee Ended shall for every default pay twelve
pence and if it be not paid next meeting then to dobl it and soe untill it is
paid.

The text is taken from *The Records of the Town of Cambridge (Formerly Newtowne)
Massachusetts, 1630–1703* (Cambridge: University Press, John Wilson and Son, 1901), 1:
4. The text is complete, with the original spelling.

12

[Dorchester Agreement]

October 8, 1633

*I*n addition to establishing a town meeting, this is the oldest surviving record of a smaller representative body being selected to
serve in place of the town meeting between meetings. The members
of this smaller representative body were usually called town "selectmen." Once these representative bodies were established, the fundamental political problem became one of controlling them so they
effectively continued to reflect popular will.

An agreement made by the
whole consent and vote of the plantation made
Mooneday 8th of October, 1633.

Inprimus it is ordered that for the generall good and well ordering of the
affayres of the Plantation their shall be every Mooneday before the Court
by eight of the Clocke in the morning, and prsently upon the beating of
the drum, a generall meeting of the inhabitants of the Plantation att the
meeteing house, there to settle (and sett downe) such orders as may tend to
the generall good as aforesayd; and every man to be bound thereby without
gaynesaying or resistance. It is also agreed that there shall be twelve men selected out of the Company that may or the greatest p't of them meete as
aforesayd to determine as aforesayd, yet so as it is desired that the most of
the Plantation will keepe the meeting constantly and all that are there although none of the Twelve shall have a free voyce as any of the 12 and that
the greate[r] vote both of the 12 and the other shall be of force and efficasy
as aforesayd. And it is likewise ordered that all things concluded as aforesayd
shall stand in force and be obeyed vntill the next monethly meeteing and
afterwardes if it be not contradicted and otherwise ordered upon the sayd
monethly meete[ing] by the greatest p'te of those that are prsent as aforesayd. Moreover, because the Court in Winter in the vacansy of the sayd

[   ] this said meeting to continue till the first Mooneday in the moneth (7) mr Johnson, mr Eltwid Pummery (mr. Richards), John Pearce, George Hull, William Phelps, Thom. ffoard.

The text is taken from the *Dorchester Town Records: Fourth Report of the Record Commissioners* (Boston: Rockwell and Churchill, City Printers, 1880), 3. The original spelling is retained. The text is complete as far as the records of the town are concerned—the gap is in the original.

13

[Cambridge Agreement on a Town Council]

February 3, 1634

S igned only thirteen months after the town meeting was institutionalized in Cambridge, this document indicates the difficulty that early colonies had with involving the entire population in day-to-day decision making, despite their small size (see *The Massachusetts Agreement on the Legislature* [10]). The move from a more or less direct democracy to a representative system closely watched by a town meeting was typical for the early colonies. The degree to which the selectmen tended to dominate the political system usually depended on the degree of religious fervor informing the colony. The more tightly religious a colony was, the more likely that the selectmen came from an oligarchy associated with the church; the more heterogeneous and open the social system was, the more likely that the town meeting continued to control the selectmen.

At A Gennerall Meeting of the whole Towne Itt was Agreed uppon by a Joynt Consent that 7 menn should be Chossen to doe the whole bussines of the Towne and soe to Continew untell the ffirst Monday in November next and untell new be Chossen in their Room soe ther was then Elected and Chossen

John Haynes Esqr
mr Symon Bradstreet
John Taylcott
Wiliam Westwood
John White
William Wadsworth
James Olmstead Constable

Itt is further Ordered by a Joynt Consent that whatsoever these Towns-men thuse Chosse [   ] shall doe In the Compas of ther tyme shall stand in as full force as if the whole Town did the same either for makeing of new orders or altering of ould ones

ffurther it is ordered that whatsoever prson they shall send for to help anny bussness and he shall refus to Come they shall have power to lay a fine uppon him and to gather [   ]

ffurther it is ordered that they shall have [   ] to attent uppon them to Imploy aboute any bussines at a publik charge

ffurther Itt is ordered that they shall meet every first Monday in a Mounth at [   ] in the After Noone accordinge to the former [   ]

Also ther was Chossen to Joyne [   ] James Olmstead Constable John Beniamen Daniell Denison Andrew Warner William Spencer which 5 acordinge to the order of Cour[t] to survey the Towne lands and enter [   ] a book Apointed for that purpose

Itt is further ordered that these 5 men meet every first Monday in the Mounth at the Constables house in the [   ] at the Ringing of the bell

---

The text is taken from *The Records of the Town of Cambridge (Formerly Newtowne) Massachusetts, 1630–1703* (Cambridge: University Press, John Wilson and Son, 1901), 1: 11–12. Spelling is the original, and the text complete, except for the undecipherable words, which are indicated by brackets.

14

[Massachusetts Agreement on the Legislature]

May 14, 1634

*W*hile not a true constitution like the Pilgrim Code of Law *[20], to be written two years later, this document contains a number of recognizably constitutional elements. A General Court, or legislature, is formally established, its powers are outlined, the manner of electing its members is described, and the frequency of its meetings is stipulated. The legislature rests ultimately on popular sovereignty, but it appears that sovereignty is passed to the legislature, much as with its apparent model—the British Parliament, and the people retain only their electoral power as the residual of their sovereignty. Even without the indecipherable passages that marred the previous document, parts of the Massachusetts Agreement remain equally obscure. Together with earlier documents, this one illustrates clearly the gradual, fitful evolution of a viable constitutional form. It is of interest that the protoconstitution is written and adopted by the legislature already sitting.*

A tt a General Courte, holden at Boston, May 14th, 1634 [   ] it is agreed, that none but the Generall Court hath power to chuse and admitt freemen.

That none but the Generall Court hath power to make and establishe lawes, nor to elect and appoynt officers, as Governor, Deputy Governor, Assistants, Tresurer, Secretary, Captain, Leiuetenants, Ensignes, or any of like moment, or to remove such upon misdemeanor, as also to sett out the dutyes and powers of the said officers.

That none but the Generall Court hath power to rayse moneyes & taxes, & to dispose of lands, viz, to give & confirme proprietyes…

It was further ordered, that the constable of every plantation shall, upon proces receaved from the Secretary, give tymely notice to the freemen of the plantation where hee dwells to send soe many of their said members as the process shall direct, to attend upon publique service; & it is agreed, that noe tryall shall passe upon any, for life or banishment, but by a jury soe summoned, or by the Generall Courte.

It is likewise ordered, that there shal be foure Generall Courts held yearely, to be summoned by the Governor, for the tyme being, & not to be dissolved without the consent of the major parte of the Court.

It was further ordered, that it shal be lawfull for the freemen of every plantation to chuse two or three of each towne before every Generall Court, to confere of & prepare such publique busines as by them shal be thought fitt to consider of at the nexte Generall Court, & that such persons as shal be hereafter soe deputed by the freemen of [the] severall plantations, to deale in their behalfe, in the publique affayres of the commonwealth, shall have the full power and voyces of all the said freemen, deryved to them for the makeing & establishing of Lawes, graunting of lands, etc., & to deale in all other affaires of the commonwealth wherein the freemen have to doe, the matter of election of magistrates & other officers onely excepted, wherein every freeman is to gyve his own voyce...

There is leave graunted to the inhabitants of Newe Towne to seek out some convenient place for them, with promise that it shal be confirmed unto them, to which they may remove their habitations, or have as an addition to that which already they have, provided they doe not take it in any place to prejudice a plantation already setled...

It was further ordered, that if any Assistant, or any man deputed by the freemen to deale in publique occasions of the commonwealthe, doe absent himselfe without leave in tyme of publique business, hee shal be fined att the discretion of the Court.

It is further ordered, that in all rates & publique charges, the townes shall have respect to levy every man according to his estate, & with consideration of all other his abilityes, whatsoever, & not according to the number of his persons.

From Shurtleff, *Massachusetts Colonial Records: Vol. 1*, 116–20. An explanation of the events surrounding this document can be found in James K. Hosmer, ed., *Winthrop's Journal*, vol. 1 (New York, 1908).

15

The Oath of a Freeman

May 14, 1634

*T*his is the oath that replaced the original 1631 version [9], and a comparison of the two is instructive. The earlier version reads as though it creates a subject, whereas this oath, at least in part because it rests on individual consent freely given, reads as though it creates a citizen with political rights and duties. Movement from the mentality of a subject to that of a citizen is one major aspect of a diverging political culture that will by 1776 make Americans and Englishmen political strangers.

Att a Genrall Courte, holden att Boston, May 14, 1634.

It was agreed & ordered, that the former oath of ffreemen shalbe revoked, soe farr as it is dissonant from the oath of ffreemen herevnder written, & that those that receaved the former oath shall stand bound noe further thereby, to any intent or purpose, then this newe oath tyes those that nowe takes ye same.

THE OATH OF A FREEMAN

I. A.B., being, by Gods providence, an inhabitant & ffreeman within the jurisdiccon of this comonweale, doe freely acknowledge my selfe to be subiect to the govermt thereof, & therefore doe heere sweare, by the greate & dreadfull name of the eurlyving God, that I wilbe true & faithfull to the same, & will accordingly yeilde assistance & support therevnto, with my pson & estate, as in equity I am bound, & will also truely indeavr to maintaine & preserue all the libertyes & previlidges thereof, submitting my selfe to the wholesome lawes & orders made & established by the same; and furthr, that I will not plott nor practise any evill aginst it, nor consent to any that shall soe doe, but will timely discovery & reveale the same to lawfull aucthority nowe here established, for the speedy preventing thereof. Moreouer, I doe solemnly binde myselfe in the sight of God, that when I shalbe called to giue my voice touching any such matter of this state, wherein ffreemen are to deale I will giue my vote & suffrage, as I shall iudge in myne owne conscience may best conduce & tend to the publique weale of the body, without respect of psons, or favr of any man. Soe helpe mee God in the Lord Jesus Christ.

Further, it is agreed that none but the Genall Court hath power to chuse and admitt freemen.

Text taken from Charles Evans, "Oaths of Allegiance in Colonial New England," *Proceedings of the American Antiquarian Society*, n.s., 31 (April 13–October 19, 1921): 394. The text is complete and unaltered.

16

[Salem Oath for Residents]

April 1, 1634

*A*lthough a part of the Massachusetts Bay Colony, Salem established its own town government early in its existence.
About the time that the Massachusetts Bay Colony was evolving a
more liberal oath, led by Cambridge (see the previous document),
Salem was moving in a contrary direction and attempting to exert
more careful control over its population. Part of this attempt took the
form of requiring even those outside the franchise to take an oath of
allegiance to the colony. The following document comprises that oath
and should be compared with the Massachusetts Agreement on the
Legislature [14].

At A Court holden att Boston, April 1th, 1634.

It was further ordered, that euy man of or above the age of twenty yeares,
whoe hath bene or shall herefter be resident within this jurisdiccon by the
space of six monethes, as an householder or soiorner, and not infranchised,
shall take the oath herevnder written, before the Gounr, or Deputy Gounr,
or some two of the nexte Assistants, whoe shall haue power to convent[1]
him for that purpose, and vpon his refuseall the second tyme, hee shalbe
banished, except the Court shall see cause to giue him further respite.

THE OATH OF RESIDENTS

I doe heare sweare, and call God to witnes, that, being nowe an inhabitant
within the lymitts of this juridiccon of the Massachusetts, I doe acknowledge myselfe lawfully subject to the aucthoritie and gouermt there established, and doe accordingly submitt my pson, family, and estate, to be
ptected, ordered, & gouerned by the lawes & constitucons thereof, and doe
faithfully pmise to be from time to time obedient and conformeable

1. In the late Middle Ages, "to convent" someone meant to call him to an assembly.

therevnto, and to the aucthoritie of the Gounr, & all other the magistrates there, and their successrs, and to all such lawes, orders, sentences, decrees, as nowe are or hereafter shalbe lawfully made, decreed, published by them or their successrs. And I will alwayes indeavr (as in duty I am bound) to advance the peace & wellfaire of this body pollitique, and I will (to my best power & meanes) seeke to devert & prevent whatsoeyer may tende to the ruine or damage thereof, or ye Gounr, or Assistants, or any of them or their successrs, and will giue speedy notice to them, or some of them, of any sedicon, violence, treacherie, or othr hurte or euill wch I shall knowe, heare, or vehemently suspect to be plotted or intended against them or any of them, or against the said Comon-wealth or goumt established. Soe helpe mee God.

Taken from Charles Evans, "Oaths of Allegiance in Colonial New England," *Proceedings of the American Antiquarian Society*, n.s., 31 (April 13–October 19, 1921): 393–94. The text is complete and unaltered.

17

[Watertown Agreement on Civil Officers]

August 23, 1634

*A*lthough at times the records of a colony may have such a richness of expression and content that one gets the impression these settlers did little else but write things down on paper, in most instances the earliest colonial records are quite sketchy. Typically, the first item in the records that survives to our time is brief and dates from a time after the political process was already well under way. The current document is exemplary in this regard. It quite clearly assumes the existence of a community with a functioning town meeting. Thus, while the community is trying to better organize itself, it already has in place a system of direct popular consent that seems not to require any explanation or justification. When reading these documents, it is useful to ask what their authors had to assume in order to write what they did.

August 23, 1634.

Agreed by the consent of the Freemen, that there shalbe Chosen three persons to be [   ] the ordering of the civill affaires in the Towne One of them to serve as Towne Clerk, and shall keep the Records and acts of the Towne. The three chosen are William Jennison, Briam Pembleton, John Eddie.

Taken from *Watertown Records: First Book, Town Proceedings* (Watertown, Mass.: Press of Fred G. Barker, 1894), 1. Spelling is the original, and the text is complete.

18

[The Enlarged Salem Covenant of 1636]

*T*he earlier covenant of 1629 (The Salem Covenant [5]) was apparently found to be inadequate. This "enlarged" version addresses the specific points of dissension that needed to be settled and thus provides a "window" into the colonists' life as a people. Because Salem in 1636 was a theocracy, what appears here to be essentially religious in nature is also political. It would be a mistake to conclude that these theocracies lacked liberty. For one thing, virtually everyone in Salem was there by choice, and the grounding of that choice was the hope to live as a good Christian. Also, this document reflects the determined attempt to use nongovernmental means of social control. Put another way, to the extent such recovenantings as this one were successful in reining in antisocial behavior, the government did not need to intervene and thus did not intrude on personal liberty. One needs to remember, however, that in colonial America liberty was not grounded in individualism but on a community able to live according to laws based on the consent of its members.*

Gather my Saints together
unto me that have made a Covenant
with me by sacrifyce. PSA. 50:5:

Wee whose names are here under written, members of the present Church of Christ in Salem, having found by said experience how dangerous it is to sitt loose to the Covenant wee make with our God: and how apt wee are to wander into by pathes, even to the looseing of our first aimes in entring into church fellowship: Doe therefore solemnly in the presence of the Eternall God, both for our own comforts, and those which shall or maybe joyned unto us, renewe that Church Covenant we find this Church bound unto at theire first beginning, viz: That We Covenant with the Lord and one with another; and doe bynd our selves in the prsence of God, to walke together in all his waies, according as he is pleased to reveale himself unto us in his Blessed word of truth. And doe more explicitely in the name and feare of God, profess and protest to walke as followeth through the power and grace of our Lord Jesus.

1. first wee avowe the Lord to be our God, and our selves his people in the truth and simplicitie of our spirits.

2. Wee give our selves to the Lord Jesus Christ, and the word of his grace fore the teaching ruleing and sanctifyeing of us in matters of worship, and Conversation, resolveing to cleave to him alone for life and glorie; and oppose all contrarie wayes, cannons and constitutions of men in his worship.

3. We promise to walk with our brethren and sisters in this Congregation with all watchfullnes and tendernes, avoyding all jelousies, suspitions, back-byteings, censurings, provoakings, secrete risings of spirite against them; but in all offences to follow the rule of the Lord Jesus, and to beare and forbeare, give and forgive as he hath taught us.

4. In publick or in private, we will willingly doe nothing to the ofence of the Church but will be willing to take advise for our selves and ours as acasion shalbe presented.

5. Wee will not in the Congregation be forward eyther to shew our gifts or parts in speaking or scrupling, or there discover the fayling of oure brethren or sisters butt atend an orderly cale there unto; knowing how much the Lord may be dishonoured, and his Gospell in the profession of it, sleighted, by our distempers, and weaknesses in publyck.

6. Wee bynd our selves to studdy the advancement of the Gospell in all truth and peace, both in regard of those that are within, or without, noe way sleighting our sister Churches, but useing theire Counsell as need shalbe: nor laying a stumbling block before any, noe not the Indians, whose good we desire to promote, and soe to converse, as we may avoyd the verrye appearance of evill.

7. We hearbye promise to carre our selves in all lawfull obedience, to those that are over us, in Church of Commonweale, knowing how well pleasing it will be to the Lord, that they should have incouragement in theire places, by our not greiveing theyre spirites through our Irregularities.

8. Wee resolve to approve our selves to the Lord in our perticular calings,

shunning ydlesness as the bane of any state, nor will we deale hardly, or oppressingly with any, wherein we are the Lord's stewards.

9. alsoe promyseing to our best abilitie to teach our children and servants, the knowledg of God and his will, that they may serve him also; and all this, not by any strength of our owne, but by the Lord Christ, whose bloud we desire may sprinckle this our Covenant made in his name.

The complete text and spelling are taken from Williston Walker, *The Creeds and Platforms of Congregationalism* (Boston: The Pilgrim Press, 1960), 116–18.

19

[Plymouth Agreement]

November 15, 1636

*O*ne might compare this text with the second paragraph of the
*Pilgrim Code of Law [20] where a version of the Plymouth
Agreement was inserted as part of the preface. It is interesting that the
paragraph in the Pilgrim Code of Law where this agreement was inserted indicates that both the Mayflower Compact (Plymouth Combination) and the original charter from King Charles (the
letters-patent) compose the legal background to what is here identified as the Plymouth Agreement of 1636. This efficient and powerful
statement of political liberty should be laid between the Mayflower
Compact and the Declaration of Independence (1776) for comparison. When we read the* entire *Declaration of Independence, its status as a later differentiation of the symbols found in the Plymouth
Agreement becomes apparent, just as the Mayflower Compact obviously stands as a precursor.*

We, the associates of New-Plymouth Coming hither as freeborn subjects of the State of England endowed with all and singular the privileges belonging to such being assembled; doe ordaine Constitute and enact
that noe act imposition law or ordinance be made or imposed upon us at
present, or to come but such as shall be imposed by Consent of the body of
associates or their representatives legally assembled; which is according to
the free liberties of England.

The text is taken from Harry M. Ward, *Statism in Plymouth Colony* (Port Washington,
N.Y.: Kennikat Press, 1973), 17. His text is complete, and his spelling and marking are
used.

20

[Pilgrim Code of Law]

November 15, 1636

*M*uch more than a code of law, this document lays out the fundamental values and political institutions of the community and is a candidate for the honor of being the first true written constitution in the modern world. It was revised in 1658 and then again in 1671. The text should be read carefully, in the context of earlier documents. On the one hand, the Pilgrim Code of Law reflects the attempt to recreate locally the English parliamentary form in a manner consistent with the provisions of its charter from the king. On the other hand, the quiet assumption of local popular sovereignty, reflected in an elected governor as well as in the inclusion of the Plymouth Agreement and the covenantal elements, is consistent with the evolving colonial political symbols going back to the Mayflower Compact. The blending of English and American forms will continue to characterize American constitutionalism. Of particular note, Plymouth Colony is by this time composed of several separate towns, so the document also establishes a federal system of government among those towns whereby each town continues to have its own assembly and officials at the same time there exists an elected colony-wide government as described here.

Whereas, at his Majesty's court held the fourth and fifth of October in the twelfth year of the reign of our sovereign lord Charles, by the grace of God, King of England, Scotland, France, and Ireland, Defender of the Faith, etc., it was ordered that Major William Brewster, Major Ralph Smith, Major John Done, and John Jenny for the town of Plymouth, Jonathan Brewster and Christopher Wadsworth for Duxborough, and James Cudworth and Anthony Annable for Scittuate should be added to the governor and assistants as committees for the whole body of this commonweal, should meet together the 15th of November at Plymouth, above-mentioned, and there to peruse all the laws, orders, and constitutions of the plantations within this government that so those that are still fitting might be established, those that time has made unnecessary might be rejected, and others that were wanting might be prepared that so the next court they might be established.

Now being assembled according to the said order, and having read the combination made at Cape Cod the 11th of November 1620 in the year of the reign of our late sovereign lord King James of England, France, Ireland, the eighteenth, and of Scotland the fifty-fourth, as also our letters patents confirmed by the honorable council, his said Majesty established and granted the 13th of January 1629 in the fifth year of the reign of our sovereign lord King Charles, and finding that, as freeborn subjects of the state of England, we hither came endowed with all and singular the privileges belonging to such, in the first place we think good that it be established for an act that, according to the... and due privileges of the subject aforesaid, no imposition, law, or ordinance be made or imposed upon us by ourselves or others at present or to come but such as shall be made or imposed by consent, according to the free liberties of the state and kingdom of England and no otherwise.

That whereas, before expressed, we find a solemn and binding combination as also letters patent derivatory from his Majesty of England, our dread sovereign, for the ordering of a body politic within the several limits of this patent, viz., from Cowahasset to the utmost bounds of Puckanokick westward, and all that tract of land southward to the southern ocean, with all and singular lands, rivers, havens, waters, creeks, ports, fishing, fowlings, etc., by virtue whereof we ordain, institute, and appoint the first Tuesday in March every year for the election of such officers as shall be thought meet for the guiding and government of this corporation.

This is altered afterwards to the first Tuesday in June yearly by a general court.

That at the day and time appointed a governor and seven assistants be chosen to rule and govern the said plantations within the said limits for one whole year and no more; and this election to be made only by the freemen according to the former custom. And that then also constables for each part and other inferior officers be also chosen.

That in every election some one of the assistants, or some other sufficient person, be chosen treasurer for the year present, whose place it shall be to receive in whatsoever sum or sums shall appertain to the royalty of the place, either coming in by way of fine, amercement, or otherwise, and shall improve the same for the public benefit of this corporation by order of the government; as also to give a just account thereof to the ensuing treasurer and to the governor whenever he shall demand it, or the court when they appoint.

That a clerk of the court also be chosen for the year.

That also one be chosen to the office of coroner to be executed as near as may be to the laws and practice of the kingdom of England, and to continue one year.

THE OFFICE OF THE GOVERNOR

The office of the governor for the time being consists in the execution of such laws and ordinances as are or shall be made and established for the good of this corporation according to the several bounds and limits thereof; viz., in calling together or advising with the assistants or council of the said corporation upon such material occasions, or so seeming to him, as time shall bring forth; in which assembly, and all other, the governor to propound the occasion of the assembly and have a double voice therein. If the assistants judge the case too great to be decided by them and refer it to the general court, then the governor to summon a court by warning all the freemen aforesaid that are then extant, and there also to propound causes, and go before the assistants in the examination of particulars, and to propound such sentence as shall be determined. Further, it shall be lawful for him to arrest and committ to ward any offenders provided that with all convenient speed he shall bring the cause to hearing either of the assisstants or general court, according to the nature of the offense. Also, it shall be lawful for him to examine any suspicious persons for evil against the colony, as also to intercept or oppose such as he conceives may tend to the overthrow of the same. And that this office continue one whole year and no more without renewing by election.

THE OATH OF THE GOVERNOR

You shall swear to be truly loyal; also, according to that measure of wisdom, understanding, and discerning given unto you faithfully, equally, and indifferently, without respect of persons, to administer justice in all cases coming before you as the governor of New Plymouth. You shall, in like manner, faithfully, duly, and truly execute the laws and ordinances of the same, and shall labor to advance and further the good of the colonies and plantations within the limits thereof to the utmost of your power and oppose any thing that shall seem to hinder the same. So help you God, who is the God of truth and punisher of falsehood.

THE OATH OF A FREEMAN

You shall be loyal. You shall not speak or do, devise or advise anything or things, act or acts, directly or indirectly, by land or water, that does, shall, or may tend to the destruction or overthrow of this present plantation, colony, or corporation of New Plymouth, neither shall you suffer the same to be spoken or done, but shall hinder, oppose, and discover the same to the governor and assistants of the said colony for the time being, or some one of them. You shall faithfully submit to such good and wholesome laws and ordinances as either are or shall be made for the ordering and government of the same, and shall endeavor to advance the growth and good of the several plantations within the limits of this corporation by all due means and courses. All which you promise and swear by the name of the great God of heaven and earth, simply, truly, and faithfully to perform as you hope for help from God, who is the God of truth and punisher of falsehood.

THE OFFICE OF AN ASSISTANT

The office of an assistant for the time being consists in appearing at the governor's summons, and in giving his best advice both in public court and private council with the governor for the good of the colonies within the limits of this government; not to disclose, but keep secret, such things as concern the public good and shall be thought meet to be concealed by the governor and council of assistants in having a special hand in the examination of public offenders and in contriving the affairs of the colony; to have a voice in the censuring of such offenders as shall not be brought to public court; that if the governor has occasion to be absent from the colony for a short time, by the governor, with consent of the rest of the assistants, he may be deputed to govern in the absence of the governor. Also, it shall be lawful for him to examine and commit to ward where any occasion arises where the governor is absent, provided the person be brought to further hearing with all convenient speed before the governor or the rest of the assistants.

Also, it shall be lawful for him in his Majesty's name to direct his warrants to any constable within the government, who ought faithfully to execute the same according to the nature and tenure thereof; and may bind over persons for matters of crime to answer at the next ensuing court of his Majesty after the fact committed or the person apprehended.

THE OATH OF THE ASSISTANTS

You shall all swear to be truly loyal to our sovereign lord King Charles, his heirs and successors. Also, you shall faithfully, truly, and justly, according to that measure of discerning and discretion God has given you, be assistant to the governor for his present year for the execution of justice in all cases and towards all persons coming before you without partiality, according to the nature of the office of an assistant read to you. Moreover, you shall diligently, duly, and truly see that the laws and ordinances of this corporation be faithfully executed; and shall labor to advance the good of the several plantations within the limits thereof and oppose anything that shall hinder the same by all due means and courses. So help you God, who is the God of truth and punisher of falsehood.

THE OATH OF ANY RESIDING WITHIN THE GOVERNMENT

You shall be truly loyal to our sovereign lord King Charles, his heirs and successors. And whereas you make choice at present to reside within the government of New Plymouth, you shall not do, or cause to be done, any act or acts, directly or indirectly, by land or water, that shall or may tend to the destruction or overthrow of the whole or any of the several colonies within the said government that are or shall be orderly erected and established, but shall, contrariwise, hinder, oppose, and discover such intents and purposes as tend thereunto to the governor for the time being, or some one of the assistants with all convenient speed. You shall also submit to and obey such good and wholesome laws, ordinances, and officers as are or shall be established within the several limits thereof. So help you God, who is the God of truth and punisher of falsehood.

THE OATH OF A CONSTABLE

You shall swear to be truly loyal to our sovereign lord King Charles, his heirs and successors, which you shall faithfully serve in the office of a constable in the ward of . . . for this present year according to that measure of wisdom understanding and discretion God has given you. In which time you shall diligently see that his Majesty's peace commanded be not broken, but shall carry the person or persons offending before the governor of this corporation, or some one of his assistants, and there attend the hearing of the case and such order as shall be given you. You shall apprehend all suspicious persons and bring them before the said governor, or someone of his assistants, as aforesaid. You shall duly and truly serve such warrants and give such summons as shall be directed to you from the governor or assistants before mentioned, and shall labour to advance the peace and happiness of this corporation and oppose any thing that shall seem to annoy the same, by all due means and courses. So help you God, who is the God of truth and punishment of falsehood.

That the annual election of officers before expressed be at a general court held in his Majesty's name of England. And that the governor in due season, by warrant directed to the several constables in his Majesty's name aforesaid, give warning to the freemen to make their appearance; and that all other our courts, warrants, summons, or commands by way of justice be all done, directed, and made in the name of his Majesty of England aforesaid, our dread sovereign.

And for default in case of appearance at the election before mentioned, without due excuse, each delinquent to be amerced in three shillings sterling.

That if at any time any shall be elected to the office of governor and will not hold according to the election that then he be amerced in twenty pounds sterling fine.

That if any elected to the office of assistant refuse to hold according to election that then he be amerced in ten pounds sterling fine.

That in case one and the same person should be elected governor a second year, having held the place the foregoing year, it should be lawful for him to refuse without amercement unless they can prevail with him by entreaty.

That the government, viz., the general courts and courts of assistants, be held at Plymouth, and that the governor hold his dwelling there for the present year, except such inferior courts as for some matters shall be allowed by this court in other places of this government.

It is enacted that no presentment hereafter shall be exhibited to the grand inquest to be brought to the bench except it be done upon oath, and that it shall be lawful for any of the assistants to administer an oath in such case.

That the constable see the highways for man and beast be made and kept in convenient repair, and therefore be also appointed surveyor for the liberty he is chosen. That two surveyors in every constablerick be chosen each year to see that the highways be mended competently. And if it fall out that a way be wanting upon due complaint, that then the governor panel a jury and upon oath charge them to lay out such way as in conscience they find most beneficial for the commonweal and as little prejudice as may be to the particular.

That the laws and ordinances of the colony and for the government of the same be made only by the freemen of the corporation and no other; provided, that in such rates and taxations as are or shall be laid upon the whole they be without partiality so as the freemen be not spared for his freedom, but the levy be equal. And in case any man finds himself aggrieved that his complaint may be heard and redressed if there be due cause.

That an oath of allegiance to the King and fidelity to the government and the several colonies therein be taken of every person that shall live within or under the same.

That all trials, whether capital or between man and man, be tried by juries according to the precedents of the law of England, as near as may be.

That the governor and two assistants, at the least, shall, as occasion shall be offered in time convenient, determine in such trivial cases, viz., under forty shillings between man and man, as shall come before them: as also in offense of small nature shall determine, do, and execute as in wisdom God shall direct them.

The original text of this document can be found in N. B. Shurtleff and David Pulsifer, eds., *Records of the Colony of New Plymouth in New England: Vol. 1, The Laws, 1623–1682* (Boston: The Press of William White, 1861), 6–12. The original is in a shorthand that is particularly tortuous even for the times in which it was written. The emended version of the text here is consistent with that found in W. Keith Kavenaugh, ed., *Foundations of Colonial America: A Documentary History* (New York: Chelsea House, 1973), 1: 247–51.

21

[Dedham Covenant]

1636

Once again we see an attempt to minimize the need for governmental intrusion into community affairs. In this instance section 3 lays out a process of mediation to regulate social conflict. Whereas section 2 reflects determination to maintain a homogeneous community with respect to values, section 3 reflects a willingness to admit newcomers on an equal footing if they subscribe to the shared community values.

One: We whose names are here unto subscribed do, in the fear and reverence of our Almighty God, mutually and severally promise amongst ourselves and each other to profess and practice one truth according to that most perfect rule, the foundation whereof is everlasting love.

Two: That we shall by all means labor to keep off from us all such as are contrary minded, and receive only such unto us as may be probably of one heart with us, [and such] as that we either know or may well and truly be informed to walk in a peacable conversation with all meekness of spirit, [this] for the edification of each other in the knowledge and faith of the Lord Jesus, and the mutual encouragement unto all temporal comforts in all things, seeking the good of each other out of which may be derived true peace.

Three: That if at any time differences shall rise between parties of our said town, that then such party or parties shall presently refer all such differences unto some one, two, or three others of our said society to be fully accorded and determined without any further delay, if it possibly may be.

Four: That every man that . . . shall have lots [and] in our said town shall pay his share in all such . . . charges as shall be imposed on him . . . , as also become freely subject unto all such orders and constitutions as shall be . . . made now or at any time hereafter from this day forward, as well for loving and comfortable society in our said town as also for the prosperous and thriving condition of our said fellowship, especially respecting the fear of God, in which we desire to begin and continue whatsoever we shall by his loving favor take into hand.

Five: And for the better manifestation of our true resolution herein, every man so received into the town is to subscribe hereunto his name, thereby obliging both himself and his successors after him forever, as we have done.

The text is taken from Kenneth A. Lockridge, *A New England Town: The First Hundred Years* (New York: W. W. Norton and Company, 1970), 4–7. Lockridge in turn drew his text from *Early Records of the Town of Dedham: III, Town and Selectmen, 1636–1659* (Dedham, Mass., 1886–1936), 2–3. Lockridge has modernized the spelling and provides only a partial text.

22

[The Massachusetts Body of Liberties]

December 1641

*B*y 1641 the colony had existed long enough to require a sys-
*tematic summary of the laws already enacted, which would
also serve as a bulwark against arbitrary government. The General
Court adopted a code that was proposed by Nathaniel Ward of Ipswitch. As a devout Puritan and a former lawyer in England, Ward
drew heavily on the code of law proposed by John Cotton in 1636,
which was based on Mosaic principles, and on the English common
law. The result of this blend was the Massachusetts Body of Liberties,
one of the most important and underappreciated documents in American history. The U.S. Bill of Rights a century and a half later would
contain twenty-six specific rights in its ten provisions. At most, seven
of these rights can be traced to Magna Carta, the English Petition of
Right (1628), or the English Bill of Rights (1689). Seven others can be
traced in their origin to the Massachusetts Body of Liberties, which
also included the seven English-originated rights and four more rights
that were first codified in Massachusetts prior to 1641. All but three
of the remaining rights in the U.S. Bill of Rights would originate in
other colonial documents.[1] The Massachusetts Body of Liberties, however, did not make these rights explicitly inalienable in that they could
be altered by the legislature—this differentiation remained for the
future. Still, Massachusetts did not abandon these rights in its later
codes, and the egalitarian nature of the Body of Liberties contrasted
sharply with English common law in 1641, when different parts of the
population had differing rights. The Massachusetts Body of Liberties
is considered the first postmedieval, or modern, bill of rights.*

---

1. A summary of these rights and their origins can be found in Donald S. Lutz, *A Preface to American Political Theory* (Lawrence: University Press of Kansas, 1992), chap. 3.

A Coppie of the Liberties of the
Massachusets Collonie in New England

The free fruition of such liberties Immunities and priveledges as human-itie, Civilitie, and Christianitie call for as due to every man in his place and proportion; without impeachment and Infringement hath ever bene and ever will be the tranquillitie and Stabilitie of Churches and Commonwealths. And the deniall or deprivall thereof, the disturbance if not the ruine of both.

We hould it therefore our dutie and safetie whilst we are about the fur-ther establishing of this Government to collect and expresse all such free-domes as for present we foresee may concerne us, and our posteritie after us, And to ratify them with our sollemne consent.

Wee doe therefore this day religiously and unanimously decree and con-firme these following Rites, liberties, and priveledges concerneing our Churches, and Civill State to be respectively impartiallie and inviolably en-joyed and observed throughout our Jurisdiction for ever.

1. No mans life shall be taken away, no mans honour or good name shall be stayned, no mans person shall be arested, restrayned, banished, dismem-bred, nor any wayes punished, no man shall be deprived of his wife or chil-dren, no mans goods or estaite shall be taken away from him, nor any way indammaged under Coulor of law, or Countenance of Authoritie, unlesse it be by vertue or equitie of some expresse law of the Country warranting the same, established by a generall Court and sufficiently published, or in case of the defect of a law in any partecular case by the word of god. And in Capitall cases, or in cases concerning dismembring or banishment, ac-cording to that word to be judged by the Generall Court.

2. Every person within Jurisdiction, whether Inhabitant or forreiner shall enjoy the same justice and law, that is generall for the plantation, which we constitute and execute one towards another, without partialitie or delay.

3. No man shall be urged to take any oath or subscribe any articles, covenants or remonstrance, of a publique and Civill nature, but such as the Generall Court hath considered, allowed, and required.

4. No man shall be punished for not appearing at or before any Civill Assembly, Court, Councell, Magistrate, or officer, nor for the omission of any office or service, if he shall be necessarily hindred, by any apparent Act or providenc of god, which he could neither foresee nor avoid. Provided that

this law shall not prejudice any person of his just cost or damage in any civill action.

5. No man shall be compelled to any publique worke or service unlesse the presse be grounded upon some act of the generall Court, and have reasonable allowance therefore.

6. No man shall be pressed in person to any office, worke, warres, or other publique service, that is necessarily and suffitiently exempted by any naturall or personall impediment, as by want of yeares, greatnes of age, defect of minde, fayling of sences, or impotencie of Lymbes.

7. No man shall be compelled to goe out of the limits of this plantation upon any offensive warres which this Commonwealth or any of our freinds or confederats shall volentarily undertake. But onely upon such vindictive and defensive warres in our owne behalfe, or the behalfe of our freinds, and confederats as shall be enterprized by the Counsell and consent of a Court generall, or by Authority derived from the same.

8. No mans Cattell or goods of what kinde soever shall be pressed or taken for any publique use or service, unlesse it be by warrant grounded upon some act of the generall Court, nor without such reasonable prices and hire as the ordinarie rates of the Countrie do afford. And if his Cattle or goods shall perish or suffer damage in such service, the owner shall be suffitiently recompenced.

9. No monoplies shall be granted or allowed amongst us, but of such new Inventions that are profitable to the Countrie, and that for a short time.

10. All our lands and heritages shall be free from all finds and licences upon Alienations, and from all hariotts,[2] wardships, Liveries,[3] Primerseisens,[4] yeare day and wast, Escheates,[5] and forfeitures, upon the deaths of parents, or Ancestors, be they naturall, casuall, or Juditiall.

11. All persons which are of the age of 21 yeares, and of right understanding and meamories, whether excommunicate or condemned shall have full power and libertie to make theire wills and testaments, and other lawfull alienations of theire lands and estates.

12. Every man whether Inhabitant or fforreiner, free or not free shall have libertie to come to any publique Court, Councell, or Towne meeting, and

2. Provision of military equipment by a feif.
3. Maintenance allowance provided by a feif.
4. A tax paid by the eldest to retain title to property.
5. Inheritance tax.

either by speech or writeing to move any lawful, seasonable, and materiall question, or to present any necessary motion, complaint, petition, Bill or information, whereof that meeting hath proper cognizance, so it be done in convenient time, due order, and respective manner.

[13.] No man shall be rated here for any estaite or revenue he hath in England, or in any forreine parties till it be transported hither.

[14.] Any conveyance or Alienation of land or other estaite what so ever, made by any woman that is married, any childe under age, Ideott, or distracted person, shall be good, if it be passed and ratified by the consent of a generall Court.

15. All Covenous or fraudulent Alienations or Conveyances of lands, tenements, or any hereditaments, shall be of no validitie to defeat any man from due debts or legacies, or from any just title, clame or possession, of that which is so fradulently conveyed.

16. Every Inhabitant that is an howse holder shall have free fishing and fowling in any great ponds and Bayes, Coves and Rivers, so farre as the sea ebbes and flowes within the presincts of the towne where they dwell, unlesse the freemen of the same Towne or the Generall Court have otherwise appropriated them, provided that this shall not be extended to give leave to any man to come upon other proprietie without there leave.

17. Every man of or within this Jurisdiction shall have free libertie, not with standing any Civill power to remove both himselfe, and his familie at their pleasure out of the same, provided there be no legall impediment to the contrarie.

18. No mans person shall be restrained or imprisoned by any Authority what so ever, before the law hath sentenced him thereto, If he can put in sufficient securitie, bayle, or mainprise, for his appearance, and good behaviour in the meane time, unlesse it be in Crimes Capitall, and Contempts in open Court, and in such cases where some expresse act of Court doth allow it.

19. If in a generall Court any miscariage shall be amongst the Assistants when they are by themselves that may deserve an Admonition or fine under 20 sh, it shall be examined and sentenced amongst themselves, If amongst the Deputies when they are by themselves, It shall be examined and sentenced amongst themselves, If it be when the whole Court is togeather, it shall be judged by the whole Court, and not severallie as before.

20. If any which are to sit as Judges in any other Court shall demeane

themselves offensively in the Court, the rest of the Judges present shall have power to censure him for it, if the cause be of a high nature it shall be presented to and censured at the next superior Court.

21. In all cases where the first summons are not served six dayes before the Court, and the cause briefly specified in the warrant, where appearance is to be made by the partie summoned, it shall be at his libertie whether he will appeare or not, except all cases that are to be handled in Courts suddainly called upon extraordinary occasions, In all cases where there appeares present and urgent cause Any Assistant or officer apointed shal have power to make out Attaichments for the first summons.

22. No man in any suit or action against an other shall falsely pretend great debts or damages to vex his Adversary, if it shall appeare any doth so, The Court shall have power to set a reasonable fine on his head.

23. No man shall be adjudged to pay for detaining any Debt from any Crediter above eight pounds in the hundred for one yeare, And not above that rate proportionable for all somes what so ever, neither shall this be a coulour or countenance to allow any usurie amongst us contrarie to the law of god.

24. In all Trespasses or damages done to any man or men, If it can be proved to be done by the meere default of him or them to whome the trespasse is done, It shall be judged no trespasse, nor any damage given for it.

25. No Summons pleading Judgement, or any kinde of proceeding in Court or course of Justice shall be abated, arested, or reversed, upon any kinde of cercumstantiall errors or mistakes, If the person and cause be rightly understood and intended by the Court.

26. Every man that findeth himselfe unfit to plead his owne cause in any Court, shall have Libertie to imploy any man against whom the Court doth not except, to helpe him, Provided he give him noe fee, or reward for his paines. This shall not exempt the partie him selfe from Answering such Questions in person as the Court shall thinke meete to demand of him.

27. If any plaintife shall give into any Court a declaration of his cause in writeing, The defendant shall also have libertie and time to give in his answer in writeing, And so in all further proceedings betwene partie and partie, So it doth not further hinder the dispach of Justice then the Court shall be willing unto.

28. The plaintife in all Actions brought in any Court shall have libertie to withdraw his Action, or to be nonsuited before the Jurie hath given in

their verdict, in which case he shall alwaies pay full cost and chardges to the defendant, and may afterwards renew his suite at an other Court if he please.

29. In all Actions at law it shall be the libertie of the plaintife and defendant by mutual consent to choose whether they will be tryed by the Bench or by a Jurie, unlesse it be where the law upon just reason hath otherwise determined. The like libertie shall be granted to all persons in Criminall cases.

30. It shall be in the libertie both of plaintife and defendant, and likewise every delinquent (to be judged by a Jurie) to challenge any of the Jurors. And if his challenge be found just and reasonable by the Bench, or the rest of the Jurie, as the challenger shall choose it shall be allowed him, and tales de cercumstantibus impaneled in their room.

31. In all cases where evidence is so obscure or defective that the Jurie cannot clearly and safely give a positive verdict, whether it be a grand or petit Jurie, It shall have libertie to give a non Liquit, or a spetiall verdict, in which last, that is in a spetiall veredict, the Judgement of the cause shall be left to the Court, and all Jurors shall have libertie in matters of fact if they cannot finde the maine issue, yet to finde and present in their verdict so much as they can, If the Bench and Jurors shall so differ at any time about their verdict that either of them can not proceed with peace of conscience the case shall be referred to the Generall Court, who shall take the question from both and determine it.

32. Every man shall have libertie to replevy his Cattell or goods impounded, distreined, seised, or extended, unlesse it be upon execution after Judgement, and in paiment of fines. Provided he puts in good securitie to prosecute his replevin, And to satisfie such demands as his Adversary shall recover against him in Law.

33. No mans person shall be Arrested, or imprisoned upon execution or judgment for any debt or fine, if the law can finde competent meanes of satisfaction otherwise from his estaite, And if not his person may be arrested and imprisoned where he shall be kept at his owne charge, not the plaintife's till satisfaction be made: unlesse the Court that had cognizance of the cause or some superior Court shall otherwise provide.

34. If any man shall be proved and Judged a common Barrator vexing others with unjust frequent and endlesse suites, It shall be in the power of Courts both to denie him the benefit of the law, and to punish him for his Barratry.

35. No mans Corne nor hay that is in the field or upon the Cart, nor his garden stuffe, nor any thing subject to present decay, shall be taken in any distresse, unles he that takes it doth presently bestow it where it may not be imbesled nor suffer spoile or decay, or give securitie to satisfie the worth thereof if it comes to any harme.

36. It shall be in the libertie of every man cast condemned or sentenced in any cause in any Inferior Court, to make their Appeale to the Court of Assistants, provided they tender their appeale and put in securitie to prosecute it before the Court be ended wherein they were condemned, And within six dayes next ensuing put in good securitie before some Assistant to satisfie what his Adversarie shall recover against him; And if the cause be of a Criminall nature, for his good behaviour and appearance, And everie man shall have libertie to complaine to the Generall Court of any Injustice done him in any Court of Assistants or other.

37. In all cases where it appeares to the Court that the plaintife hath willingly and witingly done wronge to the defendant in commenceing and prosecuting any action or complaint against him, They shall have power to impose upon him a proportionable fine to the use of the defendant, or accused person, for his false complaint or clamor.

38. Everie man shall have libertie to Record in the publique Rolles of any Court any Testimony give[n] upon oath in the same Court, or before two Assistants, or any Deede or evidence legally confirmed there to remaine in perpetuam rei memoriam, that is for perpetuall memoriall or evidence upon occasion.

39. In all Actions both reall and personall betweene partie and partie, the Court shall have power to respite execution for a convenient time, when in their prudence they see just cause so to doe.

40. No Conveyance, Deede, or promise what so ever shall be of validitie, If it be gotten by Illegal violence, imprisonment, threatenings, or any kinde of forcible compulsion called Dures.

41. Everie man that is to Answere for any Criminall cause, whether he be in prison or under bayle, his cause shall be heard and determined at the next Court that hath proper Cognizance thereof, And may be done without prejudice of Justice.

42. No man shall be twise sentenced by Civill Justice for one and the same Crime, offence, or Trespasse.

43. No man shall be beaten with above 40 stripes, nor shall any true gen-

tleman, nor any man equall to a gentleman be punished with whipping, unless his crime be very shamefull, and his course of life vitious and profligate.

44. No man condemned to dye shall be put to death within fower dayes next after his condemnation, unles the Court see spetiall cause to the contrary, or in case of martiall law, nor shall the body of any man so put to death be unburied 12 howers, unlesse it be in case of Anatomie.

45. No man shall be forced by Torture to confesse any Crime against himselfe nor any other unlesse it be in some Capitall case where he is first fullie convicted by cleare and suffitient evidence to be guilty, After which if the cause be of that nature, That it is very apparent there be other conspiratours, or confederates with him, Then he may be tortured, yet not with such Tortures as be Barbarous and inhumane.

46. For bodilie punishments we allow amongst us none that are inhumane Barbarous or cruell.

47. No man shall be put to death without the testimony of two or three witnesses, or that which is equivalent there unto.

48. Every Inhabitant of the Countrie shall have free libertie to search and veewe any Rooles, Records, or Regesters of any Court or office except the Councell, And to have a transcript or exemplification thereof written examined, and signed by the hand of the officer of the office paying the appointed fees therefore.

49. No free man shall be compelled to serve upon Juries above two Courts in a yeare, except grand Jurie men, who shall hould two Courts together at the least.

50. All Jurors shall be chosen continuallie by the freemen of the Towne where they dwell.

51. All Associates selected at any time to Assist the Assistants in Inferior Courts, shall be nominated by the Townes belonging to that Court, by orderly agreement amonge themselves.

52. Children, Idiots, Distracted persons, and all that are strangers, or new commers to our plantation, shall have such allowances and dispensations in any cause whether Criminall or other as religion and reason require.

53. The age of discretion of passing away of lands or such kinde of herediments, or for giveing of votes, verdicts or Sentence in any Civill Courts or causes, shall be one and twentie yeares.

54. When so ever anything is to be put to vote, any sentence to be pronounced, or any other matter to be proposed, or read in any Court or Assembly, If the president or moderator thereof shall refuse to performe it, the Major parte of the members of that Court or Assembly shall have power to appoint any other meete man of them to do it, And if there be just cause to punish him that should and would not.

55. In all suites or Actions in any Court, the plaintife shall have libertie to make all the titles and claims to that he sues for he can. And the Defendant shall have libertie to plead all the pleas he can in answere to them, and the Court shall judge according to the intire evidence of all.

56. If any man shall behave himselfe offensively at any Towne meeting, the rest of the freemen then present, shall have power to sentence him for his offence, So be it the mulct or penaltie exceed not twentie shilings.

57. When so ever any person shall come to any very suddaine untimely and unnaturall death, Some Assistant, or the Constables of that Towne shall forthwith sumon a Jury of twelve free men to inquire of the cause and manner of their death, and shall present a true verdict thereof to some neere Assistant, or the next Court to be helde for that Towne upon their oath.

LIBERTIES MORE PECULIARLIE
CONCERNING THE FREE MEN.

58. Civill Authoritie hath power and libertie to see the peace, ordinances and Rules of Christ observed in every church according to his word, so it be done in a Civill and not in an Ecclesiastical way.

59. Civill Authoritie hath power and libertie to deale with any Church member in a way of Civill Justice, notwithstanding any Church relation, office, or interest.

60. No church censure shall degrade or depose any man from any Civill dignitie, office, or Authoritie he shall have in the Commonwealth.

61. No Magestrate, Juror, Officer, or other man shall be bound to informe present or reveale any private crim or offence, wherein there is no perill or danger to this plantation or any member thereof, when any necessarietye of conscience binds him to secresie grounded upon the word of god, unlesse it be in case of testimony lawfully required.

62. Any Shire or Towne shall have libertie to choose their Deputies

whom and where they please for the General Court, So be it they be free men, and have taken there oath of fealtie, and Inhabiting in this Jurisdiction.

63. No Governor, Deputie Governor, Assistant, Associate, or grand Jury man at any Court, nor any Deputie for the Generall Court, shall at any time beare his owne chardges at any Court, but their necessary expences shall be defrayed either by the Towne, or Shire on whose service they are, or by the Country in generall.

64. Everie Action betweene partie and partie, and proceedings against delinquents in Criminall causes shall be briefly and destinctly entered in the Rolles of every Court by the Recorder thereof. That such actions be not afterwards brought againe to the vexation of any man.

65. No custome or prescription shall ever prevaile amongst us in any morall cause, our meaneing is maintaine anything that can be proved to bee morrallie sinfull by the word of god.

66. The Freemen of everie Towneship shall have power to make such by laws and constitutions as may concerne the wellfare of their Towne, provided they be not of a Criminall, but onely of a prudentiall nature. And that their penalties exceede not 20 sh. for one offence. And that they be not repugnant to the publique laws and orders of the Countrie. And if any Inhabitant shall neglect or refuse to observe them, they shall have power to levy the appointed penalties by distresse.

67. It is the constant libertie of the freemen of this plantation to choose yearly at the Court of Election out of the freemen all the Generall officers of this Jurisdiction. If they please to dischardge them at the day of Election by way of vote. They may do it without shewing cause. But if at any other generall Court, we hould it due justice, that the reasons thereof be alleadged and proved. By Generall officers we meane, our Governor, Deputie Governor, Assistants, Treasurer, Generall of our warres. And our Admiral at Sea, and such as are or hereafter may be of the like generall nature.

68. It is the libertie of the freemen to choose such deputies for the Generall Court out of themselves, either in their owne Townes or elsewhere as they judge fittest, And because we cannot foresee what varietie and weight of occasions may fall into future consideration, And what counsells we may stand in neede of, we decree. That the Deputies (to attend the Generall Court in the behalfe of the Countrie) shall not any time be stated or inacted, but from Court to Court, or at the most but for one yeare. that the Countrie

may have an Annuall libertie to do in that case what is most behoofefull for the best welfaire thereof.

69. No Generall Court shall be desolved or adjourned without the consent of the Major parte thereof.

70. All Freemen called to give any advise, vote, verdict, or sentence in any Court, Counsell, or Civill Assembly, shall have full freedome to doe it according to their true Judgments and Consciences, So it be done orderly and inofensively for the manner.

71. The Governor shall have a casting voice whensoever an Equi vote shall fall out of the Court of Assistants, or generall assembly, So shall the presendent or moderator have in all Civill Courts or Assemblies.

72. The Governor and Deputie Governor Joyntly consenting or any three Assistants concurring in consent shall have power out of Court to reprive a condemned malefactour, till the next quarter or generall Court. The generall Court onely shall have power to pardon a condemned malefactor.

73. The Generall Court hath libertie and Authoritie to send out any member of the Comanwealth of what qualitie, condition or office whatsoever into forreine parts about any publique message or Negotiation. Provided the partie sent be acquainted with the affaire he goeth about, and be willing to undertake the service.

74. The freemen of every Towne or Towneship, shall have full power to choose yearly or for lesse time out of themselves a convenient number of fitt men to order the planting or prudential occasions of that Towne, according to Instructions given them in writeing, Provided nothing be done by them contrary to the publique laws and orders of the Countrie, provided also the number of such select persons be not above nine.

75. It is and shall be the libertie of any member or members of any Court, Councell or Civill Assembly in cases of makeing or executing any order or law, that properlie concerne religion, or any cause capitall or warres, or Subscription to any publique Articles or Remonstrance, in case they cannot in Judgement and conscience consent to that way the Major vote or suffrage goes, to make their contra Remonstrance or protestation in speech or writeing, and upon request to have their dissent recorded in the Rolles of that Court. So it be done Christianlie and respectively for the manner. And their dissent onely be entered without the reasons thereof, for the avoiding of tediousness.

76. When so ever any Jurie of trialls or Jurours are not cleare in their Judgments or consciences conserneing any cause wherein they are to give their verdict, They shall have libertie in open Court to advise with any man they thinke fitt to resolve or direct them, before they give in their verdict.

77. In all cases wherein any freeman is to give his vote, be it in point of Election, makeing constitutions and orders, or passing sentence in any case of Judicature or the like, if he cannot see reason to give it positively one way or an other, he shall have libertie to be silent, and not pressed to a determined vote.

78. The Generall or publique Treasure or any parte thereof shall never be exspended but by the appointment of a Generall Court, nor any Shire Treasure, but by the appointment of the freemen thereof, nor any Towne Treasurie but by freemen of that Towneship.

LIBERTIES OF WOEMEN

79. If any man at his death shall not leave his wife a competent portion of his estaite, upon just complaint made to the Generall Court she shall be relieved.

80. Everie marryed woeman shall be free from bodilie correction or stripes by her husband, unlesse it be in his owne defence upon her assault. If there be any just cause of correction complaint shall be made to Authoritie assembled in some Court, from which onely she shall receive it.

LIBERTIES OF CHILDREN

81. When Parents dye intestate, the Elder sonne shall have a doble portion of his whole estate reall and personall, unlesse the Generall Court upon just cause alleadged shall Judge otherwise.

82. When parents dye intestate, haveing noe heires males of their bodies their Daughters shall inherit as Copartners, unles the Generall Court upon just reason shall judge otherwise.

83. If any parents shall wilfullie and unreasonably deny any childe timely or convenient mariage, or shall exercise any unnaturall severitie towards them, Such children shall have free libertie to complain to Authoritie for redresse.

84. No Orphan dureing their minoritie which was not committed to tuition or service by the parents in their life time, shall afterwards be absolutely disposed of by any kindred, friend, Executor, Towneship, or Church, nor by themselves without the consent of some Court, wherein two Assistants at least shall be present.

LIBERTIES OF SERVANTS

85. If any servants shall flee from the Tiranny and crueltie of their masters to the howse of any freeman of the same Towne, they shall be there protected and susteyned till due order be taken for their relife. Provided due notice thereof be speedily given to their masters from whom they fled. And the next Assistant or Constable where the partie flying is harboured.

86. No servant shall be put of for above a yeare to any other neither in the life of their master nor after their death by their Executors or Administrators unlesse it be by consent of Authoritie assembled in some Court, or two Assistants.

87. If any man smite out the eye or tooth of his man servant, or maid servant, or otherwise mayme or much disfigure him, unlesse it be by meere casualtie, he shall let them goe free from his service. And shall have such further recompense as the Court shall allow him.

88. Servants that have served diligentlie and faithfully to the benefitt of their maisters seaven yeares, shall not be sent away emptie. And if any have bene unfaithfull, negligent or unprofitable in their service, notwithstanding the good usage of their maisters, they shall not be dismissed till they have made satisfaction according to the Judgement of Authoritie.

LIBERTIES OF FORREINERS AND STRANGERS

89. If any people of other Nations professing the true Christian Religion shall flee to us from the Tiranny or oppression of their persecutors, or from famyne, warres, or the like necessary and compulsarie cause, They shall be entertayned and succoured amongst us, according to that power and prudence god shall give us.

90. If any ships or other vessels, be it freind or enemy, shall suffer shipwrack upon our Coast, there shall be no violence or wrong offered to their

persons or goods. But their persons shall be harboured, and relieved, and their goods preserved in safety till Authoritie may be certified thereof, and shall take further order therein.

91. There shall never be any bond slaverie villinage or Captivitie amongst us, unles it be lawfull Captives taken in just warres, and such strangers as willingly belie themselves or are sold to us. And these shall have all the liberties and Christian usages which the law of god established in Israell concerning such persons doeth morally require. This exempts none from servitude who shall be Judged thereto by Authoritie.

OFF THE BRUITE CREATURE

92. No man shall exercise any Tirranny or Crueltie towards any bruite Creature which are usuallie kept for mans use.

93. If any man shall have occasion to leade or drive Cattel from place to place that is far of, So that they be weary, or hungry, or fall sick, or lambe, It shall be lawful to rest or refresh them, for a competent time, in any open place that is not Corne, meadow, or inclosed for some peculiar use.

94.

1. If any man after legall conviction shall have or worship any other god, but the lord god, he shall be put to death. DUT. 13.6.10, DUT. 17.2.6, EX. 22.20

2. If any man or woeman be a witch, (that is hath or consulteth with a familiar spirit,) They shall be put to death. EX. 22.18, LEV. 20.27, DUT. 18.10

3. If any person shall Blaspheme the name of God, the father, Sonne, or Holie ghost, with direct expresse, presumptuous or high handed blasphemie, or shall curse god in the like manner, he shall be put to death. LEV. 24.15.16

4. If any person committ any wilfull murther, which is manslaughter, committed upon premeditated mallice, hatred, or Crueltie, not in a mans necessarie and just defence, nor by meere

casualtie against his will, he shall be put to death. EX. 21.12, NUMB. 35.13.14, 30.31

5. If any person slayeth an other suddainely in his anger or Crueltie of passion, he shall be put to death. NUMB. 25.20.21, LEV. 24.17

6. If any person shall slay an other through guile, either by poysoning or other such divelish practice, he shall be put to death. EX. 21.14

7. If any man or woman shall lye with any beast or brute creature by Carnall Copulation, They shall surely be put to death. And the beast shall be slaine and buried and not eaten. LEV. 19.23

8. If any man lyeth with mankinde as he lyeth with a woeman, both of them have committed abhomination, they both shall surely be put to death. LEV. 19.22

9. If any person committeth Adultery with a married or espoused wife, the Adulterer and Adulteresse shall surely be put to death. EX. 20.14

10. If any man stealeth a man or mankinde, he shall surely be put to death. EX. 21.16

11. If any man rise up by false witnes, wittingly and of purpose to take away any man's life, he shall be put to death. DUT. 19.16, 18. 19

12. If any man shall conspire and attempt any invation, insurrection, or publique rebellion against our commonwealth, or shall indeavour to surprize any Towne or Townes, fort or forts therein, or shall treacherously and perfediouslie attempt the alteration and subversion of our frame of politie or Government fundamentallie, he shall be put to death.

95. A declaration of the Liberties the Lord Jesus hath given to the Churches.

1. All the people of god within this Jurisdiction who are not in a church way, and be orthodox in Judgement, and not scandalous in life, shall have full libertie to gather themselves into a Church Estaite. Provided they doe it in a Christian way, with due observation of the rules of Christ revealed in his word.

2. Every Church hath full libertie to exercise all the ordinances of god, according to the rules of Scripture.

3. Every Church hath free libertie of Election and ordination of all their officers from time to time, provided they be able pious and orthodox.

4. Every Church hath free libertie of Admission, Recommendation, Dismission, and Expulsion, or deposall of their officers, and members, upon due cause, with free exercise of the Discipline and Censures of Christ according to the rules of his word.

5. No Injunctions are to be put upon any Church, Church Officers or member in point of Doctrine, worship or Discipline, whether for substance or cercumstance besides the Institutions of the lord.

6. Every Church of Christ hath freedome to celebrate dayes of fasting and prayer, and of thanksgiveing according to the word of god.

7. The Elders of Churches have free libertie to meete monthly, Quarterly, or otherwise, in convenient numbers and places, for conferences, and consultations about Christian and Church questions and occasions.

8. All Churches have libertie to deale with any of their members in a church way that are in the hand of Justice. So it be not to retard or hinder the course thereof.

9. Every Church hath libertie to deal with any magestrate, Deputie of Court or other officer what soe ever that is a member

in a church way in case of apparent and just offence given in their places. so it be done with due observance and respect.

10. Wee allowe private meetings for edification in religion amongst Christians of all sortes of people. So it be without just offence both for number, time, place, and other cercumstances.

11. For the preventing and removeing of errour and offence that may grow and spread in any of the Churches in this Jurisdiction. And for the preserveing of trueith and peace in the several churches within them selves, and for the maintenance and exercise of brotherly communion, amongst all the churches in the Countrie, It is allowed and ratified, by the Authoritie of this Generall Court as a lawfull libertie of the Churches of Christ. That once in every month of the yeare (when the season will beare it) It shall be lawfull for the minesters and Elders, of the Churches neere adjoyneing together, with any other of the breetheren with the consent of the churches to assemble by course in each severall Church one after an other. To the intent after the preaching of the word by such a minister as shall be requested thereto by the Elders of the church where the Assembly is held, The rest of the day may be spent in publique Christian Conference about the discussing and resolveing of any such doubts and cases of conscience concerning matter of doctrine or worship or government of the church as shall be propounded by any of the Breetheren of that church, with leave also to any other Brother to propound his objections or answeres for further satisfaction according to the word of god. Provided that the whole action be guided and moderated by the Elders of the Church where the Assemblie is helde, or by such others as they shall appoint. And that no thing be concluded and imposed by way of Authoritie from one or more Churches upon an other, but onely by way of Brotherly conference and consultations. That the trueth may be searched out to the satisfying of every man's Conscience in the sight of god according to his worde. And because such an Assembly and the worke their of can not be duely attended to if other lectures be held in the same weeke. It is therefore agreed with the consent of the Churches. That in that weeke when such an Assembly is held.

All the lectures in all the neighbouring Churches for the weeke shall be forborne. That so the publique service of Christ in this more solemne Assembly may be transacted with greater deligence and attention.

96. How so ever these above specified rites, freedomes, Immunities, Authorities and priveledges, both Civill and Ecclesiasticall are expressed onely under the name and title of Liberties, and not in the exact forme of Laws, or Statutes, yet we do with one consent fullie Authorise, and earnestly intreate all that are and shall be in Authoritie to consider them as laws, and not to faile to inflict condigne and proportionable punishments upon every man impartiallie, that shall infringe or violate any of them.

97. Wee likewise give full power and libertie to any person that shall at any time be denyed or deprived of any of them, to commence and prosecute their suite, Complaint, or action against any man that shall so doe, in any Court that hath proper Cognizance or judicature thereof.

98. Lastly because our dutie and desire is to do nothing suddainlie which fundamentally concerne us, we decree that these rites and liberties, shall be Audably read and deliberately weighed at ever Generall Court that shall be held, within three yeares next insueing, And such of them as shall not be altered or repealed they shall stand so ratified, That no man shall infringe them without due punishment.

And if any General Court within these next thre yeares shall faile or forget to reade and consider them as abovesaid. The Governor and Deputie Governor for the time being, and every Assistant present at such Courts shall forfeite 20 sh. a man, and everie Deputie 10 sh. a man for each neglect, which shall be paid out of their proper estate, and not by the Country or the Townes which choose them. And when so ever there shall arise any question in any Court amonge the Assistants and Associates thereof about the explanation of these Rites and liberties, The Generall Court onely shall have power to interprett them.

Complete text, with original spelling, taken from S. Whitmore, *Bibliographical Sketch of the Laws of Massachusetts Colony* (1889), 32–60.

23

[The Combination of the
Inhabitants upon the Piscataqua
River for Government]

October 22, 1641

I *t is instructive to compare this document with The Mayflower Compact [3]. The two are surprisingly similar, although it is certain those writing this document did not consult the earlier one. The major difference is that here God is not called upon as a witness, and therefore it is not a covenant but a compact. Note also that the king, although prominently mentioned, does not sanction this agreement either. Instead, the force of this document rests entirely on the people directly, which constitutes de facto popular sovereignty. Popular sovereignty, however, is not yet a legal or formal constitutional principle, which explains why the document is considered only temporary until the king's approval can be obtained. This is an example, like many other documents during the colonial era, in which political practice preceded political theory, although practice tended to result from the habits of mind engendered by earlier theoretical formulations. In the case of popular sovereignty, that earlier theoretical formulation was to be found in theology.*

Whereas sundry Mischiefs and Inconveniences have befallen us, and more and greater may, in regard of want of Civill Government, his gracious Majesty haveing settled no order for us, to our knowledge, we whose names are underwritten, being Inhabitants upon the River of Pascataqua have voluntarily agreed to combine ourselves into a body Politick, that wee may the more comfortably enjoy the Benefit of his Majesties Laws, and doe hereby actually engage ourselves to submit to his Royall Majesties Laws, together with all such Laws as shall be concluded by a major part of the Freemen of our Society, in Case they be not repugnant to the laws of

England, and administered in behalf of his Majestie. And this wee have mutually promised, and engaged to doe, an so to continue till his excellent Majestie shall give other orders concerning us. In witness whereof Wee have hereunto set our hands, October 22. In the 16 year of the Reigne of our Sovereigne Lord, Charles by the grace of God, King of Great Brittaine, France and Ireland, Defender of the Faith, &c.

Subscribed by Thomas Larkham,
     Richard Waldrene,
     William Waldrene, [with thirty-eight more]

Text taken from Francis N. Thorpe, ed., *The Federal and State Constitutions, Colonial Charters, and Other Organic Laws of the United States* (Washington, D.C.: Government Printing Office, 1907), 2445. The text is complete, and the spelling is as found in Thorpe.

24

[Massachusetts Bicameral Ordinance]

March 7, 1644

*I*t was not unusual for colonial legislatures to have two parts that together constituted the whole. One part elected by the towns (here the deputies) would elect the rest of the legislature (here termed the magistrates). Because the two parts sat together as the legislature, there was only an implicit bicameralism. The magistrates sat continuously to advise the governor, and only periodically would the deputies join them to form a sitting legislature. The Connecticut legislature was structured this way (see the Fundamental Orders of Connecticut, 1639 [43]), as was the Massachusetts legislature until this ordinance was passed in 1644. Here Massachusetts takes the next step and moves to two separate bodies. Note that the move to bicameralism rests on certain unspecified "inconveniences" as well as on the emulation of unspecified models rather than on theoretical principles. Americans would later develop a substantial theoretical justification for bicameralism—enhancing the pursuit of the common good through a more deliberative process as well as the preservation of liberty through separation of powers—but initially bicameralism had a practical, prudential grounding.

Forasmuch as, after long experience, wee find divers inconveniences in the manner of our proceeding in Courts by magistrates & deputies siting together, & accounting it wisdome to follow the laudable practice of other states who have layd groundworks for government & order in the issuing of business of greatest & highest consequence,—

It is therefore ordered, first, that the magistrates may sit & act busines by themselves, by drawing up bills & orders which they shall see good in their wisdome, which haveing agreed upon, they may present them to the deputies to bee considered of, how good & wholesome such orders are for the country, & accordingly to give their assent or dissent, the deputies in like manner siting apart by themselves, & consulting about such orders & lawes as they in their discretion & experience shall find meete for common good, which agreed upon by them they may present to the magistrates, who, according to their wisdome, haveing seriously considered of them, may consent unto them or disalow them; & when any orders have passed the approbation of both magistrates & deputies, then such orders to bee ingrossed, & in the last day of the Court to bee read deliberately, & full assent to bee given; provided, also, that all matters of judicature which this Court shall take cognisance of shal bee issued in like manner.

Complete text with original spelling taken from Shurtleff, *Massachusetts Colonial Records: Vol. II,* 58–59. Discussion of the historical context, as well as examples of related documents, can be found in Michael Kammen, *Deputyes & Libertyes: The Origins of Representative Government in Colonial America* (New York: Alfred A. Knopf, 1969).

25

[Massachusetts Ordinance on the Legislature]

November 13, 1644

*T*his is a comprehensive ordinance altering the size and mode of
electing the legislature (see documents 10, 14, and 24 for the
original formation of this legislature and intervening alterations).
Note that even though this is an ordinance passed by the legislature,
it must be approved by the electorate before it becomes law—"if the
freeman shall accept therof [this ordinance] . . . assenting or dissenting
to this proposition." Also note that the magistrates are elected by aggregating the votes of all the individual electors in the colony, while
the deputies are elected by aggregating the votes for each town. In this
way, the deputies represent their respective town while the magistrates
represent the entire colony (see the Fundamental Orders of Connecticut, 1639 [43] for a similar distinction). In the U.S. Constitution the House of Representatives will be elected by localities and the
Senate by statewide electorates. Although the theoretical grounding for
the national practice will be different than for colonial legislatures,
the institutional design was developed during the colonial era on
practical grounds and justified later.

I t is ordered, that the freemen of this jurisdiction shall meete in their severall townes within two months after the date hereof, to consider of whom
they would nominate to be put to vote upon the day of election of newe
magistrates, to the number of seaven, at which meeting every freeman shall
have liberty to put in his vote for whom hee thinketh fit, all which votes shal
be sealed up at that meeting, & sent by some one or two (whom they shall
choose) to the sheire townes in each sheire, upon the last 5th day of the last
month, at which meeting the said selectmen of every towne (by whom the
votes being brought) shall not have power to open them, being sealed up,
as before, but shall choose one or two from amongst themselves, by whom

they shall send the aforesaid votes, being all sealed up in one paper, unto Boston, on the last third day of the first month, at which meeting there shal be two magistrates, before whom the proxies shal be opened & sorted; & those persons nominated for magistrates that have most votes, to the number of seaven, shal be they that shal be put to vote at the day of election; & that such as have most votes to be first nominated & put to election, that the freemen may know for whom to send in their proxies. The select men of every sheire, being at this meeting, shall take care to send to the aforesaid selectmen of every towne whom they be that are to be put to vote, which select men of every towne shall call a meeting of their townes, & acquaint them whom they are, that so the freemen may have time to consider of them, & send in their proxies accordingly; & no other shal be put to vote but such as are agreed upon, as before.

Whereas wee haveing found by experience that the charge of this Generall Court groweth very great & burthensome, in regard of the continuall increase of deputies sent unto the same, & further forseeing that as townes increase the number wil be still augmented, to the unsupportable burthen of this common wealth; as also it being thought a matter worthy the triall, dureing the standing of this order, to have the use of the negative vote forborne, both by magistrates & deputies, the premisses considered, it is declared by the Court, (if the freemen shall accept thereof,) that a tryall shal be made for one yeare ensuing the day of election next, by choyce of twenty deputies out of the severall shires to equall the number of magistrates chosen upon the day of election, the choyce of them to be thus divided: Suffolke chall choose sixe, Middlesex sixe, & Essex & Norfolk, being joyned in one, shall chose eight; and further, to the end the ablest gifted men may be made use of in so weighty a worke, it shal be at the liberty of the freemen to choose them, in their own sheires, or elsewhere, as they shall see best, the choyce to be after this manner: the freemen of each shire, meeting in their owne severall townes together within two months next following, shall there give in their severall votes for so many deputies as belong unto their sheire to choose, which votes shal be forthwith sealed up, & one or two chosen to carry them sealed to their sheire town the last 5th day of the last month following, where, in the presence of one magistrate, they shal be opened & conferd togeather, & so many as shall have the major vote of the sheire are chosen, not exceeding the number aforesaid; & such as are so chosen shall assemble themselves at the next Court of Election, presented under the hands of those which were sent from the townes to the sheire meetings aforesaid, the names & severall number of vote they there had, from which assembly those onely that had the greatest number of votes, to equall the number of magistrates then chosen, shal be confirmed, & the rest dismissed from the present service, from every sheire a like number, so neare as may be; the magistrates & deputies thus chosen shall sit togeather as a full & sufficient Generall Court, to act in al things by the major vote of the whole Court; and further, it is declared, that every towne shall fourthwith, namely, by the last of the next month, send in under the hands of their late deputies their vote, assenting or dissenting to this proposition, to the house of Mr. Nowell, who, together with one of the late deputies of Charlestowne, one of Cambridge, & one of Boston, shall have power to peruse the said votes, & if they shall find that the greater number of the townes shall agree that this may be propounded to them shall proceed, they shall thereupon fourthwith certify the Governor thereof, who shall thereupon give speedy notice to every towne that they may proceed according to this declaration; & whereas it may fall out that two or more sheires may make choyce of one & the same men, it is therefore provided, that Suffolk shall begin makeing knowne to Middlesex whom they have chosen, who the next 4th day following shall make their choyce, & send word to Essex & Norfolke whom Suffolk & themselves have chosen; then the next 4th day shall Essex and Norfolke make their choyce.

The complete and original text is taken from Shurtleff, *Massachusetts Colonial Records: Vol. II*, 167–68.

26

The Laws and Liberties of Massachusetts

1647

*E*ssentially an organized codification of the laws passed in earlier years, with a number of new laws added, this organic act contains everything we might today expect in a constitution and indeed functioned as a constitution for the colony. The document has many notable features. Its preamble efficiently lays out the theoretical basis for government that underlies the document's contents, and shows the manner and extent to which theological ideas and principles are involved. Note that creating a "city upon a hill" does not involve denigrating the governments of other nations. From the very beginning of the text there is an obvious concern for life, liberty, and property. In addition to laying out the basic institutions of government, The Laws and Liberties is an extended bill of rights that mixes very advanced features with some that are less so; for example, the more than two hundred crimes punishable by death under English common law at that time is reduced to sixteen.

The Book of the General Lawes and Libertyes Concerning the Inhabitants of the Massachusets Collected Out of the Records of the General Court for the Several Years Wherein They Were Made and Established,

And now revised by the same Court and desposed into an Alphabetical order and published by the same Authoritie in the General Court held at Boston the fourteenth of the first month Anno 1647.

TO OUR BELOVED BRETHREN AND NEIGHBOURS

The Inhabitants of the Massachusets, the Governour, Assistants and Deputies assembled in the Generall Court of that Jurisdiction with grace and peace in our Lord Jesus Christ. So soon as God had set up Politicall Government among his people Israel hee gave them a body of lawes of judgement both in civil and criminal causes. These were brief and fundamental principles, yet withall so full and comprehensive as out of them clear deductions were to be drawne to all particular cases in future times. For a Common-wealth without lawes is like a Ship without rigging and steeradge. Nor is it sufficient to have principles or fundamentalls, but these are to be drawn out into so many of their deductions as the time and condition of that people may have use of. And it is very unsafe & injurious to the body of the people to put them to learn their duty and libertie from generall rules, nor is it enough to have lawes except they be also just. Therefore among other priviledges which the Lord bestowed upon his peculiar people, these he calls them specially to consider of, that God was neerer to them and their lawes were more righteous then other nations. God was sayd to be amongst them or neer to them because of his Ordnances established by himselfe, and their lawes righteous because himselfe was their Law-giver: yet in the comparison are implyed two things, first that other nations had something of Gods presence amongst them. Secondly that there was also somwhat of equitie in their lawes, for it pleased the Father (upon the Covenant of Redemption with his Son) to restore so much of his Image to lost man as whereby all nations are disposed to worship God, and to advance righteousnes: Which appears in that of the Apostle Rom. 1. 21. They knew God &c: and in the 2. 14. They did by nature the things conteined in the law of God. But the nations corrupting his ordinances (both of Religion, and Justice) God withdrew his presence from them proportionably whereby they were given up to abominable lusts Rom. 2.21. Wheras if they had walked according to that light & law of nature might have been preserved from such moral evils and might have injoyed a common blessing in all their natural and civil Ordinances: now, if it might have been so with the nations who were so much strangers to the Covenant of Grace, what advantage have they who have interest in this Covenant, and may injoye the special presence of God in the puritie and native simplicitie of all his Ordinances by which he is so neer to his owne people. This hath been no small priviledge, and advantage to us in New-England that our Churches, and civil State have been planted, and growne up (like two twinnes) together like that of Israel in the wilderness by which wee were put in minde (and had opportunitie put into our hands) not only to gather our Churches, and set up the Ordinances of Christ Jesus in them according to the Apostolick patterne by such light as the Lord graciously afforded us: but also withall to frame our civil Politie, and lawes according to the rules of his most holy word whereby each do help and strengthen other (the Churches the civil Authoritie, and the civil Authoritie the Churches) and so both prosper the better without such emulation, and contention for priviledges or priority as have proved the misery (if not ruine) of both in some other places.

For this end about nine years wee used the help of some of the Elders of our Churches to compose a modell of the Judiciall lawes of Moses with such other cases as might be referred to them, with intent to make sure of them in composing our lawes, but not to have them published as the lawes of this Jurisdiction: nor were they voted in Court. For that book intitled The Liberties &c: published about seven years since (which conteines also many lawes and orders both for civil & criminal causes, and is commonly [though without ground] reported to be our Fundamentalls that wee owne as established by Authoritie of this Court, and that after three years experience & generall approbation: and accordingly we have inserted them into this volume under the severall heads to which they belong yet not as fundamentalls, for divers of them have since been repealed, or altered, and more may justly be (at least) amended heerafter as further experience shall discover defects or inconveniences for Nihil simul natum et perfectum. The same must we lay of this present Volume, we have not published it as a perfect body of laws sufficient to carry on the Government established for future times, nor could it be expected that we should promise such a thing. For if it be no disparagement to the wisedome of that High Court of Parliament in England that in four hundred years they could not so compile their lawes, and regulate proceedings in Courts of justice &c: but that they had still new work to do of the same kinde almost every Parliament: there can be no just cause to blame a poor Colonie (being unfurnished of Lawyers and Statemen) that in eighteen years hath produced no more, nor better rules for a good, and setled Government then this Book holds forth: nor have you (our Bretheren and Neighbours) any cause, whether you look back upon our Native Country, or take your observation by other States, & Commonwealths in Europe) to complaine of such as you have imployed in this service; for the time which hath been spent in making laws, and repealing and altering them so often, nor of the charge which the Country hath been put to for those occasions, the Civilian gives you a satisfactorie reason of such continuall alterations additions &c: *Crescit in Orbe dolus.*

These Lawes which were made successively in divers former years, we have reduced under severall heads in an alphabetical method, that so they might the more readily ye be found, & that the divers lawes concerning one matter being placed together the scope and intent of the whole and of every of them might the more easily be apprehended: we must confesse we have not been so exact in placing every law under its most proper title as we might, and would have been: the reason was our hasty indeavour to satisfie your longing expectation, and frequent complaints for want of such a volume to be published in print: wherin (upon every occasion) you might readily see the rule which you ought to walke by. And in this (we hope) you will finde satisfastion, by the help of the references under the several heads, and the Table which we have added in the end. For such lawes and orders as are not of generall concernment we have not put them into this booke, but they remain still in force, and are to be seen in the booke of the Records of the Court, but all generall laws not heer inserted nor mentioned to be still of force are to be accounted repealed.

You have called us from amongst the rest of our Bretheren and given us power to make these lawes: we must now call upon you to see them executed: remembring that old & true proverb, The execution of the law is the life of the law. If one sort of you viz: non-Freemen should object that you had no hand in calling us to this worke, and therefore think yourselvs not bound to obedience &c. Wee answer that a subsequent, or implicit consent is of like force in this case, as an expresse precedent power: for in putting your persons and estates into the protection and way of subsistance held forth and exercised within this jurisdiction, you doe tacitly submit to this Government and to all the wholesome lawes thereof, and so is the common repute in all nations and that upon this Maxim.

If any of you meet with some law that seemes not to tend to your particular benefit, you must consider that lawes are made with respect to the whole people, and not to each particular person: and obedience to them must be yeilded with respect to the common welfare, not to thy private advantage, and as thou yeildest obedience to the law for comon good, but to thy disadvantage: so another must observe some other law for them good, though to his own damage; thus must we be content to bear one anothers burden and so fullfill the Law of Christ.

That distinction which is put between the Lawes of God and the laws of men, becomes a snare to many as it is mis-applyed in the ordering of their obedience to civil Authoritie; for when the Authoritie is of God and that in way of an Ordinance Rom. 13. 1. and when the administration of it is according to deductions, and rules gathered from the word of God, and the clear light of nature in civil nations, surely there is no humane law that tendeth to common good (according to those principles) but the same is mediately a law of God, and that in way of an Ordinance which all are to submit unto and that for conscience sake. Rom. 13. 5.

By order of the General Court.

INCREASE NOWEL, SECR.

The Book of the General Lauues and Libertyes Concerning &c:

> FORASMUCH as the free fruition of such Liberties, Immunities, priviledges as humanitie, civilitie & christianity call for as due to everie man in his place, & proportion, without impeachment & infringement hath ever been, & ever will be the tranquility & stability of Churches & Comon-wealthes; & the deniall or deprivall thereof the disturbance, if not ruine of both:

It is therefore ordered by this Court, & Authority thereof, That no mans life shall be taken away; no mans honour or good name shall be stayned; no mans person shall be arrested, restrained, bannished, dismembred nor any wayes punished; no man shall be deprived of his wife or children; no mans goods or estate shall be taken away from him; nor any wayes indamaged under colour of law or countenance of Authoritie unles it be by the vertue or equity of some expresse law of the Country warranting the same established by a General Court & sufficiently published; or in case of the defect of a law in any particular case by the word of God. And in capital cases, or in cases concerning dismembring or banishment according to that word to be judged by the General Court [1641]

ABILITIE.

All persons of the age of twenty one years, and of right understanding & memorie whether excommunicate, condemned or other, shall have full power and libertie to make their Wills & Testaments & other lawfull Alienations of their lands and estates. [1641]

ACTIONS.

All Action of debt, accounts, slaunder, and Actions of the case concerning debts and accounts shall henceforth be tryed where the Plantiffe pleaseth; so it be in the jurisdiction of that Court where the Plantiffe, or Defendant dwelleth: unles by consent under both their hands it appeare they would have the case tryed in any other Court. All other Actions shal be tryed within that jurisdiction where the cause of Action doth arise. [1642]

2. It is ordered by this Court & Authoritie thereof, That every person impleading another in any court of Assistants, or County court shal pay the sum of ten shillings before his case be entred, unless the court fee cause to admit any to sue in [1642]

3. It is ordered by the Authority aforesayd, That where the debt or damage recovered shall amount to ten pounds in every such case to pay five shillings more, and where it shall amount to twenty pounds or upward there to pay ten shillings more then the first ten shillings, which sayd additions shall be put to the Judgement and Execution to be levied by the Marshall and accounted for to the Treasurer. [1647]

4. In all actions brought to any court the Plantiffe shall have liberty to withdraw his action or to be non-suted before the Jurie have given in their verdict; in which case he shall always pay full cost and charges to the Defendant, and may afterward renew his sute at another Court. [1641]

AGE.

It is ordered by this Court & the Authoritie thereof, that the age for passing away of lands, or such kinde of hereditaments, or for giving of votes, verdicts or sentences in any civil courts or causes, shall be twenty and one years: but in case of chusing of Guardions, fourteen years [1641 1647]

ANA-BAPTISTS.

Forasmuch as experience hath plentifully & often proved that since the first arising of the Ana-baptists about a hundred years past they have been the Incendiaries of Common-Wealths & the Infectors of persons in main matters of Religion, & the Troublers of Churches in most places where they have been, & that they who have held the baptizing of Infants unlawful, have usually held other errors or heresies together therwith (though as hereticks used to doe they have concealed the same untill they espied a fit advantage and opportunity to vent them by way of question or scruple) and wheras divers of this kinde have since our coming into New-England appeared amongst our selvs, some whereof as others before them have denied the Ordinance of Magistracy, and the lawfulnes of making warre, others the lawfulnes of Magistrates, and their Inspection into any breach of the first Table: which opinions is conived at by us are like to be increased among us & so necessarily bring guilt up us, infection, & trouble to the Churches & hazzard to the whole Common-wealth:

It is therfore ordered by this Court & Authoritie therof, that if any person or persons within this Jurisdiction shall either openly condemn or oppose the baptizing of Infants, or goe about secretly to reduce others from the approbation or use thereof, or shall purposely depart the Congregation at the administration of that Ordinance; or shall deny the Ordinance of Magistracy, or their lawfull right or authoritie to make war, or to punish the outward breaches of the first Table, and shall appear to the Court wilfully and obstinately to continue therin, after due means of conviction, everie such person or persons shall be sentenced to Banishment. [1644] . . .

ARRESTS.

It is ordered and decreed by this Court & Authoritie thereof, That no mans person shall be arrested or imprisoned for any debt or fine if the law can finde any competent meanes of satisfaction otherwise from his estate. And if not this person may be arrested and imprisoned, where he shall be kept at his own charge, not the Plaintiffs, till satisfaction be made; unles the Court that had cognisance of the cause or some superiour Court shall otherwise determine: provided neverthelesse that no mans person shall be kept in prison for debt but when there appears some estate which he will not produce, to which end any Court or Commissioners authorized by the General Court may administer an oath to the partie or any others suspected to be privie in concealing his estate, but shall satisfie by service if the Creditor require it but shall not be solde to any but of the English nation. [1641: 1647] . . .

BOND-SLAVERY.

It is ordered by this Court and authoritie thereof, that there shall never be any bond-slavery, villenage or captivitie amongst us; unless it be lawfull captives, taken in just warrs, and such strangers as willingly sell themselves, or are solde to us: and such shall have the libertyes and christian usages which the law of God established in Israell concerning such persons doth morally require, provided, this exempts none from servitude who shall be judged thereto by Authoritie. [1641] . . .

CAPITAL LAWES.

If any man after legal conviction shall HAVE OR WORSHIP any other God, but the LORD GOD: he shall be put to death. Exod. 22. 20. Deut. 13.6. & 10. Deut. 17. 2. 6.

2. If any man or woman be a WITCH, that is, hath or consulteth with a familiar spirit, they shall be put to death. Exod. 22. 18. Levit. 20. 27. Deut. 18. 10. 11.

3. If any person within this Jurisdiction whether Christian or Pagan shall wittingly and willingly presume to BLASPHEME the holy Name of God, Father, Son or Holy-Ghost, with direct, expresse, presumptuous, or highhanded blasphemy, either by wilfull or obstinate denying the true God, or his Creation, or Government of the world: or shall curse God in like manner, or reproach the holy religion of God as if it were but a politick device to keep ignorant men in awe; or shal utter any other kinde of Blasphemy of the like nature & degree they shall be put to death. Levit. 24. 15. 16.

4. If any person shall commit any wilfull MURTHER, which is Man slaughter, committed upon premeditate malice, hatred, or crueltie not in a mans necessary and just defence, nor by meer casualty against his will, he shall be put to death. Exod. 21. 12. 13. Numb. 35. 31.

5. If any person slayeth another suddenly in his ANGER, or CRUELTY of passion, he shall be put to death. Levit. 24. 17. Numb. 35. 20. 21.

6. If any person shall slay another through guile, either by POYSONING, or other such devilish practice, he shall be put to death. Exod. 21. 14.

7. If any man or woman shall LYE WITH ANY BEAST, or bruit creature, by carnall copulation; they shall surely be put to death: and the beast shall be slain, & buried, and not eaten. Lev. 20. 15. 16.

8. If any man LYETH WITH MAN-KINDE as he lieth with a woman, both of them have committed abomination, they both shal surely be put to death: unles the one partie were forced (or be under fourteen years of age in which case he shall be seveerly punished) Levit. 20. 13.

9. If any person commit ADULTERIE with a married or espoused wife; the Adulterer & Adulteresse shall surely be put to death. Lev. 20. 19. & 18. 20 Deu. 22. 23. 27.

10. If any man STEALETH A MAN, or Man-kinde, he shall surely be put to death Exodus 21. 16.

11. If any man rise up by FALSE-WITNES wittingly and of purpose to take away any mans life: he shal be put to death. Deut. 19. 16. 18. 16.

12. If any man shall CONSPIRE, and attempt any Invasion, Insurrection, or publick Rebellion against our Common-Wealth: or shall indeavour to surprize any Town, or Townes, Fort, or Forts therin; or shall treacherously, & perfidiously attempt the Alteration and Subversion of our frame of Politie, or Government fundamentally he shall be put to death. Numb. 16. 2 Sam. 3. 2 Sam. 18. 2 Sam. 20.

13. If any child, or children, above sixteen years old, and of sufficient understanding, shall CURSE, or SMITE their natural FATHER, or MOTHER; he or they shall be put to death: unles it can be sufficiently testified that the Parents have been very unchristianly negligent in the education of such children; or so provoked them by extream, and cruel correction: that they have been forced therunto to preserve themselves from death or maiming. Exod. 21. 17. Lev. 20. 9. Exod 21. 15.

14. If a man have a stubborn or REBELLIOUS SON, of sufficient years & uderstanding (viz) sixteen years of age, which will not obey the voice of his Father, or the voice of his Mother, and that when they have chastened him will not harken unto them: then shal his Father & Mother being his natural parents, lay hold on him, & bring him to the Magistrates assembled in Court & testifie unto them, that their Son is stubborn & rebellious & will not obey their voice and chastisement, but lives in sundry notorious crimes, such a son shal be put to death. Deut. 21. 20. 21.

15. If any man shal RAVISH any maid or single woman, comitting carnal copulation with her by force, against her own will; that is above the age of ten years he shal be punished either with death, or with some other greivous punishment according to circumstances as the Judges, or General court shal determin. [1641] . . .

CHARGES PUBLICK.

And it is further ordered that the Comissioners for the severall towns in everie Shire shall yearly upon the first fourth day of the week in the seventh month, assemble at their shire Town: & bring with them fairly written the just number of males listed as aforesaid, and the assessments of estates made in their several towns according to the rules & directions in this present order expressed, and the said Comissioners being so assembled shall duly and carefully examin all the said lists and assessments of the severall towns in that Shire, and shall correct & perfect the same according to the true intent of this order, as they or the major part of them shall determine, & the same so perfected they shal speedily transmit to the Treasurer under their hands or the hands of the major part of them and therupon the Treasurer shal give warrants to the Constables to collect & levie the same; so as the whole assessment both for persons & estates may be payd in unto the Treasurer before the twentith day of the ninth month, yearly, & everie one shal pay their rate to the Constable in the same town where it shal be assessed. Nor shall any land or estate be rated in any other town but where the same shal lye, is, or was improved to the owners, reputed owners or other propietors use or behoof if it be within this Jurisdiction. And if the Treasurer canot dispose of it there, the Constable shall send it to such place in Boston, or elswhere as the Treasurer shall appoint at the charge of the Countrie to be allowed the Constable upon his accout with the Treasurer. And for all peculiars viz: such places as are not yet layd within the bounds of any town the same lands with the persons and estates therupon shall be assessed by the rates of the town next unto it, the measure or estimation shall be by the distance of the Meeting houses...

CHILDREN.

For as much as the good education of children is of singular behoof and benefit to any Common-wealth; and wher as many parents & masters are too indulgent and negligent of their duty in that kinde. It is therefore ordered that the Selectmen of every town, in the severall precincts and quarters where they dwell, shall have a vigilant eye over their brethren & neighbours, to see, first that none of them shall suffer so much barbarism in any of their families as not to indeavour to teach by themselves or others, their children & apprentices so much learning as may inable them perfectly to read the english tongue, & knowledge of the Capital laws: upon penaltie of twentie shillings for each neglect therin. Also that all masters of families doe once a week (at the least) catechize their children and servants in the grounds & principles of Religion, & if any be unable to doe so much: that then at the least they procure such children or apprentices to learn some short orthodox catechism without book, that they may be able to answer unto the questions that shall be propounded to them out of such catechism by their parents or masters or any of the Selectmen when they shall call them to a tryall of what they have learned in this kinde. And further that all parents and masters do breed & bring up their children & apprentices in some honest lawful calling, labour or imploymet, either in husbandry, or some other trade profitable for themselves, and the Common-wealth if they will not or cannot train them up in learning to fit them for higher imployments. And if any of the Selectmen after admonition by them given such masters of families shal finde them still negligent of their dutie in the particulars aforementioned, wherby children and servants become rude, stubborn & unruly; the said Selectmen with the help of two Magistrates, or the next County court for that Shire, shall take such children or apprentices from them & place them with some masters for years (boyes till they come to twenty-one, and girls eighteen years of age compleat) which will more strictly look unto, and force them to submit unto government according to the rules of this order, if by fair means and former instructions they will not be drawn unto it. [1642]

2. Wheras sundry gentlemen of qualitie, and others oft times send over their children into this country unto some freinds heer, hoping at the least therby to prevent their extravagant and riotous courses, who not with standing by means of some unadvised and ill-affected persons, which give them credit, in expectation their freinds, either in favour to them or prevention of blemish to themselves, will discharge what ever is done that way, they are no lesse lavish & profuse heer to the great greif of their freinds, dishonour of God & reproach of the Countrie.

It is therefore ordered by this Court & authoritie thereof; That if any person after publication heerof shall any way give credit to any such youth, or other person under twentie one years of age, without order from such their freinds, heer, or elswhere, under their hands in writing they shall lose their debt whatever it be. And further if such youth or other person incur any penalty by such means and have not wherwith to pay, such person, or persons, as are occasions therof shall pay it as delinquents in the like case should doe. [1647]

3. If any parents shall wilfully, and unreasonably deny any childe timely or convenient marriage, or shall exercise any unnaturall severeitie towards them such children shal have libertie to complain to Authoritie for redresse in such cases. [1641]

4. No Orphan during their minority which was not committed to tuition, or service by their parents in their life time, shall afterward be absolutely dis-

posed of by any without the consent of some Court wherin two Assistants (at least) shall be present, except in case of marriage, in which the approbation of the major part of the Selectmen, in that town or any one of the next Assistants shall be sufficient. And the minoritie of women in case of marriage shall be till sixteen years. [1646] ...

COUNCILL.

This Court considering how the weighty affairs of this Jurisdiction whether they concern this peculiarly or have reference to the rest of our confederated Colonies may be duly and speedily transacted in the vacancy of the Generall Court for the satisfaction of the Comissioners, in respect of the weighty and sodain occasions which may be then in hand, doth heerby expresse and declare, That the General Court ought to be called by the Governour, when the importancy of the busines doth require it, and that time and opportunitie will safely admit the same, and that all other necessary matters are to be ordered and dispatched by the major part of the Council of the Common-wealth, & therfore to that end letters signifying, breifly, the busines and the time and place of meeting for consultation ought to be sent unto the Assistants. Also it is heerby declared, that seven of the said Assistants meeting, the Governour or Deputy Governour being one is a sufficient Assembly to act, by impressing of soldiers or otherwise as need shall be. And in case of extream and urgent necessitie, when indeavours are reasonably used to call together the Assistants and the busines will not admit delay, then the acts of so many as do assemble are to be accounted, and are accounted valid, & sufficient. Also it is intended that the generall words aforementioned contein in them power to impresse & send forth soldiers, and all manner of victuails, vessels at sea, carriages and all other necessaries, and to send warrants to the Treasurer to pay for them. [1645]

COURTS.

For the better administration of justice and easing the Countrie of unnecessary charge and travells: it is ordered by this Court and Authoritie thereof;

That there shal be four Quarter Courts of Assistants yearly kept by the Governour, or Deputy Gover: and the rest of the Magistrates, the first of them on the first third day (viz: tuisday) in the fourth month called June: the second on the first third day of the seventh month: the third on the first third day of the tenth month: the fourth on the first third day of the first month called March. Also there be four County Courts held at Boston, by such of the Magistrates as shall reside in, or neer the same, viz: by any five, four or three of them, who shall have power to assemble together upo the last fift day of the eight, eleventh, second & fift months everie year, and there to hear & determin all civil causes & criminal, not extending to life, member or banishment according to the course of the court of Assistnts, & to summon Juries out of the neighbour towns, & the Marshall & other Officers shall give attendance there as at other Courts. And it is further ordered that there shall be four Quarter Courts kept yearly by the Magistrates of Essex, with such other persons of worth as shall fro time to time be apointed by the General Court; at the nomination of the towns in that Shire by orderly agreement among themselves, to be joyned in Commission with them so that with the Magistrates they be five in all and so that no Court be kept without one Magistrate at the least: and so any three of the Commissioners aforesaid may keep Court in the absence of the rest: yet none of all the Magistrates are excluded from any of these Courts who can, and please to attend the same. And the General Court to appoint from time to time, which of the said Magistrates shall specially belong to everie of the said Courts. Two of these Quarter Courts shall be kept at Salem, the other at Ipswitch. The first, the last third day of the week in the seventh month at Ipswitch. The second at Salem the last third day of the tenth month. The third at Ipswitch the last third day of the first month. The fourth the last third day of the fourth month at Salem. All and every which Courts shall be holden by the Magistrates of Salem and Ipswitch with the rest of that County or so many of them shall attend the same; but no Jurie men shal be warned from Ipswitch to Salem nor from Salem to Ipswitch. Also there shall be a Grand Jurie at either place, once a year. Which Courts shall have the same power in civil and criminal causes as the courts of Assistants have (at Boston) except tryalls for life, limb or banishment, which are wholy reserved unto the courts of Assistants. The like libertie for County courts and tryall of causes is graunted to the Shire town of Cambridge for the County of Midlesex, as Essex hath, to be holden by the Magistrates of Midlesex & Suffolk & such other men of worth as shall be nominated and chosen as aforesaid, one of which Courts shall be holden on the last third day of the eight month, and another on the last third day of the second month from year to year. And the like libertie for County Courts and tryall of causes is graunted to the County of Norfolk to be holden at Salisburie on the last third day of the second month;

and another at Hampton on such day as the General Court shall appoint to be kept in each place from time to time. And if any shal finde himselfe greived with the sentence of any the said County courts he may appeal to the next court of Assistants. Provided he put in sufficient caution according to law. Lastly, it is ordered by the Authoritie aforesaid that all causes brought to the courts of Assistants by way of appeal, and other causes specially belonging to the said courts, shall be first determined from time to time: & that causes of divorce shall be tryed only in the said court of Assistants. [1635 1636 1639 1641 1642]

2. For the more speedy dispatch of all causes which shall concern Strangers, who cannot stay to attend the ordinary Courts of justice, It is ordered by this Court and Authoritie therof;

That the Governour or Deputy Governour with any two other Magistrates, or when the Governour or Deputy Governour cannot attend it, that any three Magistrates shall have power to hear and determin by a Jurie of twelve men, or otherwise as is used in other Courts, all causes civil and criminal triable in County Courts, which shall arise between such Strangers, or wherin any such Stranger shall be a partie. And all records of such proceedings shall be transmitted to the Records of the Court of Assistants, to be entered as tryalls in other Courts, all which shall be at the charge of the parties, as the Court shall determin, so as the Country be no wayes charged by such courts. [1639]

3. For the electing of our Governour, Deputy Governor, Assistants and other general Officers upon the day or dayes appointed by our Pattent to hold our yearly Court being the last fourth day of the week (viz: Wednesday) of every Easter Term; it is solemnly and unanimously decreed and established,

That henceforth the Freemen of this Jurisdiction shal either in person or by proxie without any Summons attend & consummate the Elections, at which time also they shal send their Deputies with full power to consult of and determin such matters as concern the welfare of this Common-wealth; from which General Court no Magistrates or Deputy shall depart or be discharged without the consent of the major part both of Magistrates and Deputies, during the first four dayes of the first Session therof, under the penaltie of one hundred pounds for everie such default on either part. And for the after Sessions, if any be, the Deputies for Dover are at libertie whether to atted or not. [1643]

4. Forasmuch as after long experience wee finde divers inconveniences in the manner of our proceeding in Courts by Magistrates and Deputies sitting together, and account it wisedome to follow the laudable practice of other States, who have layd ground works for government and order for issuing busines of greatest and highest consequence: it is therfore ordered by this Court and Authoritie therof,

That henceforth the Magistrates may sit and act busines by themselves, by drawing up Bills and Orders which they shall see good in their wisdom, which having agreed upon, they may present them to the Deputies to be considered of, how good and wholesom such orders are for the Countrie & accordingly to give their assent or dissent. The Deputies in like manner sitting apart by themselves and consulting about such orders and laws as they in their discretion and experience shall finde meet for the common good: which agreed upon by them they may present to the Magistrates who having seriously considered of them may manifest their consent or dissent thereto. And when any Orders have passed the approbation of both Magistrates and Deputies, then to be ingrossed: which in the last day of this Court or Sessions shal be deliberately read over. Provided also that all matters of Judicature which this Court shall take cognisance of, shall be issued in like manner (unles the Court upon some particular occasion or busines agree otherwise). [1644] ...

DEPUTIES FOR THE GENERALL COURT.

For easing the body of Freemen now increasing, and better dispatching the busines of General Courts, It is ordered and by this Court declared;

That henceforth it shall be lawfull for the Freemen of everie Plantation to choose their Deputies before every Generall Court, to confer of, and prepare such publick busines as by them shall be thought fit to consider of at the next General court. And that such persons as shall be heerafter so deputed by the Freemen of the several Plantations to deal on their behalfe in the publick affairs of the Common-wealth, shall have the full power and voices of all the said Freemen derived to them for the making and establishing of Laws, graunting of lands, and to deal in all other affairs of the Comon-wealth wherin the Freemen have to doe: the matter of election of Magistrates and other officers only excepted wherin every Freeman is to give his own voice. [1634]

2. Forasmuch as through the blessing of God the number of towns are much increased, It is therfore ordered and by this Court enacted;

That henceforth no town shall send more then two Deputies to the General Court; though the number of Freemen in any town be more then twenty. And that all towns which have not to the number of twenty Freemen shall send but one Deputy, & such towns as have not ten Freemen shall send none, but such Freemen shall vote with the next town in the choice of their Deputie or Deputies til this Court take further order. [1636 1638]

3. It is ordered by this Court and Authoritie therof, That when the Deputyes for severall towns are met together before, or at any General court, it shall be lawfull for them or the major part of them to hear and determin any difference that may arise about the election of any of their members, and to order things amongst themselves that may concern the well ordering of their body. And that heerafter the Deputies for the General court shall be elected by papers as the Governour is chosen. [1634 1635]

4. It is ordered by this Court and Authoritie therof; That the Freemen of any Shire or town have liberty to choose such Deputies for the General court either in their own Shire, Town, or elsewhere, as they judge fittest, so be it they be Freemen and inhabiting within this Jurisdiction. And because wee cannot foresee what variety and weight of occasions may fall into future consideration, & what counsells we may stand in need of: wee decree that the Deputies to attend the General court in behalfe of the Coutry shall not at any time be stated and enacted but from court to court, or at the most but for one year, that the Countrie may have an annual liberty to doe in what case what is most behoofefull for the best welfare therof. [1641] . . .

ECCLESIASTICALL:

1. All the people of God within this Jurisdiction who are not in a Church way and be orthodox in judgement and not scandalous in life shall have full libertie to gather themselves into a Church estate, provided they doe it in a christian way with due observation of the rules of Christ revealed in his word. Provided also that the General Court doth not, nor will heerafter approve of any such companyes of men as shall joyne in any pretended way of Church fellowship unles they shall acquaint the Magistrates and the Elders of the neighbour Churches where they intend to joyn, & have their approbation therin.

2. And it is farther ordered, that no person being a member of any Church

which shal be gathered without the approbation of the Magistrates and the said Churches shal be admitted to the Freedom of this Common-wealth.

3. Everie Church hath free liberty to exercise all the Ordinances of God according to the rules of the Scripture.

4. Everie Church hath free libertie of election and ordination of all her Officers from time to time. Provided they be able, pious and orthodox.

5. Everie Church hath also free libertie of admission, recommendation, dismission & expulsion or deposall of their Officers and members upon due cause, with free exercise of the disciplin and censures of Christ according to the rules of his word.

6. No injuction shall be put upon any Church, church Officer or member in point of doctrine, worship or disciplin, whether for substance or circumstance besides the institutions of the Lord.

7. Everie Church of Christ hath freedom to celebrate dayes of Fasting and prayer and of Thanksgiving according to the word of God.

8. The Elders of churches also have libertie to meet monthly, quarterly or otherwise in convenient numbers and places, for conference and consultations about christian and church questions and occasions.

9. All Churches also have libertie to deal with any their members in a church way that are in the hands of justice, so it be not to retard and hinder the course therof.

10. Everie Church hath libertie to deal with any Magistrate, Deputy of court, or other Officer whatsoever that is a member of theirs, in a church way in case of apparent and just offence, given in their places, so it be done with due observance and respect.

11. Wee also allow private meetings for edification in Religion amongst christians of all sorts of people so it be without just offence, both for number, time, place and other circumstances.

12. For the preventing and removing of errour and offence that may grow and spread in any of the Churches in this jurisdiction, and for the preserving of truth & peace in the severall Churches within themselves, and for the maintainance and exercise of brotherly comunion amongst all the Churches in the country.

It is allowed and ratified by the authoritie of this Court, as a lawfull libertie of the Churches of Christ, that once in every month of the year (when the season will bear it) it shall be lawfull for the Ministers and Elders of the Churches neer adjoyning, together with any other of the Brethren, with the consent of the Churches, to assemble by course in everie several church one after another, to the intent, that after the preaching of the word, by such a Minister as shal be requested therto, by the Elders of the Church where the Assemby is held, the rest of the day may be spent in public christian conference, about the discussing and resolving of any such doubts & cases of consciences concerning matter of doctrine, or worship, or government of the Church as shall be propounded by any of the Brethren of that Church; with leave also to any other Brother to propound his objections, or answers, for further satisfaction according to the word of God. Provided that the whole action be guided and moderated by the Elders of the Church where the Assembly is held, or by such others as they shall appoint. And that nothing be concluded and imposed by way of Authoritie from one, or more Churches, upon another, but only by way of brotherly conference & consultations, that the truth may be searched out to the satisfying of every mans conscience in the sight of God according to his word. And because such an Assemblie and the work therof cannot be duly attended if other lectures be held the same week, it is therfore agreed with the consent of the Churches, that in what week such an Assembly is held all the Lectures in all the neighbouring Churches for the week dayes shall be forborne, that so the publick service of Christ in this Assembly may be transacted with greater diligence & attention. [1641]

13. Forasmuch as the open contempt of Gods word and Messengers therof is the desolating sinne of civil States and Churches and that the preaching of the word by those whom God doth send, is the chief ordinary means ordained of God for the converting, edifying and saving the souls of the Elect through the presence and power of the Holy-Ghost, therunto promised: and that the ministry of the word, is set up by God in his Churches, for those holy ends: and according to the respect or contempt of the same and of those whom God hath set apart for his own work & imployment, the weal or woe of all Christian States is much furthered and promoted; it is therefore ordered and decreed,

That if any christian (so called) within this Jurisdiction shall contemptuously behave himselfe toward the Word preached or the Messengers therof called to dispense the same in any Congregation; when he doth faithfully execute his Service and Office therin, according to the will and word of God, either by interrupting him in his preaching, or by charging him falsely with any errour which he hath not taught in the open face of the Church: or like a son of Korah cast upon his true doctrine or himselfe any reproach, to the dishonour of the Lord Jesus who hath sent him and to the disparagement of that his holy Ordinance, and making Gods wayes contemptible and ridiculous: that everie such person or persons (whatsoever censure the Church may passe) shall for the first scandall be convented and reproved openly by the Magistrate at some lecture, and bound to their good behaviour. And if a second time they break forth into the like contemptuous carriages, they shall either pay five pounds to the publick Treasurie; or stand two hours openly upon a block or stool, four foot high on a lecture day with a paper fixed on his breast, written in Capital letters [AN OPEN AND OBSTINATE CONTEMNER OF GODS HOLY ORDINANCES] that others may fear and be ashamed of breaking out into the like wickednes. [1646]

14. It is ordered and decreed by this Court and Authoritie thereof; That wheresoever the ministry of the word is established according to the order of the Gospell throughout this Jurisdiction every person shall duly resort and attend therunto respectively upon the Lords days & upon such publick Fast dayes & dayes of Thanksgiving as are to be generally kept by the appointmet of Authoritie: & if any person within this Jurisdiction shal without just and necessarie cause withdraw himselfe from hearing the publick ministry of the word after due meanes of conviction used, he shall forfeit for his absence from everie such publick meeting five shillings. All such offences to be heard and determined by any one Magistrate or more from time to time. [1646]

15. Forasmuch as the peace and prosperity of Churches and members therof as well as civil Rights & Liberties are carefully to be maintained, it is ordered by this Court & decreed, That the civil Authoritie heer established hath power and liberty to see the peace, ordinances and rules of Christ be observed in everie Church according to his word. As also to deal with any church-member in a way of civil justice notwithstanding any church relation, office, or interest; so it be done in a civil and not in an ecclesiastical way. Nor shall any church censure degrade or depose any man from any civil dignity, office or authoritie he shall have in the Commonwealth. [1641]

16. Forasmuch as there are many Inhabitants in divers towns, who leave their several habitations and therby draw much of the in-come of their estates into other towns wherby the ministry is much neglected, it is therfore ordered by this Court and the authoritie therof; That from henceforth all lands, cattle and other estates of any kinde whatsoever, shall be lyable to be

rated to all common charges whatsoever, either for the Church, Town or Comon-wealth in the same place where the estate is from time to time. And to the end there may be a convenient habitation for the use of the ministry in everie town in this Jurisdiction to remain to posterity. It is decreed by the authoritie of this Court that where the major part of the Inhabitants (according to the order of regulating valid town acts) shall graunt, build, or purchase such habitation it shall be good in law, and the particular sum upon each person assessed by just rate, shal be duly paid according as in other cases of town rates. Provided alwayes that such graunt, deed of purchase and the deed of gift therupon to the use of a present preaching Elder and his next successour and so from time to time to his successors: be entred in the town book and acknowledged before a Magistrate, and recorded in the Shire court. [1647]

ELECTIONS.

It is ordered by this Court and Authoritie therof: That for the yearly choosing of Assistants for the time to come instead of papers the Freemen shall use indian corn and beans. The indian corn to manifest election, the beans for blanks. And that if any Freeman shall put in more then one indian corn or bean for the choise or refusal of any publick Officer, he shall forfeit for everie such offence ten pounds. And that any man that is not free or otherwise hath not libertie of voting, putting in any vote shal forfeit the like sum of ten pounds. [1643]

2. For the preventing of many inconveniences that otherwise may arise upon the yearly day of Election, and that the work of that day may be the more orderly, easily and speedily issued, it is ordered by this Court and the authoritie thereof.

That the Freemen in the several towns and villages within this Jurisdiction, shall this next year from time to time either in person or by proxie sealed up, make all their elections, by papers, indian corn and beans as heerafter is expressed, to be taken, sealed up & sent to the court of Election as this order appoints, the Governour, Deputie Governour, Major Generall, Treasurer, Secretary and Comissioners for the united Colonies to be chosen by writing, open or once folded, not twisted or rolled up, that so they may be the sooner and surer perused: and all the Assistants to be chosen by indian corn and beans, the indian corn to manifest election as in Sect: I; and for such small villages as come not in person and that send no Deputies to the Court, the Constable of the said village, together with two or three of the chiefe Freemen shall receive the votes of the rest of their Freemen, and deliver them together with their own sealed up to the Deputie or Deputies for the next town, who shall carefully convey the same unto the said Court of Election. [1647]

3. For asmuch as the choice of Assistants in case of supply is of great concernment, and with all care and circumspection to be attended; It is therfore ordered by this Court and Authoritie therof,

That when any Assistants are to be supplyed, the Deputies for the General Court shall give notice to their Constables or Selectmen to call together their freemen in their severall towns: to give in their votes unto the number of seven persons, or as the General Court shall direct, who shall then and there appoint one to carrie them sealed up unto their Shire towns upon the last fourth day of the week in the first month from time to time; which persons for each town so assembled shall appoint one for each Shire to carrie them unto Boston the second third day of the second month there to be opened before two Magistrates. And those seven or other number agreed upon as aforesaid, that have most votes shall be the men which shall be nominated at the court of Election for Assistants as aforesaid. Which persons the Agents for each Shire shall forthwith signifie to the Constables of all their several towns in writing under their hands with the number of votes for each person: all which the said Constables shall forthwith signifie to their Freemen. And as any hath more votes then other so shall they be put to vote. [1647]

4. It is decreed and by this Court declared That it is the constant libertie of the Freemen of this Jurisdiction to choose yearly at the court of Election out of the Freemen, all the general Officers of this Jurisdiction, and if they please to discharge them at the court of Election by way of vote they may doe it without shewing cause. But if at any other General Court, we hold it due justice that the reason therof be alledged and proved. By general Officers we mean our Governour, Deputy Governour, Assistants, Treasurer, General of our wars, our Admirall at sea, Commissioners for the united-Colonies and such others as are, or heerafter may be of the like general nature. [1641]

FORNICATION

It is ordered by this Court and Authoritie therof, That if any man shall commit Fornication with any single woman, they shall be punished either by enjoyning to Marriage, or Fine, or corporall punishment, or all or any of these as the Judges in the courts of Assistants shall appoint most agreeble to the word of God. And this Order to continue till the Court take further order. [1642]

FREEMEN, NON-FREEMEN.

WHERAS there are within this jurisdiction many members of churches who to exempt themselves from all publick service in the Common-wealth will not come in, to be made Freemen, it is therfore ordered by this Court and the Authoritie therof,

That all such members of Churches in the severall towns within this Jurisdiction shall not be exempted from such publick service as they are from time to time chosen to by the Freemen of the severall towns: as Constables, Jurors, Select-men and Surveyors of highwayes. And if any such person shall refuse to serve in, or take upon him any such Office being legally chosen therunto, he shall pay for every such refusall such Fine as the town shall impose, not exceeding twenty shilings as Freemen are lyable to in such cases. [1647]

FUGITIVES, STRANGERS.

It is ordered by this Court and Authoritie therof, That if any people of other nations prosessing the true Christian Religion shall flee to us from the tyranie or oppression of their persecutors, or from Famine, Wars, or the like necessarie and compulsarie cause, they shall be entertained and succoured amongst us according to that power and prudence God shall give us. [1641]

GAMING.

UPON Complaint of great disorder by the use of the game called Shuffle-board, in houses of common entertainment, wherby much pretious time is spent unfruitfully and much wast of wine and beer occasioned; it is therfore ordered and enacted by the Authoritie of this Court;

That no person shall henceforth use the said game of Shuffle-board in any such house, nor in any other house used as common for such purpose, upon payn for every Keeper of such house to forfeit for everie such offence five shillings: Nor shall any person at any time play or game for any monie, or mony-worth upon penalty of forefeiting treble the value therof: one half to the partie informing, the other half to the Treasurie. And any Magistrate may hear and determin any offence against this Law. [1646 1647]

GENERAL COURT.

It is ordered, and by this Court declared that the Governour and Deputie Governour joyntly consenting, or any three Assistants concurring in consent shall have power out of Court to reprieve a condemned malefactor till the next Court of Assistants: or General Court. And that the General Court only shall have power to pardon a condemned malefactor.

Also it is declared that the General Court hath libertie and Authoritie to send forth any member of this Common-wealth, of what qualitie and condition or office whatsoever into forrein parts, about any publick Message or negociation: notwithstanding any office or relation whatsoever. Provided the partie so sent be acquainted with the affairs he goeth about, and be willing to undertake the service.

Nor shall any General Court be dissolved or adjourned without the consent of the major part therof. [1641]

GOVERNOUR.

It is ordered, and by this Court declared that the Governour shall have a casting vote whensoever an equivote shall fall out in the Court of Assistants, or general Assemblie: so shall the President or Moderatour have in all civil Courts or Assemblies [1641]

HERESIE.

ALTHOUGH no humane power be Lord over the Faith & Consciences of men, and therfore may not constrein them to beleive or professe against their Consciences: yet because such as bring in damnable heresies, tending to the subversion of the Christian Faith, and destruction of the soules of men, ought duly to be restreined from such notorious impiety, it is therfore ordered and decreed by this Court;

That if any Christian within this Jurisdiction shall go about to subvert and destroy the christian Faith and Religion, by broaching or mainteining any damnable heresie; as denying the immortalitie of the Soul, or the resurrection of the body, or any sin to be repented of in the Regenerate, or any evil done by the outward man to be accounted sin: or denying that Christ gave himself a Ransom for our sins, or shal affirm that wee are not justified by his Death and Righteousnes, but by the perfection of our own works; or shall deny the moralitie of the fourth commandement, or shall indeavour to seduce others to any the herisies aforementioned, everie such person continuing obstinate therin after due means of conviction shall be sentenced to Banishment. [1646] ...

IDLENES.

It is ordered by this Court and Authoritie therof, that no person, Housholder or other shall spend his time idlely or unproffitably under pain of such punishment as the Court of Assistants or County Court shall think meet to inflict. And for this end it is ordered that the Constable of everie place shall use speciall care and diligence to take knowledge of offenders in this kinde, especially of common coasters, unproffitable fowlers and tobacco takers, and present the same unto the two next Assistants, who shall have power to hear and determin the cause, or transfer it to the next Court. [1633]

JESUITS.

THIS court taking into consideration the great wars, combustions and divisions which are this day in Europe: and that the same are observed to be raysed and fomented chiefly by the secret underminings, and solicitations of those of the Jesuiticall Order, men brought up and devoted to the religion and court of Rome; which hath occasioned divers States to expell them their territories; for prevention wherof among our selves, It is ordered and enacted by Authoritie of this Court,

That no Jesuit, or spiritual or ecclesiastical person [as they are termed] ordained by the authoritie of the Pope, or Sea of Rome shall henceforth at any time repair to, or come within this Jurisdiction: And if any person shal give just cause of suspicion that he is one of such Societie or Order he shall be brought before some of the Magistrates, and if he cannot free himselfe of such suspicion he shall be committed to prison, or bound over to the next Court of Assistants, to be tryed and proceeded with by Banishment or otherwise as the Court shall see cause: and if any person so banished shall be taken the second time within this Jurisdiction upon lawfull tryall and conviction he shall be put to death. Provided this Law shall not extend to any such Jesuit, spiritual or ecclesiasticall person as shall be cast upon our shoars, by ship-wrack or other accident, so as he continue no longer then till he may have opportunitie of passage for his departure; nor to any such as shall come in company with any Messenger hither upon publick occasions, or any Merchant or Master of any ship, belonging to any place not in emnitie with the State of England, or our selves, so as they depart again with the same Messenger, Master or Merchant, and behave themselves inoffensively during their abode heer. [1647] . . .

IMPRESSES.

It is ordered, and by this Court declared, that no man shall be compelled to any publick work, or service, unlesse the Presse be grounded upon some act of the General Court; and have reasonable allowance therfore: nor shall any man be compelled in person to any office, work, wars, or other publick service that is necessarily and sufficiently exempted, by any natural or personal impediment; as by want of years, greatnes of age, defect of minde, failing of senses, or impotencye of lims. Nor shall any man be compelled to go out of this Jurisdiction upon any offensive wars, which this Commonwealth, or any of our freinds or confoederates shall voluntarily undertake; but only upon such vindictive and defensive wars, in our own behalf, or the behalf of our freinds and confoederates; as shall be enterprized by the counsell, and consent of a General Court, or by Authoritie derived from the same. Nor shall any mans cattle or goods of what kinde soever be pressed, or taken for any publick use or service; unles it be by Warrant grounded upon some act of the General Court: nor without such reasonable prizes and hire as the ordinarie rates of the Countrie doe afford. And if his cattle or goods shall perish, or suffer damage in such service, the Owner shall be sufficiently recompenced. [1641]

IMPRISONMENT.

It is ordered, and by this Court declared; that no mans person shall be restreined or imprisoned by any authoritie whatsoever before the Law hath sentenced him therto: if he can put in sufficient securitie, Bayle or Mainprize for his appearance, and good behaviour in the mean time: unles it be in crimes Capital, and contempt in open Court, and in such cases where some expresse Act of Court doth allow it. [1641]

INDIANS

It is ordered by Authoritie of this Court; that no person whatsoever shall henceforth buy land of any Indian, without license first had & obtained of the General Court: and if any shall offend heerin, such land so bought shall be forfeited to the Countrie.

Nor shall any man within this Jurisidiction directly or indirectly amend, repair, or cause to be amended or repaired any gun, small or great, belonging to any Indian, nor shall indeavour the same. Nor shall sell or give to any Indian, directly or indirectly any such gun, or any gun-powder, shot or lead, or shotmould, or any militarie weapons or armour: upon payn of ten pounds fine, at the least for everie such offence: and that the court of Assistants shall have power to increase the Fine; or to impose corporall punishment (where a Fine cannot be had) at their discretion.

It is ordered by the Authoritie aforesaid that everie town shall have power to restrein all Indians from profaning the Lords day. [1633 1637 1641]

2. Wheras it appeareth to this Court that notwithstanding the former Laws, made against selling of guns, powder and Ammunition to the Indians, they are yet supplyed by indirect means, it is thefore ordered by this Court and Authoritie therof;

That if any person after publication heerof, shall sell, give or barter any gun or guns, powder, bullets, shot or lead to any Indian whatsoever, or unto any person inhabiting out of this Jurisdiction without license of this Court, or the court of Assistants, or some two Magistrates, he shall forfeith for everie gun so sold, given or bartered ten pounds: and for everie pound of powder five pounds: and for everie pound of bullets, shot or lead fourty shillings: and so proportionably for any greater or lesser quantitie. [1642]

3. It is ordered by this Court and Authoritie therof, that in all places, the English and such others as co-inhabit within our Jurisidiction shall keep their cattle from destroying the Indians corn, in any ground where they have right to plant; and if any of their corn be destroyed for want of fencing, or herding; the town shall make satisfaction, and shall have power among themselves to lay the charge where the occasion of the damage did arise. Provided that the Indians shall make proof that the cattle of such a town, farm, or per-

son did the damage. And for encouragement of the Indians toward the fencing in their corn fields, such towns, farms or persons, whose cattle may annoy them that way, shall direct, assist and help them in felling of trees, ryving, and sharpening of rayls, & holing of posts: allowing one English-man to three or more Indians. And shall also draw the fencing into place for them, and allow one man a day or two toward the setting up the same, and either lend or sell them tools to finish it. Provided that such Indians, to whom the Countrie, or any town hath given, or shall give ground to plant upon, or that shall purchase ground of the English shall fence such their corn fields or ground at their own charge as the English doe or should doe; and if any Indians refuse to fence their corn ground (being tendred help as aforesaid) in the presence and hearing of any Magistrate or selected Townsmen being met together they shall keep off all cattle or lose one half of their damages.

And it is also ordered that if any harm be done at any time by the Indians unto the English in their cattle; the Governour or Deputie Governour with two of the Assistants or any three Magistrates or any County Court may order satisfaction according to law and justice. [1640 1648]

4. Considering that one end in planting these parts was to propagate the true Religion unto the Indians: and that divers of them are become subjects to the English and have ingaged themselves to be willing and ready to understand the Law of God, it is therfore ordered and decreed,

That such necessary and wholsom Laws, which are in force, and may be made from time to time, to reduce them to civilitie of life shall be once in the year (if the times be safe) made known to them, by such fit persons as the General Court shall nominate, having the help of some able Interpreter with them.

Considering also that interpretation of tongues is appointed of God for propagating the Truth: and may therfore have a blessed successe in the hearts of others in due season, it is therfore farther ordered and decreed,

That two Ministers shall be chosen by the Elders of the Churches everie year at the Court of Election, and so be sent with the consent of their Churches (with whomsoever will freely offer themselves to accompany them in that service) to make known the heavenly counsell of God among the Indians in most familiar manner, by the help of some able Interpreter; as may be most available to bring them unto the knowledge of the truth, and their conversation to the Rules of Jesus Christ. And for that end that something be allowed them by the General Court, to give away freely unto those

Indians whom they shall perceive most willing & ready to be instructed by them.

And it is farther ordered and decreed by this Court; that no Indian shall at any time powaw, or performe outward worship to their false gods: or to the devil in any part of our Jurisdiction; whether they be such as shall dwell heer, or shall come hither: and if any shall transgresse this Law, the Powawer shall pay five pounds; the Procurer five pounds; and every other countenancing by his presence or otherwise being of age of discretion twenty shillings. [1646]

INDITEMENTS.

If any person shall be indicted of any capital crime (who is not then in durance) & shall refuse to render his person to some Magistrates within one month after three Proclaimations publickly made in the town where he usually abides, there being a month betwixt Proclaimation and Proclaimation, his lands and goods shall be seized to the use of the common Treasurie, till he make his lawfull appearance. And such withdrawing of himselfe shall stand in stead of one wittnes to prove his crime, unles he can make it appear to the Court that he was necessarily hindred. [1646]

IN-KEEPERS, TIPPLING, DRUNKENES.

FORASMUCH as there is a necessary use of houses of common entertainment in every Common-wealth, and of such as retail wine, beer and victuals; yet because there are so many abuses of that lawfull libertie, both by persons entertaining and persons entertained, there is also need of strict Laws and rules to regulate such an employment: It is therfor ordered by this Court and Authoritie therof;

That no person or persons shall at any time under any pretence or colour whasoever undertake to be a common Victuailer, Keeper of a Cooks shop, or house for common entertainment, Taverner, or publick seller of wine, ale, beer or strong-water (by re-tale), nor shall any sell wine privately in his house or out of doors by a lesse quantitie, or under a quarter cask: without approbation of the selected Townsmen and Licence of the Shire Court where they dwell: upon pain of forfeiture of five pounds for everie such offence, or imprisonment at pleasure of the Court, where satisfaction cannot be had.

And every person so licenced for common entertainment shall have some inoffensive Signe obvious for strangers direction, and such as have no such Signe after three months so licensed from time to time shall lose their license: and others allowed in their stead. Any licensed person that selleth beer shall not sell any above two-pence the ale-quart: upon penaltie of three shillings four pence for everie such offence. And it is permiteed to any that will to sell beer out of doors at a pennie the ale-quart and under.

Neither shall any such licenced person aforesaid suffer any to be drunken, or drink excessively viz: above half a pinte of wine for one person at one time; or to continue tippling above the space of half an hour, or at unreasonable times, or after nine of the clock at night in, or about any of their houses on penaltie of five shillings for everie such offence.

And everie person found drunken viz: so that he be therby bereaved or disabled in the use of his understanding, appearing in his speech or gesture in any the said houses or elsewhere shall forfeith ten shillings. And for excessive drinking three shillings four pence. And for continuing above half an hour tippling two shillings six pence. And for tippling at unreasonable times, or after nine a clock at night five shillings: for everie offence in these particulars being lawfully convict therof. And for want of payment such shall be imprisoned untill they pay: or be set in the Stocks one hour or more [in some open place] as the weather will permit not exceeding three hours at one time...

JURIES, JURORS.

It is ordered by this Court and Authoritie therof, that the Constable of everie town upon Proces from the Recorder of each Court, shall give timely notice to the Freemen of their town, to choos so many able discreet men as the Proces shal direct which men so chosen he shall warn to attend the Court wherto they are appointed, and shall make return of the Proces unto the Recorder aforesaid: which men so chosen shall be impannelled and sworn truly to try betwixt partie and partie, who shall finde the matter of fact with the damages and costs according to their evidence, and the Judges shall declare the Sentence (or direct the Jurie to finde) according to the law. And if there be any matter of apparent equitie as upon the forfeiture of an Obligation, breach of covenant without damage, or the like, the Bench shall determin such matter of equitie.

2. Nor shall any tryall passe upon any for life or bannishment but by a special Jurie so summoned for that purpose, or by the General Court.

3. It is also ordered by the Authoritie aforesaid that there shall be Grand-Juries summoned everie year unto the several Courts, in each Jurisdiction; to inform the Court of any misdemeanours that they shall know or hear to be committed by any person or persons whatsoever within this Jurisdiction. And to doe any other service of the Common-wealth, that according to law they shall be injoyned to by the said Court; and in all cases wherin evidence is so obscure or defective that the Jurie cannot clearly and safely give a positive verdict, whether it be Grand, or Petty Jurie, it shall have libertie to give a [verdict] or a special verdict, in which last, that is, a special verdict the judgement of the Cause shall be left unto the Bench. And all jurors shall have libertie in matters of fact if they cannot finde the main issue yet to finde and present in their verdict so much as they can.

4. And if the Bench and Jurors shall so differ at any time about their verdict that either of them cannot proceed with peace of conscience, the Case shall be referred to the General Court who shall take the question from both and determin it.

5. And it is farther ordered that whensoever any Jurie of tryalls, or Jurors are not clear in their judgements or consciences, concerning any Case wherin they are to give their verdict, they shall have libertie, in open court to advise with any man they shall think fit to resolve or direct them, before they give in their verdict. And no Freeman shall be compelled to serve upon Juries above one ordinary Court in a year: except Grand-jurie men, who shall hold two Courts together at the least, and such others as shall be summoned to serve in case of life and death or bannishment. [1634 1641 1642]

JUSTICE.

It is ordered, and by this Court declared; that every person within this Jurisdiction, whether Inhabitant or other shall enjoy the same justice and law that is general for this Jurisdiction which wee constitute and execute one towards another, in all cases proper to our cognisance without partialitie or delay. [1641] . . .

LIBERTIES COMMON

It is ordered by this Court, decreed and declared; that everie man whether Inhabitant or Forreiner, Free or not Free shall have libertie to come to any publick Court, Counsell, or Town-meeting; and either by speech or writing, to move any lawfull, reasonable, or material question; or to present any necessarie motion, complaint, petition, bill or information wherof that Meeting hath proper cognisance, so it be done in convenient time, due order and respective manner. [1641]

2. Everie Inhabitant who is an hous-holder shall have free fishing and fowling, in any great Ponds, Bayes, Coves and Rivers so far as the Sea ebs and flows, within the precincts of the town where they dwell, unles the Freemen of the same town, or the General Court have otherwise appropriated them. Provided that no town shall appropriate to any particular person or persons, any great Pond conteining more then ten acres of land: and that no man shall come upon anothers proprietie without their leave otherwise then as heerafter expressed; the which clearly to determin, it is declared that in all creeks, coves and other places, about and upon salt water where the Sea ebs and flows, the Proprietor of the land adjoyning shall have proprietie to the low water mark where the Sea doth not ebb above a hundred rods, and not more wheresoever it ebs farther. Provided that such Proprietor shall not by this libertie have power to stop or hinder the passage of boats or other vessels in, or through any sea creeks, or coves to other mens houses or lands. And for great Ponds lying in common though within the bounds of some town, it shall be free for any man to fish and fowl there, and may passe and repasse on foot through any mans proprietie for that end, so they trespasse not upon any mans corn or meadow. [1641 1647]

3. Every man of, or within this Jurisdiction shall have free libertie, (notwithstanding any civil power) to remove both himself and his familie at their pleasure out of the same. Provided there be no legal impediment to the contrary. [1641]

LYING.

WHERAS truth in words as well as in actions is required of all men, especially of Christians who are the professed Servants of the God of Truth; and wheras all lying is contrary to truth, and some sorts of lyes are not only sinfull (as all lyes are) but also pernicious to the Publick-weal, and injurious to particular persons; it is therfore ordered by this Court and Authoritie therof,

That everie person of the age of discretion [which is accounted fourteen years] who shall wittingly and willingly make, or publish any Lye which may be pernicious to the publick weal, or tending to the damage or injurie of any particular person, or with intent to deceive and abuse the people with false news or reports: and the same duly proved in any Court or before any one Magistrate (who hath heerby power graunted to hear, and determin all offences against this Law) such person shall be fined for the first offence ten shillings, or if the partie be unable to pay the same then to be set in the stocks so long as the said Court of Magistrate shall appoint, in some open place, not exceeding two hours. For the second offence in that kinde wherof any shall be legally convicted the sum of twenty shillings, or be whipped upon the naked body not exceeding ten stripes. And for the third offence that way fourty shillings, or if the partie be unable to pay, then to be whipped with more stripes, not exceeding fifteen. And if yet any shall offend in the like kinde, and be legally convicted therof, such person, male or female, shall be fined ten shillings a time more then formerly: or if the partie so offending be unable to pay, then to be whipped with five, or six more stripes then formerly not exceeding fourty at any time.

The aforesaid fines shall be levied, or stripes inflicted either by the Marshal of that Jurisdiction, or Constable of the Town where the offence is committed according as the Court or Magistrate shall direct. And such fines so levied shall be paid to the Treasurie of that Shire where the Cause is tried.

And if any person shall finde himselfe greived with the sentence of any such Magistrate out of Court, he may appeal to the next Court of the same Shire, giving sufficient securitie to prosecute his appeal and abide the Order of the Court. And if the said Court shall judge his appeal causlesse, he shall be double fined and pay the charges of the Court during his Action, or corrected by whipping as aforesaid not exceeding fourtie stripes; and pay the costs of Court and partie complaining or informing, and of Wittnesses in Case.

And for all such as being under age of discretion that shall offend in lying contrary to this Order their Parents or Masters shall give them due correction, and that in the presence of some Officer if any Magistrate shall so appoint. Provided also that no person shall be barred of his just Action of Slaunder, or otherwise by an proceeding upon this Order. [1645]

MAGISTRATES.

THIS court being sensible of the great disorder growing in this Commonwealth through the contempts cast upon the civil Authoritie, which willing to prevent, doe order and decree;

That whosoever shall henceforth openly or willingly defame any Court of justice, or the Sentences or proceedings of the same, or any of the Magistrates or other Judges of any such Court in respect of any Act or Sentence therin passed, and being therof lawfully convict in any General Court or Court of Assistants shall be punished for the same by Fine, Imprisonment, Disfranchisement or Bannishment as the qualitie and measure of the offence shall deserve.

And if any Magistrate or other member of any court shall use any re-proachfull, or un-beseeming speeches, or behaviour towards any Magistrate, Judge, or member of the Court in the face of the said Court he shall be sharply reproved, by the Governour, or other principal Judge of the same Court for the time being. And if the qualitie of the offence be such as shall deserve a farther censure, or if the person so reproved shall reply again without leave, the same Court may proceed to punish any such offender by Fine, or Imprisonment, or it shall be presented to, and censured at the next superiour Court.

2. If in a General Court any miscarriage shall be amongst the Magistrates when they are by themselves, it shall be examined, and sentenced amongst themselves. If amongst the Deputies when they are by themselves, it shall be examined, and sentenced amongst themselves. If it be when the whole Court is together, it shall be judged by the whole Court, and not severall as before. [1637 1641]

3. And it is ordered by the Authoritie of this Court that the Governour, Deputie Governour, or greater part of the Assistants may upon urgent oc-casion call a General Court at any time. [1647]

4. And wheras there may arise some difference of judgement in doubtfull cases, it is therfore farther ordered;

That no Law, Order, or Sentence shall passe as an Act of the Court with-out the consent of the greater part of the Magistrats on the one partie, and the greater number of the Deputies on the other part.

5. And for preventing all occasions of partial and undue proceeding in Courts of justice, and avoyding of jealousies which may be taken up against Judges in that kinde, it is farther ordered,

That in everie Case of civil nature between partie and partie where there shall fall out so neer relation between any Judge and any of the parties as between Father and Son, either by nature or marriage, Brother and Brother; in like kinde Uncle and Nephew, Land-lord and Tenent in matter of con-siderable value, such Judge though he may have libertie to be present in the Court at the time of the tryall, and give reasonable advice in the Case, yet shall have no power to vote or give sentence therin, neither shall Sit as Judge, but beneath the Bench when he shall so plead or give advice in the Case. [1635]

MONOPOLIES.

It is ordered, decreed and by this Court declared; that there shall be no Monopolies graunted or allowed amongst us, but of such new inventions that are profitable for the Countrie, and that for a short time. [1641]

OATHS, SUBSCRIPTION

It is ordered and decreed, and by this Court declared; that no man shall be urged to take any oath, or subscribe any Articles, Covenants, or remonstrance of publick and civil nature but such as the General Court hath considered, allowed and required. And that no oath of Magistrate, counceller or any other Officer shall binde him any farther, or longer then he is resident, or reputed an Inhabitant of this Jurisdiction [1641]

OPPRESSION

For avoyding such mischeifs as may follow by such illdisposed persons as may take libertie to oppresse and wrong their neighbours, by taking excessive wages for work, or unreasonable prizes for such necessarie merchandizes or other commodities as shall passe from man to man, it is ordered, That if any man shall offend in any of the said cases he shall be punished by Fine, or Imprisonment according to the qualitie of the offence, as the Court to which he is presented upon lawfull tryall & conviction shall adjudge. [1635] . . .

PROFANE SWEARING.

It is ordered, and by this Court decreed, that if any person within this Jurisdiction shall swear rashly and vainly either by the holy Name of God, or any other oath, he shall forfeit to the common Treasurie for everie such severall offence ten shillings. And it shall be in the power of any Magistrate by Warrant to the Constable to call such person before him, and upon sufficient proof to passe sentence, and levie the said penaltie according to the usuall order of Justice. And if such person be not able, or shall utterly refuse to pay the aforesaid Fine, he shall be committed to the Stocks there to continue, not exceeding three hours, and not lesse then one hour. [1646] . . .

PUNISHMENT

It is ordered, decreed, and by this Court declared; that no man shall be twice sentenced by civil Justice for one and the same Crime, offence or Trespasse. And for bodily punishments, wee allow amongst us none that are in-humane, barbarous or cruel. [1641]

SCHOOLS.

It being one chief project of that old deluder, Satan, to keep men from the knowledge of the Scriptures, as in former times keeping them in an unknown tongue, so in these later times by perswading from the use of Tongues, that so at least the true sense and meaning of the Original might be clowded with false glosses of Saint-seeming-deceivers; and that Learning may not be buried in the graves of our fore-fathers in Church and Commonwealth, the Lord assisting our indeavours: it is therfore ordered by this Court and Authoritie therof;

That everie Township in this Jurisdiction, after the Lord hath increased them to the number of fifty Householders shall then forthwith appoint one within their Town to teach all such children as shall resort to him to write and read, whose wages shall be paid either by the Parents or Masters of such children, or by the Inhabitants in general by way of supply, as the major part of those that order the prudentials of the Town shall appoint. Provided that those which send their children be not oppressed by paying much more then they can have them taught for in other Towns.

2. And it is farther ordered, that where any Town shall increase to the number of one hundred Families or Householders they shall set upon a Grammar-School, the Masters therof being able to instruct youth so far as they may be fitted for the Universitie. And if any Town neglect the performance heerof above one year then everie such town shall pay five pounds per annum to the next such School, till they shall perform this Order. [1647] . . .

STRANGERS.

It is ordered by this Court and the Authoritie therof; that no Town or person shal receive any stranger resorting hither with intent to reside in this Jurisdiction, nor shall allow any Lot or Habitation to any, or entertain any such above three weeks, except such person shall have allowance under the hand of some one Magistrate, upon pain of everie Town that shall give, or sell any Lot or Habitation to any not so licenced such Fine to the Countrie as the County Court shall impose, not exceeding fifty pounds, nor lesse then ten pounds. And of everie person receiving any such for longer time then is heer expressed or allowed, in some special cases as before, or in case of entertainment of friends resorting from other parts of this Country in amitie with us, shall forfeit as aforesaid, not exceeding twenty pounds, nor lesse then four pounds: and for everie month after so offending, shal forfeit, as aforesaid not exceeding ten pounds, nor lesse then fourty shillings. Also, that all Constables shall inform the Courts of new commers which they know to be admitted without licence, from time to time. [1637 1638 1647]

SUMMONS.

It is ordered, and by this Court declared; that no Summons, Pleading, Judgement or any kinde of proceeding in Court or course of justice shall be abated, arested or reversed upon any kinde of circumstantial errors or mistakes, if the person and the Cause be rightly understood and intended by the Court.

2. And that in all cases where the first Summons are not served six dayes before the Court, and the Case briefly specified in the Warrant where appearance is to be made by the partie summoned; it shall be at his libertie whether he will appear, or not, except all Cases that are to be handled in Courts suddenly called upon extraordinarie occasions. And that in all cases where there appears present and urgent cause any Assistant or Officer appointed shall have power to make out Attachments for the first Summons. Also, it is declared that the day of Summons or Attachment served, and the day of appearance shall be taken inclusively as part of the six dayes. [1641 1647]

SUITS, VEXATIOUS SUITS.

It is ordered and decreed, and by this Court declared; that in all Cases where it appears to the Court that the Plaintiffe hath willingly & wittingly done wrong to the Defendant in commencing and prosecuting any Action, Suit, Complaint or Indictment in his own name or in the name of others, he shall pay treble damages to the partie greived, and be fined fourty shillings to the Common Treasurie. [1641 1646] . . .

TOBACCO.

This Court finding that since the repealing of the former Laws against Tobacco, the same is more abused then before doth therfore order,

That no man shall take any tobacco within twenty poles of any house, or so neer as may indanger the same, or neer any Barn, corn, or hay-cock as may occasion the fyring therof, upon pain of ten shillings for everie such offence, besides full recompence of all damages done by means therof. Nor shall any take tobacco in any Inne or common Victualing-house, except in a private room there, so as neither the Master of the said house nor any other Guests there shall take offence therat, which if any doe, then such person shall forthwith forbear, upon pain of two shillings sixpence for everie such offence. And for all Fines incurred by this Law, one half part shall be to the Informer the other to the poor of the town where the offence is done. [1638 1647]

TORTURE.

It is ordered, decreed, and by this Court declared; that no man shall be forced by torture to confesse any crime against himselfe or any other, unles it be in some Capital where he is first fully convicted by clear and sufficient evidence to be guilty. After which, if the Case be of that nature that it is very apparent there be other Conspirators or Confoederates with him; then he may be tortured, yet not with such tortures as be barbarous and inhumane.

2. And that no man shal be beaten with above fourty stripes for one Fact at one time. Nor shall any man be punished with whipping, except he have not otherwise to answer the Law, unles his crime be very shamefull, and his course of life vitious and profligate. [1641]

TOWNSHIPS.

It is ordered, decreed, and by this Court declared, that if any man shall behave himselfe offensively at any Town-meeting, the rest then present shall have power to sentence him for such offence, so be it the mulct or penalty exceed not twenty shillings.

2. and that the Freemen of everie Township, and others authorized by law, shall have power to make such Laws and Constitutions as may concern the welfare of their Town. Provided they be not repugnant to the publick Laws and Orders of the Countrie. And if any Inhabitant shall neglect or refuse to observe them, they shall have power to levie the appointed penalties by distresse.

3. Also that the Freemen of everie town or Township, with such other the Inhabitats as have taken the Oath of fidelitie shall have full power to choos

yearly, or for lesse time, within each Township a convenient number of fit men to order the planting and prudential occasions of that Town, according to instructions given them in writing.

Provided, nothing be done by them contrary to the publick Laws and Orders of the Countrie. Provided also that the number of such Select persons be not aboue nine.

4. Farther, it is ordered by the Authoritie aforesayd, that all Towns shall take care from time to time to order and dispose of all single persons, and In-mates within their Towns to service, or otherwise. And if any be greived at such order or dispose, they have libertie to appeal to the next County Court.

5. This Court taking into considerattion the usefull Parts and abilities of divers Inhabitants amongst us, which are not Freemen, which if improved to publick use, the affairs of this Common-wealth may be the easier caried an end in the severall Towns of this Jurisdiction doth order, and heerby declare;

That henceforth it shall may be lawfull for the Freemen within any of the said Towns, to make choice of such Inhabitants (though non-Freemen) who have taken, or shall take the Oath of fidelitie to this Government to be Jurie-men, and to have their Vote in the choice of the Select-men for the town Affairs, Assessements of Rates, and other Prudentials proper to the Select-men of the several Towns. Provided still that the major part of all companyes of Select-men be Free-men from time to time that shall make any valid Act. As also, where no Select-men are, to have their Vote in ordering of Schools, hearing of cattle, laying out of High-wayes and distributing of Lands; any Law, Use or Custom to the contrary notwithstanding. Provided also that no non-Freeman shall have his Vote, untill he have attained the age of twenty one years. [1636 1641 1647]

TRYALLS.

Wheras this Court is often taken up in hearing and deciding particular Cases, between partie and partie, which more properly belong to other inferiour Court. And that if the partie against whom the Judgment shall have any new evidence, or other new matter to plead, he may desire a new Tryall in the same Court upon a Bill or review. And if justice shall not be done him upon that Tryall he may then come to this Court for releif. [1642]

2. it is ordered, and by this Court declared, that in all Actions of Law it

shall be the libertie of the Plaintiffe and Defendant by mutuall consent to choos whether they will be tryed by the Bench or a Jurie, unles it be where the Law upon just reason hath otherwise determined. The like libertie shall be graunted to all persons in any criminal Cases.

3. Also it shall be in the libertie both of Plaintiffe and Defendant, & likewise everie delinquent to be judged by a Jurie, to challenge any of the Jurors, & if the challenge be found just and reasonable, by the Bench or the rest of the Jurie as the Challenger shall choos, it shall be allowed him, & impannelled in their room.

4. Also, children, Ideots, distracted persons and all that are strangers or new comers to our Plantation shall have such allowances, and dispensations in any Case, whether criminal or others, as Religion and reason require. [1641]

VOTES.

It is ordered, decreed and by this Court declared; that all, and everie Freeman, and others authorized by Law, called to give any Advice, Vote, Verdict or Sentence in any Court, Council or civil Assemblie, shall have full freedom to doe it according to their true judgements and consciences, so it be done orderly and inoffensively, for the manner. And that in all cases wherin any Freeman or other is to give his Vote be it in point of Election, making Constitutions and Orders or passing Sentence in any case of Judicature or the like, if he cannot see light or reason to give it positively, one way or other, he shall have libertie to be silent, and not pressed to a determinate vote. And farther that whensoever any thing is to be put to vote, and Sentence to be pronounced or any other matter to be proposed, or read in any Court or Assemblie, if the President or Moderator shall refuse to perform it, the major part of the members of that Court or Assemblie shall have power to appoint any other meet man of them to doe it. And if there be just cause, to punish him that should, and would not. [1641]

USERIE.

It is ordered, decreed & by this Court declared, that no man shall be adjudged for the meer forbearance of any debt, above eight pounds in the hundred for one year, and not above that rate proportionably for all sums whatsoever, Bills of Exchange excepted, neither shall this be a colour or countenance to allow any usurie amongst us contrary to the Law of God. [1641 1643] ...

WITNESSES.

It is ordered, decreed, and by this Court declared, that no man shall be put to death without the testimonie of two or three witnesses, or that which is equivalent therunto. [1641]

2. And it is ordered by this Court and the Authoritie therof, that any one Magistrate, or Commissioner authorized therunto by the General Court may take the Testimonie of any person of fourteen years of age, or above, of sound understanding and reputation, in any Case civil or criminal; and shall keep the same in his own hands till the Court, or deliver it to the Recorder, publick Notarie or Clerk of the writs to be recorded, that so nothing may be altered in it. Provided, that where any such witnesse shall have his abode within ten miles of the Court, and there living and not disabled by sicknes, or other infirmitie, the said Testimonie so taken out of court shall not be received, or made use of in the Court, except the witnes be also present to be farther examined about it. Provided also, that in all capital cases all witnesses shall be present wheresoever they dwell.

3. And it is farther ordered by the Authoritie aforesaid, that any person summoned to appear as a witnes in any civil Court between partie and partie, shall not be compellable to travell to any Court or place where he is to give his Testimonie, except he who shall so summon him shall lay down or give him satisfaction for his travell and expences, out-ward and home-ward; and for such time as he shall spend in attendance in such case when he is at such Court or place, the Court shall award due recompence. And it is ordered that two shillings a day shall be accounted due satisfaction to any Witnes for travell and expences: and that when the Witnes dwelleth within three miles, and is not at charge to passe over any other Ferrie than betwixt Charlstown and Boston then one shilling six pence per diem shall be accounted sufficient. And if any Witnes after such payment or satisfaction shall fail to appear to give his Testimonie he shall be lyable to pay the parties damages upon an action of the Case. And all Witnesses in criminal cases shall have suitable satisfaction, payd by the Treasurer upon Warrant from the Court or Judge before whom the case is tryed. And for a general rule to be observed in all criminal causes, both where the Fines are put in certain, and

also where they are otherwise, it is farther ordered by the Authoritie afore-sayd, that the charges of Witnesses in all such cases shall be borne by the parties delinquent, and shall be added to the Fines imposed; that so the Treasurer having upon Warrant from the Court or other Judge satisfied such Witnesses, it may be repayd him with the Fine: that so the Witness may be timely satisfied, and the countrie not damnified. [1647] . . .

Only about 30 percent of the original text is reproduced here. It is based on the copy of the 1648 edition in the Henry E. Huntington Library as reproduced in *The Laws and Liberties of Massachusetts* (Cambridge: Harvard University Press, 1929). The volume has an introduction by Max Farrand but no listed editor. The spelling of the original has been retained, except for replacing the use of the German *s* with the standard English form. The sections of the text here omitted contain more mundane provisions concerning such things as the price of cattle, viewers of pipe-staves, the salting of fish, and surveying.

27

[Massachusetts Ordinance on Legislative Procedure]

October 18, 1648

*T*he following ordinance qualifies as a founding document because it creates and describes the duties of elected officers of the
legislature. Very little survives concerning colonial legislative processes,
so this document is doubly interesting because it is the oldest surviving description of how a colonial legislature went about its business.
It is clear that the purpose of the ordinance is not only to maintain
orderly processes and systematic record keeping but also to ensure that
legislative proceedings and decisions are available to the public in a
form that allows them to remain informed. Earlier documents in
this collection have clearly implied a de facto popular sovereignty,
and thus, the systematic keeping of public legislative records is in
keeping with that implication. Because colonial legislatures passed
relatively few laws by today's standards and were quite small, they
could easily conduct their business without dividing into committees. Therefore it is noteworthy that the Massachusetts legislature
(General Court) was apparently already using a committee system, especially since the British Parliament, with much larger concerns and
a much heavier legislative load, had moved to an intermittent committee system only a few years earlier. The use of a committee system,
however, also made the process much more deliberative, and a deliberative decision making process was highly valued in colonial
America as a means of pursuing the consensual common good as opposed to mere majority rule. The commitment to deliberative
processes is reflected in a variety of documents, but see documents 46
and 62 for more obvious examples.

For the better carrying on the occassions of the Generall Court, & to the end that the records of the same, together with what shall be presented by way of petition, etc., or passes by way of vote, either amongst the magistrates or deputies, may hereafter be more exactly recorded, & kept for public use,—

It is hereby ordered, that as there is a secretary amongst the magistrates, (who is the generall officer of the common wealth, for the keeping the publike records of the same,) so there shall be a clarke amongst the deputies, to be chosen by them, from time to time; that (by the Court of Elections, and then the officers to begin their entryes, their recompence accordingly) there be provided, by the auditor, four large paper books, in folio, bound up with velum & pastboard, two whereof to be delivered to the secretary, & two to the clarke of the House of Deputies, one to be a journall to each of them, the other for the faire entry of all lawes, acts, & orders, etc., that shall passe the magistrates and deputies, that of the secretaries to be the publike record of the country, that of the clarkes to be a book onely of coppies.

That the secretary & clarke for the deputies shall briefly enter into their journals, respectively, the title of all bills, orders, lawes, petitions, etc., which shal be presented & read amongst them, what are referd to committees, & what are voted negatively or affirmatively, & so for any addition or alteration.

That all bills, lawes, petitions, etc, which shal be last concluded amongst the magistrates, shall remain with the Governor till the latter end of that session, & such as are last assented to by the deputies shall remain with the speaker till the said time, when the whole Courte shall meete together, or a committee of magistrates & deputies, to consider what hath passed that session, where the secretary & clarke shall be present, & by their journals call for such bils, etc, as hath passed either house, & such as shall appeare to have passed the magistrates & deputies shall be delivered to the secretary to record, who shall record the same within one month after every session, which being done, the clarke of the deputies shall have liberty, for one month after, to transcribe the same into his booke; & such bills, orders, etc, that hath only passed the magistrates, shall be delivered to the secretary to keepe upon file, & such as have onely passed the deputies shal be delivered to their clarke to be kept upon file, in like manner, or otherwise disposed of, as the whole Court shall appoint; that all lawes, orders, & acts of Courte, contained in the ould bookes, that are of force, & not ordered to be printed, be transcribed in some alphabeticall or methodicall way, by direction of some committee that this Courte shall please to appoint, & delivered to the secretary to record in the first place, in the said booke of records, & then the acts of the other sessions in order accordingly, & a coppy of all to be transcribed by the clarke of the deputies, as aforesaid.

Text taken from Shurtleff, *Massachusetts Colonial Records: Vol. II*, 194–98. Text is complete, with the original spelling.

28

[Towns of Wells, Gorgiana, and Piscataqua Form an Independent Government]

July 1649

*T*his document is typical of those written during the Cromwellian era, when the interruption of the monarchy cast into doubt the continued legality of the charters written earlier in the century and coherent instructions from England were not forthcoming. While many colonies continued under their former organic documents, other colonies like this one felt compelled to refound themselves. Unremarked in the document itself but implied in the generic title, the document is notable for creating a federation out of the three towns. Documents that created federal systems, among others, include the General Laws and Liberties of New Hampshire, 1680 [2]; the Pilgrim Code of Law, 1636 [20]; the Massachusetts Ordinance on the Legislature, 1644 [25]; the Organization of the Government of Rhode Island, 1642 [37]; the Fundamental Orders of Connecticut, 1639 [43]; the Structure of Town Governments, 1639 [45]; and the New Haven Fundamentals, 1643 [50]. Again we see the de facto use of an important American constitutional principle before there was a theoretical grounding other than that found in theology—in this case covenant theology. The three towns in this document later became part of the state of Maine, but during the colonial era were claimed by Massachusetts.

---

*W*hereas the inhabitants of Piscataqua, Gorgiana, and Wells in the province of Maine, have here begun to propogate and populate these parts of the country, did formerly by power derivative from Sir Ferdinando Gorges, Knight, exercise the regulating the affairs of the country as nigh as we could according to the laws of England, and such other ordinances as was thought meet and requisite for the better regulating thereof. Now, forasmuch as Sir Ferdinando Gorges is dead, the country by their general letters sent to his heirs in June 1647 and 48, but by the said distractions in England no return is yet come to hand, and command from the Parliament not to meddle in so much as was granted to Mr. Rigley, most of the commissioners being departed the province, the inhabitants are for present in some distraction about the regulating of the affairs of these sites. For the better ordering whereof, till further order, power, and authority shall come out of England, the inhabitants with one free and univeranimus consent do bind themselves in a body politic, a combination to see these parts of the country and province regulated according to such laws as formerly have been exercised and such others as shall be thought meet, not repugnant to the fundamental laws of our native country, and to make choice of such governor or governess and magistrates as by most voices they shall think meet. Dated in Gorgiana, alias Accomenticus, the [   ] day of July 1649. The privileges of Accomenticus' charter excepted.

Text is complete and taken from Kavenaugh, *Foundations of Colonial America,* 1: 263–64.

29

[The Cambridge Agreement
of October 4, 1652]

*T*his agreement is simultaneously a reformation of the civil polity and a set of instructions from the town meeting to those individuals selected to act in their name between meetings. The practice of town meetings giving instructions to the elected officers and representatives was a common one in the colonies and was extended to colony-wide, and later state-wide, representative bodies. Often the purpose of the town meeting was to press for specific legislation, but many, as in this case, were designed to formalize fundamental community values and principles to guide the actions of those in government. Once again we see de facto popular sovereignty implied.

At a Genrall meeting of the Towne ye 4th (10) 1652.

Theis prpositions here under written were voted, and joyntly agreed uppon by the Inhabitants, for the instructions to be given to the Townsmen.

That wt eur[1] worke or buissines is by order of Court assigned to the Townsmen or injoyned on the Town That the Townsmen shall make due care to effect the same so as may best conduce to a publique good and no damage by neglect thereof

2. That as often as they shall see needfull, they shall giue publique notice to the inhabitants to meet together and wt eur orders or determinations shalbe passed by a publique vote of the Towne, or are already made by the Towne or ye select men, that the Townsmen take due care to execute fullfill and accomplish the same with out respect of any mans person, according to yr best wisdome.

3. That wt eur damage they shall conceiue or apprehend to come to the Towne, by any person with in or with out the Towne by appropriating intruding or damnifying or exceeding there owne due prportion in any wise,

---

1. This reads, "That what our work..."

any of the Commons, landes or woodes, or other publique stocke liberties or interests of the Towne according to there best discretion they shall prvent and remoue the same.

4. That they take due care for the maintenance and reparation and well ordering of all such thinges wherin the Towne hath a Common interest, as the meeting house Common gates and high wayes, Common heards and ye like.

5. That they make such wholesome orders and impose such Penalties, and duly publish and execute the same as may best effect the execution of the premises.

6. That the necessary charges yt shalbe expended in ye execution of the premises be yearly discharged by an equall rate, made by the Townsmen, and leuied by the Cunstable on ye seurall Inhabitants

7. That The Cunstables giue in a yearly account of wt they receiue of the publique stocke of the Towne by rate or otherwise, and how they haue disbursed the same, the same to be done before ye yearly Election of the Townsmen, and kept uppon Record in a booke fairely written and in case the Cunstables shall faile herein, then to Continue in there office another yeare, except the Towne shall see meet otherwise to dispose.

8. That the Surveyours of the high wayes take due care for the reparation of all the Comon high wayes with in ye towne, and keep uppon Record the names of Such persons as are improued therein during ye yeare, and deliur the same in a list fairely written to the Townsmen then in place at ye end of there year that so no man may be wronged in doing more than his due proportion.

At the same time the buissines about stinting[2] ye Cow Comon[3] was debated, and by a publicke Vote agreed that it should be refferred to ye magestrates of the next County Cort in Midlesex, to determine wheth [   ] or Cow Common were already lawfully stinted.

also there is chosen for a committe to effect this buissines with the Magestrates by prsenting ye true state of the buissines, mr Joseph Cooke John Bridge, Gregory Stone, Edward Goffe Ri: Jacson and Edward Winship.

2. Making an allotment, apportioning, setting limits to.
3. A cow common was a field or group of fields owned by the town but set aside for anyone to graze his cattle. In effect, it was a town commons.

The complete text is taken from *The Records of the Town of Cambridge (Formerly Newtowne) Massachusetts, 1630–1703* (Cambridge: University Press, John Wilson and Son, 1901), 2: 99–100. The spelling is the same as in the original except that the German *s* has been transcribed as an English *s*, where appropriate.

30

[Puritan] Laws and Liberties

September 29, 1658

A revision of the Pilgrim Code of Law, 1636 [20], this is simultaneously a code of law, an amended version of the earlier constitution, and thus a constitution itself. The colony of Plymouth, almost from the beginning, was composed of several towns, each with its own covenant and town meeting. Thus, like the nearby Massachusetts Bay Colony, Plymouth had a functioning federal system. The Puritans begin the present document, as they did the earlier one, by rehearsing the basis for their action. They refer to both their charter and their founding covenant, the Plymouth Combination, 1620 (The Mayflower Compact [3]), as the grounding for their civil body politic. Their careful discussion in this regard implies a de facto federal relationship between the colonies and the mother country, which essentially rehearses the position that will be taken during the Stamp Act crisis and on the eve of the Revolution to explain the colonial view of that relationship. A section-by-section comparison with the earlier Code of Law it replaces reveals an essential continuity since 1620.

The Booke of the Generall Lawes and Liberties of the Inhabitants of the Jurisdiction of New Plymouth Collected out of the Records of the generall Court; and lately Reuised and established and deposed into an Alphabeticall order and published by the Authoritie of the generall Court held att New Plymouth the 29th day of September: Anno 1658

Bee Subject to every
ordinance of Man for
the Lords sake
1 peter 2cond 13th

To our beloued bretheren and Naighbours the Inhabitants of the Jurisdiction of New Plymouth; the Gour: Assistants and Deputies assembled att
the generall Court of that Jurisdiction held att the Towne of Plymouth the
29th day of September Anno: Dom: 1658, wisheth grace and peace in our
Lord Jesus Christ; it was the great privilidge of Israell of old and soe was acknowlidged by them Nehemiah the 9:13 That God gaue them right Judgments and true lawes; for God being the God of order and not of confusion
hath Comaunded in his word; and put man into a capasitie in some measure to obserue and bee guided by good and wholsome lawes which are soe
fare good and wholsome; as by how much they are deriued from and agreeable to; the Ancient platforme of Gods lawe; for although sundry pticulares
in the Judiciall law which was of old jnioyned to the Jewes: did more especially (att least in some cercomstances) befitt their Pedagogye; yett are (they
for the maine) soe exemplary being grounded on principalls of morall equitie as that all men; (Christians especially) ought alwaies to haue an eye
thervnto; in the framing of theire Politique Constitutions; and although
seuerall of the heathen National whoe were Ignorant of the true God and
of his lawe haue bine famous in theire times for the enacting and execution
of such lawes as haue proued profitable for the Gourment of theire Comon-
wealth in the times wherin they liued; yett notwithstanding theire exelen-
cye appeered so fare; as they were founded vpon grounds of morall equitie
which hath its originall from the lawe of God; and accordingly wee whoe
haue bine actors in the framing of this smale body of lawes together with
other vsefull Instruments who are gone to theire rest; can safely say; both
for ourselues and them; that wee haue had an eye principally and primarily
vnto the aforsaid platforme; and Secondaryly vnto the Right Improuement
of the liberteis graunted vnto vs by our Superiours the state of England att
the first begining of this infant plantation which was to enact such lawes as
should most befitt a state in the nonage therof; not rejecting or omiting to
obserue such of the lawes of our Natiue Countrey as would conduce vnto
the good and grouth of soe weake a begining as ours in this Wilderness as
any Impartiall eye not forestaled with prejudice may eazely descerne in the
pusall[1] of this smale booke of the lawes of our Collonie; The prmises duely
considered might worke euery consiencious sperit to faithfull obeidience;
and although wee hold and doe affeirme that both Courts of Justice and Ma-

1. Perusal.

jestrates; whoe are the minnesters of the lawe are esencially Ciuill; Notwithstanding wee conceiue that as the Majestrate hath his power from God soe
vndoubtedly hee is to Improue it for the honor of God; and that in the
vphoulding of his worship and seruice and against the contrary; with due
respect alsoe to bee had vnto those that are really consciencious; though
differing and discenting in some smaller matters; but if any really or in the
pretence of consience shall professe that which eminently tendeth to the
Invndation of Ciuill State and violation of Naturall bonds or the ouerthrow
of the Churches of God or of his Worship; that heer prudence is to bee Improued in a speciall manor in the enacting and execution of lawes; It hath
bine our endeauors in framing of our lawes that nothinge should bee found
amongst them but that which fall vnder the same pticulares; wee haue likewise reduced them to such order as they may most conduce to our vtillitie
and profitt; possibly it may bee that weaknes may appeer in the composure
of sundry of them for want of such plenty of able instruments as others are
furnished withall; howeuer lett this suffice the gentle Reader; that our ends
are to the vtmost of our powers; in these our endeauors to promote both
Church and State both att the psent and for the future; and therfore soe
fare as wee haue aimed att the glory of God and comon good; and acted
according to God; bee not found a Resister but obeident; least therby thou
Resist the ordinance of God and soe Incurr the displeasure of God vnto
damnation; Romans 13:2:

A Declaration demonstrating the warrantable grounds and proceedings of
the first associates of the Gourment of New Plymouth in theire laying the
first foundation of the Gourment in this Jurisdiction for makeing of lawes
and disposing of lands and all such thinges as shall or may Conduce to the
welbeing of this Corporation of New Plymouth;

Whereas John Carver William Bradford Edward Winslow William Brewster Isacke Allerton and diuers others the subjects of our late Sour:[2] Lord
Kinge James by the grace of God Kinge of England Scotland ffrance and Ireland Defendor of the faith did in the eighteenth yeare of his Raigne of
England ffrance and ireland; and of Scotland the fifty fourth which was in
the year of our Lord God one thousand six hundred and twenty; vndertake
a voyage into that pte of America called Verginnia or New England thervnto
adjoyning; there to erect a plantation and Collonie of English; Intending the

---

2. "Sovr," or sovereign.

Glory of God the enlargment of his Maties dominnions and the speciall good of the English Nation.

And Wheras by the good Prouidence of God the said John Caruer William Bradford Edward Winslow William Brewster Isacke Allerton and theire associates ariued in New England aforsaid in the harbour of Cape Cod or Paomett Scittuate and being in New England aforsaid; where all the said psons entered into a Ciuill Combination; being the eleuenth day of Nouember in the yeare aforemencioned; as the subjects of our said Sour: Lord the Kinge; to become a body Pollitique binding our selues to obserue such lawes and ordinances and obey such officers as from time to time should bee made and Chosen for their well ordering and guidance; and thervpon by the fauor of the Almighty; began the first Collonie in New England; there being then none other within the said Continent; att a place Called by the Natiues Apaum alliis Patuxett; and by the English New Plymouth; all which Lands being void of Inhabitants; Wee the said John Carver William Bradford Edward Winslow William Brewster Isacke Allerton and the rest of our Associates; entering into a league of Peace with Massasoiett since called Woosamequen Prince or Sachem of these ptes; hee the said Massasoiett freely gaue them all the lands adjacent to them; and theire heires for euer, acknowlidging himselfe content to become the subject of our Sour Lord the Kinge aforsaid his heires and Successors and takeing protection of vs the said John Carver William Bradford Edward Winslow William Brewster Isacke Allerton and theire Associates the naturall subjects of our Sour: Lord the Kinge aforsaid But haueing noe speciall letters Patents for the said ptes of New England but onely the generall leaue and libertie of our Consiences in the publicke worship of God where euer wee should settle; being therefore now settled and requiring speciall lycence and Comission from his Matie[3] for the ordering of our affaires vnder his graciouse protection; had sundry Comissions made and Confeirmed by his Maties Councell for New England to John Peirse and his associates; whose names wee onely made vse of and whose associates wee were in the late happy and memorable Raigne of our said Sour: Lord King James; But finding our selues still straightened;[4] and a willingnes in the honoble Councell aforsaid to enlarge vs; ptely in regard of the many difficulties wee had vndergone; and ptely in regard of the

3. Majesty.
4. In serious straits, or in serious difficulties.

good service wee had done; as well in releiueing his Maties Subjects as otherwise wee procured a further enlargement vnder the name of Willam Bradford aforsaid and his Associates whose names wee likewise vsed; and whose associates as formerly wee still are; By vertue of which said letters Pattents libertie is giuen to vs deriuatory from our Sour: Lord King Charles bearing date the thirteenth of January 1629 being the fift yeare of his raigne of England Scotland ffrance and Ireland &c and signed by the Right honoble Robert Earle of Warwicke in the behalfe of his Maties said Councell for New England; and sealed with theire Comon seale to frame and make orders ordinances and Constitutions for the ordering disposing and Gouning of our psons and distributeing of our Lands within the said Lymetts To bee holden of his Matie his heires and successors as of his mannor of East greenwich in the County of Kent in free and Comon Soccage and not in Capite nor by Knights seruice,[5] viz: all that pte of America and tract and tracts of land that lyeth within or between a sertaine Rivolett or Rundelett comonly called Coahassett alliis Conahassett towards the north; and the Riuer called Narrangansett Riuer towards the south and the great Westerne Ocean towards the East; and within and between a straight line directly extending into the maine towards the west; from the mouth of the said Riuer called Narranganssett Riuer to the vtmost bounds and lymetts of a Countrey or place in New England called Pocanacutt alliis Puckanakicke alliis Sowamsett doth extend; together with the one halfe of the said Riuer called Narrangansetts; and the said Riuolett or Rundelett called Coahassett allis Conahassett; and all lands Riuers waters hauens creekes ports ffishings fowlings; and all heredetiments profitts Comodities and emoluments whatsoeuer; Scittuate lying and being arising within or between the said lymetts or bounds or any of them; furthermore all that Tract or pte of land in New England or pte of america aforsaid which lyeth within or between; and extendeth it selfe from the vtmost lymetts of Cobbasecontee alliis Comacecontee which adjoyneth to the Riuer of Kennebecke alliis Kennebekicke towards the westerne Ocean; and a place called the falls at Nequamkicke in America aforsaid; and the space of fifteen English miles on each side of the said Riuer comonly called Kenebecke Riuer; that lyeth within the said bounds Eastwards Westwards Northwards and southwards last aboue mentioned; and all lands grounds

---

5. To be held without owing any of the traditional feudal duties, such as providing soldiers or military service.

soyles Riuers waters ffishings heridetiments and prof fitts whatsoeuer scittuate lying and being arising happening or accrewing in or within the said lymetts or bounds or either of them; together with free Ingresse egresse and Regresse with shipps boates shallops and other vessels from the sea called the westeren ocean; to the Riuer called Kennebecke and from the said Riuer to the said Westeren Occean; together with all prorogatiues Rights Royalties Jurisdictions priuilidges franchises liberties and amunities and alsoe marine liberties with the escheats and causualties therof; the Admiraltie Jurisdiction excepted; with all the Interest right title claime and demaund whatsoeuer which the said Councell and theire successors now haue or ought to haue or may haue or require heerafter in or to any of the said Tract or portion of lands heerby mencioned to bee graunted; or any the pmises in as free large ample and benificiall manor to all Intents and constructions whatsoeuer as the said Councell by vertue of his Maties said letters may or can graunt; To haue and to hold the said Tract and tracts of land and all and singulare the pmises aboue mencioned to bee graunted with theire and euery of theire appurtenances; To the said Willam Bradford his heires associates and assignes for euer To the onely proper vse and absolute behoofe of the said Willam Bradford his heires associates and assignes for euer; yeilding and paying vnto our said Sour: Lord the Kinge his heires and successors for euer; one fift pte of the Oare of the mines of Gould and siluer; and one other fift pte therof to the Presedent and Councell; which shalbee had posessed and obtained within the precincts aforsd for all seruices and demaunds whatsoeuer; allowing the said Willam Bradford his associates and assignes and euery of them his and theire agents tenants and servants; and all such as hee or they shall send or Imploy about his said pticulare plantation; shall and may from time to time freely and lawfully goe and returne trad or trafficke as well with the English as any the Natiues within the precincts aforsaid; with libertie of fishing vpon any pte of the sea coast and sea shores of any the seas or Ilands adjacent; and not being Inhabited or otherwise disposed of by order of the said Presedent and Councell forbiding all others to traffick with the Natiues or Inhabitants in any of the said Lymetts; without the speciall leaue of the said Willam Bradford his heires and associates; and allowing the said Willam Bradford his heires and associates to take apprehend seize and make prise of all such psons theire Shipes and goods as shall attempt to Inhabite or trad with the salvage people as aforsaid;

Morouer Wheras in the first begining of this Collonie diuers Marchants and others of the Citty of London and elsewhere adventured diuers sumes of money with the said John Caruer William Bradford Edward Winslow William Brewster Isacke Allerton and the rest of theire asosiates on certaine tearmes of ptenorship[6] to continew for the tearme of seauen yeares the said tearm being expired; the plantation by reason of manifold losses and Crosses by sea and land in the begining of soe great a worke being largly Indebted and noe meanes to pay the said debtes but by the sale of the whole and the same being put vpon sale; the said William Bradford Edward Winsow William Brewster Isacke Allerton and other our associates the Inhabitants of New Plymouth and elswhere being loth to bee depriued of our labours bought the same; for and in consideration of eighteen hundred pounds sterling viz: all and singulare the priuilidges lands goods Chattles ordinance amunition or whatsoeuer appertained to the said plantation or the adventures; with all and singulare the priuilidges thervnto belonging; as appeers by a deed between the said Isacke Allerton then agent for the said William Bradford and his Associates on the one pte; and John Pococke Robert Keine Edward Basse James Sherley and John Beachamp on the other pte being thervnto deputed by the said Marchants and the rest adventuring as aforsaid; as appeers by a Deed bearing date the sixt of Nouember in the third yeare of the Raigne of our Sour: Lord Charles by the grace of God Kinge of England Scotland ffrance and Ireland

Anno Dom: 1627 one thousand six hundred twenty and seauen; Bee it Knowne vnto all men by these psents that according to our first Intents for the better effecting the glory of God; the Inlargment of the dominnions of our said Sour: Lord the Kinge, and the speciall good of his subjects by vertue as well of our Combination aforsaid; as alsoe the seuerall graunts by vs procured; in the Names of John Peirce and William Bradford theire heires and associates together with our lawful right in respect of vacancye donation or Purchase of the Natiues and our full purchase of the adventures before expressed; haue giuen vnto and alloted assigned and graunted to all and euery pson and psons whose name or names shall follow vpon this publicke Record such proportion or proportions of Grounds with all and singulare the priuilidges thervnto belonging as aforsaid to him or them his or theire heires

---

6. Tenancy, held as a tenant.

and Assignes Successiuely for euer to bee holden of his Maties of England his heires and Successors as of his manor of East greenwich in the Countey of Kent in free and comon Sockage and not in Capitie nor by Knights Service yeilding and paying to our said Sou: Lord the Kinge his heires and Successors for euer one fift pte of the Oare of the mines of Gould and siluer and one other fift pte to the psedent and Councell which shalbee had possessed and obtained as aforsaid and whatsoeuer lands are graunted vnto any by the said William Bradford Edward Winslow William Brewster Isaack Allerton or their heires or Associates as aforsaid being acknowlidged in publicke Court and brought to this booke of Records of the seuerall Inheritances of the Subjects of our Soueraigne Lord the King within this Gouerment; It shalbee lawfull for the Gour of New Plymouth aforsaid from time to time and att all times for all Intents and purposes; the said ptie or pties his or theire heires or assignes for euer; To haue and to hold the said portion of lands soe graunted bounded and recorded as aforsaid with all and singulare the Apurtenances thervnto belonging to the onely proper and Absolute vse and behoofe of the said ptie or pties his or theire heires and Assignes for euer;

Wee the Associates of New Plymouth coming hether as freeborne Subjects of the State of New England Indowed with all and singulare the privilidges belonging to such being Assembled Doe ordeine constitute and enacte that noe acte Imposition law or ordinance bee made or Imposed vpon vs att prsent or to come but such as shalbee made and Imposed by consent of the body of the Associates or theire Representatives legally assembled, which is according to the free liberties of the State of England;

It is further enacted

That all our Courts bee kept att the Towne of Plymouth except the Gour and Assistants shall see Reason to keep som Courts of Assistants elswhere within this Gourment.

Whereas by the first Associates of this Gourment the Courts of Election were held in the month of January Anually and afterwards in the month of March Anually; By reason of the vnseasonablenes of those times of the yeare; It is enacted by the Court and the Authoritie therof That the election Courts bee holden the first Tusday in June Annually; And the other Generall Courts bee holden the first Tusday in October and the first Tusday in March Anually; and that the Courts of Assistants bee holden the first Tusday in August the first Tusday in December the first Tusday in ffebrewary and the first Tusday in May Anually.

It is enacted by the Court and the Authoritie therof that all such as shalbee admited freemen of this Corporation shall stand one whole yeare propounded to the Court viz: to bee propounded att one June Court and to stand so propounded vntill the June Court following and then to bee admited if the Court shall not see cause to the Contrary.

Wheras A Comittee was chosen viz: Mrh Tho: Prence Mr Willam Collyare Mr Tho: Dimmacke Mr James Cudworth Mr Josias Winslow John Dunham senir. Gorge Soule and Constant Southworth to consider of the proposition propounded by the deputies att the Court held in October 1650 concerning the major pte of the Courts to order the adjournments and desolutions of the generall Courts and the makeing and repealing of lawes they the said Comittee declared theire minds to bee that matters in the aforsaid respects to rest vnaltered as they were and that for the future as formerly in the makeing and repealing of lawes and adjornment of Courts wherin Comittes are resquisite the majestrates and deputies bee considered as one body.

Wheras diuers actes and orders touching the making and repealing of lawes att June Courts and the adjournments therof is rendered with a dubiouse Interpretation; and this Court haueing by propositions to the freemen of the seuerall Townships desired theire answares in order to the regulateing therof but not receiueing any answare from sundry of them haue seen cause to declare theire owne sence therof and therfor doe enact That fitt and able psons bee anually chosen out of the freemen to attend June courts and the seuerall adjornments therof by the approued Inhabitants quallified as in such case is prouided of this Jurisdiction in theire respectiue townshipps for deputies vnto whom with the majestrates as the body Representatiue is comitted full power for the makeing and repealing of all lawes as vpon theire seriouse considerations they shall find meet for the publicke weale of this Jurisdiction and that then onely such lawes bee enacted or repealed except the Gour for the time being shall see waightey and nessesary cause by the complaint of the freemen or otherwise to call a special Court either of the whole body of the ffreemen or theire deputies; the freemen of this Jurisdiction being left to theire liberties to send theire voate by proxey for the choise of Gour Assistants Comissioners and Treasurer in such way as by order of Court is alreddy prouided and this order to stand in full force till the whole body of ffreemen shall take further order therin; It is alsoe further provided that vpon notice giuen in an orderly way to the Gour by the major pte of the ffreemen of this Jurisdiction of theire apprehensions of a nessesitie of the body of ffreemen to come together; then the Gour for the time being shall take the first oppertunitie to Summon in the body of ffreemen to aduise and acte ther as the matter shall require;

THE OATH OF A FFREEMAN.

You shalbee truely Loyall to our Sour Lord the King his heires and Successors. You shall not speake or doe deuise or aduise Any thinge or things Act or Actes directly or Indirectly by Land or Water that doth shall or may tend to the destruction or ouerthrow of these prsent Plantations or Townshipes of the Corporation of New Plymouth neither shall you suffer the same to bee spoken or done but shall hinder oppose and descouer the same to the Gour And assistants of the said Collonie for the time being; or some one of them; you shall faithfully Submitt vnto such good and wholsome Lawes and ordinances as either are or shalbee made for the ordering and Gourment of the same; and shall Indeuor to aduance the grouth and good of the seuerall townshipes and plantations within the Lymetts of this Corporation by all due meanes and courses; All which you pmise and Sweare by the Name of the great God of heauen and earth simply truely and faithfully to pforme as you hope for healp from God who is the God of truth and punisher of falchood.

It is enacted by the Court and the Authoritie therof; That on the first Tusday in June anually there shalbee a Gour and seauen Assistants chosen to Rule and Gouerne the said Plantations and Townshipes within the Lymetts of this Corporation and this election to bee made onely by the ffreemen therof;

And that the Gour in due season by warrant directed to the seuerall Cunstables in the Name of his Matie giue warning to the ffreemen either to make their psonall appeerance att the Courts of election or to send theire voates by proxey for the choise of officers according to the following order; and that all our Courts warrants Summons and comaunds bee all done directed and made in the Name of our Sour Lord the King

Wheras in regard of age disabilletie of body vrgent occations and other Inconveniencies that doe acrew sundry of the ffreemen are hindered that they can not appeer att Courts of election, In consideration wherof it is enacted by the Court and the Authoritie therof that any freeman of this Corporation shall haue libertie to send his voate by proxy for the choise of Gour Assistants Comissioners and Treasurer; And that the deputies of the seuerall townes chosen to attend the Courts of election and the seuerall adjournments therof shall in the towne meeting in which they are chosen they or either of them giue notice vnto the freemen that those that Intend not to make theire psonall appeerance att the Court of election are now to giue in theire voates Sealed vp for the chosing of Gour Assistants Comissioners and Treasurer; and the said deputies to obserue by a list of their Names whoe hath voted and whoe hath not; The which voates soe brought in to bee ymediately Sealed vp and brought vnto and deliuered in open Court by the said deputies.

It is enacted by the Court that att Courts of election the voates of all the ffreemen prsent bee first read and Next after them the deputies of the suerall townes shall orderly prsent the proxey of theire owne towne.

It is enacted by the Court and the Authoritie therof that other public offecers besides Gour and Assistants bee chosen and established att the Court in June Anually viz: Comissioners and Treasurrer; and that other Inferior officers; as Cunstables grandjurymen and Survayors for the highwaies bee then alsoe confeirmed if approued by the Court.

It is enacted by the Court and the Authoritie therof that incase there shalbee occasion for a Corroner that the Next majestrate where such accedent falls shall sitt as Corrowner and execute that office according to the Custome of England as near as may bee.

It is enacted by the Court and the Authoritie therof that all our Courts summons and comaunds bee all done directed and made in the Name of his Matie of England our dread Sour and alsoe that all Ciuill officers and minnesters of Justice in this Jurisdiction to be sworne in his said Maties name and alsoe that the oath of fidelitie and all other oathes shall goe in that tenure.

THE OFFICE OF THE GOUR:

The office of the Gour for the time being consisteth in the execution of such lawes and ordinances as are or shalbee made and established for the good of this Corporation according to the bounds and Lymitts therof viz: in calling together or aduising with the Assistants or Councell of the said Corporation vpon such matteriall occasions (or soe seeming to him) as time shall bring forth, In wch Assembly and all other the Gour to propound the Occation of the Assembly and haue a double voyce therin; if the Assistants Judge the case too great to bee desided by them and refer it to the Genrall Court then the Gourr to Summon a Courty by warning all the ffreemen that are then extant; as alsoe incase the major pte of the ffreemen seeing waighty cause for the whole body to meet together and in an orderly way acquaint him with theire desires therof; Then hee shall Summon the whole body of ffreemen together with all convenient Speed; and there alsoe to propound causes and goe before the Assistants in the examination of pticulares and to propound such Centance as shalbee determined; further it shalbee lawfull for him to Arrest and comitt to Ward any offendors; provided that with all Convenient Speed hee shall bring the cause to hearing either of the Assistants or generall Court according to the nature of the offence; Alsoe it shalbee lawfull for him to examine any suspicious psons for euill against the Collonie as alsoe to Interupt or oppose such letters as hee conceiueth may tend to the ouerthrow of the same; and that this office continew one whole yeare and noe more without renewing by election;

THE OATH OF THE GOUR:

You Shalbee truely Loyall to our Sour Lord King Charles his heires and Successors Also according to that measure of Wisdome vnderstanding and deserning giuen vnto you shall faithfully Equally and Indifferently without respect of psons Adminnester Justice in all Cases coming before you as the Gour of New Plymouth; You shall in like manor faithfully duely and truely exequte the Lawes and ordinances of the Same; and shall laboure to Advance and further the good of The Townshipes and plantations within the Lymitts therof to the vttermost of youer power and oppose any thing that shall seeme to hinder the same Soe healp you God whoe is the God of truth and the punisher of falshood.

THE OFFICE OF ANN ASSISTANT.

The office of an Assistant for the time being consisteth in appeering att the Gournors Summons and in giueing his best advise both in publicke court and private Councell with the Gour for the good of the seuerall Townships and plantations within the lymetts of this Gourment; not to disclose but to keep secrett such things as concerne the publique good and shalbee thought meet to bee concealed by the Gour and Councell of Assistants in haueing a speciall hand in the examination of publicke offendors and in contriueing the affaires of the Collonie to haue a voyce in the censuring of such offendors as shalbee brought to publicke Court; That if the Gour haue occation to bee absent from the Collonie for a short time by the Gour with concent of the rest of the Assistants hee may bee deputed to Gouerne in the absence of the Gour alsoe it shalbee lawfull for him to examine and comitt to ward where any occation ariseth where the Gour is absent prouided the pson bee brought to hearing with all convenient Speed before the Gour and the rest of the Assistants; alsoe it shalbee lawfull for him in his Maties Name to direct his warrants to any Cunstable within the Gourment whoe ought faithfully to execute the same according to the Nature and tenure therof and may bind ouer psons for matters of crime to answare att the next ensueing Court of his said Mtie after the fact comitted or the pson apprehended;

THE OATH OF AN ASSISTANT.

You shall all sweare to bee truely Loyall to our Sour Lord King Charles his heires and Successors you shall faithfully truely and Justly according to the measure of deserning and descretion God hath giuen you bee Assistant to the Gour for this prsent yeare for the execution of Justice in all cases and towards all psons coming before you without parciallitie according to the Nature of the Office of an Assistant read vnto you; Morouer you shall dilligently duely and truely see that the Lawes and ordinances of this Corporation bee duely executed and shall labour to Advance the good of the seuerall plantations within the lymetts therof and oppose any thinge that shall hinder the same by all due meanes and courses Soe healp you God whoe is the God of truth and punisher of falshood;

It is enacted by the Court and the Authorite thereof that the Gour and two of the Assistants at the least shall as occation shalbee offered in time convenient determine in such triviall cases viz. vnder forty shillinges between man and man as shall come before them as alsoe in offences of smale Nature shall determine doe and execute as in wisdome God shall direct them;

It is enacted by the Court and the authoritie therof That att euery election Court some one of the Assistants or some other suficient man bee chosen Treasurer for the yeare following whose place it shalbee to demaund and receiue in whatsoeuer sume or sumes shall appertaine to the Royaltie of the place either coming in by way of fine Amercment or otherwise and shall Improue the same for the publicke benefitt of this Corporation by order of the Gourment.

It is further enacted by the Court that the Treasurer shall att the election Courts Anually giue in his accounts of his receipts and paiments for his yeare to any that the Court shall appoint and to bee entered vpon Record and thervpon to bee discharged.

It is likewise enacted by the Court that the Treasurer by vertue of his said office shall take order that all debts due to the Countrey bee seasonbly brought in vnto such place or places as hee shall appoint that soe all dues and debts due vnto any pson or psons from the Contrey may bee seasonably and Satisfactorily defrayed except the publice officers wages which is otherwise prouided for.

It is enacted by the Court that it shalbee in the libertie of the Treasurer after a month is past after Judgment by his warrant to require in any fine as hee shall see reason;

Wheras the Court haue taken notice that diuers of the ffreemen of this Corporation doe neither appeer att Courts of election nor send theire voates by proxey for the choise of majestrates It is enacted by the Court and the authoritie therof That whosoeuer of the ffreemen of this Corporation that shall not appeer att the Court of election att Plymouth in June annually nor send theire voate by proxey according to order of Court for the Choise of Gour Assistants Comissioners and Treasurer shall be fined to the Collonies vse the sume of ten shillinges for euery such default; vnlesse some vnavoidable Impediment hinder such in theire appeerance.

Memorand that an oath bee formed for the Treasurer and next entered.

THE OATH OF THE TREASURER.

You shall faithfully serue in the office of the Treasurer in the Jurisdiction of New Plymouth for this prsent yeare during which time you shall dillegently enquire after demaund and receiue whatsoeuer sum or sumes shall appertaine to this Gourment; arising by way of fine amersment Royaltie or otherwise and shall faithfully Improue the same for the vse of the Gourment and according to order dispose therof as occation shall require you shalbee reddy to giue in a true account vnto the Court of youer actings in youer said office yearly att June Courts; Soe healp you God

THE OATH OF A GRANDJURYMAN.

You shall true prsentment make of all thinges giuen you in charge you shall prsent Nothing of Mallice or illwill youer owne Councell and youer fellowes in reference to this oath you shall well and truely keep soe healp you God.

THE OATH OF THE CLARKE OF THE COURT.

You shall faithfully serue in the office of the Clarke of the Court for the Jurisdiction of New Plymouth You shall attend the Generall Courts held for this Gourment att Plymouth Aforsaid and the suerall Adjournments therof; and the Courts of Assistants and there Imploy youerselfe in such occasions as are behoofull to youer said place and office you shall likewise Attend such other meetings of the majestrates of like Nature as aboue expressed that shall or may fall out in the Interims of time betwixt the said Courts you shall not disclose but keep secrett such things as concerne the publicke good and shalbee thought meet to bee Concealled by the Gour and Councell of Assistants You shall faithfully Record all such thinges as you shall haue order from Authoritie to Comitte to publicke Record and shall faithfully keep the publicke Records of this Jurisdiction Soe healp you God who is the God of truth and the punisher of falshood; . . .

The text is based on the one found in Shurtleff and Pulsifer, *Vol. II, Laws,* 147–67. The text is here reproduced only in part since the document is a revision of The Pilgrim Code of Law and therefore repeats much of what is found in the earlier document. The shorthand in the earlier document is tortuous, so changes have been made for the modern reader, but these are minimal.

31

[An Act of the General Court]

June 10, 1661

*T*he charter of 1629 creating the Massachusetts Bay Company
not only had the standard provision providing for local self-
government but also had the peculiarity of failing to make any specific reference to parliamentary authority. This was interpreted to
mean, at least by the colonists, that the English Parliament had no
power over the colony. The Massachusetts Body of Liberties, 1641 [22],
also implied that the colony was bound only by laws of its own choosing. The document below was passed by the Massachusetts General
Court in a bold attempt to essentially declare their autonomy from allegiance to the king as well, or at least to render that allegiance so ten-
uous as to make it meaningless. This move to enlarge the liberties of
the colonies is one more major attempt by the colonists to create a political foundation based completely upon their own consent. Indeed,
the document spells out clearly the major principles that underlay the
evolving colonial constitutionalism. The Crown eventually revoked
the colony's charter in 1684, and this document was a major reason
for that royal action.

CONCERNING OUR LIBERTIES

1. We conceive the patent (under God) to be the first and main foundation of our civil polity here, by a Governor and Company, according as is
therein expressed.

2. The Governor and Company are, by the patent, a body politic, in fact
and name.

3. This body politic is vested with power to make freemen.

4. These freemen have power to choose annually a governor, deputy governor, assistants, and their select representatives or deputies.

5. This government has power also to set up all sorts of officers, as well superior as inferior, and point out their power and places.

6. The governor, deputy governor, assistants, and select representatives or deputies have full power and authority, both legislative and executive, for the government of all the people here, whether inhabitants or strangers, both concerning ecclesiastics and in civils, without appeal, excepting law or laws repugnant to the laws of England.

7. The government is privileged by all fitting means (yea, if need be, by force of arms) to defend themselves, both by land and sea, against all such person or persons as shall at any time attempt or enterprise the destruction, invasion, detriment, or annoyance of this plantation, or the inhabitants therein, besides other privileges mentioned in the patent, not here expressed.

8. We conceive any imposition prejudicial to the country contrary to any just law of ours, not repugnant to the laws of England, to be an infringement of our right.

CONCERNING OUR DUTIES OF ALLEGIANCE TO OUR SOVEREIGN LORD, THE KING

1. We ought to uphold and, to our power, maintain his place, as of right belonging to Our Sovereign Lord, The King, as holden of His Majesty's manor of East Greenwich, and not to subject the same to any foreign prince or potentate whatsoever.

2. We ought to endeavor the preservation of His Majesty's royal person, realms, and dominions, and so far as lies in us, to discover and prevent all plots and conspiracies against the same.

3. We ought to seek the peace and prosperity of Our King and nation by a faithful discharge in the governing of his people committed to our care.

First, by punishing all such crimes (being breaches of the First or Second Table) as are committed against the peace of Our Sovereign Lord, The King, his Royal Crown, and dignity.

Second, in propagating the Gospel, defending and upholding the true Christian or Protestant religion according to the faith given by our Lord Christ in His word; our dread sovereign being styled "defender of the faith."

The premises considered, it may well stand with the loyalty and obedience of such subjects as are thus privileged by their rightful sovereign (for Himself, His Heirs, and Successors forever) as cause shall require, to plead with their prince against all such as shall at any time endeavor the violation of their privileges... And, also, that the General Court may do safely to declare that in case (for the future) any legally obnoxious, and flying from the civil justice of the state of England, shall come over to these parts, they may not here expect shelter.

The text is taken from Shurtleff, *Massachusetts Colonial Records: Vol. IV*, 25–26.

32

[Providence Agreement]

August 20, 1637

*R*oger Williams, who refused to take any of the oaths required
by the Massachusetts Bay Colony because he believed any
oath constituted taking God's name in vain, moved with his fol-
lowers to Providence, which was founded using this document. The
simple covenant formula is familiar, but without the oath it becomes
a compact resting on implicit popular sovereignty. In addition to
being one of the first political compacts, the Providence Agreement
also contains the first expression in the new world of the separation
of church and state—achieved by limiting the town meeting to "civil
things." The following year the second Rhode Island colony was established at Aquidneck (Pocasset), using an oath in the traditional
covenant form (see the Government of Pocasset [33]). A minority
withdrew the following year from Pocasset and drew up its civil compact at Newport without an oath (see the Newport Agreement [34]).
Another colony, which was established at Portsmouth, drew up its
new agreement two days after Newport's (see the Government of
Portsmouth [35]); unlike the Newport Agreement, the Portsmouth
one contained an oath. The Providence Agreement of 1637 was replaced by the Plantation Agreement at Providence, 1640 [36].
Portsmouth and Newport joined in a federation in 1642 that allowed each town to retain its respective government and thus to preserve the differences (see the Organization of the Government of
Rhode Island [37]). Warwick formed itself in 1647 [38], and finally,
in 1647 these towns all united in the Acts and Orders [39], which
was a complete constitution.

We whose names are hereunder, desirous to inhabit in the town of Providence, do promise to subject ourselves in active and passive obedience to all such orders or agreements as shall be made for the public good of the body in an orderly way, by the major consent of present inhabitants, masters of families, incorporated together in a Towne fellowship, and others whom they shall admit unto them only in civil things.

[Signed by Richard Scott and twelve others.]

The complete text is taken from Charles Evans, "Oaths of Allegiance in Colonial New England," *Proceedings of the American Antiquarian Society,* n.s., 31 (April 13–October 19, 1921): 424. Evans's spelling is used.

33

[Government of Pocasset]

March 7, 1638

*C*onsult the comments accompanying the Providence Agreement *[32] for the historical setting of this document. A typical political covenant, this document is distinguished by references to biblical passages containing the underlying principles. The reader might want to consult these passages. The second part of the agreement was passed later in the day after a break for lunch.*

The 7th day of the first month, 1638

We whose names are underwritten do here solemnly in the presence of Jehovah incorporate ourselves into a Bodie Politick and as he shall help, will submit our persons, lives and estates unto our Lord Jesus Christ, the King of Kings and Lord of Lords and to all those perfect and most absolute laws of his given us in his holy word of truth, to be guided and judged thereby.

Exod. 24. 3, 4.

2 Cron. 11. 3

2 Kings. 11. 17

[Signed by William Coddington and eighteen others.]

The 7th of the first month, 1638.

We that are Freemen Incorporate of this Bodie Politick do Elect and Constitute William Coddington, Esquire, a Judge amongst us, and so covenant to yield all due honour unto him according to the lawes of God, and so far as in us lyes to maintaine the honour and privileges of his place which shall hereafter be ratifyed according unto God, the Lord helping us so to do. William Aspinwall, Sec'ry

I, William Coddington, Esquire, being called and chosen by the Freemen Incorporate of this Bodie Politick, to be a Judge amongst them, do covenant to do justice and Judgment impartially according to the lawes of God, and to maintaine the Fundamentall Rights and Privileges of this Body Politick, which shall hereafter be ratifyed according unto God, the Lord helping us to do so.

Wm. Coddington

William Aspinwall is appointed Secretary.

It is agreed that William Dyre shall be Clarke of this Body.

Complete text, with the original spelling, taken from J. R. Bartlett, ed., *Records of the Colony of Rhode Island and Providence Plantations in New England: Vol 1, 1636 to 1663* (Providence: A. Crawford Greene and Brother, State Printers, 1856), 52–53.

34
[Newport Agreement]

April 28, 1639

*T*his is the document drawn up by the dissenting minority that withdrew from the settlement at Pocasset (see the discussion of the Providence Agreement [32]). It is not an oath but rests on the agreement among the people, implying popular sovereignty. It was drawn up in Pocasset before they left.

Pocasset. On the 28th of the 2d [month], 1639

It is agreed.

By vs whose hands are underwritten, to propagate a Plantation in the midst of the Island or elsewhere; And doe engage ourselves to bear equall charges, answerable to our strength and estates in common; and that our determinations shall be by major voice of judge and elders; the Judge to have a double voice.

[Signed by William Coddington and eight others.]

The complete text, with the original spelling, is taken from Bartlett, *Vol. 1, 1636 to 1663,* 69.

35

[The Government of Portsmouth]

April 30, 1639

*S*ee the discussion of the Providence Agreement [32] for events leading up to this agreement. The Portsmouth agreement is unusual in that it is a compact; however, those signing it invoke the authority of the king, although he is unaware his authority is being used. The compact thus has the form of a civil compact without the legal status because the king has not signed it. We can only guess at the reason for this format, but it avoids invoking God's name as well as it avoids using an implicit popular sovereignty that might, for some reason, have made these people uneasy. It certainly would make it easier for the king to approve the document post hoc. Another unusual feature is that it appears to establish government by arbitration.

Aprill the 30th, 1639

We, whose names are under [written doe acknowledge] ourselves the legall subjects of [his Majestie] King Charles, and in his name [doe hereby binde] ourselves into a civill body politicke, unto his lawes according to matters of justice.

[Signed by William Hutchinson and thirty associates.]

According to the true intent of the [foregoing instrument, wee] whose names are above particularly [recorded, do agree] joyntly or by the major voice to g[overne ourselves by the] ruler or judge amongst us in all [transactions] for the space and tearme of one [yeare, he] behaving himselfe according to the t[enor of the same.]

We have freely made choice of [   ] to be ruler or judge among us.

We have also, for the help and ease [of the conducting of] public business and affairs for [the colony] for one yeare, allso chosen unto him William Ballston, William Freeborne, John Porter, John [   ], John Wall, Philip

Sherman, as allso William Aspinwall to lay out lands as they shall be disposed.

We have also made choice of [   ] amongst us for this yeare ensuing.

It is appoynted that there shall be [a court held every] yeare, every quarter, one for to doe right betwixt man and [man—a] jury of twelve men; as also it is [ordered, that] the eight men chosen unto him [shall hold a] meeting amongst themselves, to consult [together]; as also to put an end to any controverzy, if it amount not to the value of fortie [shillings.] The Judge, with the rest of the eight men [shall decide it] if brought to ye publicke Court.

The complete text, with original spelling, is taken from Bartlett, *Vol. 1, 1636 to 1663,* 70–71. The gaps are in the original, and brackets indicate illegible words that have been supplied on the basis of context.

36

Plantation Agreement at Providence

August 27, 1640

*T*he Providence Agreement, 1637 [32] created a highly democratic political system centered around a town meeting. This document does not replace that one but supplements it. Apparently the town meeting was spending too much time resolving disagreements between individuals, many of the disagreements involving money and property; so here the town has created an arbitration structure, with a set of guidelines for the arbiters, aimed at resolving such disagreements. In England, and in most other places, these disagreements would normally be taken to a court. Here, the panel of elected arbiters stands in for a civil court, which guarantees such disputes will be settled more by the ethic of neighborliness using community values and standards rather than on the basis of legalisms and standing precedent.

———————

Report of Arbitrators at Providence,
containing proposals for a form of government
Providence the 27th of the 5th mo.
in the yeare (so called) 1640.

Wee, Robert Coles, Chad Browne, William Harris, and John Warner, being freely chosen by the consent of our louing friends and neighbours the Inhabitants of this Towne of Providence, having many differences amongst us, they being freely willing and also bound themselves to stand to our Arbitration in all differences amongst us to rest contented in our determination, being so betrusted we have seriously and carefully indeavoured to weigh and consider all those differences, being desirous to bringe vnity and peace, although our abilities are farr short in the due examination of such weighty things, yet so farre as we conceive in laying all things together we have gone the fairest and equallest way to produce our peace.

I. Agreed, We have with one consent agreed that in parting those particler properties which some of our friends and neighbours have in Patuxit, from the general Common of our towne of Providence, to run vppon a streight line from a fresh spring being in the Gulley, at the head of that cove running by that point of land called Saxafras vnto the town of Mashipawog, to an oake tree standing neere vnto the corne field, being at this time the neerest corne field vnto Patuxit, the oake tree having four marks with an axe, till some other land marke be set for a certaine bound. Also, we agree that if any meadow ground lyeing and joineing to that Meadow, that borders uppon the River of Patuxit come within the aforesaid line, which will not come within a streight line from long Cove to the marked tree, then for that meadow to belong to Pawtuxit, and so beyond the towne of Mashipawog from the oake tree between the two fresh Rivers Pawtuxit and Wanasquatucket of an even Distance.

II. Agreed. We have with one consent agreed that for the disposeing, of those lands that shall be disposed belonging to this towne of Providence to be in the whole Inhabitants be the choise of five men for generall disposeall, to be betrusted with disposeall of lands and also of the towne Stocke, and all Generall things and not to receive in any six dayes as townesmen, but first to give the Inhabitants notice to consider if any have just cause to shew against the receiving of him as you can apprehend, and to receive none but such as subscribe to this our determination. Also, we agree that if any of our neighbours doe apprehend himselfe wronged by these or any of these 5 disposers, that at the General towne meeting he may have a tryall. Alsoe wee agree for the towne to choose beside the other five men one or more to keeppe Record of all things belonging to the towne and lying in Common.

Wee agree, as formerly hath bin the liberties of the town, so still, to hould forth liberty of Conscience.

III. Agreed, that after many Considerations and Consultations of our owne State and alsoe of States abroad in way of government, we apprehend, no way so suitable to our Condition as government by way of Arbitration. But if men agree themselves by arbitration, no State we know of disallows that, neither doe we: But if men refuse that which is but common humanity betweene man and man, then to compel such vnreasonable persons to a reasonable way, we agree that the 5 disposers shall have power to compell him either to choose two men himselfe, or if he refuse, for them to choose two men to arbitrate his cause, and if these foure men chosen by every partie do end the cause, then to see theire determination performed and the faultive to pay the Arbitrators for theire time spent in it: But if those foure men doe not end it, then for the 5 disposers to choose the 3 men, and for the certainty hereof, wee agree the major part of the 5 disposers to choose the 3 men, and the major part of the 3 men to end the cause hauing power from the 5 disposers by a note under theire hand to performe it, and the faultive not agreeing in the first to pay the charge of the last, and for the Arbitrators to follow no imployment till the cause be ended without consent of the whole that have to doe with the cause.

Instance. In the first Arbitration the offendor may offer reasonable terms of peace, and the offended may exact upon him and refuse and trouble men beyond reasonable satisfaction; so for the last arbitrators to judge where the fault was, in not agreeing in the first, to pay the charge of the last.

IV. Agreed, that if any person damnify any man, either in goods or good name, and the person offended follow not the cause vppon the offendor, that if any person giue notice to the 5 Disposers, they shall call the party delinquent to answer by Arbitration.

Instance. Thus, if any person abuse an other in person or goods, may be for peace sake, a man will at present put it vp, and it may so be resolue to revenge: therefore, for the peace of the state, the disposers are to look to it in the first place.

V. Agreed, for all the whole Inhabitants to combine ourselves to assist any man in the pursuit of any party delinquent, with all our best endeavours to attack him: but if any man raise a hubbub, and there be no just cause, then for the party that raised the hubbub to satisfy men for their time lost in it.

VI. Agreed, that if any man have a difference with any of the 5 Disposers which cannot be deferred till general meeting of the towne, then he may have the Clerk call the towne together at his [discretion] for a tryall.

Instance. It may be, a man may be to depart the land, or to a farr parte of the land; or his estate may lye vppon a speedy tryall or the like case may fall out.

VII. Agreed, that the towne, by the five men shall give every man a deed of all his lands lying within the bounds of the Plantation, to hould it by for after ages.

VIII. Agreed, that the 5 disposers shall from the date hereof, meete every month-day vppon General things and at the quarter-day to yeeld a new choise and give vp theire old Accounts.

IX. Agreed, that the Clerke shall call the 5 Disposers together at the month-day, and the generall towne together every quarter, to meete vppon general occasions from the date hereof.

X. Agreed, that the Clerke is to receive for every cause that comes to the towne for a tryall 4*d.*[1] for making each deed 12*d.* and to give vp the booke to the towne at the yeeres end, and yeeld to a new choice.

XI. Agreed, that all acts of disposall on both sides to stand since the difference.

XII. Agreed, that every man that hath not paid in his purchase money for his Plantation shall make vp his 10*s.*[2] to be 30*s.* eqval with the first purchasers: and for all that are received townsmen hereafter, to pay the like summe of money to the town stocke.

These being those things wee have generally concluded on, for our peace, we desireing our loveing friends to receive as our absolute determination, laying ourselves downe as subjects to it.

[Signed by the four writers in the document plus thirty-five others.]

1. Four pence.
2. Ten shillings.

Taken from Bartlett, *Vol. 1, 1636 to 1663*, 27–31. The text is complete, with the original spelling.

37

[Organization of the Government of Rhode Island]

March 16–19, 1642

*F*inding themselves sharing an island in Narragansett Bay, the towns of Portsmouth and Newport united using a document that mixed a few general principles and brief institutional descriptions with, among other miscellany, ordinances on the killing of foxes and deer. The most important result was the election of a common representative body. Another important feature, however, was religious toleration (it prohibited anyone from being held delinquent from doctrine). As a founding document this one is defective for two reasons—the colony-wide institutions are underspecified and the relationship between the colony governments and town governments is unclear. Although defective in these respects, as well as confusing in its organization and content, the document served as a kind of constitution for five years but was later replaced by the Acts and Orders of 1647 [39].

The Generall Court of Election began and held at Portsmouth, from the 16th of March, to the 19th of the same mo., 1641.

1. It was ordered and agreed, before the Election, that an Ingagement by oath should be taken of all the officers of this Body now to be elected, as likewise for the time to come; the ingagement which the severall officers of the State shall give is this; To the Execution of this office, I Judge myself bound before God to walk faithfully and this I profess in ye presence of God.

BY ELECTION.

2. Mr. Will'm Coddington is chosen Governour for one whole yeare, or till a new be chosen.

172

Mr. Wm. Brenton is chosen Dep'ty Governour, for one whole yeare, or, &c.

Mr. John Coggshall is chosen Assistant for one whole yeare, or, &c.

Mr. Rob't Harding is chosen Assistant for one whole yeare, or, &c.

Mr. Wm. Balston is chosen Assistant and Treasurer for one whole yeare, etc.

Mr. John Porter is chosen Assistant for one whole yeare, or until, &c.

Wm. Dyre is chosen Secretary for one whole yeare, or until, &c.

Mr. Rob't Jeoffreys is chosen Treasurer for one whole yeare, or, &c.

Thomas Gorton and Henry Bull are chosen Sergeant Attendants of Portsmouth for one yeare, or till a new be chosen.

Thomas Cornell and Henry Bishop are chosen Constables of Nuport, for one yeare, or till a new be chosen.

3. It is ordered and unanimously agreed upon, that the Government which this Bodie Politick doth attend vnto in this Island, and the Jurisdiction thereof, in favour of our Prince is a DEMOCRACIE, or Popular Government; that is to say, It is in the Powre of the Body of Freemen orderly assembled, or the major part of them, to make or constitue Just Lawes, by which they will be regulated, and to depute from among themselves such Ministers as shall see them faithfully executed between Man and Man.

4. It was further ordered, by the authority of this present Courte, that none bee accounted a Delinquent for *Doctrine:* Provided, it be not directly re-pugnant to ye Government or Lawes established.

5. It was further ordered, that all such who shall kill a Fox shall have six shillings and eight pence, for his paines, duly paid vnto him by the Treasurer of ye Towne in which lands it was killed: Provided, that he bring the Head thereof to said Treasurer; and this order shall be of sufficient authority to the Treasurer to pay and discharge the said summ.

6. It is further ordered, that all Men who shall kill any Deare (except it be upon his own proper Land), shall bring and deliver half the said Deare into the Treasurie, or pay Forty shillings; and further it is ordered, that the Governour and Deputy Governour shall have authority to give forth a War-rant to some one deputed of each Towne to kill some against the Court times for the Countries use, who shall by his Warrant have Libertie to kill wher-ever he find; Provided, it be not within any man's enclosure, and to be paid by the Treasurer: Provided, also, that no Indian shall be suffered to kill or destroy at any time or any where.

7. It is ordered from henceforth, that the Quarter Session Courts shall alway be kept the first, the first Tuesday in March; the second, the first Tuesday in June; the third, the first Tuesday in September; the last, the first Tuesday in December.

8. It is ordered, that Eight Gunns and their furniture with two corsletts, now in the hands of Mr. Willbore, shall be taken off by the Threasurie Jointlie, as part of satisfaction for what debts from him is now dew thereto: and that the said Armes be equally divided to each Towne.

9. It is ordered, that the Deputie Governour and Mr. Willbore, and Mr. Coggshall, and Mr. Jeremy Clarke, shall be joyned in commission with the Two Treasurers that now bee, to examine the Treasurie, and to even the accounts, and then to present them so rectified to the next General Court; and what oneveness there is found to bee, the one Treasurer shall make payment to the other Treasurer within twentie dayes after the period of their commission: the limits which are set for the performance of this, shall be three weeks from the date hereof.

10. It is ordered, that Mr. Porter, Mr. Balston, Mr. Easton, and Mr. Jeoffreys shall runn the line between the two Towns within twentie dayes after the date hereof, or else shall forfeit a Mark a peece; and performing it within the (time or) tearme they shall have a Mark a peace for their Labour.

11. It is ordered, that each Towne shall provide a Towne Book, wherein they shall Record the Evidences of the Lands by them impropriated; and shall also have Powre to give forth a Coppie thereof, which shall be a clear evidence for them and theirs, to whom it is so granted.

12. It is ordered, that the Officers of Justices of the Peace is confirmed to the Magistrates.

13. It is ordered, that no Fiers shall be kindled by any whatsoever to runn at Randome, eyther in Meadows or Woods; but what by him that so kindled it shall forthwith be put out, that it damnifie none. And that if damage shall accrew, satisfaction to the utmost shall be awarded.

14. It is ordered, that a Booke shall be provided, wherein the Secretary shall write all such Lawes and Acts, as are made and constituted by the Body, to be left alway in that Towne where the said Secretary is not resident; and also that coppies of such Acts as shall be made now or hereafter, at the Generall Courts concerning necessary uses and ordinances to be observed, shall be fixed upon some public place where all men may see and take no-

tice of them; or that coppies thereof be given to the Clerks of the Band, who shall read them at the head of the Companie.

15. It is ordered, that a Manual Seale shall be provided for the State, and that the Signett or Engraving thereof, shall be a sheafe of Arrows bound up, and in the Liess or Bond, this motto indented: *Amor vincent omnia.*

16. It is ordered, that Ingagement shall be taken by the Justices of the Peace in their Quarter Sessions of all men or youth above fifteen years of age, eyther by the oath of Fidelity, or some other strong cognizance.

17. It is ordered, that a Line be drawen and a way be cleared between the Townes of Nuport and Portsmouth, by removing of the wood and mowing it; that drift Cattle may sufficiently pass; and for the performance thereof, Capt. Morris, of the one Towne, and Mr. Jeoffreys of the other, are appointed to draw the Line, and to be paid therefore, and the Townes to perform the rest.

18. It is ordered, that the Traine Bands shall choose among the Freemen, one or more such as shall be for their commanders, and present them to the Towne. The Major vote of the Towne, by the Authority of this Court, shall have the negative voise for the Establishment of them, and shall order their Powre till the next Generall Courte.

19. It is ordered, that the major part of the Courts, being lawfully assembled at the place and houre appointed, shall have full Powre to transact the business that shall be Presented: Provided, it be the Major part of the Body entire, if it be the Generall Court (present) or the Major part of the Magistrates, with the Jury in the inferior Courts; and that such acts concluded and issued be of as full authority as if there were all present. Provided, there be due and seasonable notice given of every such Court.

Complete text, with the original spelling, taken from Bartlett, *Vol. I, 1636 to 1663*, III–15.

38

[Warwick Agreement]

August 8, 1647

*U*nlike Providence, Pocasset, Portsmouth, and Newport, Warwick did not write its own founding document prior to the
granting of an official charter in 1644 because its inhabitants did not
feel it lawful to erect their own government without explicit authority from England. Written three years after Rhode Island was chartered as a colony, the Warwick Agreement reflects the need to fit into
the frame of that charter. The result is the purest example during the
colonial era of a civil covenant sanctioned by the king.

KNOW ALL MEN, Colonies, Peoples, and Nations, unto whom the same
hereof shall come; that wee, the chiefe Sachems, Princes or Governours
of the Nanhigansets (in the part of America, now called New-England), together with the joynt and unanimous consent of all our people and subjects, inhabitants thereof, do upon serious consideration, mature and
deliberate advise and counsell, great and weighty grounds and reasons moving us thereunto, whereof one most effectual unto us, is, that noble fame
we have heard of that Great and mighty Prince, Charles, King of Great
Britaine, in that honorable and princely care he hath all his servants, and
true and loyall subjects, the consideration whereof moveth and bendeth
our hearts with one consent, freely, voluntarily, and most humbly to submit,
subject, and give over ourselves, peoples, lands, rights, inheritances, and pos-
sessions whatsoever, in ourselves and our heires successively for ever, unto
the protection, care and government of that worthy and royal Prince,
Charles, King of Great Britaine and Ireland, his heires and successors forever, to be ruled and governed according to the ancient and honorable
lawes and customes, established in that so renowned realme and kingdome
of Old England; we do, therefore, by these presents, confesse, and most willingly and submissively acknowledge ourselves to be the humble, loving and

obedient servants and subjects of his Majestie; to be ruled, ordered, and disposed of, in ourselves and ours, according to his princely wisdome., counsell and lawes of that honorable State of Old England;

and wrighting us of what wrong is, or may be done unto us, according to his honorable lawes and customes, exercised amongst his subjects, in their preservation and safety, and in the defeating and overthrow of his, and their enemies; not that we find ourselves necessitated hereunto, in respect of our relation, or occasion we have, or may have, with any of the natives in these parts, knowing ourselves sufficient defence, and able to judge in any matter or cause in that respect; but have just cause of jealousy and suspicion of some of His Majesty's pretended subjects. Therefore our desire is, to have our matters and causes heard and tried according to his just and equall lawes, in that way and order His Highness shall please to appoint:

having ourselves been the chief Sachems, or Princes successively, of the country, time out of mind; and for our present and lawfull enacting hereof, being so farre remote from His Majestie, wee have, by joynt consent, made choice of foure of his loyall and loving subjects, our trusty and well-beloved friends, Samuel Gorton, John Wickes, Randall Houlden and John Warner, whom we have deputed, and made our lawful Attornies or Commissioners, not only for the acting and performing of this our Deed, in the behalfe of his Highnesse, but also for the safe custody, careful conveyance, and declaration hereof unto his grace: being done upon the lands of the Nanhigansett, at a Court or Generall Assembly called and assembled together, of purpose, for the publick enacting, and manifestation hereof.

And for the further confirmation, and establishing of this our Act and Deed, wee, the abovesaid Sachems or Princes, have, according to that commendable custome of Englishmen, subscribed our names and sett our seals hereunto, as so many testimonies of our fayth and truth, our love and loyalty to that our dread Soveraighne, and that according to the Englishmen's account.

Complete text, with the original spelling, taken from Bartlett, *Vol. 1, 1636–1663*, 134–35.

39

Acts and Orders of 1647

*T*he Acts and Orders of 1647, like the Pilgrim Code of Law, 1636 [20] and Fundamental Orders of Connecticut, 1639 [43], is a complete document of foundation and qualifies as a true constitution. Like these other early colonial constitutions, the Acts and Orders creates a federal system wherein the towns composing it continue to have functioning governments with their own powers and competencies. In 1663 Rhode Island received a new charter from the king, which essentially ratified the government established by the Acts and Orders. In 1776 Rhode Island retained this charter as the constitution for its new independent statehood simply by removing any references to the king, and the charter was not replaced until 1842. Scholars of American constitutionalism thus put the duration of the Acts and Orders, Rhode Island's first constitution, at 195 years, which was a record duration for a modern constitution until the Massachusetts Constitution of 1780 turned 196 in 1976. The Acts and Orders is also notable in that it was the first colonial foundation document specifically based on English principles of law instead of principles and practices derived from religion.

Acts and Orders

Made and agreed upon at the Generall Court of Election, held at Portsmouth, in Rhode Island, the 19, 20, 21 of May, Anno. 1647, for the Colonie and province of Providence.

Mr. John Coggeshall is chosen Moderator of the present Assembly.

2. It was Voted and found, that the major part of the Colonie was present at this Assemblie, whereby there was full power to transact.

3. It was further agreed, that in case the Assemblie departe unto the number of Fortie; those fortie shall stay and act as if the whole were present, and be of as full authoritie.

4. It was agreed, that all should set their hands to an engagement to the Charter.

5. It was agreed and ordered, that a week before any General Courte, notice should be given to every Towne by the head officer, that they chuse a Committee for the Transaction of the affaires there, except it bee for the Election of Generall Officers; and such as go not, may send their votes sealed.

6. It was ordered, upon the request of the Commissioners of the Towne of Providence, that their second instruction should be granted and established unto the, Vidg't. Wee do voluntarily assent, and are freely willing to receive and to be governed by the Lawes of England, together with the way of the Administration of them, soe far as the nature and constitution of this Plantation will admit, desiring (soe far as possible may be,) to hold a correspondence with the whole Colonie in the modell that hath been latelie shewn vnto us by our worthy Friends of the Island, if the Generall Court shall compleate and confirm the same, or any other Modell as the Generall Courte shall agree vpon according to our Charter.

7. It was unanimously agreed, That we do all owne and submit to the Lawes, as they are contracted in the Bulke with the Administration of Justice, according thereto, which are to stand in force till the next Generall Courte of Election, and every Towne to have a Coppie of them, and then to present what shall appeare therein not to be suitable to the Constitution of the place, and then to amend it.

8. It was agreed, that Warwick should have the same priviledges as Providence.

9. It was agreed, that the Generall Courte of Tryall should be held at Newport vpon the second Tuesday of June next ensuing.

10. It was agreed, that the Election of Offices should be by papers.
Mr. John Coggeshall is chosen President of this Province, or Colonie.
Mr. Roger Williams is chosen Assistant of Providence,
Mr. John Samford is chosen Assistant of Portsmouth,
Mr. Wm. Coddington is chosen Assistant of Newport,
Mr. Randall Holden is chosen Assistant of Warwick,
William Dyre is chosen Gen. Recorder,
Mr. Jeremy Clerke is chosen Treasurer.

11. It is ordered, that all cases presented, concerning General Matters for the Colony, shall be first stated in the Townes, Vigd't, That is, when a case is propounded, The Towne where it is propounded, shall agitate and fully

discuss the matter in their Towne Meetings and conclude by Vote; and then shal the Recorder of the Towne, or Towne Clerk, send a coppy of the agreement to every of the other three Townes, who shall agitate the case likewise in each Towne and vote it, and collect the votes. Then shall they commend it to the Committee for the General Courte (then a meeting called,) who being assembled and finding the Major parte of the Colonie concurring in the case, it shall stand for a Law till the next Generall Assembly of all the people, then and there to be considered, whether any longer to stand yea or no; Further it is agreed, that six men of each Towne shall be the number of the Committe premised, and to be freely chosen. And further it is agreed, that when the General Courte thus assembled, shall determine the cases before hand thus presented, It shall also be lawful for the said General Court, and hereby are they authorized, that if vnto them or any of them some case or cases shall be presented that may be deemed necessary for the public weale and good of the whole, they shall fully debate, discuss and determine ye matter among themselves; and then shall each Committee returning to their Towne declare what they have done in the case or cases premised. The Townes then debating and concluding, the votes shall be collected and sealed up, and then by the Towne Clarke of each Towne shall be sent with speed to the General Recorder, who, in the presence of the President shall open the votes; and if the major vote determine the case, it shall stand as a Law till the next General Assemblie then or there to be confirmed or nullified.

12. It is ordered, that the Courte of Election shall alway be held upon the first Tuesday after the 15th of May, annually, if wind or weather hinder not. Then the General Court of Tryall immediately to succeed vpon the dissolving of the said General Court, Vidg't: the next day; and that the next General Court of Election shall be held at Providence Towne. Further, it is agreed, that forasmuch as many may be necessarily detained, that they cannot come to the General Court of Election, that then they shall send their votes sealed upon unto the said Court, which shall be as effectual as their personal appearances.

13. It is ordered, that each Towne shall choose and order ye authoritie of two Surveyors for the Highways, and appoint time to mend them; also that they are to have notice of all cattle that shall be exported, and returne the marks of them unto the Towne; and if any shall presume to export any without giving notice of it to the men appointed, or their Deputies he shall forfeit all such Cattle so exported, or the worth of them.

14. It is ordered, that the Inhabitants of Portsmouth and Newport here present doe presently choose their officers of the Island; but that this act shall be not precedent for the future, but that the constant course of choosing shall be hereafter, when as the year is out, as the Major votes of the Townes of Portsmouth and Newport shall order it sometimes before the year is out, in some peaceable and moderate way which they shall agree upon.

THE ENGAGEMENT OF THE OFFICERS

You. A. B _____, being called and chosen vnto public employment, and the office of _____, by the free vote and consent of ye Inhabitants of the Province of Providence Plantations (now orderly met), do, in the present Assemblie, engage yourself faithfully and truly to the utmost of your power to execute the commission committed vnto you; and do hereby promise to do neither more nor less in that respect than that which the Colonie [authorized] you to do according to the best of your understanding.

We, the Inhabitants of the Province of Providence Plantations being here orderly met, and having by free vote chosen you _____, to public office and officers for the due administration of Justice and the execution thereof throughout the whole Colonie, do hereby engage ourselves to the utmost of our power to suport and vphold you in your faithful performance thereof.

15. It is ordered, that the Councills of Newport and Portsmouth, shall consult and agree how and in what manner (within these thirtie dayes) the monthly and quarterly Courts shall be ordered, and who shall sit therein; further, it is agreed, that all cases depending shall be heard and issued at the next Generall Court of Tryall.

16. It is ordered, that the Townes shall appoint men to view all Goates and Swine killed or to be killed, and shew the eare markes of them unto the said persons or one of them, whereby it may appeare to be their own; and if any shall presume to conceale eyther Swine or Goats so killed or to be killed, shall forfeit five pounds; one half to the State, the other to him that will sue for it, eyther by action or bill. It shall be lawfull also, for those that are appointed to the service being necessarily detayned, to make, constitute, and appoint a Deputie.

17. It is ordered, that John Cooke and Thomas Brownell, are chosen Water Bailies for the Colonie.

18. It is ordered, that the Seale of the Province shall be an Anchor.

19. It is ordered, that the Councils of the Townes consisting of six men shall be chosen at their next Towne Meetings.

20. It is ordered, that the Sea Lawes, otherwise called the Lawes of Oleron, shall be in force among us for the benefit of Seamen (vpon ye Island,) and the Chief Officers in the Towne shall have power to summon the Court and determine the cause or causes presented.

21. It is ordered, that none shall goe out of the Court without leave; or if any do depart, he shall leve his vote behind him, that his power remain, though his person be absent.

22. It is ordered, forasmuch as Mr. Roger Williams hath taken great paines and expended much time in the obtayning of the Charter for this Province of Noble Lords and Governors; be it enacted and established, that in regard of his so great travaile, charges and good endeavours, we do freely give and grant to the said Roger Williams one hundred pounds, to be levied out of the three townes, Vidg't: Fifty pounds out of Newport, thirtie pounds out of Portsmouth, and twentie pounds out of Providence, which rate is to be levied and paid in by the last of November next.

23. It is ordered, that forasmuch as there are some remote places inhabited and possessed within our Charter, and it is found necessary that a vigilant eye be had over them, it is ordered, that Newport shall take into their custody the Trading house or houses of the Narragansett Bay; Portsmouth to take in Prudence; and Patuxet shall be left to their choice, whether they will have Providence, Portsmouth or Newport over them. And it is ordered, that the officers of each Towne shall have full power and authoritie in them or eyther of them, according to their precincts, by this present Court assyned.

24. It is ordered, that there is free Libertie granted for the free Inhabitants of ye Province (if they will) to erect an Artillery Garden, and those that are desirous to advance the Art Military, shall have freedom to exercise themselves therein, and to agree of their forme, and choose their officers, as they shall agree among themselves.

25. Provided, [   ] shall choose their officers after the 15th of June next, vpon paine of forfeiting Tenn pounds a Town, if neglected.

26. It is ordered, that in cases of necessity without the bounds of the Townes, a special officer for ye execution of Justice, may be authorized by any of the Generall Officers for a general case.

27. It is ordered, that ye General Officers shall write to the Bay about

Patuxet Inhabitants; and also write to the Inhabitants thereof to owne and choose the Government of the Province.

28. It is ordered, that the Dutch, French or other Alliants, or any Englishman inhabiting among them, shall pay the like customs and duties, as we doe among them for all such goods as shall be imported for the English, excepting beaver. Also, we do absolutely prohibit them or any of them to trade or barter with the Indians within our Jurisdiction, upon paine of forfeiture of Shipp and Goods; and this to take effect after due notice given. The Generall Officers are ordered to write to the Dutch Governor, and upon the returne of the answer it shall be commended to the Townes to consider of.

29. It is ordered, that all ye Inhabitants in each Towne shall choose their Military Officers from among themselves on the first Tuesday after the 12th of March; and that eight sevarall times in the yeare, the Bands of each plantation or Towne, shall, openlie in the field, be exercised and disciplined by their Commanders and Officers, in the months of May, August, January and February excepted; and on the first Monday of ye other months, all the Train Bands to make their personal appearances completely armed, to attend their colors, by 8 o'clock in the morning, at the second beate of ye Drum; and if any appear not, they shall forfeit and pay five shillings into the hands of the Clarke of ye Band; and if any shall come defective in his Armes or furniture, he shall forfeit and pay ye sum of twelve pence, after the Town Council have caused them to be supplied; and that all men who shall come and remaine ye space of twenty days, shall be liable to ye injunction of this order; Provided, herdsmen, fighter-men and such as be left of necessity at Farmes, shall pay two shilings and sixpence for every dayes absence: And that the two Chief officers in each Towne, to witt: one of the Commonweale, the other of the Band, upon the exhibition of the complaint by ye Clark (which shall be within three dayes after the fault committed,) shall judge and determine of ye reasons of the excuses, who, upon the hearing thereof, shall determine whether every such person shall pay five shillings, two shillings and sixpence, or nothing; and according as they find any defective, shall give their warrants to ye Clark to distraine their Goods if they shall refuse to pay what is ordered. And if the Clarke shall neglect to gather up what is ordered, he shall forfeit and pay so much into the hands of the Captain, the next training day; And that all the fines and forfeitures shall be imployed to the use and service of the Band. And the Towne Councils shall have power to cause those which are defective in armes, to be supplied in an equal way according to

Estate and strength. And if any of ye Traine Band after his appearance shall refuse or neglect the command of his Captain, to be exercised and disciplined, he shall forfeit as much as if he had not appeared: And that the Town Council shall order the power of the Military Officers within the Towne, and in all caes that concerne ye whole, the President and ye foure assistants, and ye Captains of every Band shall be the Councill of Warr; that if any of the Officers of ye Band be at any time left out, they shall beare Armes again, for ye Constitution of our place will not beare the contrary: that every Inhabitant of the Island above sixteen or under sixty yeares of age, shall alwayes be provided of a Musket, one pound of powder, twenty bullets, and two fadom of Match, with sword, rest, bandaleers all completely furnished.

30. It is ordered, that in regard of ye many incursions that we are subjected vnto, and that an Alarum for ye giving of notice thereof is necessary when occasion is offered. It is agreed, that this form be observed. Vidg't: Three Muskets distinctly discharged, and a Herauld appointed to go speedilie threw the Towne, and crie, Alarum! Alarum!! and the Drum to beate incessantly; upon which, all to repair (upon forfeiture and the Town Councill shall order) unto the Town House, there to receive information of the Town Councill what is farther to be done.

31. It is ordered and agreed, that if any person or persons, shall sell, give deliver, or any otherwayes convey any powder, shott, lead, gunn, pistoll, sword, dagger, halberd or pike to the Indians that are or may prove offensive to this Colonie, or any member thereof, he or they, for the first offence, shall forfeit ye sum of five pounds; and for his second offence, offending in the same kind, and being lawfully convicted, shall forfeit ten pounds; half to the State, and half to him that will sew for it, and no wager of Law by any means to be allowed to the offender. And, it is further ordered, that if any person shall mend or repaire their Guns, or [   ] he shall forfeit the same penaltie.

32. It is ordered, that the Towne Officers shall given their engagements in their severall Townes to ye General Officer in that Towne, before they execute their office.

33. It is ordered, that if the Indians shall offer to putt away upon exchange or barter, their false peag for good, and warrant it so to be, and it be found otherwise, it shall be confiscated to the Public Treasury.

34. It is ordered, that every Towne shall have a coppy of the Lawes and Orders, and that each Towne shall pay for their coppy; and also, that the

Councell for the Townes shall order the fees for their Officers, and the Generall Officers shall order the fees of the General Officers: Provided, that nothing already concluded in the Bulck of Lawes be any wayes crossed or envaded.

FOR THE PROVINCE OF PROVIDENCE.

Forasmuch as we have received from our Noble Lords and Honored Governours, and that by virtue of an ordinance of the Parliament of England, a free and absolute Charter of Civill incorporation, &c. Wee do joyntlie agree to incorporate ourselves, and soe to remaine a Body Politicke by the authoritie thereof, and therefore do declare to own ourselves and one another to be Members of the same Body, and to have right to the Freedome and priviledges thereof by subscribing our names to these words, following: vidg't.

Wee, whose names are here vnder written, doe engage ourselves to the vttmost of our Estates and Strength, to mainteyne the authority and to enjoy the Libertie granted to vs by our Charter, in the extent of itt according to the Letter, and to mainteyne each other by the same authoritie, in his lawfull right and Libertie.

And with this our Charter gives vs powre to governe ourselves and such other as come among vs, and by such a forme of Civill Government as by the Voluntarie consent, &c., shall be found most suitable to our Estate and condition,

It is agreed, by this present Assembly thus incorporate, and by this present act declared, that the forme of Government established is DEMOCRATICALL; that is to say, a Government held by ye free and voluntarie consent of all, or the greater parte of the free Inhabitants.

And now to the end that we may give, each to other, (notwithstanding our different consciences, touching the truth as it is in Jesus, whereof, upon the point we all make mention,) as good and hopeful assurance as we are able, touching each man's peaceable and quiett enjoyment of his lawfull right and Libertie, we doe agree vnto, and by the authoritie above said, Inact, establish, and confirme these orders following.

TOUCHING LAWES.

That no person, in this Colonie, shall be taken or imprisoned, or be disseized of his Lands or Liberties, or be Exiled, or any other otherwise molested or destroyed, but by the Lawfull judgment of his Peeres, or by some known Law, and according to the Letter of it, Ratified and confirmed by the major part of the Generall Assembly lawfully met and orderly managed.

2. That no person shall (but at his great perill,) presume to beare or execute any office, that is not lawfuly called to it, and confirmed in it; nor though he be lawfully called and confirmed, presume to doe more or less than those that had powre to call him, or did authorize him to doe.

3. That no Assembly shall have powre to constitute any Lawes for the binding of others, or to ordaine Officers for the execution thereof, but such as are founded upon the Charter and rightlie derived from the General Assemblie, lawfully met and orderly managed.

4. That no person be employed in any service for the Publick Administration of Justice and Judgment vpon offenders, or between Man and Man, without good encouragement, and due satisfaction from the Publick, eyther out of the common stock, or out of the stocks of those that have occasioned his service; that so, those that are able to serve, may not be unwilling, and those that are able and willing, may not be disabled by being overburthened. And then, in case a man be called vnto Office by a lawfull Assemble, and refuse to beare office, or be called by an officer to assist in the execution of his office, and refuse to assist him, he shall forfeit as much again as his wages would have amounted unto, or be otherwise fined by the judgment of his Peers, and to pay his fine or forfeiture, unless the Colony, or that lawful Assembly release him. But in case of eminent danger, no man shall refuse.

And now, forasmuch as our Charter gives us powre to make such Lawes, Constitutions, Penalties, and Officers of Justice for the execution thereof as we, or the greater part of vs shall, by free consent, agree vnto, and yet does premise that those Lawes, Constitutions, and Penalties soe made shall be conformable to the Lawes of England, soe far as the nature and constitution of our place will admit, to the end that we may show ourselves not only unwilling that our popularity should prove (as some conjecture it will,) an Anarchie, and so a common Tyranny, but willing and exceedingly desirous to preserve every man safe in his person, name and estate; and to show ourselves, in soe doing, to be also vnder authoritie, by keeping within the verge and limitts prescribed us in our Charter, by which we have Authoritie in this respect to act; Wee do agree and by this present act determine, to make such Lawes and Constitutions soe conformable, &c., or rather to make those Lawes ours, and better known among us; that is to say, such of them, and so farr, as the nature and constitution of our place will admit.

TOUCHING THE COMMON LAW.

It being the common right among common men, and is profitable eyther to direct or correct all, without exception; and it being true, which that Great Doctor of the Gentiles once said, that the Law is made or brought to light, not for a righteous man, who is a Law vnto himselfe, but for the Lawless and disobedient in the Generall, but more particularly for murderers of Fathers and Mothers; for Manslayers, for whoremongers, and those that defile themselves with mankind; for Menstealers, for Lyars and perjured persons, vnto which, vpon the point, may be reduced the common Law of the Realme of England, the end of which is, as is propounded, to preserve every man safe in his own person, name and estate; Wee doe agree to make, or rather to bring such Lawes to light for the direction or correction of such lawless persons, and for their memories sake to reduce them to these five generall Lawes or Heads; viz.:

1. Under that head of murdering Fathers and Mothers, being ye highest and most unnatural, are comprehended those Lawes that concerne High Treason, Pettie Treason, Rebellion, Misbehaviour, and their accessaries.

2. Under the Law for Manslayers, are comprehended those Lawes that concerne Self-murder, Murder, Homicide, Misadventure, casual death, cutting out the Tongue or Eyes, Witchcraft, Burglarie, Robberie, Burning of Houses, Forcible entryes, Rescues and Escape, Riotts, Routs and Unlawfull Assemblies, Batteries, Assaults and Threats and their accessaries.

3. Under the Law for Whoremongers, and those that defile themselves with mankind, being the chief of that nature, are comprehended those Lawes that concerne Sodomie, Buggerie, Rape, Adulterie, Fornication, and their Accessaries.

4. Under the Law for Menstealers, being the chief of that nature, are comprehended those Lawes that concern Theft of men, Larcenie, Trespasses by Men or beasts, Fraudulent dealing by deceitfull bargaine, Covenants, Conveyances by Barratrie, Conspiracie, Champertie and Maintenance, by forging or rasing records, Writs, Deeds, Leases, Bills, &c., and by using fallse weights and measures and their accessaries.

5. Under the Law for Lyars and perjured persons, being the chiefe of that

nature, are comprehended such as concerne perjurie itselfe, breach of covenant, Slander, False witnesse-bearing, and their accessories.

And as necessary concomitants hereof, to prevent Murder, Theft and Perjury, We do joyntlie agree in this present Assemblie, to make or produce such Laws as concerne provision for the poore, soe that the impotent shall be mainteyned and the able employed. And to prevent Poverties, it is agreed, that such Lawes be made and produced as concernes ye ordering of Ale-houses, and Taverns, Drunkenness and unlawfull gaming therein; and in-stead of such to propagate Archerie, which is both man-like and profitable; and to prevent whoredom and those evils before mentioned, it is agreed by this present Assemble to constitute and establish some ordinance touching Marriage, Probate of Wills, and Intestates . . .

Rebellion.

It is agreed and enacted by this present Assemblie, that no inferiour shall rise up or rebell against his superiour, especially such to whom he more di-rectlie owes faith, dutie, and ready obedience; it being altogether unsuit-able to civill order, which by the authoritie of our Charter we purpose to propagate; wherefore, we doe declare that we counte it a kind of Rebellion for a servant to threat, assault, or strike his master; and the penaltie for a threat or assault shall be, to be bound to his good behaviour; for striking especially if it be malitiouslie, to be sent to the House of Correction, there to remaine for six months, or to satisfie his master. It is allso Rebellion for a child to threat, assault, or strike his Parents, and his Penaltie shall be, to be sent to the House of Correction, there to remaine a twelve-month, or to humble himself to his parents' satisfaction. It is allso Rebellion to threat, assault or strike a Judge of Record; and the penaltie to be bound to his good behaviour, and further fined by his Peers. It is also a kind of Rebellion to withstand an arrest, and the execution of Judgment; the penaltie to be bound to his good behaviour, and to be judged by his Peers.

Misbehaviour.

It is agreed by this present Assemblie, and by this act declared, that for any man to sue words of contempt against a chief officer, especially in the exe-cution of his office, is against good manners, and misbehaviour; and his penaltie shall be, to be bound to appear at the next Court, where such matters are to be Tryed: where, being lawfully convict by his Peers, he shall be bound to his good behaviour, so to remaine for three months space, or till the next Court following...

Touching Whoremongers.

First of Sodomie, which is forbidden by this present Assemblie threwout the whole Colonie, and by Sundry Statutes of England. 25 Hen. viii. 6; 5 Eliz. xvii. It is a vile affection, whereby men given up thereto, leave the natural use of woman, and burne in their lusts, one toward another; and so men with men worke that which is vnseemly, as that Doctor of the Gentiles in his letter to the Romans once spake, i. 27; The Penaltie concluded by that State under whose authoritie we are, is Felonie of death, without remedye. See 5 Eliz. 17.

Buggerie.

Buggerie is forbidden by this present Assembly threwout the whole Colonie, and also strengthened by the same Statute of England. It is a most filthy lying with a beast as with a woman, and is abomination and confusion; the just reward whereof prepared to our hands, is Felonie of death, without remedie. See 5 Eliz. 17.

Rape.

Rape is forbidden by this present Assembly threwout the whole Colonie; and we do hereby declare, that it is when a man through his vile and unbridled affection, lyeth with, forceth a woman against her will; like hereunto is the knowing of a maid carnally who is vnder ye age of Tenn yeares, though it be with her consent. The penaltie we do declare to be Felonie of death. See, for confirmation, 13 Edw. i. 34; and if the Woman consent after, she loseth her dowre of Lands. See 6 Rich. ii. 6. And so doth a married wife that elopeth with her adventurer. 13 Edw. i. 34.

Adulterie and Fornication.

Is forbidden by this present Assembliy threwout the Colonie, with this memento, that the Most High will judge them. 13 Hen. iv. Adultery is declared to be a vile affection, whereby men do turn aside from ye naturall use of their own wives, and do burn in their lusts towards strange flesh; and we do agree, that what penaltie the Wisdome of the State of England have or shall appoint touching these transgressions, the accessarie and effects shall stand in force threwout the whole Colonie.

Touching Menstealers.

It is agreed, and by this present Assembly enacted, that the taking away, deflouring or contracting in marriage a maid under sixteen yeares of age, against the will of, or vnknown to the Father or Mother of the Maid, is a kind of stealing of her; and that the penaltie shall be eyther five years' imprisonment or satisfaction of her parents. 4 Will. and Mary, 8 . . .

Touching Liars and Perjured Persons.

Forasmuch as the consciences of sundry men, truly conscienable, may scruple the giving or taking of an oath, and it would be noways suitable to the nature and constitution of our place (who professeth ourselves to be men of different consciences, and no one wiling to force another) to Debar such as cannot do so, eyther from bearing office amongst vs, or from giving in testimony in a case depending.

Be it enacted by the authority of this present Assembly, that a solemn profession or Testimony in a Court of Record, or before a Judge of Record, shall be accounted, threwout the whole Colonie of as full force as an oath; and because many, in giving engagement or testimony, are usually more over awed with the Penaltie which is known, than with the most High, who is little known in the Kingdoms of men.

It is, therefore, further agreed and ordered, that he that falsifieth such a solemn profession or testimony, shall be accounted among vs as a perjured person, and his penaltie shall be that, looke what detriment is or might be brought vpon others by falsifying his engagement or testimony, the same shall fall upon himself. He shall also forfeit five pounds, and be disenabled eyther to beare office, or to give in Testimony in any Court of Record, vntill the Colonie release him; and this forfeiture and determinet, (the partie being lawfully convicted,) shall be, one halfe to the King's Custome, and the other shall go to the partie grieved that sues for it, by action of debt or bill: but in case the partie be not worth so much, then shall he be imprisoned in the House of Correction till it be wrought out, or else sett in the

Pillory in some open place, and have his Eares nayled thereto; and then may the partie grieved receive his dammages; and the procurer shall have the like penaltie. See 5 Eliz. 9.

Breach of Covenant.

Breach of Covenant is by the present Assembly, forbidden threwout the whole Colonie.

It is enacted, and agreed, that they that perform not their Covenants made eyther by word or writing, (excepting those before excepted,) shall be liable to satisfie what the other can prove he is damnified by reason of the non-performance thereof, which he may recover upon an action of the case.

And be it further enacted, that no person retayning a servant, shall putt their servant away, nor no person retayned shall depart from their master, mistress or dame, untill the end of the term covenanted for, vss it be for some reasonable and sufficient cause, witnessed before and allowed by the Head Officer or Officers of the Towne, and three or foure able and discreet men of the Comon Councill or Towne appointed thereto, vnder their hands in writing, for the discharge eyther of Master or Servant.

And be it enacted further, that that Master, Mistress or Dame, that putts away their servant without sufficient cause, and so allowed with such a discharge, shall forfeit the sum of forty shillings; and if any servant departe from his or her Master, Mistress or Dame's service before the end of the Terme covenanted for, vnless it be for some sufficient cause allowed of as before, or not serve according to the Tenure of the promise or covenant, vpon complaint vnto the Head Officers of the Towne and their associates, the matter being fully proved, he shall be committed to Ward without Baile or Mainprize, vntill by sufficient sureties he be bound to his Master, Mistress or Dame, to perform the engagement.

Be it enacted, by the authoritie above said, that he that shall retaine a Servant now lawfully dismissed and sett at liberty from his Master, shall forfeit for every such offence five pounds, which the Master may recover by an action of Debt. See 5 Eliz. 4...

Slaunder.

Forasmuch as a good name is better than precious ointment, and Slaunderers are worser than dead flies to corrupt and alter the savour thereof, it is agreed, by this present Assembly, to prohibitt the raysing or spreading of false reports, Slaunderers and Libells throwout the whole Colonie; and we further declare that the partie offended or grieved by such False reports, Slaunders, and Libells as hereafter followeth, may bring his action of slaunder against the reporter and speaker thereof, in case vpon demand he reaveale not the author, but if revealed, then against the Author, and shall recover sufficient damages. The cases actionable are these; for a man to say eyther by word or writing, and yet not able to prove it, that another is a Traytor, a Fellon, a Thiefe, a Cutt-purse, or hath stole something; a perjured person, or hath forsworn himselfe in any man's case; a Bankrupt, a Cheater, or one that lives by cheating; to call and be not able to prove it, an unmarried woman a whore; a young man unmarried, a whoremaster; to say a young man keepeth a House of Bawdery; or that a Tradesman maketh nothing but bad wares; or that a Merchant or shop-keeper hath nothing but rotten, bad and vnsound wares in his house or shopp, or to speak any thing in the dispragement of a Man's goods that he putts to sale whereby he may be damnified.

Poore.

It is agreed and ordered, by this present Assembly, that each Towne shall provide carefully for the reliefe of the poore, to maintaiyne the impotent, and to employ the able, and shall appoint an overseer for the same purpose. See 43 Eliz. 2.

Scoulds.

It is ordered, Common Scoulds shall be punished with the Ducking Stoole.

Ale Houses.

It is ordered, by the authority of this present Assembly, that no Taverne, Alehouse or Victualling House, shall be kept threwout the whole Colonie without Licence or Allowance; and whosoever shall keep Taverne or Alehouse, or Victualling house without licence, shall forfeit twenty shillings, which shall be levied to the vse of the poore, and shall by the head officer of the Towne be forthwith discharged. See 3 Car. 3.

Licenses.

Be it also enacted by the authority of this present Assembly, that each Towne shall have power to allow Tavernes, Alehouses, and Victualling houses within its own precincts; and the Head officer of the Towne shall binde by Recognizance every such Taverne, Alehouse keeper and Victualler so allowed, with two such sufficient sureties to keep good order in his house, and not to vse such games as are judged by the Lawes of England to be vnlawfull in such Common houses, as Carding, Dicing, Slide, Groat, &c., and not to suffer any Townsmen to remeine tipling therein for one hours space, vnder the penaltie of ten shillings for every such default, vpon the view of the head officers, or vpon the information of sufficient witnesses vpon their solemn testimony, or by his owne confession; And every Townsman so taken, shall forfeit for every time, three shillings and four pence; which forfeitures shall be taken by distreint and given to the overseer for the use of the Poore.

Drunkenness.

Drunkenness is forbidden throwout this whole Colonie; and it is further agreed, that the head officer of each Towne, or any other Magistrate shall have powre upon his owne view, confession of the partie or proof vpon one witness his Testimony, to convict a person of drunkenness, who shall be by him enjoyned to pay five shillings, for that fact into the hands of the overseer for the vse of the poore, within one week after the same conviction; and in case the partie refuse so to do or be not able; then shall he be sett in the Stocks, and there remaine for the space of six houres; and for the second offence, being convicted as aforesaid, he shall forfeit ten shillings, to be paid as before; and shall be bound by the head officer or magistrate before whom he is convicted, to his good behaviour, with two sufficient sureties in the summe of tenpounds. 21 Jac. 7 . . .

Marriage.

It is agreed, and ordered by this present Assemblie, for the preventing of many evills and mischiefs that may follow thereon, that no contract or agreement between a Man and a Woman to owne each other as Man and Wife, shall be owned from henceforth threwout the Whole Colonie as a lawfull marriage, nor their Children or Issue so coming together to be legitimate or lawfullie begotten, but such as are, in the first place, with the parents, then orderly published in two severall meetings of the Townsmen, and lastly confirmed before the head officer of the Towne, and entered into the Towne clerk's Booke. And that man that goes contrarie to this present Ordinance established, shall forfeit five pounds to the parents of the Maid, and be bound to his good behavior; and all the accessories shall forfeit five pounds a man, halfe whereof shall go to the grieved parents and the other halfe of the Towne...

Touching the Public Administration of Justice
According to the Lawes Agreed Upon and
Established Throwout the Whole Colonie.

Be it enacted by this present Assemblie, that for matters of greater weight and moment, there shall be erected a Generall Court of Tryalls for the whole Colonie, and Generall Officers for the Administration of Justice therein.

The Court shall be held twice in the yeare, in case there be matters that are then and there to be Tryed, Sci: upon the next day after the dissolving of the Court of Election held in May, and the other upon the last Tewsday of the eighth moneth, commonly called October, and these Courts to be held at _____

It is further agreed, that to these Colonie Courts of Tryall, shall appertaine the Tryall of such Crimes as may hazard Life, Limbe, Disfranchisement or Bannishment; and such Trespasses, Debts, and differences (as by the Common Councill eyther of Towne or Townes shall be judged too weightie for a more private determining). Also, such matters of difference as fall out betweene Towne and Towne, or between parties dwelling in two Townes more remote, or in the case of an arrest of a man belonging to a neighbour Colonie, or, in cases of great importance; also, attaints of Inquests, and Tryalls of perjuries, and finally all such matters as are not referred, by any charter or order, vnto any Towne apart, or to the Island, or two Townes joyntlie.

Be it enacted further by the authority of this present Assemblie, that the Generall Officer for the whole Colonie shall be these, Sci: One President, foure Assistants, in every Towne one, one General Recorder, one Publick Treasurer, and a General Sargent; which Officers shall be chosen every yeare in the General Assembly, and towards the latter end of that Session. They shall also be chosen after this matter: for President, Recorder, Treasurer and Serjant each Towne shall present one; and he which the major part of the General Assembly pitcheth upon by paper, shall stand and be confirmed in his Office for that yeare; and for Assistant, each Towne shall present two, and he which the vote by paper pitcheth upon, shall be the Assistant in that Towne.

Be it further enacted, that the President and Assistants shall have such a Commission by which they shall be conservators of the peace in the same Towne where they live and throwout the whole Colony. By this Commission, they shall keep the peace, and in case it be broke by threats, assaults, or affrayes, eyther before any of them or vpon lawfull complaint, he or they shall bind the parties by recognizance with two sufficient sureties vnto the peace, and to prepare at that Court where such matters are to be tryed, and soe to remaine, vntill by proclamation in open Court he shall be acquitted . . .

PRESIDENT'S COMMISSION.

By a speciall commission, the President shall sitt as Chief Judge in the Colonie Courts of Tryall, to see that order and course of Law appointed thereto be dulie observed, and the verdict being given in, he is to pronounce the sentence.

In case it be a matter of Felonie, to deliver vp to the Generall Sargent to the execution, or see it done and performed.

In case it be a matter of Trespass, debt or any other difference betweene Man and Man; he is, together with the Assistants, to tax the costs and to send forth a Writ of Execution unto the Generall Sargant at least tenn dayes before, to give the whole Colonie notice, to the end they may prepare for the Generall Assemblie.

ASSISTANTS.

By a speciall commission, all the assistants, if not necessarily deteyned, shall sit with the President in ye Generall Courts of Tryall, and shall supply the roome of a Coroner in each Towne where they dwell.

TOUCHING THE GENERALL RECORDER.

Be it enacted by this present Assemblie, that the Generall Recorder's Office shall be in the generall, to keep a Coppie of all the Records or Acts of the Generall Assemblie, Generall and particular Courts of Judicature, Rolles of the Freemen of the Colonie, Records, Evidences, Sales and Bargaines of Land, Wills and Testaments of the Testators, and orders of the Townsmen touching the Intestate, Records of the Limitts and Bounds of Townes, their Highways, Driftwayes, Commons and Fencings, Priviledges and Liberties. And forasmuch as matters of greatest concernement ought to be kept and preserved with the greatest vigilance: Be it enacted, that the Generall purchases, (which are all we can shew for our right to our Lands, and the Charter which is that which gives vs who are Subjects right to exercise authority one over another,) be kept in a strong chest, having foure severall Locks annexed thereto, and that each Towne keep a key thereof, that soe, as there is a common right and interest therein, there may be no access vnto them in a divided way, (lest also, they be divided) but with a common consent. And let it be further enacted, that this chest be placed in the safest place of the Colonies; and the Generall Recorder, also, shall have the key to the Roome in which it is placed.

Be it also enacted, that he that is Generall Recorder, shall supply the roome of the Clerke of the peace or assizes, in the Generall Court of Tryall, as it is a Court of Assize or Goale delivery. And as Clark of assize, his office shall be to receive examination, information, recognizances and bailments, presented by the Officer who committed the Felon to prison. He shall also receive the bill of indictments presented by him who was bound to prosecute the prisoner; he shall read the indictments and enroll the acts of the Court itself, the indictment, the process, the answer, the traverse itself, the verdict, the judgment thereupon, and the execution. And as this Court is a Court of Common Please, soe he shall supply the roome of the master of the office, and in that regard his office shall be, vpon the request of the plaintiff or his Attorney, (in matters that clearly appertaine vnto that Court,) to direct a Writ to the General Sargant to arrest the defendant, in such an action, of such a man, and to take baile for his appearance by such a day as the writ makes mention to be returnable; and in case the General Sargant returne ye defendants Bond by the day appointed, then shall he enter into his appearance, and in case they proceed, his office shall be, to file such declarations and answers. But in case after a declaration is filed in expectation of an answer, or to make his defence, and he doth not, then the plaintiff taketh him by fault, which is called confessing the action; and then the Recorders office shall be, to enter and record a nihil dicit (id est,) he saith nothing thereon, and so shall be send out a writ of enquiry of dammages vnto the Towne where the defendant lives. And the head officer of the Towne, at the next Towne Court, shall enquire of damages, and by a writ of destringes to the Sargant, shall cause the defendant for that purpose to come to the Court, and in case he appeare not, he shall forfeit the distraint, and the head officer of the Towne may distraine again and again. The matter being issued in the Towne, it shall be returned into the office, and the Recorder shall then enter the postia returne, and give forth to the General Sargent a writ of Execution.

TOUCHING THE PUBLICK TREASURER.

Be it enacted, that the Publick Treasurer shall only receive such finds, forfeitures, amercements and taxes, as fall vpon such as are not within the liberties of the three Townes specified in the Charter; and Warwick, that is invested with the like priviledges and powre; and that the Townes mentioned shall receive and keep safe in their custody all finds, forfeitures and amercements that shall be levied upon the Inhabitants thereof vntill they be called for by the authority from England; but if vpon our humble petition, they be granted to the Colony, then shall they enjoy them as a helpe in their Government as their custom forever. Moreover, looke what comes into the Publick Treasury by that way, he shall give account of in the Generall Assembly.

TOUCHING THE GENERALL SARGANT.

Be it enacted by this present Assemblie, that he that is chosen Generall Sargant shall be an able man of Estate, for so ought a Sheriff to be, whose place he supplies; whose office shall be to attend all Colonye Courts of Tryall, and to serve eyther by himselfe or the Serjants of each Towne, all Writts originall or judiciall; who having arrested a man for that which he is bailable, he shall take baile by an obligation to himselfe, with sufficient sureties; the condition of which shall be, to make appearance in the place, and at the time, the bill, writt, or warrant specifies. He shall also gather vp all fines, forfeitures and amercements, that are made at the Colonie Courts of Tryall, and shall returne them faithfully unto the Treasurie to which they appertaine. When he is chosen, he shall be solemnly engaged to exact no more than his wages, and to take no more than is forfeited; for not serving writts and warrants, he shall lose to the party grieved, treble damages, forfeit Forty Pounds; twentie whereof is the King's Custome, and twentie shall be to the party that sueth. And he that summons or doth arrest without warrant, shall be imprisoned till he pay to the party grieved ten pounds, his costs and damages, and twentie pounds to the King. See the 43 Eliz. 6. He shall also have the charge of the prison for the Colony, and the prisoners therein.

But forasmuch as Justice cannot be had in the general Court of Judicature, notwithstanding these Officers, without Pleaders and Tryars, be it enacted, that there shall be both, and rules given for their orderly proceedings.

TOUCHING THE INQUEST FOR TRYARS.

To save needless expenses and travailes, be it enacted, by the authority of this present Assemblie, that all Traitors, Felons, and such as are suspected thereof shall be indicted by twelve or sixteen honest and lawful men of, and also in the Towne where the person was taken, or of, and in the Towne where his Tryall shall be, and at the Court of Tryall. And that three of the most sufficient and least suspicious persons in each Towne bee chosen by the Townsmen tenn days before, and sent to that Court to attend the Tryall of such matters as shall be presented, and that these be returned and arrayed by the General Sargent, so that the parties may have knowledge of them foure dayes before the Sessions of the Justices upon paine of ten pounds; and that they be chosen by neyther old men above seventy yeares, nor mean men, nor such as have a charter of exemption, nor an indictor, nor interested in the deliverance of an indictee. See 42 Edw. iii. 11; 13 Edw. i. 37; 25 Edw. iii. 3; 3 Hen. v. 3; 23 Hen. vi. 9.

And be it further enacted, that no man shall pass vpon the Life of a Man in this Colonie, nor in plea real, no, nor personal in any issue joyned, that amounts in the dammage to the value of forty marks, nor touching forcible entry, nor touching Riotts, who is not clear worth forty pounds, nor in smaller matters in the Towne that is not clearly worth twenty pounds.

And be it further enacted, that men have their peremptory and other challenges, to the full, as they have them in England, where for petty Treason, Murder and Felony, they may challenge to the number of twentie. See 32 Hen. viii. 3.

And be it enacted, that the inquest upon the Tryall of persons indicted of Felonie, shall eyther allow of, or reject the witnesses according to their consciences, of all or the major part of them. 4 Jac. 3.

And be it further enacted, that the inquest being thus chosen by the Townes, and summoned by the Sargant, in case any of them appeare not, their roome shall be supplied by such among those that stand about, or that live in the same Towne (and they refusing, the same fine,) where the Colonie Court of Tryall is held, and every man soe chosen and summoned, if he appeares not, shall lose and forfeit five shillings and ten pence; or what he might have gott if he had attended the service which the Court shall determine, which, by a distringas from the Court, the Serjant shall require, and levie and deliver into the Treasury to which it belongs.

And be it further enacted by the authority of this present Assemblie, that if any false verdict be given in any action, suit, or demand, either in this or in any other Court of the Colonie, in any thing personall, as Trespass, Debt, Difference, &c.; the party grieved shall have a writ of attaint out of this Court of the Colonie, putting in sufficient security against each partie giving in such an untrue verdict, whereby yee parties shall be summoned by great distresses; and in case the thing in demand and the verdict surmounts forty pounds, to the three able men of each Towne shall be added twelve of the same Towne, where the Colonie Court of Tryall shall be, being worth three score pounds a piece, if such and so many are to be had, and in case these find they gaven an vntrue verdict, every one of the former inquest shall forfeit twenty pounds, ten whereof is the King's custome, and ten pounds shall go to the partie grieved, that sues for it; he shall be also not of credence, neither shall his solemn testimony be taken in any Court, vntill the Colonie release him. But if, eyther the demand or verdict be vnder forty pounds, then shall the inquest be worth fifty pounds a man; and every one of the petty inquest being found guilty, shall forfeit five pounds, the like punishment as is before specified. See 23 Hen. viii. 3; 37 Hen. viii. 5. And in case he that sues for the writ of attaint makes it not good, every party attainted may have his action against him, and recover sufficient dammages.

TOUCHING PLEADERS.

Be it enacted by the authority of this present Assembly, that any man may plead his own case in any Court, or before any Judge of Record Throwout the whole Colonie, or may make his Attorney to plead for him, or may vse the Attorney that belongs to the Court which may be two in a Towne, to wit; discreet, honest and able men for understanding, chosen by the Townsmen of the same Towne, and solemnly engaged by the head officer thereof, not to vse any manner of deceit to beguile eyther Court or partie. And these being thus chosen and confirmed, shall be authorized, being entertayned, to plead to any Court in the Colonie; but in case such pleader or Attorney shall vse any manner of deceit as is aforesaid, and be thereof attainted, or that shall be notoriously in any default of record, he shall forfeit his place, and never more be admitted to plead in any Court of the Colonie. See 3 Edw. 1, 28; 4 Hen. iv. 18.

Be it also further enacted, that in matters of oversie betweene partie and partie, or Towne and Towne, that belongs to the hearing and determination of the Colony Court of Tryall, the partie complaining, or his attorney, shall goe to the General Record, and in his office shall enter his action; then shall he request a writ to arrest the defendant as is abovesaid, returnable at least twenty dayes before the Court; the bond of the defendant being returned into the Recorder's Office, the plaintiff or his Attorney, shall, within foure dayes after, file his declaration in the Recorder's Office (or he shall be non-suited) where the defendant or his Attorney may see it and take forth a coppie thereof; then shall the defendant or his Attorney, file the answer eight dayes before the Court. And so shall they join issue, that Court, and proceed to Tryall, where the witnesses to prove or disprove the issue being produced, the plaintiff and defendant may plead their own cause, or have their Attorneys plead for them before ye Bench, and the inquest; and the verdict and judgment being given, the Recorder shall enter it. But in case the defendant puts in his answer, and at the Court makes his demurr, then shall the Court judge of the sufficiency thereof, and so shall accept the demurr, or proceed; but in case he neyther puts in his answer, nor demurr, or gives in his answer, but puts not in his demurr, and yet appeares not, then shall be entered, he saith nothing; and so shall it be taken for granted he confesseth the action, and then shall go forth a writ from the Court vnto the Towne in which he lives, to enquire of dammages, which being returned to the Recorder, a process or writ shall go forth for Execution.

And now forasmuch as we have prescribed Rules and orders, whereby are declared both the authoritie, office and duty of every person that shall be employed about this Colonie Court of Tryall, and have likewise declared, that the President's and foure assistants' office (among other things that belong to their care) is to see that order and course of Law appointed to this Court be dewly observed.

It is agreed, and by the authority of this present Assemblie enacted, that as the former Lawes are committed to their custodie to see them observed or executed, soe are these constitutions, so farr, as they have a respect vnto an orderly finding out of Justice and the administration thereof, committed to their charge, to see them observed.

And furthermore be it enacted, as that which adds to the comely and commendable order of this Court of Judicature, that at eight of the clock in the morning of those dayes vpon which the Court is appointed at the farthest, the President, the Towne Assistants, and the Head Officers of the same Towne where the Court shall be kept, (for their Councill and helpe,) shall sit in the publicke Sessions house, and also the Generall Recorder, where shall attend those that seeke for justice, their pleaders, witnesses, Tryars and the Generall Sarjant with his prisoners ready either to rid his hands of them, or else to doe execution vpon them or others as Justice shall require.

In the first place, the Recorder shall present, and if there be time read over the bills of indictment; and if, in case they have been examined or presented by an inquest before, then shall he pass them over; if not, then shall the President sett apart the honest and lawfull men prepared for that purpose, by a solemn engagement, faithfully to enquire touching the bills, and soe shall send them forth with the same.

Then, in case there be any controversies or difficulties between partie and partie that are lawfully and orderly presented to that Court for Tryall, the Recorder shall read them over in the open Courte, and that which was first joyned for issue, shall come first to the hearing. And because the twelve men are to have the hearing and determining of all controversies and differences depending between partie and partie, they shall be first called forth by the President and placed in order before those that are to be judged, from whom they shall receive a solemn charge vpon the perill and penaltie the law hath provided, to do justice between the parties contending, according to evidence. This done, then shall the parties, (having first had their lawfull challenges,) or their Attornies plead their cases before them, produced their witnesses for what they affirme, which shall be taken upon the like perill. When they have sufficiently discussed the difference, then shall the President or any other of the Assistants mind the inquest of the most material passages and arguments that are brought by one and other for the case and against it, without alteration or leaning to one party or another, (which is too commonly seene,) and soe shall the President advise the inquest to goe forth and do justice and right between their neighbours, according to the evidence that has been brought, for what has been pleaded. These being gone forth, then may the Court proceed to deale with such as are bound by recognizance eyther to release them or to continue their Bonds, according as there is just cause, and may read over the Indictments that have been enquired into before, and are now presented as true bills, or that were committed to the inquest in the beginning of the Court and are returned true bills, The twelve men returning with a verdict it shall be recorded, and soe shall they be employed, vntill all the differences be ended.

And forasmuch as it belongs to the Justices to taes the costs, lett the vacant times be so employed.

These controversies, differences and demands being thus all issued, then let the Recorder call to ye Sarjant to bring forth ye Prisoners. Before each prisoner lett his inductment be read, and he demanded what he saieth to the indictment, whether Guilty or not. If he answer Guilty, his confession shall be recorded. If he sayeth not Guilty, then lett him be demanded if he will be tryed by God and the Country, sci: his countrymen. If he consents, the President shall call forth the twelve men before him, wish him to look upon them, and ask if he have any thing against them; if not, then he shall charge them vpon the former perill, to deale faithfully and truly in the matter; it being a matter of consequence and moment, and to proceed to determine according to the light of their consciences, vpon the evidence given in, and if any be found Guilty of death, to be reprieved to the next Court. And thus having issued all matters depending, the President with the assistants and councellors shall give forth writs vnto the Generall Sarjant for the severall executions, and so break vp the Court for that time and sitting.

And be it further enacted, by the authoritie of this present Assemblie, that the perill that any officer shall susteyne, for going without, besides, or beyond his Commission, shall be first lawfuly and orderly judged. And that no officer employed in this Colonie shall think it strange or hard dealing to be brought to his faire Tryall, and Judgment for what he hath done amiss.

Be it enacted, that the Cheife Officers of the Colonie, Island, or Townes, shall be tryed and judged in the Generall Assembly by a committe of the most able and impartiall men, chosen out from among them, against whom they may have also their lawfull challenges: and that all other officers abusing their offices, shall be tryed and judged eyther in the Towne by which they were chosen; or, if the Towne please, or if not chosen by the Towne, then shall they be tryed and judged by the Colonie Courts of Tryalls, And in case any man sues for Justice against an officer or other, and he cannot be heard, or is heard and cannot be righted by any Law extant among vs, then shall the partie grieved petition to the Generall or Law making Assemblie, and shall be relieved.

And now forasmuch as the choice of all the officers that are to be employed in this Colonie, like the Colonies about vs, once a year, whereby it may be easily collected, that he that hath an office or charge this yeare, may have none another; and it would be too prejudicial to the peace of the place or quiet Government thereof, for a man out of a discontented selfwill, or other pretence, not to resigne, together with his office, belonging to the Colonie, Island or Towne, to him that is chosen and appointed thereto . . .

Spelling is as it appears in Bartlett, *Vol. 1, 1636 to 1663*, 38–65. The text is quite lengthy and herein is reproduced only in part. Sections excluded deal with more standard or mundane aspects of law, such as fraud, forgery, trespassing, larceny, assault, robbery, and burglary.

40

Charter of Providence

March 14, 1649

*T*his is not a true charter insofar as it does not proceed from the king. Rather it is typical of many early colonial documents because it proceeds from powers of self-government frequently granted in the original charters from England. It is one of the earliest examples of a town charter being granted from what we would today consider the state level—equivalent to the state of Texas granting Houston a city charter. Note the inhabitants are taking it upon themselves to act on their own and are careful to cite their authority to do so under the charter granted by the king, implying that the king is sanctioning this document. The colonists see a federal relationship between the king and colony and therefore have no difficulty imagining a federal relationship between the colony government and its town governments.

Charter of Providence

*W*hereas, by virtue of a free and absolute charter of civill incorporation, granted to the free inhabitants of the colonie of Providence, by the Right Honorable Robert, Earl of Warwick, Governor in chiefe with the rest of the Honorable Commoners, bearing the date the 7th day of March, Anno 1643, givinge and grantinge full power and authoritie vnto the said inhabitants to governe themselves and such others as shall come among them, as also to make, constitute and ordaine such lawes, orders and constitutions, and to inflict such punishments and penalties as is conformable to the lawes of England, so neare as the nature and constitution of the place will admit, and which may best suite the estate and condition thereof, and whereas the said towns of Providence, Portsmouth, Newport and Warwick are far remote from each other, whereby so often and free intercourse of help, in decidinge of differences and trying of causes and the like, cannot easilie and at all times be had and procured of that kind is requisite; therefore, upon the petition and humble request of the freemen of the Town of Providence, exhibited unto this present session of the General Assembly, wherein they desire freedome and libertie to incorporate themselves into a body politicke, and we, the said Assembly, having duly weighed and seriously considered the premises, and being willing and ready to provide for the ease and libertie of the people, have thought fit, and by the authoritie aforesaid, and by these presents, do give, grant and confirme unto the free Inhabitants of the towne of Providence, a free and absolute charter of civill incorporation and government, to be knowne by the Incorporation of Providence Plantation in the Narrangansett Bay, in New-England, together with full power and authoritie to governe and rule themselves, and such others as shall hereafter inhabit within any part of the said Plantation, by such a form of civill government, as by voluntarie consent of all, or the greater part of them, shall be found most suitable unto their estate and condition; and, to that end, to make and ordaine such civill orders and constitutions, to inflict such punishments upon transgressors, and for execution thereof, and of the common statute lawes of the colonye agreed unto, and the penalties and so many of them as are not annexed already unto the colonye court of trialls, so to place and displace officers of justice, as they or the greater parte of them shall, by one consent, agree unto. Provided, nevertheless, that the said lawes, constitutions and punishments, for the civill government of the said plantation, be conformable to the lawes of England, so far as the nature and constitution of the place will admit, yet, always reserving to the aforesaid General Assemblie power and authoritie so to dispose the generall governmente of that plantation as it stands in reference to the rest of the plantations, as they shall conceive, from time to time, most conducing to the generall good of the said plantations. And we the said Assemblie, do further authorise the aforesaid inhabitants to elect and engage such aforesaide officers upon the first second day of June, annually. And, moreover, we authorize the said inhabitants, for the better transacting of their publicke affaires, to make and use a publicke seal as the knowne seale of Providence Plantation, in the Narrangansett Bay, in New-England.

In testimonie whereof, we the said Generall Assemblie, have hereunto sett oure handes and seales the 14th of March, anno 1648.

John Warner
Clerk of the Assemblie.

Taken from Bartlett, *Vol. 1, 1636 to 1663*, 214–16. The text, with the original spelling, is complete.

41

[General Assembly of Rhode Island
Is Divided into Two Houses]

March 27, 1666

Several colonies independently made this important move to a bicameral legislature—Massachusetts (Massachusetts Bicameral Ordinance [24]) and Connecticut (Division of the Connecticut General Assembly [54]) are others noted in this collection. To a certain extent these moves to bicameralism were attempts to emulate the structure and processes of the British Parliament, and to a certain extent they were a response to colonial political inclinations. The documents provide only vague reasons for bicameralism, but it is certain that the British model was not so much slavishly imitated as it was studied for beneficial design characteristics. In British North America, with no true aristocracy to serve as the basis for an upper house, bicameralism was grounded in the desire for a careful, deliberative process as well as in a desire to distinguish representation of specific geographical units, such as towns and counties, from representation of the interests of the entire colony. In short, bicameralism provided a way for the colonists to respond simultaneously to two of their fundamental values—localism and the common good.

The Assembly having taken notice of the motion from the townes of Portsmouth and of Warwick, desiring the Assembly would order that the deputyes may sitt apart from the magistrates as a House by themselves; and consequently the magistrates to sitt as a House by themselves; and that of these two houses may consist the law makeing power, called in the Charter the Gennerall Assembly, of this body, collony, or corporation of Rhode Island and Providence Plantations. At this present Assembly haveing well weighed such conveniances, and such consideratione as may perswade to grant the same, and yett to provide against such inconveniancyes as may for want of mature and sound advice proceed therefrom, doe in this presant Assembly enacte and declare that it is freely agreed, that the request of the townes aforesaid, be granted and ordered, that the magistrates sitt by themselves, and the deputyes by themselves, and that each house soe sitting have equal power and priviledge in the proposeing, composing and propagating any act, order and law in Gennerall Assembly; and that neither house in Gennerall Assembly shall have power without the concurrance of the majour part of the other House, to make any law or order to be accounted as an acte of the Gennerall Assembly. This in gennerall, is fully ordered, with a recommendation of the more pertickelar and methodicall settleing the ways and circumstances of ordering and regulating the afaires in each house and addresses, &c., from the one house to the other, vnto the consideration of the Gennerall Assembly, that is to sitt the first Wednesday in the month of May, now next ensuinge: where it is hopefully expected the matter may be fully debated and sett in a good way vpon more deliberation than this presant time can afford. The Court haveing alredye sate long on other weighty matters that lay before them.

Ordered, that the Recorder shall have for his atendance on the Gennerall Assembly in October, and for the Assembly now in March, 1666, for coppies of both, twenty five shillings from each towne.

Ordered, that coppies shall spedily goe forth vnder the seale to each towne.

Taken without alteration from Bartlett, *Vol. II, 1664 to 1677*, 110.

42

Plantation Covenant at Quinnipiack

April 1638

*A*lthough the framers used the title shown above, it is more frequently referred to in history books as the "New Haven Plantation Covenant." This document was adopted shortly after the group arrived from Boston. It was to function as a temporary, general agreement until the people could become familiar enough with each other's religious views, sentiments, and moral conduct to adopt a written frame of government and code of laws, which they did fourteen months later (see the New Haven Fundamentals, 1643 [50]). The earlier document, reproduced below, was not actually a covenant because there was no oath. The settlers, not knowing each other well, did not want to force an oath on each other until they were certain they all had agreed on what was to be covenanted. Thus the authors termed the document a "plantation covenant" to indicate its lesser status.

We the assembly of free planters do solemnly covenant] thatt as [in] matters thatt Concerne the gathering and ordering of a Chur. so Likewise in all publique offices wch concerne Cuill orders as Choyce of magistrates and officers makeing and repealing of Lawes devideing allotmts of Inheritance and all things of Like nature we would all of vs be ordered by those Rules wch the scripture holds forth to vs.

The text is taken from Isabel Macbeath Calder, *The New Haven Colony* (New Haven: Yale University Press, 1934), 51. Calder in turn cites the *New Haven Colonial Records, 1638–1649,* 12. The first part of the first sentence, in brackets, has been added by this editor on the basis of information found in Calder and elsewhere. The spelling and punctuation are Calder's.

43

Fundamental Orders of Connecticut

January 14, 1639

*A*long with the Pilgrim Code of Law *[20] and the Fundamental Articles of New Haven [46], this document is a candidate for being the earliest written constitution in America. It describes itself internally as a "combination" and "confederation," although one could with equal truth call it a compact. It should be noted that this document, as well as the Pilgrim Code of Law, prominently displays oaths for officeholders as an essential part of the agreement, which underscores the importance of the other oaths for establishing government (see, for example, documents 4, 9, 15, 16, 47, and 65). In 1662 the king signed a new charter for the combined colonies of Connecticut and New Haven that essentially ratified the political system defined here. In 1776 the people of Connecticut adopted the charter as their new state constitution after removing references to the king. The 1776 constitution was replaced in 1816, which means that the Fundamental Orders of Connecticut effectively served as a constitution for 177 years. Like many of the colonial founding compacts and constitutions, the Fundamental Orders of Connecticut was not written in as orderly a manner as we would expect in modern documents. The reader must carefully consider the entire document, because institutions described toward the beginning of the document often have important components described later. As was usually the case with colonial constitutions, this document creates a federal political system.*

FORASMUCH as it hath pleased the Allmighty God by the wise disposi-
tion of his diuyne[1] pruidence so to Order and dispose of things that we
the Inhabitants and Residents of Windsor, Harteford and Wethersfield are
now cohabiting and dwelling in and vppon the River of Conectecotte and
the Lands thereunto adioyneing; and Well knowning where a people are
gathered togather the word of God requires that to mayntayne the peace and
vnion of such a people there should be an orderly and decent Gouerment
established according to God, to order and dispose of the affayres of the people at all seasons as occation shall require; doe therefore assotiate and con-
ioyne our selues to be as one Publike State or Commonwelth; and doe, for
our selues and our Successors and such as shall be adioyned to vs att any
tyme hereafter, enter into Combination and Confederation togather, to
mayntayne and prsearue the liberty and purity of the gospell of our Lord
Jesus wch we now prfesse, as also the disciplyne of the Churches, wch according to the truth of the said gospell is now practised amongst vs; As also
in o[u]r Cieuell[2] Affaires to be guided and gouerned according to such Lawes,
Rules, Orders and decrees as shall be made, ordered & decreed, as followeth:—

1. It is Ordered, sentenced and decreed, that there shall be yerely two generall Assemblies or Courts, the [first] on the second thursday in Aprill, the other
the second thursday in September, following; the first shall be called the Courte
of Election, wherein shall be yerely Chosen fro[m] tyme to tyme soe many
Magestrats and other publike Officers as shall be found requisitte: Whereof
one to be chosen Gouernour for the yeare ensueing and vntill another be chosen, and noe other Magestrate to be chosen for more then one yeare; pruided
allwayes there be sixe chosen besids the Gouernour; wch being chosen and
sworne according to an Oath recorded for that purpose shall haue power to administer iustice according to the Lawes here established, and for want thereof
according to the rule of the word of God, wch choise shall be made by all that
are admitted freemen and haue taken the Oath of Fidellity, and doe cohabitte
wthin this Jurisdiction, (Hauing been admitted Inhabitants by the major prt of
the Towne wherein they liue,) or the mayor prte of such as shall be then prsent.

2. It is Ordered, sentensed and decreed, that the Election of the aforesaid
Magestrats shall be on this manner: euery prson prsent and quallified for

---

1. In this document, as in others, the letters *u* and *v* are often interchanged. Divine
is here effectively rendered divyne. The letters *i* and *j* are likewise often interchanged.
2. Civil.

choyse shall bring in (to the prsons deputed to receaue them) one single papr wth the name of him written in yt whome he desires to haue Gouernour, and he that hath the greatest number of papers shall be Gouernor for that yeare. And the rest of the Magestrats or publike Officers to be chosen in this manner: The Secrtary for the tyme being shall first read the names of all that are to be put to choise and then shall seuerally nominate them distinctly, and euery one that would haue the prson nominated to be chosen shall bring in one single paper written vppon, and he that would not haue him chosen shall bring in a blanke: and euery one that hath more written papers than blanks shall be a Magistrat for that yeare; wch papers shall be receaued and told by one or more that shall be then chosen by the court and sworne to be faythfull therein; but in case there should not be sixe chosen as aforesaid, besids the Gouernor, out of those wch are nominated, then he or they wch haue the most written paprs shall be a Magestrate or Magestrats for the ensueing yeare, to make vp the aforesaid number.

3. It is Ordered, sentenced and decreed, that the Secretary shall not nominate any prson, nor shall any prson be chosen newly into the Magestracy wch was not prpownded in some Generall Courte before, to be nominated the next Election; and to that end yt shall be lawfull for ech of the Townes aforesaid by their deputyes to nominate any two who they conceaue fitte to be put to election; and the Courte may ad so many more as they iudge requisitt.

4. It is Ordered, sentenced and decreed that noe prson be chosen Gouernor aboue once in two years, and that the Gouernor be always a member of some approved congregation, and formerly of the Magestracy wthin this Jurisdiction; and all the Magestrats Freemen of this Comonwelth: and that no Magestrate or other publike officer shall execute any prte of his or their Office before they are seuerally sworne, wch shall be done in the face of the Courte if they be prsent, and in case of absence by some deputed for that purpose.

5. It is Ordered, sentenced and decreed, that to the aforesaid Courte of Election the seurall Townes shall send their deputyes, and when the Elections are ended they may prceed in any publike searuice as at other Courts. Also the other Generall Courte in September shall be for makeing of lawes, and any other publike occation, wch conserns the good of the Commonwealth.

6. It is Ordered, sentenced and decreed, that the Gournor shall, ether by himselfe or by the secretary, send out summons to the Constables of eur[3]

3. Every.

Towne for the cauleing of these two standing Courts, on month at lest before their seurall tymes: And also if the Gournor and the gretest prte of the Magestrats see cause vppon any spetiall occation to call a generall Courte, they may giue order to the secretary soe to do wthin fowerteene dayes warneing; and if vrgent necessity so require, vppon a shorter notice, giueing sufficient grownds for yt to the deputyes when they meete, or else be questioned for the same; And if the Gournor and Mayor⁴ prte of Magestrats shall ether neglect or refuse to call the two Generall standing Courts or ether of them, as also at other tymes when to occations of the Commonwelth require, the Freemen thereof, or the Mayor prte of them, shall petition to them soe to doe: if then yt be ether denyed or neglected the said Freemen or the Mayor prte of them shall haue power to giue order to the Constables of the seuerall Townes to doe the same, and so may meete togather, and chuse to themselues a Moderator, and may prceed to do any Acte of power, wch any other Generall Courte may.

7. It is Ordered, sentenced and decreed that after there are warrants giuen out for any of the said Generall Courts, the Constable or Constables of ech Towne shall forthwth give notice distinctly to the inhabitants of the same, in some Publike Assembly or by goeing or sending from howse to howse, that at a place and tyme by him or them lymited and sett, they meet and assemble themselues togather to elect and chuse certen deputyes to be att the Generall Courte then following to agitate the afayres of the comonwelth; wch said Deputyes shall be chosen by all that are admitted Inhabitants in the seurall Townes and haue taken the oath of fidellity; pruided that non be chosen a Deputy for any Generall Courte wch is not a Freeman of this Commonwelth.

The a-foresaid deputyes shall be chosen in manner following: euery prson that is prsent and quallified as before exprssed, shall bring the names of such, written in seurall papers, as they desire to haue chosen for that Imployment, and these 3 or 4, more or lesse, being the number agreed on to be chosen for that tyme, that haue greatest number of papers written for them shall be dputyes for that Courte; whose names shall be endorsed on the backe side of the warrant and returned into the Courte, wth the Constable or Constables hand vnto the same.

8. It is Ordered, sentenced and decreed, that Wyndsor, Hartford and

---

4. Major.

Wethersfield shall haue power, ech Towne, to send fower of their freemen as deputyes to euery Generall Courte; and whatsoeuer other Townes shall be hereafter added to this Jurisdiction, they shall send so many deputyes as the Courte shall judge meete, a resonable prportion to the number of Freemen that are in the said Townes being to be attended therein; wch deputyes shall have the power of the whole Towne to giue their voats and alowance to all such lawes and orders as may be for the publike good, and unto wch the said Townes are to be bownd.

9. It is ordered and decreed, that the deputyes thus chosen shall haue power and liberty to appoynt a tyme and a place of meeting togather before any Generall Courte to aduise and consult of all such things as may concerne the good of the publike, as also to examine their owne Elections, whether according to the order, and if they or the gretest prte of them find any election to be illegall they may seclud such for prsent from their meeting, and returne the same and their resons to the Courte; and if yt proue true, the Courte may fyne the prty or prtyes so intruding and the Towne, if they see cause, and giue out a warrant to goe to a newe election in a legall way, either whole or in prte. Also the said deputyes shall haue power to fyne any that shall be disorderly at their meetings, or for not coming in due tyme or place according to appoyntment; and they may return the said fynes into the Courte if yt be refused to be paid, and the tresurer to take notice of yt, and to estreete or levy the same as he doth other fynes.

10. It is Ordered, sentenced and decreed, that euery Generall Courte, except such as through neglecte of the Gournor and the greatest prte of Magestrats the Freemen themselves doe call, shall consist of the Gouernor, or some one chosen to moderate the Court, and fower other Magestrats at lest, wth the mayor prte of the deputyes of the seuerall Townes legally chosen; and in case the Freemen or mayor prte of them through neglect or refusall of the Gouernor and mayor prte of the magestrats, shall call a Courte, that yt shall consist of the mayor prte of Freemen that are prsent or their deputyes, wth a Moderator chosen by them: *In wch said Generall Courts shall consist the supreme power of the Commonwelth,* and they only shall haue power to make laws or repeale them, to graunt leuyes, to admitt of Freemen, dispose of lands vndisposed of, to seuerall Townes or prsons, and also shall haue power to call ether Courte or Magestrate or any other prson whatsoeuer into question for any misdemeanour, and may for just causes displace or deale otherwise according to the nature of the offence; and also may deale in any

other matter that concerns the good of this commonwelth, excepte election of Magestrats, wch shall be done by the whole boddy of Freemen: In wch Courte the Gouernour or Moderator shall haue power to order the Courte to giue liberty of spech, and silence vnceasonable and disorderly speakeings, to put all things to voate, and in case the vote be equall to haue the casting voice. But non of these Courts shall be adiorned or dissolued wthout the consent of the major prte of the Court.

11. It is ordered, sentenced and decreed, that when any Generall Courte vppon the occations of the Commonwelth haue agreed vppon any sume or somes of mony to be leuyed vppon the seuerall Townes wthin this Jurisdiction, that a Committee be chosen to sett out and appoynt wt shall be the prportion of euery Towne to pay of the said leuy, prvided the Committees be made vp of an equall number out of each Towne.

14th January, 1638, the 11 Orders abouesaid are voted.

The Oath of the Gournor, for the Prsent

I N.W. being now chosen to be Gournor wthin this Jurisdiction, for the yeare ensueing, and vntil a new be chosen, doe sweare by the greate and dreadful name of the everliueing God, to prmote the publicke good and peace of the same, according to the best of my skill; as also will mayntayne all lawfull priuiledges of this Commonwealth: as also that all wholsome lawes that are or shall be made by lawfull authority here established, be duly executed; and will further the execution of Justice according to the rule of Gods word; so helpe me God, in the name of the Lo: Jesus Christ.

The Oath of a Magestrate, for the Prsent

I, N.W. being chosen a Magestrate wthin this Jurisdiction for the yeare ensueing, doe sweare by the great and dreadfull name of the euerliueing God, to prmote the publike good and peace of the same, according to the best of my skill, and that I will mayntayne all the lawfull priuiledges therof according to my vnderstanding, as also assist in the execution of all such wholsome lawes as are made or shall be made by lawfull authority heare established, and will further the execution of Justice for the tyme aforesaid according to the righteous rule of Gods word; so helpe me God, etc.

The text, complete and with the original spelling, is taken from Thorpe, *Federal and State Constitutions*, 519–23.

44

Guilford Covenant

June 1, 1639

*S*igned aboard ship before the colonists reached America, this agreement essentially creates a people who agree to form a future government. The rather vague covenant form used here (there is no true oath) was supplemented in 1643 by a political compact that laid out the government (see The Government of Guilford [49]).

June 1. Individuals who, the next September, purchase Menunkatuck, afterwards Guilford, enter into the following covenant: We whose names are hereunder written, intending by God's gracious permission to plant ourselves in New England, and, if it may be, in the southerly part about Quinnipiack, we do faithfully promise each to each, for ourselves and our families, and those that belong to us, that we will, the Lord assisting us, sit down and join ourselves together in one entire plantation,[1] and to be helpful each to the other in any common work, according to every man's ability, and as need shall require; . . . As for our gathering together in a church way, and the choice of officers and members to be joined together in that way, we do refer ourselves until such time as it shall please God to settle us in our plantation.

[Signed by Henry Whitfield and twenty-four others.]

---

1. In New England a plantation was a farming community composed of many separate farms and not a single agricultural enterprise using slaves, as in the southern colonies.

Text is complete, with spelling as found in Champlin Burrage, *The Church Covenant Idea: Its Origin and Development* (Philadelphia: American Baptist Publication Society, 1904), 94.

45

Structure of Town Governments

October 10, 1639

*M*ost of the so-called colonies were actually collections of towns, each of which had established its own form of self-government. The establishment of a colony-wide government, usually a legislature in which each town was represented, in effect created what we would now recognize as a federal system. The Fundamental Orders of Connecticut [43] should be viewed in this light because it established the "confederation" that is acting in this document. The Structure of Town Governments amplifies and clarifies the nature of the relationship between the towns and colony-wide governments mainly by focusing on respective jurisdictions. Other documents (2, 20, 28, 37, 39, 43, 46, and 50) similarly created federations of towns.

The Townes of Hartford, Windsore and Wethersfield, or any other of the Townes within this jurisdiction, shall each of them haue power to dispose of their owne lands vndisposed of, and all other comodityes arysing out of their owne lymitts bounded out by the Court, the libertyes of the great River excepted, as also to choose their owne officers, and make such orders as may be for the well ordering of their owne Townes, being not repugnant to any law here established, as also to impose penaltyes for the breach of the same, and to estreat and levy the same, and for non-payment to distrayne, and yf there be noe personall estate, to sue to the Court to sell his or their house or land, for making satisfaction. Also each of the aforesayd Townes shall haue power by a generall consent once every yeare to choose out 3, 5, or 7 of their cheefe Inhabitants, whereof one to be chosen moderator, who having taken an oath prouided in that case, shall haue a casting voice in case they be equall, wch sayd prsons shall meett once in every 2 monthes & being mett together, or the major part of them, whereof the moderator to be one, they shall haue power to heare, end and determine all controversies, eyther trespasses or debts not exceeding 40s. provided both partyes live in the same Towne; also any two of them or the moderator may graunt out summons to the party or partyes to come to their meetings to answere the actions; also to administer oath to any witnesses for the clearing of the cause, and to giue judgment and execution against the party offending. But yf eyther party be grieved att the sentence, he shall haue liberty to appeale to a higher Court, prvided it be before judgment and execution be graunted. But yf it fall out there be noe ground for the appeale, the Court to confirme the judgment and giue good costs, and fine or punish the prty appealing.

The Townes aforesayd shall each of them prvide a Ledger Booke, with an Index or alphabett vnto the same: Also shall choose one who shall be a Towne Clerke or Register, who shall before the Generall Court in Aprill next, record every man's house and land already graunted and measured out to him, with the bounds & quantity of the same, and whosoever shall neglect 3 monthes after notice given to bring into the sayd Towne Clerke or Register a note of his house and land, with the bounds and quantity of the same, by the nearest estimacion, shall forfeit 10s. and soe 10s. a month for ever month he shall soe neglect. The like to be done for all land hereafter graunted and measured to any; and all bargaines or morgages of land whatsoever shall be accounted of noe value vntill they be recorded, for wch entry the Register shall receaue 6d. for every parcell, delivering every owner a coppy of the same vnder his hand, whereof 4d. shall be for himselfe and 2d. for the Secretary of the Court. And the sayd Register shall, every Generall Court, in Aprill and September, deliver into the same a transcript fayrely written of all such graunts, bargaines or ingagements recorded by him in the Towne Booke, and the Secretary of the Court shall record it in a booke fayrely written prvided for that purpose, and shall preserue the coppy brought in vnder the hand of the Town Clerke. Also the sayd Towne Clerke shall haue for every serch of a parcell 1d. and for every coppy of a parcell 1d.; and a coppy of the same vnder the hands of the sayd Register or Towne Clerk and two of the men chosen to governe the Towne, shall be a sufficient evidence to all that haue the same.

After the death and decease of any person possessed of any estate, be it more or lesse, and who maketh a will in writing or by word of mouth, those men wch are appointed to order the affayres of the Towne where any such person deceaseth, shall within one month after the same, at furthest, cause a true Inventory to be taken of the sayd estate in writing, as also take a coppy of the sayd will or testament and enter it into a booke or keepe the coppy in safe custody, as also enter the names vppon record of the Children and Legatees of the Testator or deceased prson, and the sayd orderers of the Affayres of the Towne are to see every such will and Inventory to be exhibited into the publique Court, within one quarter of a yeare, where the same is to be registered; and the sayd orderers of the affayres of the Towne shall doe their indeauour in seeing that the estate of the Testator be not wasted nor spoyled, but improved for the best advantage of the Children or Legatees of the Testator, according to the mind of the Testator, for their and euery of their use, by their and every of their allowance and approbacion. But when any prson dyeth intestate, the sayd orderers of the affayres of the Townes shall cause an Inventory to be taken, and then the publique Court may graunt the administracion of the goodes and Chattells to the next of kin, jointly or severally, and divide the estate to the wiefe (yf any be), children or kindred, as in equity they shall see meet; and yf noe kindred be found, the Court to administer for the publique good of the Common, prvided there be an Inventory registered, that yf any of the kindred in future tyme appeare they may haue justice and equity done vnto them; and all charges that the publique Court or the orderers of the affayres of the Townes are att about the trust committed to them, eyther for writing or otherwise, it is to be payd out of the estate.

Within 20 days after the end of this Court, the Secretary shall provide a coppy of all the penall lawes or orders standing in force, and all other that are of generall concernement for the governement of the Commonwealth, and shall giue direction to the Constables of every Towne to publish the same within 4 dayes more, att some publique meeting in their severall Townes, and then shall cause the sayd lawes and orders to be written into a booke in their severall Townes, and kept for the use of the Towne, and soe for future tyme for all lawes or orders that are made as aforesayd, each session of the Generall Courts; and once every yeare the Constables, in their severall Townes, shall read or cause to be read in some publique meeting all such lawes as then stand in force and are not repealed; and the Secretary of the

Court shall haue 12d. for the coppy of the orders of each session of every generall Court, from each of the Townes.

Also, the Secretary of the Court shall have xid.[1] for every action that is entred, to be payed by him that enters the action, and he that is cast in the suit to allow it in costs.

1. Ten pence. The symbol "id.," or "d.," stands for pence.

The complete text is taken from J. H. Trumbull and C. J. Hoadley, eds., *The Public Records of the Colony of Connecticut Prior to the Union with New Haven Colony, 1636–1776*, vol. 1 (Hartford: Brown & Parsons, 1850), 36–39. The spelling is without emendation.

46

Fundamental Articles of New Haven

June 4–14, 1639

*O*riginally organized under the Plantation Covenant at
Quinnipiack [42] written about a year earlier, the settlers
had cause to reconsider the nature of their government. Specifically,
they considered whether full citizenship should be limited to members
of the church. Carefully going over the commitments embodied in
the earlier document, they concluded in the affirmative. This document is notable for the careful deliberation it records as well as for the
careful attention to biblical precedent. Although they had lived together for over a year, there was still considerable concern that those
signing the document not be forced to agree contrary to conscience.
The extraordinary care they took in this regard is revealed in their response to a person who, toward the end of the discussion, expressed
some doubts. Although these religious people were determined to produce a community with a high level of value homogeneity, their view
of freedom of conscience was not merely legalistic but rooted in the
Protestant commitment to individual interpretation of the Bible as
the cornerstone of religious belief.

The 4th day of the 4th moneth called June 1639, all the free planters assembled together in a ge[neral] meetinge to consult about settling
civill Government according to God, and about the nomination of persons
thatt might be founde by consent of all fittest in all respects for the foundation worke of a church w[hich] was intend to be gathered in Quinipieck.
After solemne invocation of the name of God in prayer [for] the presence
and help of his speritt, and grace in those weighty businesses, they were re-
minded of t[he] busines whereabout they mett [viz] for the establishment
of such civill order as might be most p[leas]ing unto God, and for the chuseing the fittest men for the foundation worke of a church to be gather[ed].

For the better inableing them to discerne the minde of God and to agree accordingly concerning the establishment of civill order, Mr. John Davenport propounded divers quaeres[1] to them publiquely praying them to consider seriously in the presence and feare of God the weight of the busines they met about, and nott to be rash or sleight in giveing their votes to things they understoode nott, butt to digest fully and thoroughly whatt should be propounded to them, and without respect to men as they should be satisfied and perswaded in their owne mindes to give their answers in such sort as they would be willing they should stand upon recorde for posterity.

This being earnestly pressed by Mr. Davenport, Mr. Robt. Newman was intreated to write in carracters and to read distinctly and audibly in the hearing of all the people whatt was propounded and accorded on that itt might appeare thatt all consented to matters propounded according to words written by him.

QUAER. 1. Whether the Scripturs doe holde forth a perfect rule for the direction and government of all men in all duet[ies] which they are to performe to God and men as well in the government of famyles and commonwealths as in matters of the chur.

This was assented unto by all, no man dissenting as was expressed by holding up of hands. Afterward itt was read over to them thatt they might see in whatt words their vote was expressed: They againe expressed their consent thereto by holdeing up their hands, no man dissenting.

QUAER. 2. Whereas there was a covenant solemnly made by the whole assembly of free-planters of this plantation the first day of extraordenary humiliation which wee had after wee came together, thatt as in matters thatt concerne the gathering and ordering of a chur. so likewise in all publique offices which concerne civill order, as choyce of magistrates and officers, makeing and repealing of lawes, devideing allottments of inheritance and all things of like nature we would all of us be ordered by those rules which the scripture holds forth to us. This covenant was called a plantation covenant to distinguish itt from [a] chur. covenant which could nott att thatt time be made, a chur. nott being then gathered, butt was deferred till a chur. might be gathered according to God: Itt was demaunded, whether all the free planters doe holde themselves bound by thatt covenant in all busi-

1. Queries, or questions.

nesses of thatt nature which are expressed in the covenant to submitt them-selves to be ordered by the rules held forth in the scripture.

This also was assented unto by all, and no man gainsaid itt, and they did testefie the same by holde[ing] up their hands both when itt was first pro-pounded, and confirmed the same by holdeing up their hands when itt was read unto them in publique...

QUAER. 3. Those who have desired to be received as free planters, and are settled in the plantation with a purp[ose,] resolution and desire thatt they may be admitted into a chur. fellowship according to Christ as soone [as] God shall fitt them thereunto: were desired to express itt by holdeing up of hands: Accordingly a[ll] did express this to be their desire and purpose by holdeing up their hands twice, both att the [pro]posall of itt, and after when these written words were read unto them.

QUAER. 4. All the free planters were called upon to expresse whether they held themselves bound to esta[blish] such civill order as might best con-duce to the secureing of the purity and peace of the ordina[nces] to them-selves and their posterity according to God. In answer hereunto they expressed by hold[ing] up their hands twice as before, thatt they held them selves bound to establish such [civil order] as might best conduce to the ends aforesaid.

Then Mr. Davenport declared unto them by the scripture whatt kinde of persons might best be trusted with matters of government, and by sundry arguments from scripture proved that such men as were discrib[ed] in Exod. 18.2. Deut. 1.13, with Deut 17.15, and 1. Cor. 6: 1 to 7, ought to be intrusted by them, seeing [they] were free to cast themselves into thatt mould and forme of common wealth which appeareth best for them in referrence to the secureing of the pure and peaceable injoyment of all Christ his ordinances [in] the church according to God, whereunto they have bound themselves as hath beene acknowledged. Having thus said he satt downe, praying the company freely to consider whether they would have [it] voted att this time or nott: After some space of silence Mr. Theophilus Eaton answered itt mi[ght] be voted, and some other allso spake to the same purpose, none att all opposeing itt. Then itt was propounded to vote.

QUAER. 5. Whether Free Burgesses shalbe chosen out of chur. members they thatt are in the foundat[ion] worke of the church being actually free burgesses, and to chuse to themselves out of the li[ke] estate of church fellowship and the power of chuseing magistrates and officers from among themselves and the power off makeing and repealing lawes according to the worde, and the devideing of inheritances and decideing of differences thatt may arise, and all the businesses of like nature are to be transacted by those free burgesses.

This was putt to vote and agreed unto by the lifting up of hands twice as in the former itt was done. Then one man stood up after the vote was past, and expressing his dissenting from the rest in part yett grantinge 1. That magistrates should be men fearing God. 2. Thatt the church is the company whence ordenaryly such men be expected. 3. Thatt they that chuse them ought to be men fearing God: onely att this he stuck, That free planters ought nott to given this power out of their hands: Another stood up and answered that in this case nothing was done but with their consent. The former answered thatt all the free planters ought to resume this power into their owne hands againe if things were not orderly carryed. Mr. Theophilus Eaton answered thatt in all places they chuse committyes, in like manner the companyes of London chuse the liveryes by whom the publique magistrates are chosen. In this the rest are not wronged because they expect in time to be of the livery themselves, and to have the same power. Some other intreated the former to give his arguments and reasons whereupon he dissented. He refused to doe itt and said they might nott rationally demaund itt, seeing he lett the vote passe on freely and did nott speake till after itt was past, because he would nott hinder whatt they agreed upon. Then Mr. Davenport, after a short relation of some former passages betweene them two about this quest. prayed the company thatt nothing might be concluded by them in this weighty quest. butt whatt themselves were perswaded to be agreeing with the minde of God and they had heard whatt had beene said since the voteing, intreated them againe to consider of itt, and putt itt againe to vote as before.—Againe all of them by holding up their hands did shew their consent as before, And some of them professed that whereas they did waver before they came to the assembly they were now fully convinced thatt itt is the minde of God. One of them said that in the morning, before he came, reading Deut. 17.15. he was convinced att home, another said thatt he came doubting to the assembly butt he blessed God by whatt had beene saide he was now fully satisfied thatt the choyce of burgesses out of chur. members, and to intrust those with the power before spoken off is according to the minde of God revealed in the scriptures. All haveing spoken their apprehensions, itt was agreed upon, and Mr. Robert Newman was desired to write itt as an order whereunto every one that hereafter should be admitted here as planters should submitt and testefie the same by subscribeing their names to the order, namely that church members onely shall be free burgesses, and that they onely shall chuse magistrates & officers among themselves to have the power of transacting all the publique civill affayres of this Plantation, of makeing and repealing lawes, devideing of inheritances, decideing of differences thatt may arise and doeing all things or businesses of like nature.

This being thus settled as a foundamentall agreement concerning civill government: Mr. Davenport proceeded to propound some things to consideration aboute the gathering of a chur. And to prevent the blemishing of the first beginnings of the chur. worke, Mr. Davenport advised thatt the names of such as were to be admitted might be publiquely propounded, to the end thatt they who were most approved might be chosen, for the towne being cast into severall private meetings wherein they thatt dwelt nearest together gave their accounts one to another of Gods gracious worke upon them, and prayed together and conferred to their mutuall ediffication, sundry of them had knowledg one of another, and in every meeting some one was more approved of all then any other, For this reason, and to prevent scandalls, the whole company was intreated to consider whom they found fittest to nominate for this worke.

QUAER. 6. Whether are you all willing and doe agree in this thatt twelve men be chosen that their fitnesse for the foundation worke may be tried, however there may be more named yett itt may be in their power who are chosen to reduce them to twelve, and itt be in the power of those twelve to chuse out of themselves seaven that shall be most approved of the major part to begin the church.

This was agreed upon by consent of all as was expressed by holdeing up of hands, and thatt so many as should be thought fitt for the foundation worke of the church shall be propounded by the plantation, and written downe and passe without exception unlesse they had given publique scandall or offence, yett so as in case of publique scandall or offence, every one should have liberty to propound their exception att thatt time publiquely against any man that should be nominated when all their names should be writt downe butt if the offence were private, thatt mens names might be tendered, so many as were offended were intreated to deale with the offender privately, and if he gave nott satisfaction, to bring the matter to the twelve thatt they might consider of itt impartially and in the feare of God. The names of the persons nominated and agreed upon were Mr. Theoph. Eaton, Mr. John Davenport. Mr. Robert Newman, Mr. Math. Gilbert, Mr. Richard Malbon, Mr. Nath: Turner, Eze: Chevers, Thomas Fugill, John Ponderson, William Andrewes, and Jer. Dixon. Noe exception was brought against any of those in publique, except one about takeing an excessive rate for meale which he sould to one of Pequanack in his need, which he confessed with griefe and declared thatt haveing beene smitten in heart and troubled in his conscience, he restored such a part of the price back againe with confession of his sin to the party as he thought himselfe bound to doe. And itt being feared thatt the report of the sin was heard farther th[an] the report of his satisfaction, a course was concluded on to make the satisfaction known to as many as heard of the sinn. Itt was also agreed upon att the said meeting thatt if the persons above named did finde themselves straitened in the number of fitt men for the seaven, thatt itt should be free for them to take into tryal of fitnes such other as they should thinke meete, provided thatt it should be signified to the towne upon the Lords day who they take in, thatt every man may be satisfied of them according to the course formerly taken.

The text is taken from C. J. Hoadly, ed., *Records of the Colony and Plantation of New Haven, from 1638 to 1649* (Hartford, 1857), 11–17. It is reproduced here completely and with the original spelling.

47
[Connecticut Oath of Fidelity]

1640

*T*his document is sometimes referred to as the Connecticut Oath
of Agreement. It can be compared with documents 4, 5, 9, 15,
16, and 65, as well as with the oaths internal to such longer codes,
compacts, and constitutions, as found in documents 20, 26, 39, and
43. At least a dozen other long documents, including those adopted
in middle and southern colonies, refer to citizenship oaths and oaths
of other types that must be taken but are not reproduced in the documents themselves. To these oaths must be added the oaths of shorter
political covenants. Colonial America was flooded with oath taking
as a primary means of achieving compliance, membership, citizenship, and accountability.

An Oath for Paqua' and the Plantations There:

I A.B. being by the Pruidence of God an inhabitant wthin the Jurisdiction of Conectecotte, doe acknowledge my selfe to be subject to the gourment thereof, and doe sweare by the great and dreadfull name of the eur
liueing God to be true and faythfull vnto the same, and doe submitt boath
my Prson & estate thereunto, according to all the holsome lawes & orders that ether are or hereafter shall be there made by lawfull authority:
And that I will nether plott nor practice any euell agaynst the same, nor
consent to any that shall so doe, but will tymely discour the same to lawfull authority established there; and that I will maynetayne, as in duty I
am bownd, the honor of the same & of the lawfull Magestrats thereof, pro-
moteing the publike good thereof, whilst I shall so continue an Inhabitant there, and whensour I shall give my vote, suffrage or prxy, being cauled
thereunto touching any matter wch conserns this Commonwelth, I will

giue yt as in my conscience may conduce to the best good of the same, wch out of respect of prson or favor of any man; So helpe me God in the Lo: Jesus Christ.

Text taken in full, with the original spelling, from Trumbull and Hoadly, *Public Records*, vol. 1, 54.

48

Capitall Lawes of Connecticut, Established by the Generall Court the First of December, 1642

*T*he text is a portion of a longer ordinance passed on that day by
the legislature. This document should be compared with the
equivalent section in The Massachusetts Body of Liberties [22]. To
some people today these lists of capital laws look harsh. Colonial codes
of law, however, usually had such lists, and they are important for several reasons. For one thing, they expressed fundamental values. It is
worth knowing that blasphemy was considered a more serious crime
than theft. For another thing, in Britain theft could, at that time, be
punishable by death, whereas in Connecticut it could not. The list of
crimes for which one could possibly be put to death in the mother
country was extremely long, so colonial lists are a radical departure
from the common law. This attitude was not only in accord with
Christian redemptive theology but also was prudent in the colonies,
where putting people to death for common crimes made no sense given
the serious, chronic shortage of labor. Finally, these lists are part of
what today we might consider bills of rights. The death penalty was
severely limited in scope, and everyone knew the limits. Also, the person had to be properly convicted in court, which probably explains
why the death penalty was rarely used in colonial America. Instead,
blasphemers, for example, were likely to be told to leave town per-
manently. The infamous witchcraft trials in Salem, Massachusetts,
occurred in large part because normal government, including the regular court system, had broken down. When effective government was
restored the "trials" stopped overnight.

---

1. Yf any man after legall conviction, shall have or worship any other
God but the Lord God, he shall be put to death. Deu. 13; 6, and 17. 2 Ex.
22; 20.

2. Yf any man or woman be a Witch, (that is) hath or consulteth w'th a familliar spirit, they shall be put to death. Ex. 22; 18. Lev. 20; 27. Deu. 18; 10, 11.

3. If any p'son shall blaspheme the name of God the ffather, Son or Holy Goste w'th direct, expres pr'sumptuous or highanded blasphemy, or shall curse God in the like manner, he shall be put to death. Lev. 24; 15, 16.

4. Yf any p'son shall comitt any willfull murther, w'ch is manslaughter comitted vppon mallice, hatred or cruelty, not in a mans necessary and just defence, nor by mere casualty against his will, he shall be put to death. Ex. 21; 12, 13, 14. Num. 35; 30, 31.

5. Yf any person shall slay another through guile, ether by poysonings or other such Devlish (devilish) practices, he shall be put to death. Ex. 21; 14.

6. Yf any man or woman shall ly w'th any Beast or brut creature by car-nall copulation, they shall surely be put to death, and the Beast shall be slayne and buried. Lev. 20; 15, 16.

7. Yf any man lye w'th mankind as he lyeth w'th a woman, both of them have comitted abomination, they both shall surely be put to Death. Lev. 20; 13.

8. Yf any p'son comiteth Adultery w'th a married or espoused wife, the Adulterer and the Adulteres shall surely be put to Death. Lev. 20; 10 and 18, 20. Deu. 22; 23, 24.

9. Yf any man shall forcibly and w'thout consent rauishe any mayd or Woman that is lawfull married or contracted, he shall be put to Death. Deu. 22; 25.

10. Yf any man stealeth a man or mankind, he shall be put to Death. Ex. 21; 16.

11. Yf any man rise vp by false witness, wittingly and of purpose to take away any man's life, he shall be put to Death. Deu 19; 16, 18, 19.

12. Yf any man shall conspire or attempte any Inuasion, Insurrection or Rebellion against the comonwelth, he shall be put to Deth.

13. Yf any childe or children aboue sixteene yeers old, and of sufficient un-derstanding, shall curse or smite their natural father or mother, hee or they shall bee put to Death; unlesse it can bee sufficiently testified that the par-ents have been very vnchristianly negligent in the education of such chil-dren, or so provoake them by extreme and cruel correction that they have beene foreced thereunto to preserve themselues from Death or maiming. Ex. 21; 17. Lev. 20. Ex. 20; 15.

14. Yf any man have a stubborne and rebellious sonne, of sufficient yeares and vnderstanding, viz., sixteene yeares of age, which will not obey the voice of his father or the voice of his mother, and that when they haue chastened him, will not hearken vnto them; then may his father and mother, being his naturall parents, lay hold on him and bring him to the Magestrates assembled in courte, and testify vnto them, that theire sonne is stubborne and rebellious, and will not obey their voyce and chastisement, but lives in sundry notorious crimes, such a sonne shall bee put to Death. Deu. 21; 20, 21.

The text is taken from *The Blue Laws of New Haven Colony,* compiled by "An Antiquarian" (Hartford: Case, Tiffany & Co., 1838), 102–4. The spelling is the original.

49
The Government of Guilford

June 19, 1643

*U*ntil this time the government of Guilford had been in conformity with the grant from Lord Say and Brook to
Theophilus Eaton. As a part of New Haven Colony, the government
of Guilford was entitled to one Magistrate in whom was invested all
executive and judicial powers. The settlers were either freemen or
planters. Freemen were restricted to church members, and from their
ranks were chosen all public officers, including the Magistrate and the
three or four deputies chosen to sit with the Magistrate in General
Courts. The planters were all those inhabitants above the age of
twenty-one, with a certain estate, which qualified them to vote in
town meetings. This unusually strict division into classes helps explain the restrictive language in this document as well as why the
town meeting is relatively unimportant compared with the General
Court. The present document shows that popular sovereignty was not
assumed everywhere in the colonies (see the Guilford Covenant [44]
for Guilford's first agreement).

A church was here gathered at Guilford consisting of these 7 persons:—
Mr. Henry Whitfield, Mr. John Higginson, Mr. Samuel Desborow, Mr.
William Leete, Mr. Jacob Sheaffe, John Mepham and John Hoadley.

The nineteenth day of the fourth moneth, 1643, the ffeoffeesl[1] in trust
for purchasing the plantation resigned up their right into the hands of the
church, and these foure of them, also wch were chosen to the exercise of civil
power, did also express that their right and power for that worke was now
terminated and ended, whereof notice being taken at the public meeting, it
was further prpounded, agreed and concluded, that whereas, for the time

---

1. A feudal term used to describe those holding a right of ownership, use, or control.

past (while as yet there was no church gathered amongst us) we did choose out foure men to wit Robert Kitchel, William Chittenden, John Bishop and William Leete, into whose hands we did put full power and authority to act, order and dispatch all matters, respecting the publicke weale and civill government of this plantation, until a church was gathered amongst us, wch the Lord in mercy having now done, according to the desire of or hearts, and the said foure men at this publicke meeting, having resigned up their trust, and power to the intent that all power and authority might be rightly settled within the church, as most safe and suitable for securing of those mayne ends wch wee prpounded to orselves in or coming hither and sitting downe together, namely, that wee might settle and uphold all the ordinances of God in an explicit congregational church way, wth most purity, peace and liberty, for the benefit both of orselves and our posterities after us. We do now therefore, all and every of us agree, order and conclude that only such planters, as are also members of the church shall bee, and be called freemen, and that such freemen only shall have power to elect magistrates, Deputies and all other officers of public trust or authority in matters of importance, concerning either the *civill officers or government here, from amongst themselves and not elsewhere*, and to take an account of all such officers, for the honest and faithful discharge of their several places respectively, and to deale with and prceed against them for all misdemeanors and delinquencies in their several places according to rule, unto which Magistrates Deputies or officers we doe freely subject orselves in all lawfull commands, prvided that they bee yearly chosen, from time to time, and prvided also that no lawes nor orders bee by them made, but before all the planters, then and there inhabiting and residing have had due warning and notice of their meeting, or of what is to bee done so that all weighty objections may be duly attended, considered and according to righteousness, satisfyingly removed.

It is since further agreed and ordered, that in all general courts (consisting of the Magistrates and Deputies who are also appointed to keep particular courts) all orders shall be made, in general courts by the major part of the ffreemen, and all actions in particular courts, sustained by the major vote of the Magistrates and Deputies, it provided for issue sake that when the votes fall equall in either of those courts, then the magistrate shall have a double or casting vote.

Also it is agreed that there shall bee one fixed genrall Court yearly for election of officers &c when shall be chosen the Deputies for the particular court, Treasurer, Secretary, Sureveyors of highways, Marshall, Viewers of fences, &c.

It is ordered that there shall be foure fixed prticulr Courts every yeare (viz.) the first Thursdays in ffebruary, May, September and December, when and where all the members of the Court are to attend, from time to time, at eight o'clock in the forenoon upon the penalty of five shillings for every such default.

It was further ordered that all the freemen and planters should attend each and all of these courts, and remain to their close—unless dismissed—under suitable but severe penalties.

And it was further ordered that whosoever so appearing and attending shall have just cause to speake to or transact any business wth the Court or company, or to or with any person or persons in their presence, they shall both in expressions and in all other manner of their behavyor, so comely and respectfully demeane themselves, as may hold forth an honorable esteem of the Authority then present, and a due attendance to peace, not speaking untill called or allowed to speake, nor addressing their speech to any but the Court, or Magistrate, or such as they shall allow him or them to speake unto, nor continuing by impertinencies, needless repetitions or multiplications of words, wch rather tends to darken than cleare the truth, or right of the matter upon such penalty as the Court, considering the fact or carriage wth the aggravating circumstances adjoyned shall see cause to impose and inflict.

The text, complete and with the original spelling, is taken from Bernard Christian Steiner, *A History of the Plantation of Menunkatuck and of the Original Town of Guilford, Connecticut* (Baltimore: The Friedenwald Company, 1897), 35–37.

50

New Haven Fundamentals

October 27, 1643

While not as well known as the Fundamental Orders of Connecticut [43], the New Haven Fundamentals is every bit as interesting. Both should be seen as the primary constitutional precursors to the 1662 Connecticut Charter, which was formed when the colonies of Connecticut and New Haven were united into a royal colony. In effect, the 1662 charter was written by the combined citizens of the two older colonies, or at least written to satisfy them. The blend of Connecticut and New Haven was so careful that for almost half a century the legislature alternated its meetings yearly between Hartford and New Haven. For discussion of the relatively restricted political class in New Haven, see The Government of Guilford [49].

It was agreed and concluded as a fundamental order not to be disputed or questioned hereafter that none shall be admitted to be free burghesses in any of the plantations within this jurisdiction for the future but such planters as are members of some or other of the approved churches of New England; nor shall any but such free burghesses have any vote in any election, the six present freemen at Milford enjoying the liberty with the cautions agreed; nor shall any power or trust in the ordering of any civil affairs be at any time put into the hands of any other than such church members, though as free planters all have right to their inheritance and to commence according to such grants, orders, and laws as shall be made concerning the same.

2. All such free burghesses shall have power in each town or plantation within this jurisdiction to choose fit and able men among themselves, being church members as before, to be the ordinary judges to hear and determine all inferior cases, whether civil or criminal, provided that no civil cause to be tried in any of these plantation courts in value exceed £20; and that the punishment in such criminals, according to the mind of God revealed in

his word touching such offenses, do not exceed stocking and whipping, or, if the fine be pecuniary, that it exceed not five pounds. In which court, the magistrate or magistrates, if any be chosen by the free burghesses or the jurisdiction for that plantation, shall sit and assist, with due respect to their place, and sentence shall be according to the vote of the major part of each such court. Only if the parties, or any of them, be not satisfied with the justice of such sentences or executions, appeals or complaints may be made from and against these courts to the court of magistrates for the whole jurisdiction.

3. All such free burghesses through the whole jurisdiction shall have vote in the election of all magistrates, whether governor, deputy-governor, or other magistrates, with a treasurer, a secretary, and a marshal, etc., for the jurisdiction. And for the ease of those free burghesses, especially in the more remote plantations, they may by proxy vote in these elections, though absent, their votes being sealed up in the presence of the free burghesses themselves, that their several liberties may be preserved and their votes directed according to their own particular light, and these free burghesses may, at every election, choose so many magistrates for each plantation as the weight of affairs may require, and as they shall find fit men for that trust. But it is provided and agreed that no plantation shall at any election be left destitute of a magistrate if they desire one to be chosen out of those in church fellowship with them.

4. All the magistrates for the whole jurisdiction shall meet twice a year at New Haven, namely the Monday immediately before the sitting of the two fixed general courts hereafter mentioned, to keep a court called the Court of Magistrates for the trial of weighty and capital cases, whether civil or criminal, above those limited to the ordinary judges in the particular plantations; and to receive and try all appeals brought to them from the aforesaid plantation courts; and to call all the inhabitants, whether free burghesses, free planters, or others, to account for the breach of any laws established, and for other misdemeanors, and to censure them according to the quality of the offense. In which meetings of magistrates less than four shall not be accounted a court, nor shall they carry on any business as a court. But it is expected and required that all the magistrates in this jurisdiction do constantly attend the public service at the times before mentioned, and if any of them be absent at one of the clock in the afternoon on Monday aforesaid when the court shall sit, or if any of them depart the town without leave

while the court sits, he or they shall pay for any such default twenty shillings fine, unless some providence of God occasion the same, which the court of magistrates shall judge of from time to time. And all sentences in this court shall pass by the vote of the major part of the magistrates therein. But from this court of magistrates appeals and complaints may be made and brought to the general court as the last and highest of this jurisdiction. But in all appeals or complaints from or to what court soever due costs and damages shall be paid by him or them that make appeal or complaint without just cause.

5. Besides the plantation courts and court of magistrates, there shall be a general court for the jurisdiction which shall consist of the governor, deputy-governor, and all the magistrates within the jurisdiction, and two deputies for every plantation in the jurisdiction, which deputies shall from time to time be chosen against the approach of any such general court by the aforesaid free burghesses, and sent with due certificate to assist in the same. All which, both governor and deputy-governor, magistrates and deputies, shall have their vote in the said court. This general court shall always sit at New Haven, unless upon weighty occasion the general court see cause for a time to sit elsewhere, and shall assemble twice every year, namely the first Wednesday in April and the last Wednesday in October. In the latter of which courts the governor, deputy-governor, and all the magistrates for the whole jurisdiction, with a treasurer, a secretary, and marshal, shall yearly be chosen by all the free burghesses before mentioned. Besides which two fixed courts, the governor, or in his absence the deputy-governor, shall have power to summon a general court at any other time as the urgent and extraordinary occasions of the jurisdiction may require. And at all general courts, whether ordinary or extraordinary, the governor and deputy-governor, and all the rest of the magistrates for the jurisdiction with the deputies for the several plantations, shall sit together til the affairs of the jurisdiction be dispatched or may safely be respited. And if any of the said magistrates or deputies shall either be absent at the first sitting of the said general court, unless some providence of God, hinder, which the said court shall judge of, or depart or absent at the first sitting of the said general court, unless some providence of God, hinder, which the said court shall judge of, or depart or absent themselves disorderly before the court be finished, he or they shall each of them pay twenty shillings fine, with due considerations of further aggravations if there shall be cause. Which general court shall, with all care and diligence,

provide for the maintenance of the purity of religion and suppress the contrary, according to their best light from the word of God and all wholesome and sound advice which shall be given by the elders and churches in the jurisdiction so far as may concern their civil power to deal therein.

Secondly, they shall have power to make and repeal laws and, while they are in force, to require execution of them in all the several plantations.

Thirdly, to impose an oath upon all the magistrates for the faithful discharge of the trust committed to them according to their best abilities, and to call them to account for the breach of any laws established or for other misdemeanors and to censure them as the quality of the offense shall require.

Fourthly, to impose an oath of fidelity and due subjection to the laws upon all the free burghesses, free planters, and other inhabitants within the whole jurisdiction.

Fifthly, to settle and levy rate and contributions upon all the several plantations for the public service of the jurisdiction.

Sixthly, to hear and determine all causes, whether civil or criminal, which by appeal or complaint shall be orderly brought to them from any of the other courts or from any of the other plantations. In all which, with whatsoever else shall fall within their cognizance or judicature, they shall, proceed according to the scriptures, which is the rule of all righteous laws and sentences. And nothing shall pass an act of the general court but by the consent of the major part of the magistrates and the greater part of the deputies.

These generals being thus laid and settled, though with purpose that the circumstntials such as the value of the causes to be tried in the plantations courts, the ordinary and fixed times of meetings both for the general courts and courts of magistrates, how often and when they shall sit, with the fines for absences or default, be hereafter considered of, continued, or altered as may best and most advance the course of justice and best suit the occasions of the plantations, the court proceed to present particular business of the jurisdiction.

The text is reproduced from Thorpe, *Federal and State Constitutions*, 526–29. Thorpe in turn drew upon Hoadly, *Records of the Colony and Plantation of New Haven*, 112–16.

51

[Majority Vote of Deputies and Magistrates Required for the Passage of Laws in Connecticut]

February 5, 1645

*T*he Fundamental Orders of Connecticut, 1639 [43] created a unicameral legislature with two parts. The Deputies, elected by the towns, were to represent local interests and assemble periodically with the Magistrates to form the full, legal General Court. The Magistrates, elected in an indirect colony-wide manner, were to represent the common good and sat more or less continuously to advise the Governor. The incipient bicameralism of the General Court is sharpened in this document. Whereas between 1639 and 1645 legislation required a majority of the Magistrates and Deputies combined, the Magistrates are now viewed together as a unit, as are the Deputies, and each unit must approve every bill. If a majority of Deputies does not approve a proposal it is defeated in the legislature. The same is true of the Magistrate unit; that is, a majority in the legislature must include a majority of the Deputies and a majority of the Magistrates. Still, the Deputies and Magistrates sit together as a unicameral legislature. The curious hybrid produced by the document below records the kind of institutional evolution toward bicameralism that probably took place in other colonies but was not formalized until the process was over (see, for example, documents 24, 41, and 54). Complete bicameralism was not achieved until 1698 (see Division of the Connecticut General Assembly [54]).*

---

*W*hereas it is said in the Fundamental Orders that the general court shall consist of the governor or some one chosen to moderate and four other magistrates at least, it is now ordered and adjudged to be a lawful court if the governor or deputy with other magistrates be present in court with the major part of deputies lawfully chosen. But no act shall pass or stand for a law which is not confirmed both by the major part of the said magistrates, and by the major part of the deputies there present in court, both magistrates and deputies being allowed, either of them, a negative vote. Also the particular court may be kept by the governor or deputy with [3] other magistrates.

Text taken from Trumbull and Hoadly, *Public Records,* vol. 1, 119. Text is complete, and the spelling is unaltered.

52

Connecticut Code of Laws

1650

*T*his code, sometimes cited as "Mr. Ludlow's code," after the man
who drew it up, or "The Code of 1650," appears at the end of
volume 2 of The Public Records of the Colony of Connecticut. It
is immediately preceded by the Fundamental Orders of Connecticut
[43], which is termed the "Constitution of 1639" and serves as a preface to this text. In effect, then, this document is an extension of the
constitution, which underlines the constitutional status of colonial
codes of law. Although the text is too long to reproduce in full, it is
hoped that these selections will establish its rightful place as a foundation document. The portions omitted deal with the more mundane aspects of law, such as penalties for burglary and theft, weights
and measures, heights of fences, fines, the militia, swearing, murder,
and the keeping of records. The portions included deal more directly
with rights, values, and other aspects of self-definition in which a
people might engage.

ESTABLISHED BY THE GENERAL COURT, MAY, 1650

Forasmuch as the free fruition of such Libberties, Immunities, Privileges, as
Humanity, Civillity and Christianity, call for, as due to euery man in his
place and proportion, without Impeachmt and infringement, hath euer
beene and euer will bee the Tranquillity and Stabillity of Churches and Common wealths, and the denyall or deprivall thereof, the disturbance if not
ruine of both:

It is therefore ordered by this Courte and Authority thereof, that no
mans life shall bee taken away, no mans honor or good name shall bee
stained, no mans person shall be arrested, restrained, banished, dismembered
nor any way punished; no man shall bee deprived of his wife or children,

no mans goods or estate shall bee taken away from him, nor any wayes indamaged, vnder colour of Law or countenance of Authority, vnless it be by the vertue or equity of some express Law of the Country warranting the same, established by a Generall Courte, and sufficiently published, or in case of the defect of a Law in any perticular case, by the word of God...[1]

It is ordered and decreed by this Court and Authority thereof, that wheresoeuer the ministry of the word is established according to the order of the Gospell throughout this Jurissdiction, euery person shall duely resorte and attend therevnto respectiuely vppon the Lords day, and vppon such publique fast dayes and dayes of Thanksgiuing as are to bee generally kept by the appointment of Authority. And if any person within this Jurissdiction shall without just and necessary cause withdraw himselfe from hearing the publique ministry of the word, after due meanes of conviction vsed, he shall forfeit for his absence from euery such publique meeting, fiue shillings: All such offences to bee heard and determined by any one Magistrate or more, from time to time.

Forasmuch as the peace and prosperity of Churches and members thereof, as well as Ciuill rights and Libberties are carefuly to bee maintained,—It is ordered by this Courte and decreed, that the Civill Authority heere established hath power and libberty to see the peace, ordinances and rules of Christe bee obserued in euery Church according to his word; as allso to deale with any Church member in a way of Ciuill [justice] notwithstanding any church relation, office or interest, so it bee done in a Ciuill and not in an Eclesiasticall way; nor shall any church censure degrade or depose any man from any Ciuill dignitye, office or authority hee shall haue in the Commonwealth...

IDLENESS

It is ordered by this Courte and Authority thereof, that no person, howseholder or other, shall spend his time idlely or unprofitably, under paine of such punishment as the Courte shall thinke meet to inflict: and for this end, it is ordered, that the Constable of euery place shall vse speciall care and diligence to take knowledge of offendors in this kinde, especially of com-

---

1. At this point the capital laws are reproduced word for word from the December, 1642 ordinance (see the Capitall Lawes of Connecticut [48]).

mon Coasters, vnprofitable fowlers, and Tobacko takers, and present the same vnto any Magistrate, who shall haue power to heare and determine the case or transferr it to the [next] Courte.

INDIANS

It is ordered and decreed, that where any company of Indians doe sitt downe neare any English Plantations, that they shall declare whoe is their Sachem or Chiefe, and that the said Chiefe or Sachem shall pay to the saide English such tresspasses as shall be comitted by any Indian in the said plantation adioyning, either by spoyling or killing any Cattle or Swyne, either with trapps, doggs or arrowes; And they were not to pleade that it was done by strangers, vnless they can produce the prtye and deliuer him or his goods into the custody of the english: And they shall pay the double dammage if it were done voluntarily. The like ingagement this Courte all so makes to them in case of wrong or iniury done to them by the English, wch shall bee paid by the prty by whome it was done, if hee can bee made to appeare, or otherwise by the Towne in whose limmitts such facts are committed.

Forasmuich as or lenity and gentlnes towards Indians hath made them growe bold and insolent, to enter into Englishmens howses, and vnadvisedly handle swords and peeces and other instruments, many times to the hazzard of limbs or liues of English or Indians, and allso oft steale diuerse goods out of such howses where they resorte; for the preventing whereof, It is ordered, that whatsoeuer Indian shall hereafter meddle with or handle any English mans weapons, of any sorte, either in theire howses or in the fields, they shall forfeitt for euery such defaulte halfe a fathom of wampum; and if any hurte or injurye shall therevppon follow to any persons life or limbe, wound for wound, and shall pay for the healing such wounds and other dammages. And for anythinge they steale, they shall pay double, and suffer such further punnishment as the Magistrates shall adiudge them. The Constable of any Towne may attache and arrest any Indian that shall transgress in any such kinde before mentioned; and bring them before some Magistrate, whoe may execute the penalty of this order vppon offendors in any kinde beforementioned; and bring them before some Magistrate, whoe may execute the penalty of this order vppon offendors in any kinde except life or limbe, and any person that doth see such defaults may prosecute, and shall haue halfe the forfeiture.

It is ordered by this Courte and Authority thereof, that no man within this Jurissdiction shall, directly or indirectly, amend, repaire, or cause to bee amended or repaired, any gunn, small or great, belonging to any Indian, nor shall indeauor the same; nor shall sell nor giue to any Indian, directly or indirectly, any such gunn, nor any gunpowder, or shott, or lead, or shott mould, or any military weapon or weapons, armor, or arrowe heads; nor sell nor barter nor giue any dogg or doggs, small or great; vppon paine of ten pounds fyne for euery offence, at least in any one of the aforementioned perticulars; and the Courte shall haue power to increase the fyne, or to impose corporall punnishment where a fyne cannott bee had, at theire discretion.

And it is allso ordered, that no person nor persons shall trade with them at or about theire wigwams, but in there vessells or pinnaces, or at theire owne howses, vnder penalty of twenty shillings for each default...

Whereas diuerse persons departe from amongst vs, and take vp theire aboade with the Indians, in a prophane course of life; for the preventing whereof,

It is ordered that whatsoeuer person or persons that now inhabiteth, or shall inhabitt within this Jurissdiction, and shall departe from vs and settle or joine with the Indians, that they shall suffer three yeares imprisonment at least, in the Howse of Correction, and vndergoe such further censure, by fyne or corporall punishment, the perticular Courte shall judge meet to inflict in such cases...

This Courte, judging it necessary that some meanes should bee vsed to conuey the lighte and knowledge of God and of his Worde to the Indians and Natiues amongst vs, doe order that one of the teaching Elders of the Churches in this Jurissdiction, with the helpe of Thomas Stanton, shall bee desired, twise at least in every yeare to goe amongst the neighbouring Indians and indeauor to make knowne to them the Councells of the Lord, and thereby to draw and stirr them vp to direct and order all theire wayes and coversations according to the rule of his Worde; And Mr. Gouernor and Mr. Deputy, and the other Magistrates are desired to take care to see the things attended, and with theire owne presence so farr as may bee convenient, incourage the same.

This Courte hauing duly weighed the joint determination and argument of the Commissioners of the United English Colonyes at New Hauen, in Anno 1646, in reference to the Indians, and judging it to bee both according to rules of prudence and righteousness, doe fully assent thervnto, and order, that it bee recorded amongst the Acts of this Courte, and attended in future practice as occasions may present and require: The said conclusion is as followeth;—The Commissioners seriously considering the many willfull wrongs and hostile practices of the Indians against the English, together with theire interteining, protecting and rescuing of offenders, as late our experience showeth, (wch if suffered, the peace of the Colonyes cannot bee secured,) It is therefore concluded, that in such cases the Magistrates of any of the Jurissdictions may, at the charge of the Plaintiff, send some convenient strength of English, and according to the nature and value of the offence and damage, seize and bring away any of that plantation of Indians that shall interteine, protect or rescue the offender, though it should bee in another Jurissdiction, when through distance of place, commission or direction cannot bee had, after notice and due warning giuen them, as actors, or at least accessary to the iniurye and damage done to the English, onely women and children to bee sparingly seized, vnless knowne to bee some way guilty. And because it will bee chargeable keeping Indians in prison, and if they should escape they are like to prove more insolent and dangerous after, It was thought fitt that vppon such seizure, the delinquent or satisfaction bee againe demaunded of the Sagamore or plantation of Indians guilty or accessory as before; and if it bee denyed, that then the Magistrates of the Jurissdiction deliuer vp the Indian seized to the party or partyes endammaged, either to serue or be shipped out and exchanged for neagers, as the case will justly beare. And though the Comissioners foresee that such severe though just proceeding may provoake the Indians to an vniust seizing of some of ours, yet they could not at present finde no better meanes to preserue the peace of the Colonyes, all the aforementioned outrages and insolences tending to an open warr: Onely they thought fitt that before any such seizure bee made in any plantation of Indians, the ensuing Declaration bee published, and a Coppye giuen to the perticular Saggamores: the Commissioners for the Vnited Colonyes, considering how peace with righteousness may bee preserued betweixt all the English and the severall plantations of the Indians, thought fitt to declare and publish, as they will doe no iniurye to them, so if any Indian or Indians of what plantation so euer, doe any willfull dammage to any of the English colonyes, vppon proofe, they will in a peaceable way require just satisfaction, according to the nature of the offence and dammage. But if any Saggamore or plantation of Indians, after notice and due warninge, interteine, hyde, protect, keepe, conuey away or further the escape of any such offendor or offendors, the English will require satisfaction of such Indian and Saggamore or Indian plantation; and if they deny it, they will right themselues as they may, vppon such as so meinteine them that doe the wrong, keeping peace and all tearmes of Amity and Greement with all other Indians.

INNKEEPERS

Forasmuch as there is a necessary vse of howses of Common Interteinment in euery Common wealth, and of such as retaile wine, beare and victualls, yet because there are so many abuses of that lawfull liberty, both by persons interteining and persons interteined, there is allso need of strict lawes and rules to regulate such an imployment;

It is therefore ordered by this Courte and Authority thereof, that no person or persons licensed for Common Interteinement shall suffer any to bee drunken or drinke excessiuely, viz: aboue halfe a pointe of wyne for one person at one tyme, or to continue tipling aboue the space of halfe an houre, or at vnseasonable times, or after nine of the clock at night, in or about any of theire howses, on penalty of fiue shillings for euery such offence. And euery person found drunken, viz: so that hee bee thereby bereaued or dissabled in the vse of this vnderstanding, appearing in his speech or gesture, in any of the said howses or elsewhere, shall forfeitt ten shillings; and for excessive drinking, three shillings, foure pence; and for continnuing aboue halfe an houre tipling, two shillings six pence; and for tipling at vnseasonable times, or after nien a clock at night, fiue shillings, euery offence in these perticulars, being lawfully convicted thereof; and for want of payment, such shall bee imprisoned vntill they pay, or bee set in the stocks, one houre or more, in some open place, as the weather will permitt, not exceeding three houres at one time; Provided notwithstanding, such licensed persons may interteine seafaring men or land trauellers in the night season when they come first on shoare, or from theire journye, for theire necessary refreshment, or when they prepare for theire voyage or journeye the next day early, [if there] bee no dissorder amongst them; and allso strangers and other persons in an orderly way may continnue [in] such howses of Common Interteinement during m[eal] times or vppon lawful buisines, what time their occasions shall require...

JURYES AND JURORS

It is ordered by the Authority of this Courte, that in all cases wch are entred vnder forty shillings, the sute shall bee tryed by the Courte of Magistrates as they shall judge most agreeable to equity and righteousness. And in all cases that are tryed by Juries, it is left to the Magistrates to impannell a Jury of sixe or twelue, as they shall judge the nature of the case shall require; and if four of sixe, or eight of twelue, agree, the verdict shall bee deemed to all intents and purposes sufficient and full; vppon wch judgement may bee entred and execution graunted, as if they had all concurred; but if it fall out that there bee not such a concurrence as is before mentioned, the Jurors shall returne the case to the Courte with theire reasons, and a speciall verdict is to bee drawne therevpon, and the voate of the greater number of Magistrates shall carrye the same; and the judgement to bee entred and other proceedings as in case of a verdict by a Jury...

GRAND JURY

It is ordered and decreed, that there shall bee a Grand Jury of twelue or fourteene able men warned to appeare euery Courte yearely in Septembr, or as many and oft as the Gouernor or Courte shall thinke meete, to make presentments of the breaches of any Lawes or orders or any other misdemeanors they shall know of in this Jurissdiction...

MAGISTRATES

This Courte being sensible of the great disorder growing in this Common wealth, through the contempts cast vppon the Civill Authority, wch willing to prevent, doe order and decree:

That whosoeuer shall henceforth openly or willingly defame any courte of Justice, or the sentences and proceedings of the same, or any of the Magistrates or judges of any such Courte, in respect of any Act or sentence therein passed, and being thereof lawfully convicted in any Generall Courte or Courte [of] Magistrates, shall bee punnished for the same by fyne, imprisonment, dissfranchisement or bannishment, as the quality and measure of the offence shall deserue.

SCHOOLES

It being one chiefe project of that old deluder Sathan, to keepe men from the knowledge of the Scriptures, as in former times keeping them in an unknown tongue, so in these latter times by perswading them from the vse of Tongues, so that at least the true sence and meaning of the originall might bee clouded with false glosses of saint seeming deceiuers; and that Learning may not bee buried in the Graue of or Forefathers, in Church and Common wealth, the Lord assisting our indeauers,—It is therefore ordered by this Courte and Authority thereof, that euery Towneshipp within this Jurissdiction, after the Lord hath increased them to the number of fifty houshoulders, shall then forthwith appoint one within theire Towne to teach all such children as shall resorte to him, to write and read, whose wages shall bee paid either by the parents or masters of such children, or by the inhabitants in generall by way of supplye, as the maior parte of those who order the prudentialls of the Towne shall appointe; provided that those who send theire children bee not oppresed by more than they can haue them taught for in other Townes. And it is further ordered, that where any Towne shall increase to the number of one hundred families or housholders, they shall sett vp a Grammer Schoole, the masters thereof being able to instruct youths so farre as they may bee fitted for the Vniversity. And if any Towne neglect the Performance hereof aboue one yeare, then euery such Towne shall pay fiue pounds pr Annum, to the next such Schoole, till they shall performe this order...

SECRETARY

It is ordered and decreed, that within twenty dayes after the session of euery Generall Courte, the Secretary thereof shall send forth Coppies of such Lawes and orders as are or shall bee made at either of them, wch are of generall concernement for the gouernement of this Commonwealth, to the Constables of each Towne within this Jurissdiction, for them to publish within fourteene dayes more, at some publique meeting in theire seuerall Townes, and cause to bee written into a Booke and kept for the Vse of the Towne. And once euery yeare the Constables in each Towne shall read or cause to bee read in some publique meeting all the Capitall Lawes, and giue notice to all the Inhabitants where they may at any time see the rest of the Lawes and orders and acquaint themselues therewith: And the Secretary of the Courte Shall haue twelue pence for the Coppy of the orders of each Session aforesaid, from each of the Townes...

TOBACKO

Forasmuch as it is obserued that many abuses are crept in and committed by frequent taking of Tobacko, It is ordered by the Authority of the Courte, that no person vnder the age of twenty yeares, nor any other that hath not allready accustomed himselfe to the use thereof, shall take any Tobacko, vntill hee hath brought a certificate vnder the hands of some who are approued for knowledge and skill in phisick, that it is usefull for him, and allso that hee hath receiued a lycense from the Court for the same. And for the regulating of those whoe either by theire former taking it haue to theire owne aprehensions made it necessary to them, or vppon due advice are perswaded to the vse thereof, It is ordered, that no man within this Colonye, after the publication hereof, shall take any Tobacko publiquely in the street, high wayes, or any barne yards, or vppon training dayes in any open places, vnder the penalty of six pence for each offence against this order in any the perticulares thereof, to bee paid without gainsaying vppon conviction, by the testimony of one wittness that is without just exception, before any one Magistrate. And the Constables in the severall Townes are required to make presentment to each particular courte of such as they doe vnderstand and euict to bee transgressors of this order...

VOATES

It is ordered by this Courte and decreed, that if any person within these Libberties haue been or shall be fyned or whipped for any scandalous offence, hee shall not bee admitted after such time to haue any voate in Towne or Common wealth, nor to serue on the Juiry untill the Courte shall manifest theire satisfaction...

Partial text, with the original spelling, taken from Trumbull and Hoadly, *Public Records*, vol. 1, 509–63.

53

Preface to the General Laws and Liberties of Connecticut Colony Revised and Published by Order of the General Court Held at Hartford in October 1672

After Connecticut and New Haven colonies merged in 1662 so that the combined colony had approximately the borders we associate with the state of Connecticut today (a later agreement with New York would trade the Connecticut towns on Long Island for what are now the westernmost towns of Connecticut), there was a need to more fully articulate a government for the combined colony. This was a delicate and slow process because the political cultures of the two former colonies were at some variance. This code of law was part of that evolution. Only the preface is reproduced here; it serves to illustrate the animating principles of the document as well as to show that even after unification the documents of the united colonies were still seen as deriving from, and operating under, the umbrella of the original foundation covenants.

To our Beloved Brethren and Neighbours, the Inhabitants of the Colony of Connecticut, The GENERAL COVRT of that Colony with Grace and Peace in our Lord Jesus.

The Serious Consideration of the Necessity of the Establishment of wholesome Lawes, for the Regulating of each Body Politick, Hath enclined us mainly in Obedience unto JEHOVAH the Great Law-giver: Who hath been pleased to set down a Divine Platforme, not onely of the Morall but also of Judicial Lawes, suitable for the people of Israel; As also in conformity to the manifest pleasure of our Soveraign Lord the King, in his Majesties Gracious Charter, requiring and Granting Liberty thereby of makeing of Laws and Constitutions suiting our State & condition, for the Safety & Welfare of the people of the Colony of Conecticut. We say the sense of these Weighty

Inducemnts hath moved us, notwithstanding the exceeding great difficulties of the Work, Looking up to God for wisedom and strength to engage in this solemn Service, To Exhibit and take care concerning the sufficient Promulgation of such needfull Lawes, that a more full and plain way may be set for execution of, and judgement thereby.

Wherefore although in our former Initial times (while this Colony was deemed distinct in Jurisdiction from that of New-haven,) We contented ourselves with keeping our Lawes in Manuscripts, and in the Promulgation of them by written Copies sent unto those Townes who then acknowledg themselves to be setled within our limits, But since by Divine Providence We and New-haven have agreed, according to his Majesties Pleasure manifested in our Patent, to vnite as one Body Politick: From whence and from other increasings of Plantations and Persons, together with the addition of more Lawes and Orders, an occasion is given to think it convenient if not necessary for further or full Publication, that so as well Forreigners occasionally comming hither, as the more settled Inhabitants, may have ready meanes in forming how to demean themselves and observe.

From hence and such like Considerations urging, This Court have seen cause to put these our Lawes in Print, so far as they are at present prepared; Being willing that all concerned by this Impression may know what they may expect at our hands as Justice, in the Administration of our Government here. We have endeavoured not onely to Ground our Capital Laws upon the Word of God, but also all our other Laws upon the Justice and Equity held forth in that word, which is a most perfect Rule.

Now in these our LAWS, although we may seem to vary or differ, yet it is not our purpose to Repugn the Statute Laws of England, so far as we understand them; professing ourselves always ready and willing to receive Light for Emendation or Alteration as we may have oportunity: Our whole aim in all being to Please and Glorifie God, to approve ourselves Loyal Subjects to our Soveraign, and to promote the Welfare of this People in all Godliness and Honesty, in Peace, which will be the more establishing to his Majesties Crown and Dignity, and best Answer his Religious Directions to us in our Charter: And that pure Religion and undefiled before God, according to the Gospel of our Lord Jesus, may be maintained amongst us, which was the end of the first Planters, who settled these Foundations; and ought to be the endeavours of those that shall succeed to Vphold and Encourage unto all Generations.

We need no other Inducments to lay before you, to bespeak your Obedience to what follows but that of the apostle, 1 Pet. 2, 13, 17. submit yourselves to every Ordinance of man for the Lord's sake, &c., Love the Brotherhood, Fear God, Honour the King.

By order of the General Court,
John Allin, Secrt.

The text is from Trumbull and Hoadly, *Public Records*, vol. 2 (1852), 567–68.

54

[Division of the Connecticut
General Assembly into Two Houses]

October 13, 1698

*I*n this document Connecticut altered somewhat the joint government that had resulted from the 1662 charter. Because the
charter was given by the king, there was a danger that such a uni-
lateral amendment might be viewed as disloyalty. The colonists, therefore, were careful to reaffirm their allegiance to the king and to note
that his charter permitted them to erect and conduct their own local
government. The implicit but half-formed bicameralism found in
the Fundamental Orders of Connecticut, 1639 [43] and New Haven
Fundamentals, 1643 [50] is now explicitly and fully developed (see
also Majority Vote of Deputies and Magistrates [51]). For bicameralism in other colonies, see the Massachusetts Bicameral Ordinance
[24] and General Assembly of Rhode Island [41].

It is ordered by this court, and the authority thereof, that for the future its
general assembly shall consist of two houses. The first shall consist of the
governor, or, in his absence of the deputy-governor, and assistants, which
shall be known by the name of the Upper House. The other shall consist of
such deputies as shall be legally returned from the several towns within this
colony to serve as members of this general assembly, which shall be known
by the name of the Lower House wherein a speaker chosen by themselves shall
preside. Which houses so formed shall have a distinct power to apoint all needful officers and to make such rules as they shall severally judge necessary for
the regulating of themselves. And it is further ordered that no act shall be passed
into a law of this colony, nor any law already enacted be repealed, nor any
other act proper to this general assembly, but by the consent of both houses.

Taken from Trumbull and Hoadly, *Public Records of the Colony of Connecticut*, vol. 4
(1850), 267.

55

[A Letter from Governor Richard Nicolls to the Inhabitants of Long Island]

February 1665

*C*olony-wide governments were often, but not always, built up
*from below through federations of already existing towns or
colonies. William Penn organized his colony of Pennsylvania from
above, as did Lord Calvert, in Maryland. Richard Nicolls was not a
charter holder like Penn and Calvert but was instead a governor deputed by the charter holder, the Duke of York. Here he established a
legislature for New York through the simple device of a letter. It is
notable, however, that even the governors of Royal colonies instinc-
tively felt the need to organize the population through elective bodies rather than govern them by edict. The legislature that eventually
emerged from the complicated process initiated by this letter would a
number of years later write a constitution for the colony (see Charter of Liberties and Privileges [56]). See also the discussion of Fundamentals of West New Jersey [57].*

Whereas the Inhabitants of Long Island, have for a Long time groaned
under many grievous inconveniences, and discouragements occasioned partly from their subjection, partly from their opposition to a forraigne Power, in which distracted condition, few or no Lawes could bee putt
in due Execution, Bounds and Titles to Lands disputed, Civill Libertyes in-
terrupted, and from this Generall Confusion, private dissentions and ani-
mosityes, have too much prevailed against Neighborly Love, and Christian
Charity; To the preventing of the future growth of like Evils, his Majesty as
a signall grace and honor to his subjects upon Long Island, hath at his
owne charge reduc't the forraigne Power to his obedience and by Pattent hath
invested his Royall Highness the Duke of York with full and absolute Power,
in and over all and every the Particular Tracts of Land therein mentioned,

which said Powers by Comission from his Royall Highnesse the Duke of York, I am deputed to put in execution. In discharge therefore of my Trust and Duty, to Settle good and knowne Laws within this government for the future, and receive your best advice and Information in a General Meeting, I have thought fitt to Publish unto you, That upon the last day of this present February, at Hempsteed upon Long Island, shall be held a Generall Meeting, which is to consist of Deputyes chosen by the major part of the freemen only, which is to be understood of all Persons rated according to their Estates, whether English, or Dutch, within your severall Towns and precincts, whereof you are to make Publication to the Inhabitants, foure dayes before you proceed to an Election appointing a certain day to that purpose; You are futher to impart to the Inhabitants from mee, that I do heartily recommend to them the choice of the most sober, able and discreet persons, without partiality or faction, the fruite & benefitt whereof will return to themselves in a full and perfect settlement and composure of all controversyes, and the propagation of true Religion amongst us. They are also required to bring with them a Draught of each Towne Limits, or such writings as are necessary to evidence the Bounds and Limitts, as well as the right by which they challenge such Bounds and Limits, by Grant or Purchase, or both, as also to give notice of this meeting to Sachems of the Indyans, whose presence may in some cases bee accessary. Lastly I do require you to Assemble your Inhabitants and read this Letter to them, and then and there to nominate a day for the Election of two Deputyes from your Towne, who are to bring a certificate of their due election, (with full power to conclude any cause or matter relating to their serveral Townes) to mee at Hempsteed upon the last day of February, where (God willing) I shall expect them.

Taken from E. B. O'Callaghan, ed., *Documents Relating to the Colonial History of the State of New York* (Albany, 1883), 14: 564–65. The text is complete, with the spelling as found in O'Callaghan.

56

Charter of Liberties and Privileges

October 30, 1683

A *lthough essentially based on the British parliamentary
model, the structure of New York's government described in
this document looks quite similar to that developed elsewhere in the
colonies. The true bicameralism, however, that developed in some of
the other colonies is missing in New York because the Governor's
Council is not elective and is really a privy council. The bill of rights
is derived from English common law, and although quite liberal by
European standards, is less robust than those developed in other
colonies using a theological grounding. Also, an appeal to popular
sovereignty, implicit or otherwise, is conspicuously missing. Authority instead rests explicitly with the governor, council, and assembly
combined under the implied sovereignty of the monarch.*

FOR The better Establishing the Government of this province of New
Yorke and that Justice and Right may be Equally done to all persons
within the same.

BEE It Enacted by the Governour Councell and Representatives now in
General Assembly mett and assembled and by the authority of the same.

THAT The Supreme Legislative Authority under his Majesty and Royall
Highnesse James Duke of Yorke Albany &c Lord proprietor of the said
province shall forever be and reside in a Governour, Councell, and the people mett in General Assembly.

THAT The Exercise of the Cheife Magistracy and Administration of the
Government over the said province shall bee in the said Governour assisted
by a Councell with whose advice and Consent or with at least four of them
he is to rule and Governe the same according to the Lawes thereof.

THAT in Case the Governour shall dye or be absent out of the province
and that there be noe person within the said province Comissionated by

his Royal Hignesse his heirs or Successours to be Governour or Comander in Cheife there That then the Councell for the time being or Soe many of them as are in the Said province doe take upon them the Administration of the Governour and Execution of the Lawes thereof and powers and authorityes belonging to the Governour and Councell the first in nomination in which Councell is to preside untill the said Governour shall returne and arrive in the said province againe, or the pleasure of his Royall Highnesse his heires or Successours Shall be further knowne.

THAT According to the usage Custome and practice of the Realme of England a session of a Generall Assembly be held in this province once in three yeares at least. THAT Every ffreeholder within this province and ffreeman in any Corporation Shall have his free Choise and Vote in the Electing of the Representatives without any manner of constraint or Imposition. And that in all Elections the Majority of Voices shall carry itt and by freeholders is understood every one who is Soe understood according to the Lawes of England.

THAT the persons to be Elected to sitt as representatives in the Generall Assembly from time to time for the severall Cittyes townes Countyes Shires or Divisions of this province and all places within the same shall be according to the proportion and number hereafter Expressed that is to say for the Citty, and County of New Yorke four, for the County of Suffolke two, for Queens County two, for Kings County two, for the County of Richmond two for the County of West Chester two, for the County of Ulster two for the County of Albany two and for Schenectade within the said County one, for Dukes County two, for the County of Cornwall two and as many more as his Royall Highnesse shall think fitt to Establish.

THAT All persons Chosen and Assembled in manner aforesaid or the Major part of them shall be deemed and accounted the Representatives of this province which said Representatives together with the Governour and his Councell Shall forever be the Supreame and only Legislative power under his Royall Hignesses of the said province.

THAT The said Representatives may appoint their owne Times of meeting dureing their sessions and may adjourne their house from time to time to such time as to them shall seeme meet and convenient.

THAT The said Representatives are the sole Judges of the Qualifications of their owne members, and likewise of all undue Elections and may from time to time purge their house as they shall see occasion dureing the said sessions.

THAT noe member of the general Assembly or their servants dureing the time of their Sessions and Whilest they shall be goeing to and returning from the said Assembly shall be arrested sued imprisoned or any wayes molested or troubled nor be compelled to make answere to any suite, Bill plaint, Declaration or otherwise, (Cases of High Treason and felony only Excepted) provided the number of the said servants shall not Exceed three.

THAT All bills agreed upon by the said Representatives or the Major part of them shall be presented unto the Governour and his Councell for their Approbation and Consent All and Every which Said Bills soe approved or Consented to by the Governour and his Councell shall be Esteemed and accounted the Lawes of the province, Which said Lawes shall continue and remaine of force untill they shall be repealed by the authority aforesaid that is to say the Governour Councell and Representatives in General Assembly by and with the Approbation of his Royal Highnesse or Expire by their owne Limittations.

THAT In All Cases of death or removall of any of the said Representatives The Governour shall issue out Sumons by Writt to the Respective Townes Cittyes Shires Countryes or Divisions for which he or they soe removed or deceased were chosen willing and requireing the ffreeholders of the Same to Elect others in their place and stead.

THAT Noe freeman shall be taken and imprisoned or be disseized of his ffreehold or Libertye or ffree Customes or be outlawed or Exiled or any other wayes destroyed nor shall be passed upon adjudged or condemned But by the Lawfull Judgment of his peers and by the Law of this province. Justice nor Right shall be neither sold denyed or deferred to any man within this province.

THAT Noe aid, Tax, Tallage, Assessment, Custome, Loane, Benevolence or Imposition whatsoever shall be layed assessed imposed or levyed on any of his Majestyes Subjects within this province or their Estates upon any manner of Colour or pretence but by the act and Consent of the Governour Councell and Rpresentatives of the people in Generall Assembly mett and Assembled.

THAT Noe man of what Estate or Condition soever shall be putt out of his Lands or Tenements, nor taken, nor imprisoned, nor dishereited, nor banished nor any wayes distroyed without being brought to Answere by due Course of Law.

THAT A ffreeman Shall not be amerced for a small fault, but after the manner of his fault and for a great fault after the Greatnesse thereof Saveing to him his freehold, And a husbandman saveing to him his Wainage and a merchant likewise saveing to him his merchandize, And none of the said Amerciaments shall be assessed but by the oath of twelve honest and Lawfull men of the Vicinage provided the faults and misdemeanours be not in Contempt of Courts of Judicature.

ALL Tryalls shall be by the verdict of twelve men, and as neer as many be peers or Equalls And of the neighbourhood and in the County Shire or Division where the Fact Shall arise or grow Whether the Same be by Indictment Information Declaration or otherwise against the person Offender or Defendant.

THAT In all Cases Capitall or Criminall there shall be a grand Inquest who shall first present the offence and then twelve men of the neighbourhood to try the Offender who after his plea to the Indictment shall be allowed his reasonable Challenges.

THAT In all Cases whatsoever Bayle by sufficient Suretyes Shall be allowed and taken unlesse for treason or felony plainly and specially Expressed and menconed in the Warrant of Committment provided Always that nothing herein contined shall Extend to discharge out of prison upon bayle any person taken in Execution for debts or otherwise legally sentenced by the Judgment of any of the Courts of Record within the province.

THAT Noe ffreeman shall be compelled to receive any Marriners or Souldiers into his house and there suffer them to Sojourne, against their willes provided Always it be not in time of Actuall Warr within this province.

THAT Noe Comissions for proceeding by Marshall Law against any of his Majestyes Subjects within this province shall issue forth to any person or persons whatsoever Least by Colour of them any of his Majestyes Subjects bee destroyed or putt to death Except all such officers persons and Soldiers in pay throughout the Government.

THAT from hence forward Noe Lands Within this province shall be Esteemed or accounted a Chattle or personall Estate but an Estate of Inheritance according to the Custome and practice of his Majesties Realme of England.

THAT Noe Court or Courts within this province have or at any time hereafter Shall have any Jurisdiction power or authority to grant out any Execution or other writt whereby any mans Land may be sold or any other way disposed of without the owners Consent provided Always That the issues or meane proffitts of any mans Lands shall or may be Extended by Execution or otherwise to satisfye just debts Any thing to the Contrary hereof in any wise Notwithstanding.

THAT Noe Estate of a feme Covert shall be sold or conveyed But by Deed Acknowledged by her in Some Court of Record the Woman being secretly Examined if She doth it freely without threats or Compulsion of her husband.

THAT All Wills in writing attested by two Credible Witnesses shall be of the same force to convey Lands as other Conveyances being registered in the Secretaryes Office within forty dayes after the testators death.

THAT A widdow after the death of her husband shall have her Dower And shall and may tarry in the Cheife house of her husband forty dayes after the death of her husband within which forty dayes her Dower shall be assigned her And for her Dower shallbe assigned unto her the third party of all the Lands of her husband dureing Coverture, Except shee were Endowed of Lesse before Marriage.

THAT All Lands and Heritages within this province and Dependencyes shall be free from all fines and Lycences upon Alienations and from all Herriotts Ward Shipps Liveryes primer Seizins yeare day and Wast Escheates and forfeitures upon the death of parents and Ancestors naturall unaturall casuall or Judiciall, and that forever; Cases of High treason only Excepted.

THAT Noe person or persons which professe ffaith in God by Jesus Christ Shall at any time be any wayes molested punished disquieted or called in Question for Difference in opinion or Matter of Religious Concernment, who doe not actuall disturb the Civill peace of the province, But that all and Every such person or prsons may from time to time and at all times freely have and fully enjoy his or their Judgments or Consciencyes in matters of Religion throughout all the province, they behaveing themselves peaceably and quietly and not useing this Liberty to Lycentiousnesse nor to the civill Injury or outward disturbance of others provided Always that this liberty or any thing contained therein to the Contrary shall never be Construed or improved to make void the Settlement of any publique Minister on Long Island Whether Such Settlement be by two thirds of the voices in any Towne thereon which shall always include the Minor part Or by Subscriptions of perticuler Inhabitants in Said Townes provided they are the two thirds thereon Butt that all such agreements Covenants and Subscriptions that are there already made and had Or that hereafter shall bee in this Manner Consented to agreed and Subscribed shall at all time and times hereafter be firme and Stable And in Confirmation hereof

It is Enacted by the Governour Councell and Representatives; That all Such Sumes of money soe agreed on Consented to or Subscribed as aforesaid for maintenance of said public Ministers by the two thirds of any Towne on Long Island Shall alwayes include the Minor part who shall be regulated thereby And also Such Subscriptions and agreements as are before mentioned are and Shall be always ratified performed and paid, And if any Towne on said Island in their publick Capacity of agreement with any Such minister or any perticuler persons by their private Subscriptions as aforesaid Shall make default deny or withdraw from Such payment Soe Covenanted to agreed upon and Subscribed That in Such Case upon Complaint of any Collector appointed and Chosen by two thirds of Such Towne upon Long Island unto any Justice of that County Upon his hearing the Same he is hereby authorized impowered and required to issue out his warrant unto the Constable or his Deputy or any other person appointed for the Collection of Said Rates or agreement to levy upon the goods and Cattles of the Said Delinquent or Defaulter all such Sumes of money Soe covenanted and agreed to be paid by distresse with Costs and Charges without any further Suite in Law Any Lawe Custome or usage to the Contrary in any wise Notwithstanding.

PROVIDED Always the said sume or sumes be under forty shillings otherwise to be recovered as the Law directs.

AND WHEREAS All the Respective Christian Churches now in practice within the City of New Yorke and the other places of this province doe appeare to be priviledged Churches and have beene Soe Established and Confirmed by the former authority of this Government BEE it hereby Enacted by this Generall Assembly and by the authority thereof That all the Said Respective Christian Churches be hereby Confirmed therein And that they and Every of them Shall from henceforth forever be held and reputed as priviledged Churches and Enjoy all their former freedomes of their Religion in Divine Worshipp and Church Discipline And that all former Contracts made and agreed upon for the maintenances of the severall ministers of the Said

Churches shall stand and continue in full force and virtue And that all Contracts for the future to be made Shall bee of the same power And all persons that are unwilling to performe their part of the said Contract Shall be Constrained thereunto by a warrant from any Justice of the peace provided it be under forty Shillings Or otherwise as this Law directs provided allsoe that all Christian Churches that Shall hereafter come and settle within this province shall have the Same priviledges.

Complete text is taken from *The Colonial Laws of New York*, vol. 1, 111–16. For the circumstances surrounding this document and the similar charter of 1691, see Charles M. Andrews, *The Colonial Period of American History*, vol. 3 (New Haven: Yale University Press, 1936), chap. 3; and David S. Lovejoy, "Equality and Empire: The New York Charter of Libertyes, 1683," *William and Mary Quarterly*, 3d ser., 21 (1964): 493–515.

57

Fundamentals of West New Jersey

1681

The middle colonies, developed later than those in New England and the South, did not have the freedom to develop from the bottom up on their own as some of the early colonies did. A strong governor was a central reality from the beginning. In New Jersey, as in New York, the legislature and constitution were added to the political system rather than founding it, and the English system was essentially used as a model. Central to that model was the principle that there should be no taxation without representation. Because the Glorious Revolution had not yet occurred in Britain, the colonies were still under the king through the charters he had granted them rather than under Parliament. Financial support was therefore not forthcoming for the king's colonial governors unless the king asked for it—and he would rather do other things with any levy he could extract—hence the need for local legislatures to vote such support from the colonists. In order for a meaningful, viable legislature to exist, however, some major chunks had to be carved out of the governor's powers. As a result, the New Jersey document is interesting because its central focus is a set of limits on the governor, which together make room for the legislature.

Forasmuch as it hath pleased God, to bring us into this Province of West New Jersey, and settle us here in safety, that we may be a people to the praise and honour of his name, who hath so dealt with us, and for the good and welfare of our posterity to come, we the Governor and Proprietors, freeholders and inhabitants of West New Jersey, by mutual consent and agreement, for the prevention of innovation and oppression, either upon us or our posterity, and for the preservation of the peace and tranquility of the same; and that all may be encouraged to go chearfully in their several places: We do make and constitute these our agreements to be as fundamentals to us and our posterity, to be held inviolable, and that no person or persons whatsoever, shall or may make void or disanul the same upon any pretence whatsoever.

I. That there shall be a General Free Assembly for the Province aforesaid, yearly and every year, at a day certain, chosen by the free people of the said Province, whereon all the representatives for the said Province, shall be summoned to appear, to consider of the affairs of the said Province, and to make and ordain such acts, and laws, as shall be requisite and necessary for the good government and prosperity of the free people of the said Province; and (if necessity shall require) the Governor for the time being, with the consent of his Council, may and shall issue out writts to convene the Assembly sooner, to consider and answer the necessities of the people of the said Province.

II. That the Governor of the Province aforesaid, his heirs or successors for the time being, shall not suspend or defer the signing, sealing and confirming of such acts and laws as the General Assembly (from time to time to be elected by the free people of the Province aforesaid) shall make or act for the securing of the liberties and properties of the said free people of the Province aforesaid.

III. That it shall not be lawful for the Governor of the said Province, his heirs or successors for the time being, and Council, or any of them, at any time or times hereafter, to make or raise war upon any accounts or pretence whatsoever, or to raise any military forces within the Province aforesaid, without the consent of the General Free Assembly for the time being.

IV. That it shall not be lawful for the Governor of the said Province, his heirs or successors for the time being, and Council, or any of them, at any time or times hereafter, to make or enact any law or laws for the said Province, without the consent, act and concurrence of the General Assembly; and if the Governor for the time being, his heirs or successors and Council, or any of them, shall attempt to make or enact any such law or laws of him or themselves without the consent, act and concurrence of the General Assembly; that from thenceforth, he, they, or so many of them as shall be guilty thereof, shall, upon legal conviction, be deemed and taken for enemies to the free people of the said Province; and such act so attempted to be made, to be of no force.

V. That the General Free Assembly from time to time to be chosen as aforesaid, as the representatives of the people, shall not be prorogued or dissolved (before the expirance of one whole year, to commence from the day of their election) without their own free consent.

VI. That it shall not be lawful for the Governor of the said Province, his heirs or successors for the time being, and Council, or any of them, to levy or raise any sum or sums of money, or any other tax whatsoever, without the act, consent and concurrence of the General Assembly.

VII. That all officers of State, or trust, relating to the said Province, shall be nominated and elected by the General Free Assembly for the time being, or by their appointment; which officer and officers shall be accountable to the General Free Assembly, or to such as the said Assembly shall appoint.

VIII. That the Governor of the Province aforesaid, his heirs, or successor for the time being, or any of them, shall not send ambassadors, or make treaties, or enter into an alliance upon the publick account of the said Province, without the consent of the said General Free Assembly.

IX. That no General Free Assembly hereafter to be chosen by the free people of the Province aforesaid, shall give to the Governor of the said Province for the time being, his heirs or successors, any tax, or custom for a longer time than for one whole year.

X. That liberty of conscience in matters of faith and worship towards God, shall be granted to all people within the Province aforesaid; who shall live peaceably and quietly therein; and that none of the free people of the said Province shall be rendered uncapable of office in respect of their faith and worship.

Upon the Governors acceptance and performance of the proposals herein before expressed, we the General Free Assembly Proprietors and freeholders of the Province of West New Jersey aforesaid, do accept and receive Samuel Jenings as Deputy Governor.

In testimony whereof I have hereunto put my hand and seal, the day and year above written.

SAMUEL JENNINGS,
Deputy Governor.

Thomas Ollive, Speaker, to the General Free Assembly per order and in the name of the whole Assembly.

The fundamentals aforesaid being signed and sealed by the Deputy Governor, were ordered and appointed by the said Deputy Governor, and General Free Assembly, to be recorded the day and year first aforesaid, by me Thomas Revell, clerk to the General Assembly.

The text is reproduced as found in Thorpe, *Federal and State Constitutions,* 2565–67.

58

Concessions to the Province of Pennsylvania

1681

illiam Penn sought to create a refuge in America for Quakers and other dissenting religious minorities. Regardless of his intent, he, like all colonial founders, had to induce enough people to migrate for the colony to be viable. As documents 58–61 show, Penn was of a generous bent of mind and did not hesitate to provide the strongest inducements possible—political, religious, and those of economic liberty. The document below lays out the original inducements, which are largely of an economic nature. In return Penn extracts his own concessions—free, fair, and orderly economic behavior plus equitable treatment of the Indians. His plan worked. Pennsylvania grew more rapidly than any other colony and in less than a century, even though starting three-quarters of a century after Virginia, surpassed Virginia and Massachusetts in population (not counting slaves). On the eve of the Revolution Philadelphia was the largest city in the colonies, with approximately 40,000 inhabitants versus runners-up New York City (25,000) and Boston (16,000).

Certain conditions, or concessions, agreed upon by William Penn, Proprietary and Governor of the province of Pennsylvania, and those who are the adventurers and purchasers in the same province, the eleventh of July, one thousand six hundred and eighty-one.

FIRST

That as soon as it pleaseth God that the abovesaid persons arrive there, a certain quantity of land, or ground plat, shall be laid out, for a large town or city, in the most convenient place, upon the river, for health and navigation; and every purchaser and adventurer shall, by lot, have so much land therein as will answer to the proportion, which he hath bought, or taken up, upon rent: but it is to be noted, that the surveyors shall consider what roads or high-ways will be necessary to the cities, towns, or through the lands. Great roads from city to city not to contain less than forty foot, in breadth, shall be first laid out and declared to be for high-ways, before the dividend of acres be laid out for the purchaser, and the like observation to be had for the streets in the towns and cities, that there may be convenient roads and streets preserved, not to be encroached upon by any planter or builder, that none may build irregularly to the damage of another. In this, custom governs.

II. That the land in the town be laid out together after the proportion of ten thousand acres of the whole country, that is, two hundred acres, if the place will bear it: however, that the proportion be by lot, and entire, so as those that desire to be together, especially those that are, by the catalogue, laid together may be so laid together both in the town and country.

III. That, when the country lots are laid out, every purchaser, from one thousand, to ten thousand acres, or more, not to have above one thousand acres together, unless in three years they plant a family upon every thousand acres; but that all such as purchase together, lie together; and, if as many as comply with this condition, that the whole be laid out together.

IV. That, where any number of purchasers, more or less, whose number of acres amounts to five or ten thousand acres, desire to sit together in a lot, or township, they shall have their lot, or township, cast together, in such places as have convenient harbours, or navigable rivers attending it, if such can be found; and in case any one or more purchasers plant not according to agreement, in this concession, to the prejudice of others of the same township, upon complaint thereof made to the Governor, or his Deputy, with assistance, they may award (if they see cause) that the complaining purchaser may, paying the survey money, and purchase money, and interest thereof, be entitled, enrolled and lawfully invested, in the lands so not seated.

V. That the proportion of lands, that shall be laid out in the first great town, or city, for every purchaser, shall be after the proportion of ten acres for every five hundred acres purchased, if the place will allow it.

VI. That nowithstanding there be no mention made, in the several deeds made to the purchasers; yet the said William Penn does accord and declare, that all rivers, rivulets, woods, and underwoods, waters, watercourses, quarries, mines, and minerals, (except mines royal) shall be freely and fully enjoyed, and wholly by the purchasers, into whose lot they fall.

VII. That, for every fifty acres, that shall be allotted to a servant, at the end of his service, his quit-rent shall be two shillings per annum, and the master, or owner of the servant, when he shall take up the other fifty acres, his quit-rent, shall be four shillings by the year, or, if the master of the servant (by reason of the indentures he is so obliged to do) allot out to the servant fifty acres in his own division, the said master shall have, on demand, allotted him, from the governor, the one hundred acres, at the chief rent of six shillings per annum.

VIII. And, for the encouragement of such as are ingenious and willing to search out gold and silver mines in this province, it is hereby agreed, that they have liberty to bore and dig in any man's property, fully paying the damages done; and in case a discovery should be made, that the discoverer have one-fifth, the owner of the soil (if not the discoverer) a tenth part, the Governor two-fifths, and the rest to the public treasury, saving to the king the share reserved by patent.

IX. In every hundred thousand acres, the Governor and Proprietary, by lot, reserveth ten to himself, what shall lie but in one place.

X. That every man shall be bound to plant, or man, so much of his share of land as shall be set out and surveyed, within three years after it is so set out and surveyed, or else it shall be lawfull for new comers to be settled thereupon, paying to them their survey money, and they go up higher for their shares.

XI. There shall be no buying and selling, be it with an Indian, or one among another, of any goods to be exported, but what shall be performed in public market, when such places shall be set apart, or erected, where they shall pass the public stamp, or mark. If bad ware, and prized as good, or deceitful in proportion or weight, to forfeit the value, as if good and full weight and proportion, to the public treasury of this province, whether it be the merchandize of the Indian, or that of the planters.

XII. And forasmuch, as it is usual with the planters to over-reach the poor natives of the country, in trade, by goods not being good of the kind, or debased with mixtures, with which they are sensibly aggrieved, it is agreed, whatever is sold to the Indians, in consideration of their furs, shall be sold in the market place, and there suffer the test, whether good or bad; if good, to pass; if not good, not to be sold for good, that the natives may not be abused, nor provoked.

XIII. That no man shall, by any ways or means, in word, or deed, affront, or wrong any Indian, but he shall incur the same penalty of the law, as if he had committed it against his fellow planter, and if any Indian shall abuse, in word, or deed, any planter of this province, that he shall not be his own judge upon the Indian, but he shall make his complaint to the governor of the province, or his lieutenant, or deputy, or some inferior magistrate near him, who shall, to the utmost of his power, take care with the king of the said Indian, that all reasonable satisfaction be made to the said injured planter.

XIV. That all differences, between the planters and the natives, shall also be ended by twelve men, that is, by six planters and six natives; that so we may live friendly together as much as in us lieth, preventing all occasions of heart-burnings and mischief.

XV. That the Indians shall have liberty to do all things relating to improvement of their ground, and providing sustenance for their families that any of the planters shall enjoy.

XVI. That the laws, as to slanders, drunkenness, swearing, cursing, pride in apparel, trespasses, distriesses, replevins, weights, and measures, shall be the same as in England, till altered by law in this province.

XVII. That all shall mark their hogs, sheep and other cattle, and what are not marked within three months after it is in their possession, be it young or old, it shall be forfeited to the governor, that so people may be compelled to avoid the occasions of much strife between the planters.

XVIII. That, in clearing ground, care be taken to leave one acre of trees for every five acres cleared, especially to preserve oak and mulberries, for silk and shipping.

XIX. That all ship-masters shall give an account of their countries, names, ships, owners, freights and passengers, to an officer to be appointed for that purpose, which shall be registered within two days after their arrival, and if they shall refuse so to do, that then none presume to trade with them, upon forfeiture thereof; and that such masters be looked upon as having an evil intention to the province.

XX. That no person leave the province, without publication being made thereof, in the market place, three weeks before, and a certificate from some justice of the peace, of his clearness with his neighbours and those he dealt withal, so far as such an assurance can be attained and given: and if any master of a ship shall, contrary hereunto, receive and carry away any person, that hath not given that public notice, the said master shall be liable to all debts owing by the said person so secretly transported from the province.

Lastly, That these are to be added to, or corrected, by and with the consent of the parties hereunto subscribed.

WILLIAM PENN.

Sealed and delivered in the presence of—

WILLIAM BOELHAM,

HARBERT SPRINGET,

THOMAS PRUDYARD.

Sealed and delivered in the presence of all of the proprietors, who have hereunto subscribed, except Thomas Farrinborrough and John Goodson, in presence of—

HUGH CHAMBERLEN,	WILLIAM POWEL,
R. MURRAY,	RICHARD DAVIE,
HARBERT SPRINGET,	GRIFFITH JONES,
HUMPHREY SOUTH,	HUGH LAMBE,
THOMAS BARKER,	THOMAS FARRINBORROUGH,
SAMUEL JOBSON,	JOHN GOODSON.
JOHN JOSEPH MOORE,	

Text is taken from *Votes and Proceedings of the House of Representatives of the Province of Pennsylvania, 1682–1776,* vol. I (Philadelphia: B. Franklin and D. Hall, printers, 1752), xxiv–xxvi.

59

Charter of Liberties and
Frame of Government of the
Province of Pennsylvania in America

May 5, 1682

*I*t is an understatement to term the following document impres-
sive. *The preface clearly and efficiently lays out its underlying
theory, which blends biblical principles with contemporary political
theory. Although it is his colony, Penn establishes the principle of popular sovereignty. Innovations abound, including term limits and separation of powers. The large upper house of the bicameral legislature,
the Provincial Council, has staggered three-year terms so that one-
third of its members are elected each year. The Council sits continuously. Aside from representing the people rather than states, the
Charter of Liberties is the most direct precursor to the U.S. Senate in
its institutional characteristics. The Council had four standing committees at a time when specialized, standing committees did not exist
anywhere else in the colonies or in the British Parliament. The General Assembly, initially consisting of all the freemen (the town meeting writ large), started with as many as two hundred members and
could grow to five hundred as the population grew. Article xxxix created the first formal amendment process in history. Before composing
his bill of rights, Penn consulted the Massachusetts, New York, and
Virginia constitutions. He synthesized these lists and highlighted religious freedom for anyone who believed in a deity. With these constitutional roots and the principle of free economic development
outlined in the previous document [58], Pennsylvania developed into
a prosperous, highly diverse constitutional democracy.*

The frame of the government of the province of Pensilvania, in America: together with certain laws agreed upon in England, by the Governor and divers freemen of the aforesaid province. To be further explained and confirmed there, by the first provincial Council that shall be held, if they see meet.

THE PREFACE

When the great and wise God had made the world, of all his creatures, it pleased him to chuse man his Deputy to rule it: and to fit him for so great a charge and trust, he did not only qualify him with skill and power, but with integrity to use them justly. This native goodness was equally his honour and his happiness; and whilst he stood here, all went well; there was no need of coercive or compulsive means; the precept of divine love and truth, in his bosom, was the guide and keeper of his innocency. But lust prevailing against duty, made a lamentable breach upon it; and the law, that before had no power over him, took place upon him, and his disobedient posterity, that such as would not live comfortable to the holy law within, should fall under the reproof and correction of the just law without, in a judicial administration.

This the Apostle teaches in divers of his epistles: "The law (says he) was added because of transgression," In another place, "Knowing that the law was not made for the righteous man, but for the disobedient and ungodly, for sinners, for unholy and prophane, for murderers, for whoremongers, for them that defile themselves with mankind, and for man-stealers, for lyers, for perjured persons," &c., but this is not all, he opens and carries the matter of government a little further: "Let every soul be subject to the higher powers; for there is no power but of God. The powers that be are ordained of God: whosoever therefore resisteth the power, resisteth the ordinance of God. For rulers are not a terror to good works, but to evil: wilt thou then not be afraid of the power? do that which is good, and thou shalt have praise of the same." "He is the minister of God to thee for good." "Wherefore ye must needs be subject, not only for wrath, but for conscience sake."

This settles the divine right of government beyond exception, and that for two ends: first, to terrify evil doers: secondly, to cherish those that do well; which gives government a life beyond corruption, and makes it as durable in the world, as good men shall be. So that government seems to me a part of religion itself, a thing sacred in its institution and end. For, if it does not directly remove the cause, it crushes the effects of evil, and is as such, (though a lower, yet) an emanation of the same Divine Power, that is both author and object of pure religion; the difference lying here, that the one is more free and mental, the other more corporal and compulsive in its operations: but that is only to evil doers; government itself being otherwise as capable of kindness, goodness and charity, as a more private society. They weakly err, that think there is no other use of government, than correction, which is the coarsest part of it: daily experience tells us, that the care and regulation of many other affairs, more soft, and daily necessary, makeup much of the greatest part of government; and which must have followed the peopling of the world, had Adam never fell, and will continue among men, on earth, under the highest attainments they may arrive at, by the coming of the blessed *Second Adam*, the Lord from heaven. Thus much of government in general, as to its rise and end.

For particualar frames and models it will become me to say little; and comparatively I will say nothing. My reasons are:

First. That the age is too nice and difficult for it; there being nothing the wits of men are more busy and divided upon. It is true, they seem to agree to the end, to wit, happiness; but, in the means, they differ, as to divine, so to this human felicity; and the cause is much the same, not always want of light and knowledge, but want of using them rightly. Men side with their passions against their reason, and their sinister interests have so strong a bias upon their minds, that they lean to them gainst the good of the things they know.

Secondly. I do not find a model in the world, that time, place, and some singular emergences have not necessarily altered; nor is it easy to frame a civil government, that shall serve all places alike.

Thirdly. I know what is said by the several admirers of *monarchy, aristocracy* and *democracy*, which are the rule of one, a few, and many, and are the three common ideas of government, when men discourse on the subject. But I chuse to solve the controversy with this small distinction, and it belongs to all three: *Any government is free to the people under it* (whatever be the frame) *where the laws rule, and the people are a party to those laws,* and more than this is tyranny, oligarchy, or confusion.

But, lastly, when all is said, there is hardly one frame of government in the world so ill designed by its first founders, that, in good hands, would not do well enough; and [hi]story tells us, the best, in ill ones, can do nothing that is great or good; witness the said states. Governments, like clocks, go from the motion men give them; and as governments are made and moved by men, so by them they are ruined too. Wherefore governments rather depend upon men, than men upon governments. Let men be good, and the government cannot be bad; if it be ill, they will cure it. But, if men be bad, let the government be never so good, they will endeavor to warp and spoil it to their turn.

I know some say, let us have good laws, and no matter for the men that execute them: but let them consider, that though good laws do well, good men do better: for good laws may want good men, and be abolished or evaded[1] by ill men; but good men will never want good laws, nor suffer ill ones. It is true, good laws have some awe upon ill ministers, but that is where they have not power to escape or abolish them, and the people are generally wise and good: but a loose and depraved people (which is the question) love laws and an administration like themselves. That, therefore, which makes a good constitution, must keep it, viz: men of wisdom and virtue, qualities, that because they descend not with worldly inheritances, must be carefully propagated by a virtuous education of youth; for which after ages will owe more to the care and prudence of founders, and the successive magistracy, than to their parents, for their private patrimonies.

These considerations of the weight of government, and the nice and various opinions about it, made it uneasy to me to think of publishing the ensuing frame and conditional laws, foreseeing both the censures, they will meet with, from men of differing humours and engagements, and the occasion they may give of discourse beyond my design.

But, next to the power of necessity, (which is a solicitor, that will take no denial) this induced me to a compliance, that we have (with reverence to God, and good conscience to men) to the best of our skill, contrived and composed the frame and laws of this government, to the great end of all government, viz: *To support power in reverence with the people, and to secure the people from the abuse of power,* that they may be free by their just obedience, and the magistrates honourable, for their just adminstration: for liberty, without obedience is confusion, and obedience without liberty is slavery. To carry this evenness is partly owing to the constitution, and partly to the

1. Invaded in Franklin's print.

magistracy: where either of these fail, government will be subject to convulsions; but where both are wanting, it must be totally subverted; then where both meet, the government is like to endure.

Which I humbly pray and hope *God* will please to make the lot of this Pensilvania. Amen.

WILLAM PENN.

THE FRAME, &C—APRIL 25, 1682

To all Persons, to whom these presents may come. WHEREAS king Charles the Second, by his letters patents, under the great seal of England bearing date the fourth day of March in the Thirty and Third Year of the King, for divers consideration therein mentioned, hath been graciously pleased to give and grant unto me William Penn, by the name of William Penn, Esquire, son and heir of Sir William Penn, deceased, and to my heirs and assigns forever, all that tract of land, or Province called Pennsylvania, in America, with divers great powers, preheminences, royalties, jurisdictions, and authorities, necessary for the well-being and government thereof: Now know ye, that for the well-being and government of the said province, and for the encouragement of all the freemen and planters that may be therein concerned, in pursuance of the powers aforementioned, I, the said William Penn have declared, granted, and confirmed, and by these presents, for me, my heirs and assigns, do declare, grant, and confirm unto all the freemen, planters and adventurers of, in and to the said province, these liberties, franchise, and properties, to be held, enjoyed and kept by the freemen, planters, and inhabitants of the said province of Pennsylvania for ever.

Imprimis. That the government of this province shall, according to the powers of the patent, consist of the Governor and freemen of the said province, in form of a provincial Council and General Assembly, by whom all laws shall be made, officers chosen, and public affairs transacted, as is hereafter respectively declared, that is to say—

II. That the freemen of the said province shall, on the twentieth day of the twelfth month, which shall be in the present year one thousand six hundred eighty and two, meet and assemble in some fit place, of which timely notice shall be before hand given by the Governor or his Deputy; and then, and there, shall chuse out of themselves seventy-two persons of most note for their wisdom, virtue and ability, who shall meet, on the tenth day of the first month next ensuing, and always be called, and act as, the provincial Council of the said province.

III. That, at the first choice of such provincial Council, one-third part of the said provincial Council shall be chosen to serve for three years, then next ensuing; one-third party, for two years then next ensuing; and one-third party, for one year then next ensuing each election, and no longer; and that the said third part shall go out accordingly; and on the twentieth day of the twelfth month, as aforesaid, yearly for ever afterwards, the freemen of the said province shall, in like manner, meet and assemble together, and then chuse twenty-four persons, being one-third of the said number, to serve in provincial Council for three years: it being intended, that one-third part of the whole provincial Council (always consisting, and to consist, of seventy-two persons, as aforesaid) falling off yearly, it shall be yearly supplied by such new yearly elections, as aforesaid; and that no one person shall continue therein longer than three years: and, in case any member shall decease before the last election during his time, that then at the next election ensuing his decease, another shall be chosen to supply his place, for the remaining time, he has to have served, and no longer.

IV. That, after the first seven years, every one of the said third parts, that goeth yearly off, shall be uncapable of being chosen again for one whole year following: that so all may be fitted for government and have experience of the care and burden of it.

V. That the provincial Council, in all cases and matters of moment, as their arguing upon bills to be passed into laws, erecting courts of justice, giving judgment upon criminals impeached, and choice of officers, in such manner as is hereinafter mentioned, not less than two-thirds of the whole provincial Council shall make a quorum and that the consent and approbation of two-thirds of such quorum shall be had in all such cases and matters of moment. And moreover that, in all cases and matters of lesser moment, twenty-four Members of the said provincial Council shall make a quorum the majority of which twenty-four shall, and may, always determine in such cases and causes of lesser moment.

VI. That, in this provincial Council, the Governor or his Deputy, shall or may, always preside, and have a treble voice; and the said provincial Council shall always continue, and sit upon its own adjournments and committees.

VII. That the Governor and provincial Council shall prepare and propose to the General Assembly, herafter mentioned, all bills, which they shall, at any time, think fit to be passed into laws, within the said province; which bills shall be published and affixed to the most noted places, in the inhabited parts thereof, thirty days before the meeting of the General Assembly, in order to the passing them into laws or rejecting of them, as the General Assembly shall see meet.

VIII. That the Governor and provincial Council shall take care, that all laws, statutes and ordinances, which shall at any time be made within the said province, be duly and diligently executed.

IX. That the Governor and provincial Council shall, at all times, have the care of the peace and safety of the province, and that nothing be by any person attempted to the subversion of this frame of government.

X. That the Governor and provincial Council shall, at all times, settle and order the situation of all cities, ports, and market towns in every county, modelling therein all public buildings, streets, and market places, and shall appoint all necessary roads, and high-ways in the province.

XI. That the Governor and provincial Councill shall, at all times, have power to inspect the management of the public treasury, and punish those who shall convert any part thereof to any other use, than what hath been agreed upon by the Governor, provincial Council, and General Assembly.

XII. That the Governor and provincial Council, shall erect and order all public schools, and encourage and reward the authors of useful sciences and laudable inventions in the said province.

XIII. That, for the better management of the power and trust aforesaid, the provincial Council shall, from time to time, divide itself into four distinct and proper committees, for the more easy administration of the affairs of the Province, which divides the seventy-two into four eighteens, every one of which eighteens shall consist of six out of each of the three orders, or yearly elections, each of which shall have a distinct portion of business, as followeth: *First*, a committee of plantations, to situate and settle cities, ports, and market towns, and high-ways, and to hear and decide all suits and controversies relating to plantations. *Secondly*, a committee of justice and safety, to secure the peace of the Province, and punish the mal-administration of those who subvert justice to the prejudice of the public, or private, interest. *Thirdly*, a committee of trade and treasury, who shall regulate all trade and commerce, according to law, encourage manufacture and country growth, and defray the public charge of the Province. And, *Fourthly*, a committee of manners, education, and arts, that all wicked and scandalous living may be prevented, and that youth may be successively trained up in virtue and useful knowledge and arts: the *quorum* of each of which committees being six, that is, two out of each of the three orders, or yearly elections, as aforesaid, make a constant and standing Council of *twenty-four* which will have the power of the provincial Council, being the quorum of it, in all cases not excepted in the fifth article; and in the said committees, and standing Council of the Province, the Governor, or his Deputy, shall, or may preside, as aforesaid; and in the absence of the Governor, or his Deputy, if no one is by either of them appointed, the said committees or Council shall appoint a President for that time, and not otherwise; and what shall be resolved at such committees, shall be reported to the said Council of the province, and shall be by them resolved and confirmed before the same shall be put in execution; and that these respective committees shall not sit at one and the same time, except in cases of necessity.

XIV. And, to the end that all laws prepared by the Governor and provincial Council aforesaid, may yet have the more full concurrence of the freemen of the province, it is declared, granted and confirmed, that, at the time and place or places, for the choices of a provincial council, as aforesaid, the said freemen shall yearly chuse Members to serve in a General Assembly, as their representatives, not exceeding two hundred persons, who shall yearly meet on the twentieth day of the second month, which shall be in the year one thousand six hundred eighty and three following, in the capital town, or city, of the said province, where, during eight days, the several Members may freely confer with one another; and, if any of them see meet, with a committee of the provincial Council (consisting of three out of each of the four committees aforesaid, being twelve in all) which shall be, at that time, purposely appointed to receive from any of them proposals, for the alterations or amendment of any of the said proposed and promulgated bills: and on the ninth day from their so meeting, the said General Assembly, after reading over the proposed bills by the Clerk of the provincial Council, and the occasions and motives for them being opened by the Governor or his Deputy, shall give their affirmative or negative, which to them seemeth best, in such manner as hereinafter is expressed. But not less than two-thirds shall make a *quorum* in the passing of laws, and choice of such officers as are by them to be chosen.

XV. That the laws so prepared and proposed, as aforesaid, that are assented to by the General Assembly, shall be enrolled as laws of the Province, with this stile: *By the Governor, with the assent and approbation of the freemen in provincial Council and General Assembly.*

XVI. That, for the establishment of the government and laws of this province, and to the end there may be an universal satisfaction in the laying of the fundamentals thereof: the General Assembly shall, or may, for the first year, consist of all the freemen of and in the said province; and ever after it shall be yearly chosen, as aforesaid; which number of two hundred shall be enlarged as the country shall increase in people, so as it do not exceed five hundred, at any time; the appointment and proportioning of which, as also the laying and methodizing of the choice of the provincial Council and General Assembly, in future times most equally to the divisions of the hundreds and counties, which the country shall hereafter be divided into, shall be in the power of the provincial Council to propose, and the General Assembly to resolve.

XVII. That the Governor and the provincial Council shall erect, from time to time, standing courts of justice, in such places and number as they shall judge convenient for the good government of the said province. And that the provincial Council shall, on the thirteenth day of the first month, yearly, elect and present to the Governor, or his Deputy, a double number of persons, to serve for Judges, Treasurers, Masters of Rolls, within the said province, for the year next ensuing; and the freemen of the said province, in the county courts, when they shall be erected, and till then, in the General Assembly, shall, on the three and twentieth day of the second month, yearly, elect and present to the Governor, or his Deputy, a double number of persons, to serve for Sheriffs, Justices of the Peace, and Coroners, for the year next ensuing; out of which respective elections and presentments, the Governor or his Deputy shall nominate and commissionate the proper number for each office, the third day after the said presentments, or else the first named in such presentment, for each office, shall stand and serve for that office the year ensuing.

XVIII. But forasmuch as the present condition of the province requires some immediate settlement, and admits not of so quick a revolution of officers; and to the end the said Province may, with all convenient speed, be well ordered and settled, I, William Penn, do therefore think fit to nominate and appoint such persons for Judges, Treasurers, Masters of the Rolls, Sheriffs, Justices of the Peace, and Coroners, as are most fitly qualified for those employments; to whom I shall make and grant commissions for the said offices, respectively, to hold to them, to whom the same shall be granted, for so long time as every such person shall well behave himself in the office, or place, to him respectively granted, and no longer. And upon the decease or displacing of any of the said officers, the succeeding officer, or officers, shall be chosen, as aforesaid.

XIX. That the General Assembly shall continue so long as may be needful to impeach criminals, fit to be there impeached, to pass bills into laws, that they shall think fit to pass into laws, and till such time as the Governor and provincial Council shall declare that they have nothing further to propose unto them, for their assent and approbation: and that declaration shall be a dismiss to the General Assembly for that time; which General Assembly shall be, notwithstanding, capable of assembling together into laws, and till such time as the Governor and provincial Council shall declare that they have nothing further to propose unto them, for their assent and approbation: and that declaration shall be a dismiss to the General Assembly for that time; which General Assembly shall be, notwithstanding, capable of assembling together upon the summons of the provincial Council, at any time during that year, if the said provincial Council shall see occasion for their so assembling.

XX. That all the elections of members, or representatives of the people, to serve in provincial Council and General Assembly, and all questions to be determined by both, or either of them, that relate to passing of bills into laws, to the choice of officers, to impeachments by the General Assembly, and judgment of criminals upon such impeachments by the provincial Council, and to all other cases by them respectively judged of importance, shall be resolved and determined by the ballot, and unless on sudden and indispensible occasions, no business in provincial Council, or its respective committees, shall be finally determined the same day that it is moved.

XXI. That at all times when, and so often as it shall happen that the Governor shall or may be an infant, under the age of one and twenty years, and no guardians or commissioners are appointed in writing, by the father of the said infant, or that such guardians or commissioners shall be deceased; that during such minority, the provincial Council shall, from time to time, as they shall see meet, constitute and appoint guardians or commissioners, not exceeding three, one of which three shall preside as deputy and chief guardian, during such minority, and shall have and execute, with the consent of the other two, all the power of a Governor, in all the public affairs and concerns of the said province.

XXII. That, as often as any day of the month, mentioned in any article of this charter, shall fall upon the first day of the week, commonly called the Lord's Day, the business appointed for that day shall be deferred till the next day, unless in case of emergency.

XXIII. That no act, law, or ordinance whatsoever, shall at any time hereafter, be made or done by the Governor of this province, his heirs or assigns, or by the freemen in the provincial Council, or the General Assembly, to alter, change, or diminish the form, or effect, of this charter, or any part, or clause thereof, without the consent of the Governor, his heirs, or assigns, and six parts of seven of the said freemen in provincial Council and General Assembly.

XXIV. And lastly, that I, the said for myself, my heirs and assigns, have solemnly declared, granted and confirmed, and do hereby solemnly declare, grant and confirm, that neither I, my heirs, nor assigns, shall procure to do any thing or things, whereby the liberties, in this charter contained and expressed, shall be infringed or broken; and if any thing be procured by any person or persons contrary to these premises, it shall be held of no force or effect. In witness whereof, I, the said William Penn, have unto this present character of liberties set my hand and broad seal, this five and twentieth day of the second month, vulgarly called April, in the year of our Lord one thousand six hundred and eighty-two.

WILLIAM PENN.

LAWS AGREED UPON IN ENGLAND, &C.

I. That the charter of liberties, declared, granted and confirmed the five and twentieth day of the second month, called April, 1682, before divers witnesses, by William Penn, Governor and chief Proprietor of Pennsylvania, to all the freemen and planters of the said province, is hereby declared and approved, and shall be for ever held for fundamental in the government thereof, according to the limitations mentioned in the said charter.

II. That every inhabitant in the said province, that is or shall be, a purchaser of one hundred acres of land, or upwards, his heirs and assigns, and every persons who shall have paid his passage, and taken up one hundred acres of land, at one penny an acre, and have cultivated ten acres threof, and every person, that hath been a servant, or bondsman, and is free by his service, that shall have taken up his fifty acres of land, and cultivated twenty thereof, and every inhabitant, artificer, or other resident in the said province, that pays scot and lot to the government; shall be deemed and accounted a freeman of the said province: and every such person shall, and may, be capable of electing, or being elected, representatives of the people, in provincial Council, or General Assembly, in the said province.

III. That all elections of members, or representatives of the people and freemen of the province of Pennsylvania, to serve in provincial Council, or General Assembly, to be held within the said province, shall be free and voluntary: and that the elector, that shall receive any reward or gift, in meat, drink, monies, or otherwise, shall forfeit his right to elect: and such person as shall directly or indirectly give, promise, or bestow any such reward as aforesaid, to be elected, shall forfeit his election, and be thereby incapable to serve as aforesaid: and the provincial Council and General Assembly shall be the sole judges of the regularity, or irregularity of the elections of their own respective Members.

IV. That no money or goods shall be raised upon, or paid by, any of the people of this province by way of public tax, custom or contribution, but by a law, for that purpose made; and whoever shall levy, collect, or pay any money or goods contrary thereunto, shall be held a public enemy to the province and a betrayer of the liberties of the people thereof.

V. That all courts shall be open, and justice shall neither be sold, denied or delayed.

VI. That, in all courts all persons of all persuasions may freely appear in their own way, and acording to their own manner, and there personally plead their own cause themselves; or, if unable, by their friends: and the first process shall be the exhibition of the complaint in court, fourteen days before the trial; and that the party, complained against, may be fitted for the same, he or she shall be summoned, no less than ten days before, and a copy of the complaint delivered him or her, at his or her dwelling house. But before the complaint of any person be received, he shall solemnly declare in court that he believes, in his conscience, his cause is just.

VII. That all pleadings, processes and records in courts, shall be short, and in English, and in an ordinary and plain character, that they may be understood, and justice speedily administered.

VIII. That all trials shall be by twelve men, and as near as may be, peers or equals, and of the neighborhood, and men without just exception; in cases of life, there shall be first twenty-four returned by the sheriffs, for a grand inquest, of whom twelve, at least, shall find the complaint to be true; and then the twelve men, or peers, to be likewise returned by the sheriff, shall have the final judgment. But reasonable challenges shall be always admitted against the said twelve men, or any of them.

IX. That all fees in all cases shall be moderate, and settled by the provincial Council, and General Assembly, and be hung up in a table in every respective court; and whosoever, shall be convicted of taking more, shall pay twofold, and be dismissed his employment; one moiety of which shall go to the party wronged.

X. That all prisons shall be work-houses, for felons, vagrants, and loose and idle persons; whereof one shall be in every county.

XI. That all prisoners shall be bailable by sufficient sureties, unless for capital offences, where the proof is evident, or the presumption great.

XII. That all persons wrongfully imprisoned, or prosecuted at law, shall have double damages against the informer, or prosecutor.

XIII. That all prisons shall be free, as to fees, food, and lodging.

XIV. That all lands and goods shall be liable to pay debts, except where there is legal issue, and then all the goods, and one-third of the land only.

XV. That all wills, in writing, attested by two witnesses, shall be of the same force as to lands, as other conveyances, being legally proved within forty days, either within or without the said province.

XVI. That seven years quiet possession shall give an unquestionable right, except in cases of infants, lunatics, married women, or persons beyond the seas.

XVII. That all briberies and extortion whatsoever shall be severely punished.

XVIII. That all fines shall be moderate, and saving men's contenements, merchandize, or wainage.

XIX. That all marriages (not forbidden by the law of God, as to nearness of blood and affinity by marriage) shall be encouraged; but the parents, or guardians, shall be first consulted, and the marriage shall be published before it be solemnized; and it shall be solemnized by taking one another as husband and wife, before credible witnesses; and a certificate of the whole, under the hands of parties and witnesses, shall be brought to the proper register of that county, and shall be registered in his office.

XX. And, to prevent frauds and vexatious suits within the said province, that all charters, gifts, grants, and conveyances (except leases for a year or under) and all bills, bonds, and specialties above five pounds, and not under three months, made in the said province, shall be enrolled, or registered in the public enrolment office of the said province, within the space of two months next after the making thereof, else to be void in law, and all deeds, grants, and conveyances of land (except as aforesaid) within the said province, and made out of the said province, shall be enrolled or registered, as aforesaid, within six months next after the making thereof, and settling and constituting an enrolment office or registry within the said province, else to be void in law against all persons whatsoever.

xxi. That all defacers or corrupters of charters, gifts, grants, bonds, bills, wills, contracts, and conveyances, or that shall deface or falsify any enrolment, registry or record, within this province, shall make double satisfaction for the same; half whereof shall go to the party wronged, and they shall be dismissed of all places of trust, and be publicly disgraced as false men.

xxii. That there shall be a register for births, marriages, burials, wills, and letters of administration, distinct from the other registry.

xxiii. That there shall be a register for all servants, where their names, time, wages, and days of payment shall be registered.

xxiv. That all lands and goods of felons shall be liable, to make satisfaction to the party wronged twice the value; and for want of lands or goods, the felons shall be bondmen to work in the common prison, or work-house, or otherwise, till the party injured be satisfied.

xxv. That the estates of capital offenders, as traitors and murderers, shall go, one-third to the next of kin to the sufferer, and the remainder to the next of kin to the criminal.

xxvi. That all witnesses, coming, or called, to testify their knowledge in or to any matter or thing, in any court, or before any lawful authority, within the said province, shall there give or delivery in their evidence, or testimony, by solemnly promising to speak the truth, the whole truth, and nothing but the truth, to the matter, or thing in question. And in case any person so called to evidence, shall be convicted of wilful falsehood, such person shall suffer and undergo such damage or penalty, as the person, or persons, against whom he or she bore false witness, did, or should, undergo; and shall also make satisfaction to the party wronged, and be publicly exposed as a false witness, never to be credited in any court, or before any Magistrate, in the said province.

xxvii. And, to the end that all officers chosen to serve within this province, may, with more care and dilligence, answer the trust reposed in them, it is agreed, that no such person shall enjoy more than one public office, at one time.

xxviii. That all children, within this province, of the age of twelve years, shall be taught some useful trade or skill, to the end none may be idle, but the poor may work to live, and the rich, if they become poor may not want.

xxix. That servants be not kept longer than their time, and such as are careful, be both justly and kindly used in their service, and put in fitting equipage at the expiration thereof, according to custom.

xxx. That all scandalous and malicious reporters, backbiters, defamers and spreaders of false news, whether against Magistrates, or private persons, shall be accordingly severely punished, as enemies to the peace and concord of this province.

xxxi. That for the encouragement of the planters and traders in this province, who are incorporated into a society, the patent granted to them by William Penn, Governor of the said province, is hereby ratified and confirmed.

xxxii. * * *

xxxiii. That all factors or correspondents in the said province, wronging their employers, shall make satisfaction, and one-third over, to their said employers: and in case of the death of any such factor or correspondent, the committee of trade shall take care to secure so much of the deceased party's estate as belongs to his said respective employers.

xxxiv. That all Treasurers, Judges, Masters of the Rolls, Sheriffs, Justices of the Peace, and other officers and persons whatsoever, relating to courts, or trials of causes, or any other service in the government; and all Members elected to serve in provincial Council and General Assembly, and all that have right to elect such Members, shall be such as possess faith in Jesus Christ, and that are not convicted of ill fame, or unsober and dishonest conversation, and that are of one and twenty years of age, at least; and that all such so qualified, shall be capable of the said several employments and privileges, as aforesaid.

xxxv. That all persons living in this province, who confess and acknowledge the one Almighty and eternal God, to be the Creator, Upholder and Ruler of the world; and that hold themselves obliged in conscience to live peaceable and justly in civil society, shall, in no ways, be molested or prejudiced for their religious persuasion, or practice, in matters of faith and worship, nor shall they be compelled, at any time, to frequent or maintain any religious worship, place or ministry whatever.

xxxvi. That, according to the good example of the primitive Christians, and the case of the creation, every first day of the week, called the Lord's day, people shall abstain from their common daily labour, that they may better dispose themselves to worship God according to their understandings.

xxxvii. That as a careless and corrupt administration of justice draws the wrath of God upon magistrates, so the wildness and looseness of the people provoke the indignation of God against a country: therefore, that all such offences against God, as swearing, cursing, lying, prophane talking, drunkenness, drinking of healths, obscene words, incest, sodomy, rapes, whoredom, fornication, and other uncleanness (not to be repeated) all treasons, misprisions, murders, duels, felony, seditions, maims, forcible entries, and other violences, to the persons and estates of the inhabitants within this province; all prizes, stage-plays, cards, dice, May-games, gamesters, masques, revels, bull-baitings, cock-fightings, bear-baitings, and the like, which excite the people to rudeness, cruelty, looseness, and irreligion, shall be respectively discouraged, and severely punished, according to the appointment of the Governor and freemen in provincial Council and General Assembly; as also all proceedings contrary to these laws, that are not here made expressly penal.

xxxviii. That a copy of these laws shall be hung up in the provincial Council, and in public courts of justice: and that they shall be read yearly at the opening of every provincial Council and General Assembly, and court of justice; and their assent shall be testified, by their standing up after the reading thereof.

xxxix. That there shall be, at no time, any alteration of any of these laws, without the consent of the Governor, his heirs, or assigns, and six parts of seven of the freemen, met in provincial Council and General Assembly.

xl. That all other matters and things not herein provided for, which shall, and may, concern the public justice, peace, or safety of the said province; and the raising and imposing taxes, customs, duties, or other charges whatsoever, shall be, and are, hereby referred to the order, prudence and determination of the Governor and freemen, in Provincial Council and General Assembly, to be held, from time to time, in the said province.

Signed and sealed by the Governor and freemen aforesaid, the fifth day of the third month, called one thousand six hundred and eighty-two.

Taken from *Votes and Proceedings,* vol. i, xxvii–xxviii. The complete text retains the original spelling.

60

An Act for Freedom of Conscience

December 7, 1682

*W*illiam Penn was deeply committed to religious freedom, but his commitment was not absolute. Although anyone who professed a belief in God could live undisturbed, one had to believe in Jesus Christ in order to vote and hold office (see the Pennsylvania Frame of Government [59], Articles xxxiv and xxxv of the Laws Agreed Upon in England). Coupled with a belief in toleration was the belief that true liberty, political virtue, and civil justice rested on Christian principles. The following ordinance is an attempt to further explicate freedom of religion and its limits.

Wheras the glory of almighty God and the good of mankind is the reason and end of government and, therefore, government in itself is a venerable ordinance of God. And forasmuch as it is principally desired and intended by the Proprietary and Governor and the freemen of the province of Pennsylvania and territories thereunto belonging to make and establish such laws as shall best preserve true christian and civil liberty in opposition to all unchristian, licentious, and unjust practices, whereby God may have his due, Caesar his due, and the people their due, from tyranny and oppression on the one side and insolence and licentiousness on the other, so that the best and firmest foundation may be laid for the present and future happiness of both the Governor and people of the province and territories aforesaid and their posterity.

Be it, therefore, enacted by William Penn, Proprietary and Governor, by and with the advice and consent of the deputies of the freemen of this province and counties aforesaid in assembly met and by the authority of the same, that these following chapters and paragraphs shall be the laws of Pennsylvania and the territories thereof.

Chap. 1. Almighty God, being only Lord of conscience, father of lights and spirits, and the author as well as object of all divine knowledge, faith, and worship, who can only enlighten the mind and persuade and convince the understandings of people. In due reverence to his sovereignty over the souls of mankind;

Be it enacted, by the authority aforesaid, that no person now or at any time hereafter living in this province, who shall confess and acknowledge one almighty God to be the creator, upholder, and ruler of the world, and who professes him or herself obliged in conscience to live peaceably and quietly under the civil government, shall in any case be molested or prejudiced for his or her conscientious persuasion or practice. Nor shall he or she at any time be compelled to frequent or maintain any religious worship, place, or ministry whatever contrary to his or her mind, but shall freely and fully enjoy his, or her, christian liberty in that respect, without any interruption or reflection. And if any person shall abuse or deride any other for his or her different persuasion and practice in matters of religion, such person shall be looked upon as a disturber of the peace and be punished accordingly.

But to the end that looseness, irreligion, and atheism may not creep in under pretense of conscience in this province, be it further enacted, by the authority aforesaid, that, according to the example of the primitive Christians and for the ease of the creation, every first day of the week, called the Lord's day, people shall abstain from their usual and common toil and labor that, whether masters, parents, children, or servants, they may the better dispose themselves to read the scriptures of truth at home or frequent such meetings of religious worship abroad as may best suit their respective persuasions.

Chap. II. And be it further enacted by, etc., that all officers and persons commissioned and employed in the service of the government in this province and all members and deputies elected to serve in the Assembly thereof and all that have a right to elect such deputies shall be such as profess and declare they believe in Jesus Christ to be the son of God, the savior of the world, and that are not convicted of ill-fame or unsober and dishonest conversation and that are of twenty-one years of age at least.

Chap. III. And be it further enacted, etc., that whosoever shall swear in their common conversation by the name of God or Christ or Jesus, being legally convicted thereof, shall pay, for every such offense, five shillings or suffer five days imprisonment in the house of correction at hard labor to the behoof of the public and be fed with bread and water only during that time.

Chap. v. And be it further enacted, etc., for the better prevention of corrupt communication, that whosoever shall speak loosely and profanely of almighty God, Christ Jesus, the Holy Spirit, or the scriptures of truth, and is legally convicted thereof, shall pay, for every such offense, five shillings or suffer five days imprisonment in the house of correction at hard labor to the behoof of the public and be fed with bread and water only during that time,

Chap. vi. And be it further enacted, etc., that whosoever shall, in their conversation, at any time curse himself or any other and is legally convicted thereof shall pay for every such offense five shillings or suffer five days imprisonment as aforesaid.

Text is from J. T. Mitchell and Henry Flanders, eds., *Statutes at Large of Pennsylvania from 1682 to 1801,* vol. 1 (Harrisburg, 1896), 107–9. The sections are misnumbered in the original, so that there is no section iv.

61

[Pennsylvania Charter of Liberties]

1701

*T*he 1682 *Frame of Government [59], amplified by the Frame of 1683, was replaced by the 1696 Frame. The 1683 document is not reproduced in this collection because its changes were minor. The 1696 document is not reproduced because of its considerable length and essential redundancy with the 1682 document. The present document replaced the 1696 Frame and defined the Pennsylvania political system until 1776. One major difference vis à vis the 1682 Frame is the creation of a unicameral legislature. Eliminating the Council was part of the successful attempt by the freemen to eliminate the proprietor's legislative veto. The Pennsylvania Constitution of 1776 returned to two elected bodies, but the elected Council, instead of being an upper house, was part of the executive branch—effectively an elected privy council, which in this instance provided a means for the people to keep the executive branch under control. The document below is also notable for the care Penn takes in outlining its status with respect to earlier foundation documents in both England and America, thus establishing its pedigree and its legitimacy. Penn's concern for liberty of conscience is again underlined—it is the first substantive matter addressed, and the guarantee of religious liberty is repeated at length later in the document. As with earlier Pennsylvania foundation documents, the Charter of Liberties was formulated by Penn and then consented to by the people or their elected representatives. That Penn consulted carefully with the Assembly while formulating his constitutions made popular acceptance a foregone conclusion.*

Charter of Privileges Granted by William Penn, Esquire, to the Inhabitants of Pennsylvania and Territories October 28, 1701

William Penn, Proprietary and Governor of the province of Pennsylvania and territories thereunto belonging, to all to whom these presents shall come, sends greeting.

Whereas King Charles the Second, by his letters patents under the great seal of England, bearing date the fourth day of March in the year one thousand six hundred and eighty-one, was graciously pleased to give and grant unto me and my heirs and assigns, forever, this province of Pennsylvania, with diverse great powers and jurisdictions for the well government thereof.

And whereas the King's dearest brother, James Duke of York and Albany, etc., by his deeds of feoffment, under his hand and seal duly perfected, bearing date the twenty-fourth day of August, one thousand six hundred eighty and two, did grant unto me, my heirs and assigns, all that tract of land now called the territories of Pennsylvania, together with powers and jurisdictions for the good government thereof.

And whereas for the encouragement of all the freemen and planters that might be concerned in the said province and territories and for the good government thereof, I, the said William Penn, in the year one thousand six hundred eighty and three, for me, my heirs and assigns, did grant and confirm unto all the freemen, planters, and adventurers therein diverse liberties, franchises, and properties, as by the said grant, entitled, *The Frame of the Government of the Province of Pennsylvania, and Territories Thereunto Belonging, in America,* may appear; which charter or frame, being found in some parts of it not so suitable to the present circumstances of the inhabitants, was in the third month in the year one thousand seven hundred delivered up to me, by six parts of seven of the freemen of this province and territories in General Assembly met, provision being made in the said charter for that end and purpose.

And whereas I was then pleased to promise that I would restore the said charter to them again with necessary alterations, or, in lieu thereof, give them another better adapted to answer the present circumstances and conditions of the said inhabitants; which they have now, by their representatives in General Assembly met at Philadelphia, requested me to grant.

Know you, therefore, that for the further well-being and good government of the said province and territories, and in pursuance of the rights and powers before mentioned, I, the said Wiliam Penn, do declare, grant, and confirm unto all the freemen, planters, and adventurers, and other inhabitants of this province and territories, these following liberties, franchises, and privileges, so far as in me lies, to be held, enjoyed, and kept by the freemen, planters, and adventurers, and other inhabitants of and in the said province and territories thereunto annexed, forever.

First

Because no people can be truly happy, though under the greatest enjoyment of civil liberties, if abridged of the freedom of their consciences as to their religious profession and worship. And Almighty God being the only lord of conscience, father of light and spirits, and the author as well as object of all divine knowledge, faith, and worship, who only does enlighten the minds and persuade and convince the understandings of people, I do hereby grant and declare that no person or persons inhabiting in this province or territories, who shall confess and acknowledge one almighty God, the creator, upholder and ruler of the world; and profess him or themselves obliged to live quietly under the civil government, shall be in any case molested or prejudiced in his or their person or estate because of his or their conscientious persuasion or practice, nor be compelled to frequent or maintain any religious worship, place, or ministry contrary to his or their mind, or to do or suffer any other act or thing contrary to their religious persuasion.

And that all persons who also profess to believe in Jesus Christ, the saviour of the world, shall be capable, notwithstanding their other persuasions and practices in point of conscience and religion, to serve this government in any capacity, both legislatively and executively, he or they solemnly promising, when lawfully required, allegiance to the King as sovereign and fidelity to the proprietary and Governor, and taking the attests as now established by the laws made at Newcastle, in the year one thousand and seven hundred, entitled *An Act Directing the Attests of Several Officers and Ministers*, as now amended and confirmed this present Assembly.

II,

For the well-governing of this province and territories there shall be an Assembly yearly chosen by the freemen thereof, to consist of four persons out of each county, of most note for virtue, wisdom, and ability, or of a greater number at any time as the Governor and assembly shall agree, upon the first day of October, forever; and shall sit on the fourteenth day of the same month at Philadelphia, unless the Governor and Council for the time being shall see cause to appoint another place within the said province or territories. Which Assembly shall have power to choose a speaker and other their officers and shall be judges of the qualifications and elections of their own members, sit upon their own adjournments, appoint committees, prepare bills in order to pass into laws, impeach criminals and redress grievances, and shall have all other powers and privileges of an Assembly, according to the rights of the freeborn subjects of England and as is usual in any of the King's plantations in America.

And if any county or counties shall refuse or neglect to choose their respective representatives, as aforesaid, or, if chosen, do not meet to serve in Assembly, those who are so chosen and met shall have the full power of an Assembly, in as ample manner as if all the representatives had been chosen and met, provided they are not less than two-thirds of the whole number that ought to meet.

And that the qualifications of electors and elected, and all other matters and things relating to elections of representatives to serve in Assemblies, though not herein particularly expressed, shall be and remain as by a law of this government made at Newcastle in the year one thousand seven hundred entitled, *An Act to Ascertain the Number of Members of Assembly and to Regulate the Elections.*

III.

That the freemen in each respective county, at the time and place of meeting for electing their representatives to serve in Assembly, may, as often as there shall be occasion, choose a double number of persons to present to the Governor for sheriffs and coroners to serve for three years, if so long they behave themselves well. Out of which respective elections and presentments the Governor shall nominate and commissionate one for each of the said offices, the third day after such presentment, or else the first named in such presentment for each office, as aforesaid, shall stand and serve in that office for the time before respectively limited; and in case of death or default, such vacancies shall be supplied by the Governor to serve to the end of the said term.

Provided always, that if the said freeman shall at any time neglect or decline to choose a person or persons for either or both of the aforesaid offices, then and in such case the persons that are or shall be in the respective offices of sheriffs or coroners, at the time of election, shall remain therein until they be removed by another election, as aforesaid.

IV.

That the laws of this government shall be in this style, viz., By the Governor, with the consent and approbation of the Freemen of the General Assembly met; and shall be, after confirmation by the Governor, forthwith recorded in the Rolls Offices and kept at Philadelphia, unless the Governor and Assembly shall agree to appoint another place.

V.

That all criminals shall have the same privileges of witnesses and counsel as their prosecuters.

VI.

That no person or persons shall or may, at any time hereafter, be obliged to answer any complaint, matter, or thing, whatsoever relating to property, before the Governor and Council or in any other place, but in ordinary course of justice, unless appeals thereunto shall be hereafter by law appointed.

VII.

That no person within this government shall be licensed by the Governor to keep an ordinary, tavern, or house of public entertainment, but such who are first recommended to him under the hands of the justices of the respective counties, signed in open court. Which justices are and shall be hereby empowered to supress and forbid any person keeping such public house, as aforesaid, upon their misbehavior, on such penalties as the law does or shall direct; and to recommend others from time to time as they shall see occasion.

VIII.

If any person, through temptation or melancholy, shall destroy himself, his estate, real and personal, shall, notwithstanding, descend to his wife and children or relations as if he had died a natural death; and if any person shall be destroyed or killed by casualty or accident, there shall be no forfeiture to the Governor by reason thereof.

And no act, law, or ordinance whatsoever shall at any time hereafter be made or done to alter, change, or diminish the form or effect of this charter, or of any part or clause therein, contrary to the true intent and meaning thereof, without the consent of the Governor for the time being and six parts of seven of the Assembly met.

But because the happiness of mankind depends so much upon the enjoying of liberty of their consciences, as aforesaid, I do hereby solemnly declare, promise, and grant, for me, my heirs and assigns, that the first article of this charter relating to liberty of conscience, and every part and clause therein, according to the true intent and meaning thereof, shall be kept and remain without any alteration, inviolably forever.

And lastly, I, the said William Penn, Proprietary and Governor of the province of Pennsylvania and territories thereunto belonging, for myself, my heirs and assigns, have solemnly declared, granted, and confirmed, and do hereby solemnly declare, grant, and confirm, that neither I, my heirs or assigns, shall procure or do anything or things whereby the liberties in this charter contained and expressed, nor any part thereof, shall be infringed or broken. And if anything shall be procured or done by any person or persons contrary to these presents, it shall be held of no force or effect.

In witness whereof, I, the said William Penn, at Philadelphia in Pennsylvania, have unto this present charter of liberties, set my hand and broad seal, this twenty-eighth day of October, in the year of our Lord, one thousand seven hundred and one, being the thirteenth year of the reign of King William the Third, over England, Scotland, France, and Ireland, etc., and the twenty-first year of my government.

And notwithstanding the closure and test of this present charter, as aforesaid, I think fit to add this following proviso thereunto, as part of the same, that is to say, that, notwithstanding any clause or clauses in the abovementioned charter obliging the province and territories to join together in legislation, I am content and do hereby declare that if the representatives of the province and territories shall not hereafter agree to join together in legislation, and if the same shall be signified unto me or my Deputy in open Assembly, or otherwise from under the hands and seals of the representatives, for the time being, of the province and territories, or the major part of either of them, at any time within three years from the date hereof, that in such case the inhabitants of each of the three counties of this province shall not have less than eight persons to represent them in Assembly for the province; and the inhabitants of the town of Philadelphia, when the said town is incorporated, two persons to represent them in Assembly for the province; and the inhabitants of each county in the territories shall have as many persons to represent them in a distinct Assembly for the territories, as shall by them requested as aforesaid.

Notwithstanding which separation of the province and territories, in respect of legislation I do hereby promise, grant, and declare that the inhabitants of both province and territories shall separately enjoy all other liberties, privileges, and benefits, granted jointly to them in this charter, any law, usage or custom of that government heretofore made and practiced, or any law made and passed by this General Assembly, to the contrary hereof notwithstanding.

William Penn

The charter of privileges being distinctly read in Assembly, and the whole and every part thereof being approved and agreed to by us, we do thankfully receive the same from our proprietary and Governor, at Philadelphia, this twenty-eighth day of October, one thousand seven hundred and one. Signed on behalf and by order of the Assembly.

Per Joseph Growden
Speaker

Edward Shippen	*Griffith Owen*
Phineas Pemberton	*Caleb Pusey*
Samuel Carpenter	*Thomas Story*

Proprietary and Governor's Council

The text is complete and as found in Thorpe, *Federal and State Constitutions*, 3076–81.

62

Orders Devised and Published by the House of Assembly to be Observed During the Assembly

February 25, 1638

*O*ne of the core commitments in American political thought is
to a political process that is highly deliberative. To a certain
extent the English commitment to rule of law lay behind colonial decision making processes, as well as the pragmatic belief that several
heads are better than one; however, the extraordinary care the colonists
took in this regard (see Fundamental Articles of New Haven [46] for
a good example) also resulted from another influence. The theological
perspective dominant in the American colonies held that as a result of
original sin humans could see only "as through a glass darkly," because
sinful pride and self-interest tended to cloud individual judgment.
The belief in a fallen human nature plus the commitment to seeking
the common good led colonists to rely more heavily than most peoples
on public discussions structured so as to minimize passion, self-interest,
and incomplete information. The inclination toward open public
records, as well as toward open political gatherings, is a reflection of the
colonial commitment to a deliberative process. The document below
is one of several examples surviving from seventeenth-century colonial
America that illustrate the concern for calm, open, fair, and orderly
processes during collective decision making. It is perhaps no accident
that the behavior elicited tended to resemble that found in church.

The Lieutenant General shall be called President of the Assembly and
shall appoint & direct all things that Concern Form and decency to
be used in the house and shall Command Observance thereof as he shall
see Cause upon pain of imprisonment or fine as the house shall take Precedence according to this Order.

When any one of the house is to speak to any Bill he shall stand up and be Bareheaded and direct his speech to the President only and if two or more stand up together the President shall appoint who shall speak.

No man shall stand up to speak to any Bill until the party that last spake have sat down nor shall any One refute another with any nipping or vn-civill terms nor shall name another but by some Circumloquation as the Gentleman or Burgess that spake last or that argued for or against this Bill or the Bill

The house shall sit every day holy days excepted unless it be adjourned at eight of the Clock in the morning at the furthest and at two of the Clock in the afternoon & if any Gentlemen or Burgess not appearing upon call at such time as the President is set at or after either of the said hours shall be amerced 20lb of Tobacco to be forthwth paid to the use of the house

After any Bill hath been once read in the house the Bill shall be read in-grossed or utterly rejected and upon any day or day appointed for a Session all Bills engrossed shall be put to the question and such as are assented to by the Greater part of the house and if the Votes be equal that shall be judged the Greater part which hath the Consent of the Lieutenant General shall be undersigned by the Secretary in these words ["]the freemen have as-sented["] and after that the President shall be demanded his assent in the name of the Lord proprietary and if his assent be to the Bill, the Bill shall be undersigned by the said Secretary in these words ["]the Lord Proprietary willeth that this be a Law["]

The text is complete and with the spelling found in W. H. Browne et al., eds., *Archives of Maryland: Vol. 1, Proceedings and Acts of the General Assembly of Maryland, January, 1637/8–September, 1664* (Baltimore: Maryland Historical Society, 1883), 32–33.

63

Act for Establishing the House of Assembly and the Laws to Be Made Therein

1638

*T*here had been an assembly of some sort in Maryland since 1635, but this document begins the recorded history of representative government in the colony. The proprietary government in Maryland was much like that in Pennsylvania, which is to say the governor representing the proprietor had almost unlimited power. The charters for both colonies, however, required that the proprietor pass laws with the advice and approbation of the freemen. In Pennsylvania William Penn took this part of the charter seriously, whereas in Maryland the absentee proprietor did not. His appointed governor, called Lieutenant General, essentially used the legislature created by this document as a rubber stamp. It is emblematic in the document below that certain specific individuals were invited to the Assembly by the Lieutenant General, while the freemen at large were not called but instead allowed to show up as they wished. Nevertheless, the mere existence of the legislature and the realities of colonial existence led the freemen to demand more and more real power. Gradually the legislature evolved into a true representative body, beginning with an act of the assembly that defined more clearly the relationship between the governor and the Assembly and laid out an orderly, systematic electoral process (see An Act Concerning the Calling of General Assemblies [66]).

---

*Memorandum That at the first meeting of the Assembly
on the 25th day of February 1638 was Enacted and
ordeined one Act as followeth*

*An Act For the Establishing the house of Assembly
and the Laws to be made therein*

Whereas the Kings Majestie by his Letters pattents hath given and granted full free and absolute power and authority to the Lord Proprietary of this province to make and ordeine any laws apperteining to the state of this Province by and with the advice assent and approbation of the freemen of the same or of the greater part of them or of their Deligates or deputies in such sort and forme as to the said Lord proprietarie should seem best. By Vertue Whereof Severall writts or Summons have been directed to certain Gentlemen to appear personally at this Assembly and to the rest of the free men inhabiting within the Severall hundreds of this Colony and the Isle of Kent to elect their delegates or deputies in their names and steeds to be present at the same and accordingly all the freemen of the said severall hundreds and of the Isle of Kent (some few excepted) have elected certain persons to that end and the same their Election have subscribed and returned upon record and their said Dellegates and Deputies are now assembled accordingly. Be it therefore Enacted and ordeined by the said Lord Proprietarie of and with the advice assent and approbation of the Freemen and of the delegates and deputies assembled at this present Assembly that the said Severall Persons so elected and returned as aforesaid shall be and be called Burgesses and shall supply the places of all the freemen consenting or subscribing to such their election in the same manner and to all the same intents and purposes as the Burgesses of any burrough in England in the Parliament of England useth to Supply the place of the Inhabitants of the Burroughe whereof he is Elected Burges and that the said Gentlemen and Burgesses and such other Freemen (not having Consented to any the Elections as aforesaid) as now are or shall be at any time Assembled or any twelve or more of them whereof the Lieutenant Generall and Secretary of the Province to be allwaies two shall be called the house of Assembly; and that all Acts and ordinances assented unto and approved by the said house or by the Major part of the Persons assembled and afterward assented unto by the Lieutenant Generall in the name of the said Lord proprietarie and shall be adjudged and established for laws to all the same force and effect as if the said Lord proprietary and all the freemen of this Province were personally present and did assent to and approve of the same...

[Approved by the freemen, and the Lieutenant General in behalf of the Lord Proprietor, March 12, 1638.]

Text, complete and with the original spelling, taken from Browne, *Archives of Maryland: Vol. 1,* 81–82.

64

An Act for Church Liberties

1638

*O*ne of the first colonial statements on religious freedom, this
act is notable for extending the principle to Catholics. Later
in the century a Protestant majority would temporarily rescind the
right for Catholics but a few years later would include them again.
In 1638, because the proprietor, Lord Calvert, was a Catholic, the
Assembly had no choice but to include Catholics.

Be it enacted by the Lord Proprietarie of this Province by and with the
Advice and approbation of the ffreemen of the same that Holy Church
within this Province shall have all her rights liberties and immunities safe
whole and inviolable in all things This act to continue till the end of the next
Generall Assembly and then with the Consent of the Lord Proprietarie to
be perpetuall.

Text complete as found in Browne, *Archives of Maryland: Vol. 1*, 40.

65

An Act for Swearing Allegeance

1638

*T*he problem of political obligation was handily solved in this
era not by some formal theory of consent but rather by the expedient of having all inhabitants take an oath if they wished to remain inhabitants. Colonists were supposedly required to take an oath
of fidelity to the king of England, a requirement that engendered some
controversy among the colonists. The source of the controversy lay not
in swearing allegiance to the king but in the genesis of such oaths,
which were instituted originally to recognize the monarch as head of
the Church. The Catholics in Maryland were no less hesitant about
such matters than the radical Protestant dissenters in New England,
who had left England primarily to escape the established Church.
This oath should be compared with those contained in documents 4,
9, 15, and 47. Comparison with oaths internal to longer documents,
such as the Pilgrim Code of Law [20], should also prove instructive.

B e it Enacted and ordeined by the Lord Proprietarie of this Province by
and with the Consent and approbation of the ffreemen of the same
that all and every person or persons of the age of eighteen years and upwards
Inhabitants or that Shall come hereafter to Inhabite within this Province shall
within one month next after this present Assembly shall be dissolved or
within one month after such person or persons shall land or come into this
Province take an oath to our Soveraigne Lord King Charles his heirs and
Successors in these words following (I: A B doe truly acknowledge professe
testifie and declare in my concience before God and the World that our
Soveraigne Lord King Charles is lawfull and rightfull King of England and
of all other his Majesties Dominions and Countries and I will bear true faith
and allegeance to his Majestie his heirs and lawfull Successors and him and
them will defend to the uttermost of my power against all conspiracies and

such attempts whatsoever which shall be made against his or their Crowne or dignity and shall and will doe my best endeavour to disclose and make known to his Majestie his heirs and lawfull Successors all Treasons and traiterous consperacies which I shall know or heare to be intended against his Majestie his heirs and lawfull Successors And I doe make this recognition and acknowledgement heartily willingly and truely upon the faith of a Christian So help me God) And Be it further Enacted By the authority aforesaid that if any person or persons to whom the Said oaths Shall be tendred by Virtue of this present act Shall willfully refuse to take the same that then Upon such tender and refusall the said person or persons so refuseing to take the said Oath shall be imprisoned till the next County Court or hundred Court of Kent and if at such Court such partie shall upon the Second tender refuse again to take the said oath the partie or parties so refuseing shall forfeit and lose all his Lands goods and Chattells within this Province to the Lord Proprietarie and his heirs and Shall be banished the said Province for ever (except women covert who Shall be committed only to prison untill such time as they will take the same oath).

To which end Be it further Enacted by the authority aforesaid that the Lieutent Generall or other officer Governour or Governours (for the time being) of this Province or two of the Councill or the Secretary of the Province for the time being or any Judge sitting in Court or the Commander of the Isle of Kent for persons being or that Shall be in the Ile of Kent Shall have full power to administer the said oath in manner aforesaid according to the intention of this present act This Act to continue till the end of the next assembly

---

The complete text, with original spelling, is from Browne, *Archives of Maryland: Vol. 1,* 40–41.

66

An Act What Persons Shall Be Called to Every General Assembly and an Act Concerning the Calling of General Assemblies

1638

*T*his simple act comes close to defining the entire form of government in Maryland at the time. The nature and role of the legislature, the process of elections, the definition of the suffrage, the process of passing legislation—all are established here. The result is one of the earliest representative assemblies to be established in America, although as of 1638 the legislature was still essentially a rubber stamp for the proprietor's appointed colonial representative, titled the Lieutenant General. For further discussion of the significance and historical context of this document, see the comments on Act for Establishing the House of Assembly [63].

Be it enacted by the Lord Proprietary of this province, of and with the advice and approbation of the freemen of the same, that, from henceforth, everyone being of the council of this province and any other gentlemen of able judgment and quality summoned by writ and the lord of every manor within this province after manors be erected shall or may have his voice, seat, and place in every General Assembly to be hereafter called in this province and shall be called by summons or writ unto the same. And also be it further enacted, by the authority aforesaid, that, from henceforth forever, after such time that any summons or writ shall issue for the calling or summoning a General Assembly of the freemen of this province, the commander or, in defect of a commander, the high constable of every hundred within this province or, in defect of a constable, the sheriff of the county, shall within every hundred summon all the freemen inhabiting within every hundred, as soon as conveniently may be, to assemble at a certain place and time to be by him appointed and prefixed. Which freemen so assembled, or the major part of them, shall elect and chose some one, two, or more able and sufficient men for the hundred, as the said freemen or the major part of them so assembled shall think good, to come to every such General Assembly at the time and place in such writ or summons limited and appointed, then and there, for him or themselves and all the freemen of the hundred and in their names and stead, to consult concerning the affairs of this province; and shall make a return in writing of the name or names of the persons so to be from time to time elected and chosen, and such person and persons so to be from time to time elected and chosen shall and may have a voice, place, and seat in every such General Assembly. And from henceforth such person or persons only so elected and chosen out of and for every hundred within this province, and such persons as shall be personally called by writ as afore, shall have a place, voice, and seat in all or any General Assembly hereafter to be held within this province. And every art and ordinance made in such General Assemblies by persons so called, elected, and chosen as aforsaid, or the major part of them, and assented to by the Lord Proprietary or his heirs, lords and proprietaries of this province, or by his or their lieutenant-general thereunto authorized by special warrant from the said Lord Proprietary or his heirs, shall be judged, deemed, and taken to be of as good force and strength and as effectual to all intents and purposes as if the Lord Proprietary himself and all the freemen within the said province had been personally present at such General Assemblies and had consented to and approved of the making and enacting of such laws and ordinances. Provided, that all acts approved by the freemen and by the Lieutenant-General in the name of the Lord Proprietary, as aforesaid, shall be of force until the Lord Proprietary shall signify his disassent to the same under the great seal, and no further or longer.

AN ACT CONCERNING THE CALLING
OF GENERAL ASSEMBLIES, 1638

Be it enacted by the Lord Proprietary of this province, of and with the assent and approbation of the freemen of the same, that from and after this General Assembly shall be dissolved, a General Assembly of the freemen of this province shall be called and summoned once in every three years at the least to consult of the affairs and public good of this province and for the enacting of laws and ordinances for the better government of the same. And that the said freemen so assembled shall, from and after the summoning of such assembly and assemblies until the dissolution of the same, have the like power, privileges, authority, and jurisdiction in all causes and matters arising or to arise or happen within this province as the House of Commons within the realm of England at any time heretofore assembled in that kingdom have had, used, or enjoyed or of right ought to have, use, or enjoy in, about, or concerning any matters, things, and causes whatsoever which have at any time happened or risen within the realm of England. This act to continue till the end of the next General Assembly.

The text, complete and with the original spelling, is taken from Browne, *Archives of Maryland: Vol. 1,* 74–75.

67

An Act for the
Liberties of the People

1638

*A*long with the Pilgrim Code of Law [20] and the Massachusetts Body of Liberties [22], this is one of the earliest attempts to specify and protect the rights of citizens inhabiting a colony
as distinct from the rights of proprietors. Each of these three documents takes a different approach to the problem. The document
below, as well as the others from colonial Maryland reproduced in this
volume, is notable for placing a time limit on the duration of rights.
The implication is quite straightforward that the rights being protected, far from being inalienable, result from action by the body
politic and can be rescinded for reasons acceptable to the legislature.

---

*B*e it Enacted By the Lord Proprietarie of this Province of and with the
advice and approbation of the ffreemen of the same that all the Inhabitants of this Province being Christians (Slaves excepted) Shall have and enjoy
all such rights liberties immunities priviledges and free customs within this
Province as any naturall born subject of England hath or ought to have or
enjoy in the Realm of England by force or vertue of the common law or
Statute Law of England (saveing in such Cases as the same are or may be
altered or changed by the Laws and ordinances of this Province)

And Shall not be imprisoned nor disseissed or dispossessed of their freehold goods or Chattels or be out Lawed Exiled or otherwise destroyed fore
judged or punished then according to the Laws of this province saveing to
the Lord proprietarie and his heirs all his rights and prerogatives by reason
of his domination and Seigniory over this Province and the people of the
same. This Act to Continue till the end of the next Generall Assembly.

Taken from Browne, *Archives of Maryland: Vol. I*, 41.

68

[Maryland Toleration Act]

April 21, 1649

*P*assed in accordance with instructions from Lord Baltimore, this document protected Maryland from the charge of intolerance toward Protestants. When the Protestants were in charge of the colony for a time after 1654, Catholics were not protected in their faith, but this document was reinstated with the restoration of Lord Baltimore as proprietor. The Maryland Toleration Act constitutes the broadest definition of religious freedom during the seventeenth century and was an important step toward true freedom of religion. It sounds strange to our ears that such a harshly worded document should be called a toleration act, but the breadth of toleration defended also required that the sensibilities of religious people not be offended regardless of denomination. Aside from prohibitions on the calling of names, the meat of the act is found near the end of the text—no one will be punished or disadvantaged because of his religious beliefs. In any case, the harsh blasphemy provisions were never enforced.

Acts and Orders of Assembly assented vnto
Enacted and made at a Generall Sessions of the said
Assembly held at St Maries on the one and twentieth day
of Aprill Anno Domini 1649 as followeth viz:

AN ACT CONCERNING RELIGION

fforasmuch as in a well governed and Xpian[1] Common Weath[2] matters concerning Religion and the honor of God ought in the first place to bee taken, into serious consideracion and endeavoured to bee settled. Be it there-

---

1. Christian. An *X* followed by a subscript *p* was a common symbol for Christ.
2. In the original text there was a line over the letter *e*. In the shorthand practice of the day, a line over a letter meant that one or more letters to follow have been omitted.

fore ordered and enacted by the Right Noble Cecilius Lord Baron of Balte-
more absolute Lord and Proprietary of this Province with the advise and consent of this Generall Assembly. That whatsoever pson or psons within this
Province and the Islands thereunto belonging shall from henceforth blaspheme God, that is Curse him, or deny our Saviour Jesus Christ to bee the
sonne of God, or shall deny the holy Trinity the ffather sonne and holy
Ghost, or the Godhead of any of the said Three psons of the Trinity or the
Vnity of this Godhead, or shall use or utter any reproachfull Speeches, words
or language concerning the said Holy Trinity, or any of the said three psons
thereof, shalbe punished with death and confiscation or forfeiture of all his
or her lands and goods to the Lord Proprietary and his heires, And bee it
also Enacted by the Authority and with the advise and assent aforesaid. That
whatsoever pson or psons shall from henceforth use or utter any reproachfull words or Speeches concerning the blessed Virgin Mary the Mother of
our Saviour or the holy Apostles or Evangelists or any of them shall in such
case for the first offence forfeit to the said Lord Proprietary and his heirs
Lords and Proprietaries of this Province the sume of ffive pound Sterling or
the value thereof to be Levyed on the goods and chattells of every such
pson soe offending, but in case such Offender or Offenders, shall not then
have such goods and chattells sufficient for the satisfyeing of such forfeiture, or that the same bee not otherwise speedily satisfyed that then such Offender or Offenders shalbe publiquely whipt and bee ymprisoned during the
pleasure of the Lord Proprietary or the Leivet[3] or cheife Governor of this
Province for the time being. And that every such Offender or Offenders for
every second offence shall forfeit tenne pound sterling or the value thereof
to bee levyed as aforesaid, or in case such offender or Offenders shall not
then haue goods and chattells within this Province sufficient for that purpose then to be publiquely and severly whipt and imprisoned as before is expressed. And that every pson or psons before mentioned offending herein
the third time, shall for such third Offence forfeit all his lands and Goods
and bee for ever banished and expelled out of this Province. And be it also
further Enacted by the same authority advise and assent that whatsoever pson
or psons shall from henceforth vppon any occasion or otherwise in a reproachful manner or Way declare call or denominate any pson or psons whatsoever inhabiting residing traffiqueing trading or comerceing within this

3. Lieutenant.

Province or within any the Ports, Harbors, Creeks or Havens to the same belonging to an heritick, Scismatick, Idolator, Puritan, Independent, Prespiterian popish prest, Jesuite, Jesuited Papist, Lutheran, Calvenist, Anabaptist, Brownist, Antinomian, Barrowist, Roundhead, Sepatist, or any other name or terme in a reproachfull manner relating to matter of Religion shall for every such Offence forfeit and loose the some of tenne shillings sterling or the value thereof to bee levyed on the goods and chattells of every such Offender and offenders, the one half thereof to be forfeited and paid unto the person and persons of whom such reproachfull words are or shalbe spoken or vttered, and the other half thereof to the Lord Proprietary and his heires Lords and Proprietries of this Province, But if such pson or psons who shall at any time vtter or speake any such reproachful words or Language shall not have Goods or Chattells sufficient and overt within this Province to bee taken to satisfie the penalty aforesaid or that the same bee not otherwise speedily satisfied, that then the pson or psons soe offending shalbe publickly whipt, and shall suffer imprisonmt without baile or maineprise vntill hee shee or they respectively shall satisfy the party soe offended or grieved by such reproachfull Language by asking him or her respectively forgivenes publiquely for such his Offence before the Magistrate or chiefe Officer or Officers of the Towne or place where such Offence shalbe given. And be it further likewise Enacted by the Authority and consent aforesaid That every person and persons within this Province that shall at any time hereafter prophane the Sabbath or Lords day called sunday by frequent swearing, drunkennes or by any uncivill or disorderly recreacion, or by working on that day when absolute necessity doth not require it shall for every such first offence forfeit 2s. 6d 4 sterling or the value thereof, and for the second offence 5s sterling or the value thereof, and for the third offence and soe for every time as shall offend in like manner afterwards 10s sterling or the value thereof. And in case such offender and offenders shall not have sufficient goods or chattels within this Province to satisfy any of the said Penalties respectively hereby imposed for prophaning the Sabbath or Lords day called Sunday as aforesaid, That in Every such case the partie soe offending shall for the first and second offence in that kinde be imprisoned till hee or shee shall publickly in open court before the chiefe Commander Judge or Magistrate, or that County Towne or precinct where such offence shalbe committed acknowledge the Scandall and offence he hath in that respect given against God and the good and civill Govern[m]ent of this Province And for the third

offence and for every time after shall also bee publickly whipt. And whereas
the inforceing of the conscience in matters of Religion hath frequently fallen
out to be of dangerous Consequence in those commonwealthes where it hath
been practised, And for the more quiett and peaceable government of this
Province, and the better to preserve mutuall Love and amity amongst the
Inhabitants thereof. Be it Therefore also by the Lo: Proprietary with the advise and consent of this Assembly Ordeyned & enacted (except as in this
psent Act is before Declared and sett forth) that noe person or psons whatsoever within this Province, or the Islands, Ports, Harbors, Creekes, or havens
thereunto belonging professing to beleive in Jesus Christ, shall from henceforth bee any waies troubled, Molested or discountenanced for or in respect of his or her religion not in the free exercise thereof within this Province
or the Islands thereunto belonging nor any way compelled to the beliefe or
exercise of any other Religion against his or her consent, soe as they be not
unfaithfull to the Lord Proprietary, or molest or conspire against the civill
Govern[m]ent established or to bee established in this Province vnder him
or his heires. And that all & every pson and psons that shall presume contrary to this Act and the true intent and meaning thereof directly or indirectly either in person or estate willfully to wrong disturbe trouble or molest
any person whatsoever within this Province professing to believe in Jesus
Christ for or in respect of his or her religion or the free exercise thereof within
this Province other than is provided for in this Act that such pson or psons
soe offending, shalbe compelled to pay trebble damages to the party soe
wronged or molested, and for every such offence shall also forfeit 20s sterling in money or the value thereof, half thereof for the vse of the Lo: Proprietary, and his heires Lords and Propietaries of this Province, and the other
half for the vse of the party soe wronged or molested as aforesaid, Or if the
ptie soe offending as aforesaid shall refuse or bee vnable to recompense the
party soe wronged, or to satisfy such ffyne or forfeiture, then such Offender shalbe severely punished by publick whipping & imprisonmt during the pleasure of the Lord Proprietary, or his Leivetenant or cheife
Governor of this Province for the tyme being without baile or maineprise
And bee it further alsoe Enacted by the authority and consent aforesaid That
the Sheriff or other Officer or Officers from time to time to bee appointed
& authorized for that purpose, of the County Towne or precinct where every
particular offence in this psent Act conteyned shall happen at any time to
bee committed and wherevppon there is hereby a fforfeiture ffyne or penalty

imposed shall from time to time distraine and seise the goods and estate of every such pson soe offending as aforesaid against this psent Act or any part thereof, and sell the same or any part thereof for the full satisfaccion of such forfeiture, ffine, or penalty as aforesaid, Restoring vnto the ptie soe offending the Remainder or overplus of the said goods or estate after such satisfaccion soe made as aforesaid

> The freemen haue assented. Tho: Hatton
> Enacted by Governor Wllm Stone

Text, complete and with original spelling, taken from Browne, *Archives of Maryland: Vol. I*, 244–47.

69

Articles, Laws, and Orders, Divine, Politic, and Martial for the Colony in Virginia

1610–1611

*U*nder its initial charter, Virginia was run by a cumbersome double council. A thirteen-member royal council in London appointed a thirteen-member council in Virginia to carry out its will. The system did not work, and the Virginia governor had to become a virtual dictator to maintain order. The following document was issued under martial law but still reflects the values that were generally accepted by the colonists. It is equivalent to a code of law and may be fruitfully compared with other codes of law in this collection, such as documents 2, 20, 22, 26, 30, 39, and 52. Religion plays an important role in this Virginia document, as it did in codes elsewhere, and the moral content looks similar to that of New England codes. Virginia, however, was not a Puritan colony but Church of England country—Anglicanism was for a long while the colony's established church. The similarities with the Puritans may have been due to the predominance of "low church" members who, while remaining securely in the fold, shared many of the Puritan inclinations against pomp, statues, and other vestiges of what was termed covert popery. The extent of this low church influence was revealed when in the 1690s the king proposed sending an Anglican bishop to Virginia, and every pastor in the colony signed a letter asking that the bishop not be sent. Despite its determined attempt to re-create English country life in America, Virginia society did not include members of the English aristocracy, and its religious inclinations were similarly nonhierarchical compared with the English at home. Still, this was not New England Puritanism, which is reflected in the large number of capital crimes typical of English common law at the time rather than the restricted list of capital crimes listed in, for example, the Massachu-setts *Body of Liberties [22]. Many laws are aimed at preserving the extremely limited goods in the colony, which reflects the desperate sit-uation faced in the early years of colonization.*

Articles, Lawes, and Orders, Divine, Politique, and Martiall for the Colony in Virginea: first established by Sir Thomas Gates Knight, Lieutenant Generall, the 24th of May 1610. exemplified and approved by the Right Honourable Sir Thomas West Knight, Lord Lawair, Lord Governor and Captaine Generall the 12th day of June 1610. Againe exemplified and enlarged by Sir Thomas Dale Knight, Marshall, and Deputie Governour, the 22nd of June, 1611.

Whereas his Majestie like himselfe a most zealous Prince hath in his owne Realmes a principall care of true Religion, and reverence to God, and hath alwaies strictly commaunded his Generals and Governours, with all his forces wheresoever, to let their waies be like his ends for the glorie of God.

And forasmuch as no good service can be performed, or warre well man-aged, where militarie discipline is not observed, and militarie discipline cannot be kept, where the rules or chiefe parts thereof, be not certainely set downe, and generally knowne, I have (with the advise and counsell of Sir Thomas Gates Knight, Lieutenant Generall) adhered unto the lawes di-vine, and orders politique, and martiall of his Lordship (the same exempli-fied) an addition of such others, as I have found either the necessitie of the present State of the Colonie to require, or the infancie, and weaknesses of the body thereof, as yet able to digest, and doe now publish them to all persons in the Colonie, that they may as well take knowledge of the Lawes themselves, as of the penaltie and punishment, which without partialitie shall be inflicted upon the breakers of the same.

1 First since we owe our highest and supreme duty, our greatest, and all our allegeance to him, from whom all power and authoritie is derived, and flowes as from the first, and onely fountaine, and being especiall souldiers emprest in this sacred cause, we must alone expect our successe from him, who is only the blesser of all good attempts, the King of kings, the com-maunder of commaunders, and Lord of Hostes, I do strictly commaund and

charge all Captaines and Officers, of what qualitie or nature soever, whether commanders in the field, or in towne, or townes, forts or fortresses, to have a care that the Almightie God bee duly and daily served, and that they call upon their people to heare Sermons, as that also they diligently frequent Morning and Evening praier themselves by their owne exemplar and daily life, and duties herein, encouraging others thereunto, and that such, who shall often and wilfully absent themselves, be duly punished according to the martiall law in that case provided.

2 That no man speake impiously or maliciously, against the holy and blessed Trinitie, or any of the three persons, that is to say, against God the Father, God the Son, and God the holy Ghost, or against the knowne Articles of the Christian faith, upon paine of death.

3 That no man blaspheme Gods holy name upon paine of death, or use unlawful oathes, taking the name of God in vaine, curse, or banne,[1] upon paine of severe punishment for the first offence so committed, and for the second, to have a bodkin[2] thrust through his tongue, and if he continues the blaspheming of Gods holy name, for the third time so offending, he shall be brought to a martiall court, and there receive censure of death for his offence.

4 No man shall use any traiterous words against his Majesties Person, or royall authority upon paine of death.

5 No man shall speake any word, or do any act, which may tend to the derision, or despight[3] of Gods holy word upon paine of death: Nor shall any man unworthily demeane himself unto any Preacher, or Minister of the same, but generally hold them in all reverent regard, and dutiful intreatie,[4] otherwise he the offender shall openly be whipt three times, and ask publike forgivenesse in the assembly of the congregation three several Saboth Daies.

6 Everie man and woman duly twice a day upon the first towling of the Bell shall upon the working daies repair unto the Church, to hear divine Service upon pain of losing his or her dayes allowance for the first omission, for the second to be whipt, and for the third to be condemned to the Gallies for six Moneths. Likewise no man or woman shall dare to violate or breake the Sabboth by any gaming, publique or private abroad, or at home,

1. Calling down evil upon a person.
2. A small dagger or stiletto.
3. Open defiance.
4. Treatment.

but duly sanctifie and observe the same, both himselfe and his familie, by preparing themselves at home with private prayer, that they may be the better fitted for the publique, according to the commandements of God, and the orders of our Church, as also every man and woman shall repaire in the morning to the divine service, and Sermons preached upon the Saboth day, and in the afternoone to divine service, and Catechising, upon paine for the first fault to lose their provision, and allowance for the whole weeke following, for the second to lose the said allowance, and also to be whipt, and for the third to suffer death.

7 All Preachers or Ministers within this our Colonie, or Colonies, shall in the Forts, where they are resident, after divine Service, duly preach every Sabbath day in the forenoone, and Catechise in the afternoone, and weekly say the divine service, twice every day, and preach every Wednesday, likewise every Minister where he is resident, within the same Fort, or Fortresse, Townes or Towne, shall chuse unto him, foure of the most religious and better disposed as well to informe of the abuses and neglects of the people in their duties, and service to God, as also to the due reparation, and keeping of the Church handsome, and fitted with all reverent observances thereunto belonging: likewise every Minister shall keepe a faithful and true Record, or Church Booke of all Christnings, Marriages, and deaths of such our people, as shall happen within their Fort, or Fortresses, Townes or Towne at any time, upon the burthen of a neglectfull conscience, and upon paine of losing their Entertainment.[5]

8 He that upon pretended malice, shall murther or take away the life of any man, shall bee punished with death.

9 No man shal commit the horrible, and detestable sins of Sodomie upon pain of death; and he or she that can be lawfully convict of Adultery shall be punished with death. No man shall ravish or force any woman, maid or Indian, or other, upon pain of death, and know that he or shee, that shall commit fornication, and evident proofe made thereof, for their first fault shall be whipt, for the second they shall be whipt, and for their third they shall be whipt three times a weeke for one month, and aske publique forgivenesse in the Assembly of the Congregation.

10 No man shall bee found guilty of Sacriledge, which is a Trespasse as well committed in violating the abusing any sacred ministry, duty or office of the Church, irreverently, or prophanely, as by beeing a Church robber,

5. Provisions.

to filch, steale or carry away anything out of the Church appertaining there-unto, or unto any holy, and consecrated place, to the divine Service of God, which no man should doe upon paine of death: likewise he that shall rob the store of any commodities therein, of what quality soever, whether provisions of victuals, or of arms, Trucking stuffe,[6] Apparrell, Linnen, or Wollen, Hose or Shooes, Hats or Caps, Instruments or Tooles of Steele, Iron, etc. or shall rob from his fellow souldier, or neighbor, any thing that is his, victuals, apparell, household stuffe, toole, or what necessary else soever, by water or land, out of boate, house, or knapsack, shall bee punished with death.

11 Hee that shall take an oath untruly, or beare false witnesse in any cause, or against any man whatsoever, shall be punished with death.

12 No manner of person whatsoever, shall dare to detract, slaunder, co-lumniate, or utter unseemly, and unfitting speeches, either against his Majesties Honourable Councell for this Colony, resident in England, or against the Committees, Assistants unto the said Councell, or against the zealous indeavors, and intentions of the whole body of Adventurers for this pious and Christian Plantation, or against any publique book, or bookes, which by their mature advise, and grave wisdomes, shall be thought fit, to be set foorth and publisht, for the advancement of the good of this Colony, and the felicity thereof, upon paine for the first time so offending, to be whipt three severall times, and upon his knees to acknowledge his offence and to aske forgivenesse upon the Saboth day in the assembly of the con-gregation, and for the second time so offending to be condemned to the Gal-ley for three yeares, and for the third time so offending to be punished with death.

13 No manner of person whatsoever, contrarie to the word of God (which tyes every particular and private man, for conscience sake to obedience, and duty of the Magistrate, and such as shall be placed in authoritie over them, shall detract, slaunder, calumniate, murmur, mutenie, resist, disobey, or neglect the commaundments, either of the Lord Governour, and Cap-taine Generalle, the Lieutenant Generall, the Martiall, the Councell, or any authorised Captaine, Commaunder or publike Officer, upon paine for the first time so offending to be whipt three severall times, and upon his knees

6. Materials for barter or exchange.

to acknowledge his offence, with asking forgivenesse upon the Saboth day in the assembly of the congregation, and for the second time so offending to be condemned to the Gally for three yeares: and for the third time so offending to be punished with death.

14 No man shall give any disgraceful words, or commit any act to the disgrace of any person in this Colonie, or any part thereof, upon paine of being tied head and feete together, upon the guard everie night for the space of one moneth, besides to bee publikely disgraced himselfe, and be made incapable ever after to possesse any place, or execute any office in this imployment.

15 No man of what condition soever shall barter, trucke, or trade with the Indians, except he be thereunto appointed by lawful authority upon paine of death.

16 No man shall rifle or dispoile, by force or violence, take away any thing from any Indian coming to trade, or otherwise, upon paine of death.

17 No Cape Marchant,[7] or Provant Master,[8] or Munition Master, or Truck Master, or keeper of any store, shall at any time imbezell, sell, or give away any thing under his Charge to any Favorite, of his, more than unto any other, whome necessity shall require in that case to have extraordinary allowance of provisions, nor shall they give a false accompt unto the Lord Governour, and Captaine Generall, unto the Lieutenant Generall, unto the Marshall, or any deputed Governor, at any time having the commaund of the Colony, with intent to defraud the said Colony, upon paine of death.

18 No man shall imbezel or take away the goods of any man that dyeth, or is imployed from the town or Fort where he dwelleth in any other occasioned remote service, for the time, upon pain of whipping three severall times, and restitution of the said goods againe, and in danger of incurring the penalty of the tenth Article, if so it may come under the construction of theft. And if any man die and make a will, his goods shall be accordingly disposed; if hee die intestate, his goods shall bee put into the store, and being valued by two sufficient praisors, his next of kinne (according to the common Lawes of England), shall from the Company, Committees, or adventurers, receive due satisfaction in moneys, according as they were praised, by which means the Colonie shall be better furnished; and the goods more

7. An officer who supervised the provision house of a fort.
8. The master of the provisions, who also provided the soldiers' allowance.

carefully preserved, for the right heire, and the right heire receive content for the same in England.

19 There shall be no Capttain, Master, Marriner, saylor, or any else of what quality or condition soever, belonging to any Ship or Ships, at this time remaining, or which shall hereafter arrive within this our River, bargaine, buy, truck, or trade with any one member in this Colony, man, woman, or child, for any toole or instrument of iron, steel, or what else, whether appertaining to Smith Carpenter, Joyner, Shipwright, or any manuall occupation, or handicraft man whatsoever, resident within our Colonie, nor shall they buy or bargaine, for any apparell, linnen, or wollen, householdstuffe, bedde, bedding, sheete towels, napkins, brasse, pewter, or such like, eyther for ready money, or provisions, nor shall they exchange their provisions, of what quality soever, whether Butter, Cheese, Bisket, meal, Oatmele, Aquavite,[9] oyle, Bacon, any kind of Spice, or such like, for any such aforesaid instruments, or tooles, apparell, or householdstuffe, at any time, or so long as they shall here remain, from the date of these presents upon paine of losse of their wages in England, confiscation and forfeiture of such their monies and provisions, and upon peril beside of such corporall punishment as shall be inflicted upon them by verdict and censure of a martiall Court: Nor shall any officer, souldier, or Trades man, or any else of what sort soever, members of this Colony, dare to sell any such Toole, or instruments, necessary and usefull, for the businesse of the Colonie, or trucke, sell, exchange, or give away his apparell, or household stuffe of what sort soever, unto any such Seaman, either for mony, or any such foresaid provisions, upon paine of 3 times severall whipping, for the one offender, and the other upon perill of incurring censure, whether of disgrace, or addition of such punishment, as shall bee thought fit by a Court martiall.

20 Whereas sometimes heeretofore the covetous and wide affections of some greedy and ill disposed Seamen, Saylers, and Marriners, laying hold upon the advantage of the present necessity, under which the Colony sometimes suffered, have sold unto our people, provisions of Meale, Oatmeale, Bisket, Butter, Cheese etc., at unreasonable rates, and prises unconscionable: for avoiding the like to bee now put in practise, there shall no Captain, Master, Marriner, or Saylor, or what Officer else belonging to any ship, or shippes,

9. Spirits or alcoholic beverages.

now within our river, or heereafter which shall arrive, shall dare to bargaine, exchange, barter, truck, trade, or sell, upon paine of death, unto any one Landman[10] member of this present Colony, any provisions of what kind soever, above the determined valuations, and prises, set downe and proclaimed, and sent therefore unto each of your severall ships, to bee fixed uppon your Maine mast, to the intent that want of due notice, and ignorance in this case, be no excuse, or plea, for any offender herein.

21 Sithence[11] we are not to bee a little carefull, and our young Cattell, and Breeders may be cherished, that by the preservation, and incrase of them, the Colony heere may receive in due time assured and great benefite, and the adventurers at home may be eased of so great a burthen, by sending unto us yeerely supplies of this kinde, which now heere for a while, carefully attended, may turne their supplies unto us into provisions of other qualities, when of these wee shall be able to subsist our selves, and which wee may in short time, be powerful enough to doe, if we wil according to our owne knowledge of what is good for our selves, forbeare to work into our own wants, againe, by over hasty destroying, and devouring the stockes, and authors of so profitable succeeding a Commodity, as increase of Cattell, Kine, Hogges, Goates, Poultrie etc. must of necessity bee granted, in every common mans judgement, to render unto us: Now know thee therefore, these promises carefully considered, that it is our will and pleasure, that every one, of what quality or condition soever hee bee, in this present Colony, to take due notice of this our Edict, whereby wee do strictly charge and command, that no man shall dare to kill, or destroy any Bull, Cow, Calfe, Mare, Horse, Colt, Goate, Swine, Cocke, Henne, Chicken, Dogge, Turkie, or any tame Cattel, or Poultry, of what condition soever; whether his owne, or appertaining to another man, without leave from the Generall, upon paine of death in the Principall, and in the accessary, burning in the Hand, and losse of his eares, and unto the concealer of the same four and twenty houres of whipping, with addition of further punishment, as shall be thought fitte by the censure, and verdict of a Martiall Court.

22 There shall no man or woman, Launderer or Launderesse, dare to wash any uncleane Linnen, drive bucks,[12] or throw out the water or sudes of fowle

10. Literally a man of the land—not a sailor.
11. Seeing that.
12. Bleach clothes.

cloathes, in the open streete, within the Pallizadoes,[13] or within forty foote of the same, nor rench,[14] and make cleane, any kettle, pot, or pan, or such like vessell within twenty foote of the olde well, or new pump; nor shall any one aforesaid, within less than a quarter of one mile from the pallizadoes, dare to doe the necessities of nature, since by these unmanly, slothfull, and loathsome immodesties, the whole Fort may bee choaked, and poisoned with ill aires, and so corrupt (as in all reason cannot but much infect the same) and this shall they take notice of, and avoide, upon paine of whipping and further punishment, as shall be thought meete, by the censure of a martiall Court.

23 No man shall imbezell, lose, or willingly breake, or fraudulently make away, either Spade, Shovell, Hatchet, Axe, Mattocke,[15] or other toole or instrument upon paine of whipping.

24 Any man that hath any edge toole, either of his owne, or which hath heeretofore beene belonging to the store, see that he bring it instantly to the storehouse, where he shall receive it againe by a particular note, both of the toole, and of his name taken, that such a toole unto him appertaineth, at whose hands, upon any necessary occasion, the said toole may be required, and this shall he do, upon paine of severe punishment.

25 Every man shall have an especiall and due care, to keepe his house sweete and cleane, as also so much of the streete, as lieth before his door, and especially he shall so provide, and set his bedstead whereon he lieth, that it may stand three foote at least from the ground, as will answere the contrarie at a martiall Court.

26 Every tradesman in their severall occupation, trade and function, shall duly and daily attend his worke upon his said trade or occupation, upon perill for his first fault, and negligence therein, to have his entertainment checkt for one moneth, for his second fault three moneth, for his third one yeare, and if he continue still unfaithfull and negligent therein, to be condemned to the Gally for three yeare.

27 All overseers of workemen, shall be carefull in seeing that performed, which is given them in charge, upon paine of such punishment as shall be inflicted upon him by a martiall Court.

28 No souldier or tradesman, but shall be readie, both in the morning,

13. Pallisades.
14. Rinse.
15. A tool used to remove trees.

and in the afternoone, upon the beating of the Drum, to goe out unto his worke, nor shall hee return home, or from his worke, before the Drum beate againe, and the officer appointed for that business, bring him of, upon per-ill for the first fault to lie upon the Guard head and heeles together all night, for the second time so faulting to be whipt, and for the third time so offending to be condemned to the Gallies for a yeare.

29 No man or woman, (upon paine of death) shall runne away from the Colonie, to Powhathan, or any savage Weroance[16] else whatsoever.

30 He that shall conspire any thing against the person of the Lord Governour, and Captaine Generall, against the Lieutenant Generall, or against the Marshall, or against any publike service commaunded by them, for the dignitie, and advancement of the good of the Colony, shall be punished with death: and he that shall have knowledge of any such pretended act of disloyalty or treason, and shall not reveale the same unto his Captaine, or unto the Governour of that fort or Towne wherein he is, within the space of one houre, shall for the concealing of the same after that time, be not onely held an accessary, but alike culpable as the principall traitor or conspirer, and for the same likewise he shall suffer death.

31 What man or woman soever, shall rob any garden, publike or private, being set to weed the same, or wilfully pluck up therein any roote, herbe, or flower, to spoile and wast or steale the same, or robbe any vineyard, or gather up the grapes, or steale any eares of the corne growing, whether in the ground belonging to the same fort or towne where he dwelleth, or in any other, shallbe punished with death.

32 Whosoever Seaman, or Landman or what qualitie, or in what place of commaund soever, shall be imployed upon any discovery, trade, or fishing voiage into any of the rivers within the precincts of our Colonie, shall for the safety of those men who are committed to his commaund, stand upon good and carefull guard, for the prevention of any treachery in the Indian, and if they touch upon any shore, they shal be no less circumspect, and warie, with good and carefull guard day and night, putting forth good Centinell, and observing the orders and discipline of watch and ward, and when they have finished the discovery, trade, or fishing, they shall make hast with all speed, with such Barke or Barkes, Pinisse, Gallie, Ship. etc. as they shall have the commaund of, for the same purpose, to James towne againe, not pre-

---

16. A powerful chief of an Indian confederation south of the Potomac River.

suming to goe beyond their commission, or to carry any such Barke or Barkes, Gally, Pinnice, Ship. etc. for England or any other countrey in the actual possession of any Christian Prince, upon perill to be held an enemie to this plantation, and traitor thereunto, and accordingly to lie liable unto such censure of punishment (if they arrive in England) as shall be thought fit by the Right Honourable Lords, his Majesties Councell for this Colonie, and if it shall so happen, that he or they shall be prevented, and brought backe hither againe into the Colonie, their trecherous flight to be punished with death.

33 There is not one man nor woman in this Colonie now present, or hereafter to arrive, but shall give up an account of his and their faith, and religion, and repaire unto the Minister, that by his conference with them, hee may understand, and gather, whether heretofore they have beene sufficiently instructed, and catechised in the principles and grounds of Religion, whose weaknesse and ignorance herein, the Minister finding, and advising them in all love and charitie, to repaire often unto him, to receive therein a greater measure of knowledge, if they shal refuse so to repaire unto him, and he the Minister give notice thereof unto the Governour, or that chiefe officer of that towne or fort, wherein he or she, the parties so offending shall remaine, the Governour shall cause the offender for his first time of refusall to be whipt, for the second time to be whipt twice, and to acknowledge his fault upon the Saboth day, in the assembly of the congregation, and for the third time to be whipt every day until he heath made the same acknowledgement, and asked forgivenesse for the same, and shall repaire unto the Minister, to be further instructed as aforesaid: and upon the Saboth when the Minister shall catechise, and of him demaund any question concerning his faith and knowledge, he shall not refuse to make answere upon the same perill.

34 What man or woman soever, Laundrer or Laundresse appointed to wash the foule linnen of any one labourer or souldier, or any one else as it is their duties so to doe, performing little, or no other service for their allowance out of the store, and daily provisions, and supply of other necessaries unto the Colonie, and shall from the said labourer or souldier, or any one else of what qualitie whatsoever, either take any thing for washing, or withhold or steale from him any such linnen committed to her to wash, or change the same willingly and wittingly, with purpose to give him worse, old and torne linnen for his good, and proofe shall be made thereof, she shall be whipped

for the same, and lie in prison till she make restitution of such linnen, withheld or changed.

35 No Captaine, Master, or Mariner, of what condition soever, shall depart or carry out of the river, any Ship, Barke, Barge, Gally, Pinnace etc. Roaders[17] belonging to the Colonie, either now therein, or hither arriving, without leave and commission from the Generall or chiefe Commaunder of the Colonie upon paine of death.

36 No man or woman whatsoever, members of this Colonie, shall sell or give unto any Captine, Marriner, Master, or Sailer, etc. any commoditie of this countrey, of what quality soever, to be transported out of the Colonie, for his or their owne private uses, upon paine of death.

37 If any souldier indebted, shall refuse to pay his debts unto his creditor, his creditor shall informe his Captaine, if the Captaine cannot agree the same, the creditor shall informe the Marshals civill and principall officer, who shall preferre for the creditor a bill of complaint at the Marshals Court, where the creditor shal have Justice.

All such Bakers as are appointed to bake bread, or what else, either for the store to be given out in generall, or for any one in particular, shall not steale nor imbezell, loose, or defraud any man of his due and proper weight and measure, nor use any dishonest and deceiptfull tricke to make the bread weight heavier, or make it courser upon purpose to keepe backe any part or measure of the flower or meale committed unto him, nor aske, take, or detaine any one loafe more or lesse for his hire or paines for so baking, since whilest he who delivered unto him such meale or flower, being to attend the businesse of the Colonie, such baker or bakers are imposed upon no other service or duties, but onely so to bake for such as do worke, and this shall hee take notice of, upon paine for the first time offending herein of losing his eares, and for the second time to be condemned a yeare to the Gallies, and for the third time offending, to be condemned to the Gallies for three yeares.

All such cookes as are appointed to seeth,[18] bake or dresse any manner of way, flesh, fish, or what else, of what kind soever, either for the generall company, or for any private man, shall not make lesse, or cut away any part or parcel of such flesh, fish, etc. Nor detaine or demaund any party or parcell, as allowance or hire for his so dressing the same, since as aforesaid of the

---

17. A vessel used in sheltered water near the shore.
18. Boil.

baker, hee or they such Cooke or Cookes, exempted from other publike works abroad, are to attend such seething and dressing of such publike flesh, fish, or other provisions of what kind soever, as their service and duties expected from them by the Colony, and this shall they take notice of, upon paine for the first time offending herein, of losing his eares, and for the second time to be condemned a yeare to the Gallies: and for the third time offending to be condemned to the Gallies for three years.

All fishermen, dressers of Sturgeon or such like appointed to fish, or to cure the said Sturgeon for the use of the Colonie, shall give a just and true account of all such fish as they shall take by day or night, of what kinds soever, the same to bring unto the Governour: As also of all such kegges of Sturgeon or Caviare as they shall prepare and cure upon perill for the first time offending heerein, of loosing his eares, and for the second time to be condemned a yeare to the Gallies, and for the third time offending, to be condemned to the Gallies for three yeares. Every Minister or Preacher shall every Sabboth day before Catechising, read all these lawes and ordinances, publikely in the assembly of the congregation upon paine of his entertainment checkt for that weeke.

Text taken from D. H. Flaherty, ed., *Laws Divine, Moral, and Martial Compiled by William Strachey* (Charlottesville: The University Press of Virginia, 1969), 9–25. Flaherty retains the original spelling and punctuation, except to transpose *i* and *j*, and *u* and *v*, respectively, to correspond to modern usage. The usual practice is to reproduce only pages 9–25 of the Strachey version, as is done here, but the complete document is 101 pages long. The balance of the document contains a detailed discussion of the colony's martial laws and specific instructions from the marshal to every rank concerning duties and bearing. The Flaherty volume contains a discussion of the historical context surrounding this document, as well as the complete text.

70

[Laws Enacted by the
First General Assembly of Virginia]

August 2–4, 1619

*I*n 1618 the council in London instructed the Virginia governor
to initiate the first representative assembly in the colonies. It was
*felt that the colonists needed to have some voice in local affairs if order
and economic prosperity were to be reestablished in the faltering
colony. The legislature lasted until 1624, when a reorganization imposed by the king restored all power to the governor. The following
document was passed by the legislature during its initial six-year official existence. Even though adopted by what turned out to be only
a transitional institution, this document is still important because it
was the first compact of any sort adopted in the colonies and therefore was the first foundation document to use some form of consent.
After 1624 the governor continued to call the House of Burgesses for
unofficial consultations; however, he was forced to rely primarily on
the upper house, the Council of State appointed by the king, and he
could not act without its approval. In 1638 the governor was again officially ordered to call a session of the House of Burgesses, and with
this session it moved out of the shadows. The House of Burgesses, then
the lower house of a bicameral legislature, gradually gained the upper
hand over the Governor and Council—it did so primarily by gain-
ing the power to levy taxes. Within a few years its consent was necessary for the enactment of all laws. Thus, while the legislature that
passed the document below was officially terminated in 1624, it never
really went out of existence; and the first elected colonial legislature
eventually became the centerpiece of Virginia politics.*

By this present General Assembly be it enacted that no injury or oppression be wrought by the English against the Indians whereby the present peace might be distributed and ancient quarrels might be revived. And farther be it ordained that the Chicohomini are not to be excepted out of this law, until either that such order come out of England or that they do provoke us by some new injury.

Against idleness, gaming, drunkenness, and excess in apparel the assembly has enacted as follows.

First, in detestation of idlers, be it enacted that if any man be found to live as an idler or renegade, though a freed man, it shall be lawful for that incorporation or plantation to which he belongs to appoint him a master to serve for wages till he shows apparent signs of amendment.

Against gaming at dice and cards be it ordained by this present assembly that the winner or winners shall lose all his or their winnings and both winners and losers shall forfeit ten shillings a man, one ten shillings whereof to go to the discoverer and the rest to charitable and pious uses in the incorporation where the faults are committed.

Against drunkeness be it also decreed that if any private prsons be found culpable thereof, for the first time he is to be reproved privately by the minister, the second time publicly, the third time to lie in bolts 12 hours in the house of the provost marshal and to pay his fees, and if he still continue in that vice to undergo such severe punishment as the Governor and Council of Estate shall thinke fit to be inflicted on him. But if any officer offend in this crime, the first time he shall receive a reproof from the Governor, the second time he shall openly be reproved in the church by the minister, and the third time he shall first be committed and then degraded. Provided it be understood that the Governor has always power to restore him when he shall, in his discretion, think fit.

Against excess of apparel, that every man be assessed in the church for all public contributions, if he be unmarried according to his own apparel, if he be married, according to his own and his wife's or either of their apparel.

As touching the instruction of drawing some of the better disposed of the Indians to converse with our people and to live and labor among them, the assembly, who know well their dispositions, think it fit to enjoin at least to counsel those of the colony neither utterly to reject them nor yet to draw them to come in. But in case they will of themselves come voluntarily to places well peopled, there to do service in killing of deer, fishing, beating corn, and other works, that then five or six may be admitted into every such place and no more, and that with the consent of the Governor, provided that good guard in the night be kept upon them, for generally, though some among many may prove good, they are a most treacherous people and quickly gone when they have done a villainy. And it were fit a house were built for them to lodge in apart by themselves, and lone inhabitants by no means to entertain them.

Be it enacted by this present assembly that for laying a surer foundation of the conversion of the Indians to Christian religion, each town, city, borough, and particular plantation do obtain unto themselves by just means a certain number of the native's children to be educated by them in true religion and civil course of life. Of which children the most towardly boys in wit and graces of nature to be brought up by them in the first elements of literature, so as to be fitted for the college intended for them, that from thence they may be sent to that work of conversion.

As touching the business of planting corn, this present assembly does ordain that, year by year, all and every householder and householders have in store for every servant he or they shall keep, and also for his or their own persons, whether they have any servants or no, one spare barrel of corn to be delivered out yearly either upon sale or exchange, as need shall require. For the neglect of which duty he shall be subject to the censure of the Governor and Council of Estate; provided always, that for the first year of every new man this law shall not be in force.

About the plantation of mulberry trees, be it enacted that every man, as he is seated upon his division does, for seven years together, every year plant and maintain in growth six mulberry trees at the least and as many more as he shall think convenient and as his virtue and industry shall move him to plant; and that all such persons as shall neglect the yearly planting and maintaining of that small proportion shall be subject to the censure of the Governor and the Councel of Estate.

Be it further enacted, as concerning silk flax, that those men that are upon their division or settled habitation do this next year plant and dress 100 plants which being found a commodity may farther be increased. And whosoever do fail in the performance of this shall be subject to the punishment of the Governor and Council of Estate.

For hemp also, both English and Indian, and for English flax and aniseeds, we do require and enjoin all householders of this colony, that have any of those seeds, to make trial thereof the next season.

Moreover, be it enacted by this present assembly that every householder does yearly plant and maintain ten vines, until they have attained to the art and experience of dressing a vineyard, either by their own industry or by the instruction of some vigneron. And that upon what penalty soever the Governor and Council of Estate shall think fit to impose upon the neglecters of this act.

Be it also enacted that all necessary tradesmen, or so many as need shall require, such as are come over since the departure of Sir Thomas Dale or that shall hereafter come, shall work at their trades for any other man; each one being paid according to the quality of his trade and work, to be estimated, if he shall not be contented, by the Governor and officers of the place where he works.

Be it further ordained by this General Assembly, and we do by these presents enact, that all contracts made in England between the owners of land and their tenants and servants which they shall send hither may be caused to be duly performed and that the offenders be punished as the Governor and Council of Estate shall think just and convenient.

Be it established also by this present assembly that no crafty or advantageous means be suffered to be put in practice for the enticing away the tenants and servants of any particular plantation from the place where they are seated. And that it shall be the duty of the Governor and Council of Estate most severely to punish both the seducers and the seduced and to return these latter into their former places.

Be it further enacted that the orders for the magazine lately made be exactly kept and that the magazine be preserved from wrong and sinister practices and that, according to the orders of court in England, all tobacco and sassafras be brought by the planters to the cape merchant till such time as all the goods now or heretofore sent for the magazine be taken off their hands at the prices agreed on, that by this means the same going for England into one hand the price thereof may be upheld the better. And to the end that all the whol colony may take notice of the last order of court made in England, and all those whom it concerns may know how to observe it, we hold it fit to publish it here for a law among the rest of our laws, the which orders is as follows.

Upon the 26th of October 1618, it was ordered that the magazine should continue during the term formerly prefixed and that certain abuses now complained of should be reformed; and that for preventing of all impositions, save the allowance of 25 in the hundred profit the Governor shall have an invoice as well as the cape merchant, that if any abuse in the sale of goods be offered, he, upon intelligence and due examination thereof, shall see it corrected. And for the encouragement of particular hundreds, as Smith's hundred, Martin's hundred, Lawn's hundred and the like, it shall be lawful for them to return the same to their own adventurers; provided that the same commodity be of their own growing, without trading with any other, in one entire lump and not dispersed, and that at the determination of the joint stock the goods then remaining in the magazine shall be bought by the said particular colonies before any other goods which shall be sent by private men. And it is, moreover, ordered that if the Lady La warre, the Lady Dale, Captain Bargrave, and the rest would unite themselves into a settled colony, they might be capable of the same privileges that are granted to any of the foresaid hundreds. Hitherto the order.

All the General Assembly by voices concluded not only the acceptances and observation of this order, but of the instruction also to Sir George Yeardley next preceding the same; provided, first, that the cape merchant do accept of the tobacco of all and every the planters here in Virginia, either for goods or upon bills of exchange at three shillings the pound the best and 18 shillings the second sort; provided, also, that the bills be duly paid in England; provided, in the third place, that if any other besides the magazine have at any time any necessary commodity which the magazine does want, it shall and may be lawful for any of the colony to buy the said necessary commodity of the said party, but upon the terms of the magazine, viz., allowing no more gain than 25 in the hundred, and that with the leave of the Governor; provided, lastly, that it may be lawful for the governor to give leave to any mariner, or any other person that shall have any such necessary commodity wanting to the magazine, to carry home for England so much tobacco or other natural commodities of the country as his customers shall pay him for the said necessary commodity or commodities. And to the end we may not only persuade and incite men but enforce them also thoroughly and loyally to cure their tobacco before they bring it to the magazine, be it enacted, and by these presents we do enact, that if upon the judgment of four sufficient men of any corporation where the magazine shall reside, having first taken their oaths to give true sentence, two whereof to be chosen by the cape merchant and two by the incorporation, any tobacco whatsoever shall not prove vendible at the second price, that it shall there immediately be burned before the owner's face.

It shall be free for every man to trade with the Indians, servants only excepted, upon pain of whipping unless the master redeem it off with the payment of an angel, one-fourth part whereof to go to the provost marshal, one-fourth part to the discoverer, and the other moiety to the public uses of the incorporation where he dwells.

That no man do sell or give any Indians any piece, shot, or powder, or any other arms offensive or defensive, upon pain of being held a traitor to the colony and of being hanged as soon as the fact is proved, without all redemption.

That no man do sell or give any of the greater howes to the Indians, or any English dog of quality, as a mastive, greyhound, blood hound, land or water spaniel, or any other dog or bitch whatsoever, of the English race, upon pain of forfeiting five pounds sterling to the public uses of the incorporation where he dwells.

That no man may go above twenty miles from his dwelling place, nor upon any voyage whatsoever shall be absent from thence for the space of seven days together, without first having made the Governor or commander of the same place acquainted therewith, upon pain of paying twenty shillings to the public uses of the same incorporation where the party delinquent dwells.

That no man shall purposely go to any Indian towns, habitation, or places of resort without leave from the Governor or commander of that place where he lives, upon pain of paying 40 shillings to public uses as aforesaid.

That no man living in this colony but shall between this and the first of January next ensuing come or send to the Secretary of State to enter his own and all his servants names and for what term or upon what conditions they are to serve, upon penalty of paying 40 shillings to the said Secretary of State. Also, whatsoever masters or people do come over to this plantation that within one month of their arrival, notice being first given them of this very law, they shall likewise report to the Secretary of State and shall certify him upon what terms or conditions they become hither, to the end that he may record their grants and commissions and for how long time and upon what conditions their servants, in case they have any, are to serve them, and that upon pain of the penalty next above mentioned.

All ministers in the colony shall once a year, namely in the month of March, bring to the Secretary of Estate a true account of all the christenings, burials, and marriages, upon pain, if they fail, to be censured for their negligence by the Governor and Council of Estate; likewise, where there be no ministers, that the commanders of the place do supply the same duty.

No man without leave from the governor shall kill any neat cattle whatsoever, young or old, especially kine, heifers, or cow calves, and shall be careful to preserve their steers and oxen and to bring them to plough and such profitable uses, and, without having obtained leave as aforesaid, shall not kill them upon penalty of forfeiting the value of the beast so killed.

Whosoever shall take any of his neighbors boats, oars, or canoes without leave from the owner shall be held and esteemed as a felon and so proceeded against. Also, he that shall take away by violence or steals any canoes or other things from the Indians shall make valuable restitution to the said Indians and shall forfeit, if he be a freeholder, five pounds, if a servant 40 shillings, or endure a whipping; and anything under the value of 13 pence shall be accounted petty larceny.

All ministers shall duly read divine service and exercise their ministerial function according to the ecclesiastical laws and orders of the Church of England and every Sunday in the afternoon shall catechize such as are not yet ripe to come to the communion. And whosoever of them be found negligent or faulty in this kind shall be subject to the censure of the Governor and Council of Estate.

The ministers and church wardens shall seek to prevent all ungodly disorders; the committers whereof if, upon good admonitions and mild reproof, they will not forbear the said scandalous offences, as suspicions of whoredoms, dishonest company keeping with women, and such like, they are to be presented and punished accordingly.

If any person, after two warnings, does not amend his or her life in point of evident suspicion of incontinency or of the commission of any other enormous sins, that then he or she be presented by the church wardens and suspended for a time from the church by the minister. In which interim, if the same person do not amend and humbly submit him or herself to the church, he is then fully to be excommunicated and soon after a writ or warrant to be sent from the Governor for the apprehending of his person and seizing all his goods. Provided always, that all the ministers do meet once a quarter, namely at the feast of St. Michael the Archangel, of the Nativity of our

Saviour, of the Annunciation of the Blessed Virgin, and about mid-summer, at James City or any other place where the Governor shall reside, to determine whom it is fit to excommunicate, and that they first present their opinion to the Governor ere they proceed to the act of excommunication.

For reformation of swearing, every freeman and master of a family after thrice admonition shall give 5 shillings of the value upon present demand to the use of the church where he dwells, and every servant after the like admonition, except his master discharge the fine, shall be subject to whipping; provided, that the payment of the fine notwithstanding, the said servant shall acknowledge his fault publicly in the church.

No man whatsoever coming by water from above, as from Henrico, Charles City, or any place from the westward of James City, and being bound for Kiccowtan or any other part on this side of the same, shall presume to pass by either by day or by night without touching first here at James City, to know whether the Governor will command him any service, and the like shall they perform that come from Kiccowtanward or from any place between this and that to go upward, upon pain of forfeiting ten pounds sterling a time to the Governor; provided, that if a servant having had instructions from his master to observe his service does, notwithstanding, transgress the same, that then the said servant shall be punished at the governor's discretion, otherwise that the master himself shall undergo the foresaid penalty.

No man shall trade into the bay either in shallop, pinnace, or ship without the Governor's license and without putting in security that neither himself nor his company shall force or wrong the Indians, upon pain that doing otherwise they shall be censured at their return by the Governor and Council of Estate.

All persons whatsoever, upon Sabbath days, shall frequent divine service and sermons both forenoon and afternoon and all such as bear arms shall bring their pieces, swords, powder and shot. And every one that shall transgress this law shall forfeit three shillings a time to the use of the church, all lawful and necessary impediments excepted. But if a servant in this case shall willfully neglect his master's command he shall suffer bodily punishment.

No maid or woman servant, either now resident in the colony or hereafter to come, shall contract herself in marriage without either the consent of her parents or her master or masters or of the magistrate and minister of the place both together. And whatsoever minister shall marry or contract any such persons without some of the aforesaid consents shall be subject to the severe censure of the Governor and Council of Estate.

Be it enacted by the present assembly that whatsoever servant has heretofore or shall hereafter contract himself in England, either by way of indenture or otherwise, to serve any master here in Virginia and shall afterward, against his said former contract, depart from his master without leave or, being once embarked, shall abandon the ship he is appointed to come in and so being left behind shall put himself into the service of any other man that will bring him hither, that then at the same servant's arrival here, he shall first serve out his time with that master that brought him hither and afterward also shall serve out his time with his former master according to his covenant.

Complete text is taken from H. R. McIlwaine and John P. Kennedy, eds., *Journals of the House of Burgesses of Virginia*, vol. 1 (Richmond, 1905), 9–14.

71

Constitution for the Council
and Assembly in Virginia

July 24, 1621

*A*lthough this document was written in England, it is included here because it was adopted at the behest of the
colonists as to both form and content. In effect it legally ratifies what
the colonists had established in the previous document [70], which
in turn had been authorized by an order from England in 1618. The
present document clarifies the precise structure and operation of Virginia's local government, and it also reaffirms the subordination of
that government to the council in England. The governmental system
defined here parallels that established during the early years of most
colonies, including those in New England. There is a governor, with
a continuously sitting council to advise him. Once a year that council is joined by elected representatives from the towns and other localities to form a complete legislature, the General Assembly. See the
introduction to the previous document [70] for further discussion of
the historical context surrounding its enactment.

---

*To all people to whom these presents shall come, be seen, or heard, the
Treasurer, Council and Company of Adventurers and Planters of the
City of London for the first colony in Virginia send greeting.*

Know that we, the said Treasurer, Council and Company, taking into our
careful consideration the present state of the said colony in Virginia and intending, by the divine assistance, to settle such a form of government there
as may be to the greatest benefit and comfort of the people and whereby all
injustice, grievance, and oppression may be prevented and kept off as much
as possible from the said colony, have thought fit to make our entrance by
ordaining and establishing such supreme counsels as may not only be as-

sisting to the Governor for the time being in administration of justice and the executing of other duties to his office belonging, but also by their vigilant care and prudence may provide as well for remedy of all inconveniences growing from time to time, as also for the advancing of increase, strength, stability, and prosperity of the said colony,

We, therefore, the said Treasurer, Council and Company, by authority directed to us from his Majesty under his great seal, upon mature deliberation do hereby order and declare that from hence forward there be two supreme councils in Virginia for the better government of the said colony as aforesaid. The one of which councils to be called the Council of State and whose office shall be chiefly assisting, with their care, advise, and circumspection, to the said Governor shall be chosen, nominated, placed, and displaced from time to time by us, the said Treasurer, Council and Company and our successors; which Council of State shall consist for the present only of those persons are here inserted, viz. Sir Francis Wyatt, Governor of Virginia; Captain Francis West; Sir George Yeardley, Knight; Sir William Newce, Knight, Marshal of Virginia; Mr. George Sandys, Treasurer; Mr. George Thorpe, Deputy of the College; Captain Thomas Newce, Deputy for the Company; Mr Christopher Davison, Secretary; Doctor Potts, physician to the company; Mr. Paulet; Mr. Leech; Captain Nathaniel Powell; Mr. Roger Smith; Mr. John Berkley; Mr. John Rolf; Mr. Ralph Hamer; Mr. John Pountus; Mr. Michael Lapworth; Mr. Harwood; Mr. Samuel Macocke. Which said councillors and council we earnestly pray and desire, and in his Majesty's name strictly charge and command, that all factious partialities and sinister respects laid aside, they bend their care and endeavors to assist the said Governor first and principally in advancement and of the honor and service of Almighty God and the enlargement of His kingdom amongst those heathen people, and in erecting of the said colony in one obedience to his Majesty and all lawful authority from his Majesty's derived, and lastly in maintaining the said people in justice and Christian conversation among themselves and in strength and hability to withstand their enemies. And this Council is to be always, or for the most part, residing about or near the said Governor, and yearly, of course, and no oftener but for very extraordinary and important occasions, shall consist for the present of the said Council of State and of two burgesses out of every town, hundred and other particular plantation to be respectfully chosen by the inhabitants. Which Council shall be called the General Assembly, wherein, as also in the said

Council of State, all matters shall be decided, determined, and ordered by the greater part of the voices then present, reserving always to the Governor a negative voice. And this General Assembly shall have free power to treat, consult, and conclude as well of all emergent occasions concerning public weal of the said colony and every part thereof as shall from time to time appear necessary or requisite. Wherein, as in all other things, we require the said General Assembly, as also the said Council of State, to imitate and follow the policy of the form of government, laws, customs, manners of loyal and other administration of justice used in the realm of England, as near as may be even as ourselves by his Majesty's letters patents are required; provided that no laws or ordinances made in the said General Assembly shall be and continue in force and validity unless the same shall be solemnly ratified and confirmed in a general greater court of the said court here in England and so ratified and returned to them under our seal. It being our intent to afford the like measure also unto the said colony that after the government of the said colony shall once have been well framed and settled accordingly, which is to be done by us as by authority derived from his Majesty and the same shall have been so by us declared, no orders of our court afterward shall bind the said colony unless they be ratified in like manner in their General Assembly.

In witness whereof, we have hereunto set our common seal the 24th day of (July) 1621, and in the year of the reign of our governor, Lord James by the [. . .] of God of England, Scotland, France, and Ireland, King, Defender of the [. . .], viz, of England, France, and Scotland the nineteenth and of Scotland the four and fiftieth.

Complete text taken verbatim from S. M. Bemiss, *The Three Charters of the Virginia Company of London, with Seven Related Documents, 1606–1621* (Williamsburg: The University Press of Virginia, 1957), 126–28.

72

[Laws and Orders Concluded
by the Virginia General Assembly]

March 5, 1624

*S*hortly after the Virginia General Assembly passed this code of laws, the king reorganized the colony government and officially placed all power in the hands of the Governor, although in fact all of the Governor's actions had to be approved by the Crown-appointed Council of State. That the General Assembly was officially terminated might be explained in part by section 8 of the document below, in which the Assembly asserts that the Governor cannot levy taxes without Assembly approval. Although English common law had long held that there should be no taxes levied without the approval of Parliament, the king was not inclined to let parliamentary equivalents develop in the colonies. At the same time he did not assert that the colonists were represented in Parliament because he was engaged in a bitter struggle with Parliament that would eventually result in the temporary termination of the monarchy. This left the Virginia colonists in the anomalous position of not having the basic common law rights of Englishmen that had been guaranteed by their charter from the king. Resolution of the situation came only after the gradual reassertion of the power to tax by an Assembly was called back into official existence in 1638. A major factor in this development was the empty throne between 1640 and 1660.

---

1. THAT there shall be in every plantation, where the people use to meete for the worship of God, a house or roome sequestred for that purpose, and not to be for any temporal use whatsoever, and a place empaled in, sequestered only to the buryal of the dead.

2. That whosoever shall absent himselfe from divine service any Sunday

without an allowable excuse shall forfeite a pound of tobacco, and he that absenteth himselfe a month shall forfeith 50lb. of tobacco.

3. That there be an uniformity in our church as neere as may be to the canons in England; both in substance and circumstance, and that all persons yeild readie obedience unto them under paine of censure.

4. That the 22nd of March be yeerly solemnized as holliday, and all other hollidays (except when they fall two together) betwixt the feast of the annuntiation of the blessed virgin and St. Michael the archangell, then only the first to be observed by reason of our necessities.

5. That no minister be absent from his church above two months in all the yeare upon penalty of forfeiting halfe his means, and whosoever shall absent above fowre months in the year shall forfeit his whole means and cure.

6. That whosoever shall disparage a minister without bringing sufficient proofe to justify his reports whereby the mindes of his parishioners may be alienated from him, and his ministry prove the less effectual by their prejudication, shall not only pay 500lb. waight of tobacco but also aske the minister so wronged forgiveness publickly in the congregation.

7. That no man dispose of any of his tobacco before the minister be satisfied, upon pain of forfeiture double his part of the minister's means, and one man of every plantation to collect his means out of the first and best tobacco and corn.

8. That the Governor shall not lay any taxes or ympositions upon the colony their lands or comodities other way than by the authority of the General Assembly, to be levyed and ymployed as the said Assembly shall appoynt.

9. The governor shall not withdraw the inhabitants from their private labors to any service of his own upon any colour whatsoever and in case the publick service require ymployments of many hands before the holding a General Assemblie to give order for the same, in that case the levying of men shall be done by order of the governor and whole body of the counsell and that in such sorte as to be least burthensome to the people and most free from partialitie.

10. That all the old planters that were here before or came in at the last coming of sir Thomas Gates they and their posterity shall be exempted from their personal service to the warrs and any publick charge (church duties

excepted) that belong particularly to their persons (not exempting their families) except such as shall be ymployed to command in chief.

11. That no burgesses of the General Assembly shall be arrested during the time of the assembly, a week before and a week after upon pain of the creditors forfeiture of his debt and such punishment upon the officer as the court shall award.

12. That there shall be courts kept once a month in the corporations of Charles City and Elizabeth Citty for the decyding of suits and controversies not exceeding the value of one hundred pounds of tobacco and for punishing of petty offences, that the commanders of the places and such others as the governor and council shall appoint by commission shall be the judges, with reservation of apeal after sentence to the governor and counsell and whosoever shall appeal yf he be there cast in suit shall pay duble damages, The commanders to be of the quorum and sentence to be given by the major parties.

13. That every privatt planters devident shall be surveyed and laid out in several and the bounds recorded by the survey; yf there be any pettie differences betwixt neighbours about their devidents to be divided by the surveyor if of much importance to be referred to the governor and counsell: the surveyor to have 10lbs. of tobacco upon every hundred acres.

14. For the encouragement of men to plant store of corne, the prise shall not be stinted, but it shall be free for every man to sell it as deere as he can.

15. That there shall be in every parish a bulick granary unto which there shall be contributed for every planter exceeding the adge of 18 years alive at the crop after he hath been heere a year a bushell of corne, the which shall be disposed for the publique uses of every parish by the major part of the freemen, the remainder yearly to be taken out by the owners at St. Tho's his day and the new bushell to be putt in the roome.

16. That three sufficient men of every parish shall be sworne to see that every man shall plant and tende sufficient of corne for his family. Those men that have neglected so to do are to be by the said three men presented to be censured by the governor and counsell.

17. That all trade for corne with the salvages as well publick as private after June next shall be prohibited.

18. That every freeman shall fence in a quarter of an acre of ground before Whitsuntide next to make a garden for planting of vines, herbs, roots,

&c. subpoena ten pounds of tobacco a man, but that no man for his own family shall be tyed to fence above an acre of land and that whosoever hath fenced a garden and [   ] of the land shall be paid for it by the owner of the soyle; they shall also plant Mulberry trees.

19. The proclamations for swearing and drunkenness sett out by the governor and counsell are confirmed by this Assembly; and it is further ordered that the churchwardens shall be sworne to present them to the commanders of every plantation and that the forfeitures shall be collected by them to be for publique uses.

20. That a proclamation be read aboard every ship and afterwards fixed to the maste of such [   ] in, prohibiting them to break boulke or make privatt sales of any commodity until [   ] James City, without special order from the governor and counsell.

21. That the proclamation of the rates of commodities be still in force and that there be some men in every plantation to censure the tobacco.

22. That there be no weights nor measures used but such as shall be sealed by officers appointed for that purpose.

23. That every dwelling house shall be pallizaded in for defence against the Indians.

24. That no man go or send abroad without a sufficient parties well armed.

25. That men go not to worke in the ground without their arms (and a centinell upon them).

26. That the inhabitants go not aboard ships or upon any other occasions in such numbers, as thereby to weaken and endanger the plantations.

27. That the commander of every plantation take care that there be sufficient of powder and amunition within the plantation under his command and their pieces fixt and their arms compleate.

28. That there be dew watch kept by night.

29. That no commander of any plantation do either himselfe or suffer others to spend powder unneccessarily in drinking or entertainments, &c.

30. That such persons of quality as shall be found delinquent in their duties being not fitt to undergoe corporal punishment may notwithstanding be ymprisoned at the discretione of the commander & for greater offences to be subject to a ffine inflicted by the monthlie court, so that it exceed not the value aforesaid.

31. That every man that hath not contributed to the finding a man at the

castell shall pay for himself and servants five pounds of tobacco a head, towards the discharge of such as had their servants here.

32. That at the beginning of July next the inhabitants of every corporation shall fall upon their adjoyning salvages as we did the last yeare, those that shall be hurte upon service to be cured at the publique charge; in case any be lamed to be maintained by the country according to his person and quality.

33. That for defraying of such publique debts our troubles have brought upon us. There shall be levied 10 pounds of tobacco upon every male head above sixteen years of adge now living (not including such as arrived since the beginning of July last).

34. That no person within this colony upon the rumur of supposed changed and alteration, presume to be disobedient to the present government, nor servants to their private officers, masters or overseers at their uttermost perills.

35. That Mr. John Pountis, counsellor of state, goin to England, (being willing by our intreatie to accept of that imployment) to solicite the general cause of the country to his majesty and the counsell, towards the charges of which voyage, the country consente to pay for every male head above sixteen years of adge then living, which have been here a yeare ffour pounds of the best merchantable tobacco, in leafe, at or before the last of October next.

Subscripts.

Sir Francis Wyatt, Knt. Governor, &c.

Capt Fran's West,	John Pott,
Sir George Yeardley	Capt. Roger Smith,
George Sandy's Trear,	Capt. Raphe Hamer.

John Pountis.

William Tucker,	Nathaniel Bass,
Jabez Whitakers,	John Willcox,
William Peeine,	Nicho: Marten,
Rauleigh Croshaw,	Clement, Dilke,
Richard Kingsmell,	Isaeck Chaplin,
Edward Blany,	John Cew,
Luke Boyse,	John Utie,

John Pollington.	John Southerne,
Nathaniel Causey,	Richard Bigge,
Robert Addams,	Henry Watkins,
Thomas Harris,	Gabriel Holland,
Richard Stephens,	Thomas Morlatt,

Copia Test,

    R. HICKMAN, Cl. Sec. off.

Complete text, with original spelling, taken from W. H. Hening, ed., *The Statutes at Large: Being a Collection of All the Laws of Virginia from the First Session of the Legislature in 1619,* vol. 1 (New York: R. & W. & G. Bartow, 1823), 122–29.

73

Act Relating to the Biennial and Other Assemblies and Regulating Elections and Members in North Carolina

1715

*E*stablished in 1664/1665, the province of Carolina developed two widely separated settlements. Proprietary interest was focused on the Charles Town settlement in the south, with its fine port, while the northern settlement, centered in Albemarle County, received little attention. The document below deals with the northeastern part of the province of Carolina—what is now known as North Carolina. Each settlement was granted its own unicameral legislature under the original proprietary concessions, and both settlements were dominated by a council appointed from London. The provincial governor lived in the south, and his deputy governor served in the north. In 1669 John Locke and Anthony Cooper composed the Fundamental Constitutions of Carolina at the behest of the proprietors. Rather than resembling Locke's system in Two Treatises of Government, it instead used Harrington's complex system of representation based on the ownership of various amounts of property. Among other things, the Locke/Cooper document created more political offices than there were settlers. Parts of the proposal, which served as the basis for government until 1698, were adopted anyway. By this time North and South Carolina had come to be viewed as completely separate entities. In 1712 North Carolina received its own governor. In the 1715 document reproduced below, North Carolina established the form of government it would basically use until 1776. The document is notable for establishing clear districts and a careful electoral process.

Whereas his Excellency the Palatine and the rest of the true and absolute lords proprietors of Carolina, having duly considered the privileges and immunities wherewith kingdom of Great Britain is induced and being desirous that this their province may have such as may thereby enlarge this settlement and that the frequent sitting of assemblies is a principal safeguard of their peoples privileges, have thought fit to enact.

And be it enacted by the said Palatine and Lords Proprietors, by and with the advice and consent of the present Grand Assembly now met at Little River for the northeast part of the said province, and it is hereby enacted, that for the due election and constituting of members of the biennial and other assemblies, it shall be lawful for the freemen of the respective precincts of Albemarle to meet the first Tuesday in September every two years in the places hereafter mentioned, that is to say, the inhabitants of Chowan at the land laid out for a town on the fork of Queen Anne's Creek, the inhabitants of Perquimons at the upper side of the mouth of Suttons Creek, the inhabitants of Pasquotank at the plantation now in possession of Mr. Joseph Glaister on New Begunn Creek, the inhabitants of Currituck at the plantation of Mr. Thomas Vandermulin, the inhabitants of Beaufort in Bath in Bath Town, the inhabitants of Hyde precinct at the plantation at Mr. Websterson's the west side of Matchapungo, a river, the inhabitants of Craven at Swift's plantation at the mouth of Handock's Creek, the inhabitants of New Bern at the town so called, and then there to choose such members as are to sit in that Assembly, which shall be five freeholders out of every precinct in Albemarle County aforesaid.

And be it further enacted that it shall and may be lawful for the inhabitants and freemen in each precinct in every other county or counties that now is or shall be hereafter erected in this government aforesaid to meet as aforesaid at such place as shall be adjudged most convenient by the marshal of such county, unless he be otherwise ordered by the special commands of the Governor or Commander-in-Chief, to choose two freeholders out of every precinct in the county aforesaid to sit and vote in the said Assembly.

And be it further enacted that the burgesses so chosen in each precinct for the biennial Assembly shall meet and sit the first Monday in November then next following, every two years at the same place the assembly last sat, except the Palatines' Court shall, by their proclamation published twenty days before the said meeting, appoint some other place; and there, with the consent and concurrence of the Palatines' Court, shall make and ordain laws as shall be thought most necessary for the good of this government.

Provided always, and nevertheless, that the powers granted to the Lords Proprietors from the crown of calling, proroguing, and dissolving Assemblies are not hereby meant or intended to be invaded, limited, or restrained.

And it is hereby further enacted, by the authority aforesaid, that no person whatsoever, inhabitant of this government, born out of the allegiance of his Majesty and not made free, no Negro, Mulatto, or Indians shall be capable of voting for members of the Assembly and that no other person or persons shall be allowed or admitted to vote for members of Assembly in the government unless he be of the age of one and twenty years and has been one full year resident in the government and has paid one year's levy preceeding the election.

And be it further enacted that all persons offering to vote for members of Assembly shall bring a list to the marshal or deputy taking the poll containing the names of the persons he votes for and shall subscribe his own name or cause the same to be done. And if any such person or persons shall be suspected either by the marshall or any other candidates not to be qualified according to the true intent and meaning of this act then the marshal, deputy marshal, or other officer that shall be appointed to take and receive such votes or lists shall have power to administer an oath or attestation to every suspected person of his qualification and ability to choose members of Assembly and whether he has not before given in his list at that election.

And be it further enacted that every officer or marshal which shall admit of or take the vote of any person not truly qualified according to the purport and meaning of this act, provided the objection be made by any candidate or inspector, or shall make undue return of any person for member of Assembly, shall forfeit, for such vote taken and admitted and for such returns, twenty pounds, to be employed for and toward the building of any court house, church, or chapels as the governor for the time being shall think fit; but if no such building require it, then to the lords proprietors, and twenty pounds to each person of right and by a majority of votes ought to have been returned, to be recovered by action of debt, bill, plaint, or information in any court of record in this government wherein no essoin, wager of law, or protection shall be allowed or admitted.

And be it further enacted that every marshall or officer whose business and duty it is to make return of elections of members of Assembly shall attend the Assembly the first three days of their sitting, unless he have leave of the assembly to depart, to inform the Assembly of all matters and disputes as shall arise about elections and shall show to the Assembly the list of the votes for every person returned and have made complaint of false returns to the Assembly. And every marshal or other officer, as aforesaid, which shall deny and refuse to attend as aforesaid shall forfeit the sum of twenty pounds, to be recovered and disposed of in such manner and form as the forfeitures before by this act appointed.

And be it further enacted that whatsoever representative, so elected as aforesaid, shall fail in making his personal appearance and giving his attendance at the Assembly precisely at the day limited by the writ or on the day appointed for the meeting of the biennial Assembly, when the election is for a biennial Assembly, shall be fined for every day's absence during the sitting of the Assembly, twenty shilling, to be seized by a warrant from the Speaker and so to be applied to such uses as the lower house of Assembly shall think fit.

And be it further enacted that every member of the Assembly that shall be elected as aforesaid after the ratifying this act shall not be qualified to sit as a member in the House of Burgesses before he shall willingly take the oath of allegiance and supremacy, the abjuration oath, and all such other oaths as shall be ordered and directed to be taken by the members of Parliament in Great Britain.[1]

And be it further enacted that the quorum of the House of Burgesses for voting and passing up bills shall not be less than one full half of the House and that no bill shall be signed and ratified except there be present eight of the members, whereof the Speaker to be one; and in case eight members shall meet at any Assembly those eight shall have full power to adjourn from day to day till sufficient number can assemble to transact the business of government.

Charles Eden
N. Chevin

---

1. Note that as a result of the Glorious Revolution in 1688 we see for the first time Parliament mentioned as having the ability to legislate for a colony originally founded by a charter from the king.

C. Gale
Francis Foster
T. Knight
Edward Mosely, Speaker

Text taken from William L. Saunders, ed., *The Colonial Records of North Carolina,* vol. 2 (Raleigh, 1958), 213–16.

74

Act to Ascertain the
Manner and Form of Electing Members
to Represent the Province

1721

*B*y 1721 the government of South Carolina had evolved to the point where the local legislature was a fully functioning institution. Most of the foundation documents of South Carolina—like those of Virginia, North Carolina, and Georgia—had been written and adopted in London, and for this reason there are few that qualify for inclusion in this collection. As each of these four colonies reached the point of self-governance equivalent to that achieved in colonies further to the north, a refounding occurred through acts by the legislature. These acts usually took the form of defining electoral districts, the electoral process, and the relationship between the parts of the legislature and between the legislature and the governor. On the one hand, the institutional structures of the southern colonies had to a striking degree come to resemble those found in the northern colonies. On the other hand, political realities during the development of the southern colonies did not allow as much room for independent local development. Thus, while the institutions were similar up and down the coast, the theory underlying their design was less robust in the south than that articulated in New England and Pennsylvania in particular. As a result, while post-1775 state constitutions had much in common, the theory used to justify the Revolution and undergird later American constitutional development had been rehearsed in public to a far greater extent in the north than in the south—especially in foundation documents. Still, these arguments resonated everywhere in America.

Whereas the choosing members of the Commons House of Assembly for this province by parishes or precincts has been found by experience to be the most just and least expensive method that can be devised, and approaches nearest to the form and method of choosing or electing members in other his Majesty's dominions and plantations, and not liable to the inconveniencies that attend any other method heretofore used or practiced in this province; therefore, for preserving the same inviolable, we humbly pray your most sacred Majesty that it may be enacted,

I. And be it enacted by his Excellency Francis Nicholson, Esq., Governor, etc., by and with the advice and consent of his Majesty's honorable Council and the Assembly of this province, and by the authority of the same, that the persons who shall be chosen to serve as members of Assembly after the ratification of this act shall be elected and chosen after the manner and at the places appointed by this act.

II. And be it further enacted, by the authority aforesaid, that all writs for the future elections of members of Assembly shall be issued out by the Governor and Council for the time being, and shall bear date forty days before the day appointed for the meeting of the said members, and shall be directed to the church warden or church wardens of the several parishes hereafter named, or in case there should be wanted church wardens in any parish then to such other proper persons as the Governor and Councill shall think fit to nominate in the said writs to manage such elections, every one of whom are hereby empowered and required to execute the said writs faithfully according to the true intent and meaning of this act, to which every person shall be sworn by any one justice of the peace for the county, who is hereby required to administer such oath without fee or reward and shall give public notice in writing of all and every such writs two Sundays before the appointed time of election at the door of each parish church, or at some other public place as shall be appointed in the said writs in such parishes as have yet no churches erected, to the intent the time and place of election may be better and more fully made known; which writs shall be executed upon the same days at all places where elections are appointed.

III. And be it further enacted, by the authority aforesaid, that every free white man, and no other person, professing the christian religion, who has attained to the age of one and twenty years and has been a resident and an inhabitant in this province for the space of one whole year before the date of the writs for the election he offers to give his vote at, and has a freehold of at least 50 acres of land, or has been taxed in the precedent year twenty shillings, or is taxed twenty shillings the year present to the support of this government, shall be deemed a person qualified to vote for and may be capable of electing a representative or representatives to serve as a member or members of the Commons House of Assembly for the parish or precinct wherein he actually is a resident, or in any other parish or precincts wherein he has the like qualification.

IV. And for the preventing of frauds in all elections as much as possible, it is hereby enacted, by the authority aforesaid, that the names of the electors for members of the Commons House of Assembly shall be fairly entered in a book or roll, for that purpose provided by the churchwardens or other persons appointed for managing elections, to prevent any person's voting twice at the same election; and the manner of their voting shall be as herein after is directed, shall put into a box, glass, or sheet of paper, prepared for that purpose by the said church wardens or other persons, as is above directed, a piece of paper rolled up, wherein is written the names of the representatives he votes for, and to which paper the elector shall not be obliged to subscribe his name; and if upon the scrutiny two or more papers with persons written thereon for members of Assembly be found rolled up together, or more person's names be found written in any paper than ought to be voted for, all and every such paper or papers shall be invalid and of no effect; and that those persons who, after all the papers and votes are delivered in and entered as aforesaid, shall be found, upon the scrutiny made, to have the majority of votes, are and shall be deemed and declared to be members of the succeeding Commons House of Assembly, so as they be qualified as is hereinafter directed.

V. And be it further enacted, by the authority aforesaid, that the said election shall not continue longer than two days and that the said elections shall begin at nine in the morning and end at four in the evening, and that at adjourning of the poll at convenient hours, in the time of the aforesaid election the church wardens, or other persons, as foresaid, empowered to manage the said elections, shall seal up the said box, glass, or paper wherein are put all the votes then delivered in and rolled up by the electors, as aforesaid, with their own seals and the seals of any two or more of the electors that are there present, and upon opening the poll shall unseal the said box, glass, or paper in the presence of the said electors, in order to proceed in the said elections.

VI. And be it further enacted, by the authority aforesaid, that the said church wardens, or other persons appointed in each parish to manage the elections aforesaid, shall, within seven days after the scrutiny is made, give public notice in writing at the church door, or at such other public places in the parishes that have no churches where the election was made, to the person or persons so elected that the inhabitants of the said parish have made choice of him or them to serve as their representative or representatives in the next succeeding Commons House of Assembly, under the penalty of one hundred pounds current money of this province for his default or neglect therein, to be recovered and disposed of in such manner and form as is hereafter in this act directed.

VII. And be it further enacted, by the authority aforesaid, that the inhabitants of the several parishes in this province qualified to vote for members of Assembly, as is before in this act directed, shall, upon the day of the election, according to the Governor's and Council's precept for the time being, meet at their respective parish churches, or at some other public place in such parishes as have not yet any churches erected in them, as shall be appointed by the said precept, and there proceed to choose their representatives according to the number following; that is to say, the parish of St. Philip's Charlestown, five members; for the parish of Christ church, two members; for the parish of St. John's three members; for the parish of St. Andrew's, three members; for the parish of St. George's two members; for the parish of St. James Goose Creek, four members; for the parish of St. Thomas and St. Dennis, three members, the election to be made at the parish church of St. Thomas; for the parish of St. Paul's four members; for the parish of St. Bartholomew's, at such place in the said parish as shall be appointed by the governor and Council's precept, until the parish church is erected, four members; for the parish of St. Helena, four members, the election to be made at Beauford in the said parish; and for the parish of St. James Santee, with Winyaw, two members. And the said several members who, upon a scrutiny, are found to have the majority of votes, so as they are qualified as is hereinafter directed, shall be and they are hereby declared and adjudged to be the true representatives for the said parish.

VIII. And be it further enacted, by the authority aforesaid, that every person who shall be elected and returned, as is before directed by this act, to serve as a member of the Commons House of Assembly, shall be qualified as follows; viz., he shall be a free born subject of the kingdom of Great Britain, or of the dominion thereunto belonging, or a foreign person naturalized by act of Parliament in Great Britain or Ireland, that has attained to the age of twenty-one years, and has been resident in this province for twelve months before the date of the said writs; and having in this province a settled plantation or freehold, in his own right, of a leave 500 acres of land, and ten slaves, or has in his own proper person and in his own right, to the value of 1,000 in houses, buildings, town lots, or other lands in any part of this province.

IX. And be it further enacted, by the authority aforesaid, that any of his Majesty's justices of the peace returned to serve as a member of the said Commons House of Assembly shall read over to the rest of the members returned to serve in the said house, before they be admitted to sit as such, the last mentioned qualifying clause, and then each member, before he be admitted to sit as such in the said house, shall take the following oath on the holy evangelists. I, AB, do sincerely swear that I am duly qualified to be chosen and serve as a member of the Commons House of Assembly of this province for the parish of   , according to the true intent and meaning of this act. So help me God.

X. And be it further enacted, by the authority aforesaid, that if any member or members hereafter chosen to serve in any Commons House of Assembly should die or depart this province, or refuse to qualify him of themselves as in this act directed, or be expelled by the said House of Commons, then and in such cases the said House shall by message to the Governor and Council for the time being desire them to issue out a new writ or writs, and the said Governor and Council shall, on such a message to them presented, issue out a new writ or writs, directed as before in this act is appointed, for choosing another person or persons to serve in the place or places of such member or members so dead or departed this province, or who shall refuse to qualify him or themselves, or be expelled as aforesaid. Which person or persons, so chosen and summoned as before directed, shall attend the Commons House of Assembly, as by the precept is directed, under the same fines and penalties the several church wardens or other persons appointed to manage elections according to the directions of this act are liable to the said act.

xi. And be it further enacted, by the authority aforesaid, that all and every member and members of the Commons House of Assembly of this province, chosen by virtue of this act, shall have as much power and privilege to all intents and purposes as any member or members of the Commons House of Assembly of this province heretofore of right had, might, could, or ought to have in the said province; provided the same are such as are according to his Majesty's thirty-fifth instruction.

xii. And be it further enacted, by the authority aforesaid, that if any person or persons appointed by this act to manage any election for a member or members of the Commons House of Assembly, as aforesaid, shall willingly or knowingly admit of or take the vote of any person not qualified according to the purpose of this act, or, after any vote delivered in at such election, shall open or suffer any person whatsoever to open any such vote before the scrutiny is begun to be made, or shall make an undue return of any person for a member of the Commons House of Assembly, each person so offending, shall forfeit for each such vote taken and admitted of, opened, or suffered to be opened, as aforesaid, and for each such return, the sum of one hundred pounds current money of this province, to be recovered and disposed of in such manner and form as hereafter in this act is directed.

xiii. And be it further enacted, by the authority aforesaid, that all and every person or persons appointed to take votes, or to manage elections of members to serve in the Commons House of Assembly, as aforesaid, shall for that purpose attend at the time and place of election according as he or they are directed by the said writs and attend likewise on the said Commons House of Assembly the two first days of their sitting, unless he or they have leave sooner to depart, to inform them of all such matters and disputes that did arise or may have arisen about the election of any member or members to serve as aforesaid, or at any place or places where the same was or were appointed to be managed, and shall show to said House the list of the votes of every person returned to be a representative to serve as aforesaid, or which otherwise ought to have been returned as such, if any complaint of a false return has been made to the Commons House of Assembly; and every person appointed to take votes, as aforesaid, who shall omit or refuse to attend at either of the times and places, as aforesaid, shall forfeit the sum of ten pounds current money of this province, to be recovered and disposed of in such manner and form as is hereafter directed by this act.

xiv. And be it further enacted, by the authority aforesaid, that if any person or persons whatsoever shall, on any day appointed for the election of a member or members of the Commons House of Assembly as aforesaid, presume to violate the freedom of the said election by any arrest, menaces, or threats, or endeavor or attempt to over-awe, fright, or force any person qualified to vote against his inclination or conscience, or otherwise by bribery obtain any vote, or who shall, after the said election is over, menace, despitefully use, or abuse any person because he has not voted as he or they would have had him, every such person so offending, upon due and sufficient proof made of such his violence or abuse, menacing or threatening, before any two justices of the peace, shall be bound over to the next general sessions of the peace, himself in fifty pounds current money of this province, and two sureties, each in twenty-five pounds of like money, and to be of good behaviour, and abide the sentence of the said court, where, if the offender or offenders are convicted and found guilty of such offense or offenses, as aforesaid, then he or they shall each of them forfeit the sum of fifty pounds current money of this province, and be committed to jail without bail mainprize till the same be paid; which fine so imposed shall be paid unto one of the church wardens of the parish where the offense was committed for the use of the poor thereof; and if any person offending as aforesaid shall be chosen a member of the Commons House of Assembly, after conviction of illegal practices proved before the said House, shall by a vote of the said House be rendered uncapable to sit or vote as a member of that Commons House of Assembly.

xv. And be it further enacted, by the authority aforesaid, that no civil officer whatsoever shall execute any writs or other civil process whatsoever upon the body of any person qualified to vote for members of the Commons House of Assembly, as before in this act is directed, either in his journey to or in his return from the place of such election, or during his stay there on that account, or within forty-eight hours after the scrutiny for such elections is finished, under the penalty of twenty pounds current money of his province, to be recovered of and from the officer which shall arrest or serve any process, as aforesaid, after such manner and form and to be disposed of as hereinafter is directed; and all such writs or warrants executed on the body of any person either going to or being at, within the time limited by this clause, or returning from the place of such election is appointed to be managed, he being qualified to give in his vote thereat, are hereby declared void and null.

XVI. And be it further enacted, by the authority aforesaid, that every justice of the peace who shall refuse or neglect to do his duty in and by this act enjoined and required shall, for every default, forfeit the sum of one hundred pounds current money of this province, to be recovered and disposed of as is hereinafter directed by this act.

XVII. And be it further enacted, by the authority aforesaid, that in any succeeding Commons House of Assembly, no less than nineteen members duly met shall make an House to transact the business of the same; and for passing any law therein, there shall not be less than ten affirmatives; nor shall a less number than seven members of the said House met together have power to adjourn, which number are hereby declared to have power, in the absence of the speaker, to choose a chairman to adjourn the members from day to day and to summon by their messenger any absenting member or members to appear and give their attention in the said House.

XVIII. But forasmuch as, by the great distance of the habitation of several of the members of Charlestown, through bad weather and other accidents it may often happen that such a number may not meet to make an adjournment, be it, therefore, enacted, by the authority aforesaid, that in case none of the members of the Commons House of Assembly, or a less number than seven of them, should appear in the said House according to the directions of the writs appointing their first meeting; or to their last prorogation or adjournment, that then and in such case it shall be and it is hereby declared lawful for the governor for the time being, with the advice and consent of his council, to name a further day for the meeting of the said Commons House of Assembly, and that the said House shall not be dissolved by their not meeting as aforesaid, any law, custom, or usage to the contrary thereof in anyway notwithstanding.

XIX. And be it further enacted, by the authority aforesaid, that whosoever for the future shall be elected a member to serve in the Commons House of Assembly, before he be permitted to sit and vote in the said house, shall further qualify himself for the same by taking the usual oaths and make and sign the declaration appointed by several acts of Parliament of Great Britain.

XX. And be it further enacted, by the authority aforesaid, that all the fines and forfeitures mentioned in this act and not before particularly disposed of, the one-half thereof shall be to his Majesty for the use of the poor of the parish of St. Philip's Charlestown, to be paid to the church wardens of the said parish, and the other half to him or them that will sue for the same by action of debt, suit, bill, plaint, or information in any court of record in this province, wherein no essoign, protection, privilege, or wager of law, or stay of protection shall be admitted or allowed of.

XXI. And be it further enacted by the authority aforesaid, that this present General Assembly shall determine and be dissolved at the expiration of three years next after the date of the writs issued out for calling the same, and that every General Assembly hereafter called by virtue of any writs, as aforesaid, shall determine and be dissolved every three years next after the date of the respective writs by which they were called, except sooner dissolved by the Governor.

XXII. And be it further enacted, by the authority aforesaid, that the sitting and holding of General Assemblies shall not be discontinued or intermitted above six months, but shall within that time, from and after the determination of this or any other General Assembly, or oftener if occasion require, new writs to be issued out by the Governor for the time being for calling, assembling, and holding of another General Assembly.

XXIII. And be it further enacted and declared that this present Assembly, having been elected and called together by virtue of his Majesty's royal commissions and instructions to his Excellency Francis Nicholson, Esq., his Majesty's Governor and Commander-in-Chief of this his province of South Carolina, shall in all things whatsoever be deemed and held to be a true and lawful Assembly, and all acts and ordinances duly passed by them, by and with the consent of his Majesty's honorable Council and assented to by his Excellency, shall be deemed and accounted laws and orders of the said province, anything in any former act of this province heretofore made notwithstanding.

XXIV. And be it further enacted, by the authority aforesaid, that all former acts of Assembly of this province relating to or concerning the elections of the members to serve in the Commons House of Assembly be, from and after the ratification of this act, repealed, and they are hereby declared void and repealed.

James Moore,
Speaker

Charlestown, [...] 19, 1721.
Assented to by Francis Nicholson, Governor

The text is taken from T. Cooper, ed., *Statutes at Large of South Carolina*, vol. 3 (Columbia, 1837), 135–40.

75
Act to Ascertain the
Manner and Form of Electing Members
to Represent the Inhabitants of This Province
in the Commons House of Assembly

June 9, 1761

*E*stablished by charter in 1732, Georgia was initially governed by a board of trustees in London with no provision for either a governor or a legislature. An appointed governor was in place by 1743, but an assembly was not authorized until 1751, and even then it had no real power. In 1752 the trusteeship ended and Georgia reverted to a royal colony. At this point the Crown established institutions similar to those found in the other royal colonies. In 1761 the Georgia legislature passed the act in this document to define the electoral basis underlying their government. It is very similar to the act passed by South Carolina in 1721 [74]. One feature of the present document is that it clearly describes a method of voting used throughout the colonies and reveals that votes were public rather than secret. It was not considered unusual for voters to be asked to "stand up and be counted." The secret ballot was not widely used in America until the late nineteenth century. The precise definition and careful protection of the electoral process implies that the people are the foundation of government. The care taken here and in other colonial documents in this regard indicates that the concept of the electoral process is at least emerging, if not already accepted. One needs to remember that elections were rare in the world at this time, and rules for running them are in the process of being worked out in documents like this one.

Whereas the manner and form of choosing members of the Commons House of Assembly to represent the inhabitants of this province and the qualifications of electors and those elected members of the Commons House of Assembly has never yet been appointed, fixed, and determined by any law of this province. We, therefore, pray your most sacred Majesty that it may be enacted. And be it enacted by his Honor James Wright, Esquire, Lieutenant-Governor and Commander-in-Chief of this his Majesty's province of Georgia, by and with the advice and consent of the honorable Council and the Commons House of Assembly of the said province in General Assembly met, and by the authority of the same, that from and after the passing of this act all writs for the election of members of the Commons House of Assembly shall be issued out by the Governor or Commander-in-Chief for the time being with the consent of the Council and shall bear test forty days before the day appointed for the meeting of the said members and shall be directed to the provost marshal in the said writs to cause such elections to be made and to return the names of the persons elected to be members of the Commons House of Assembly. And the provost marshal is hereby empowered and required to execute such writ to him directed and, for the faithful and due performance of which according to the true intent and meaning of this act, the provost marshal shall cause public notice in writing to be affixed at one or more noted place or places in such parish, district, town, or village for which the election of a member or members by him is to be taken, at least ten days before the day of election, of the time and place where such election is by him to be taken.

II. And be it further enacted, by the authority aforesaid, that every free white man, and no other, who has attained to the age of twenty-one years and has been resident in the province six months and is legally possessed in his own right of fifty acres of land in the said parish, district, town, or village for which the member or members is or are to be elected to represent in the General Assembly, shall be deemed a person qualified for electing a representative or representatives to serve as member or members of the Commons House of Assembly for the parish, district, town, or village wherein he is possessed of the above qualification.

III. And for preventing frauds, as much as may be, in all elections, it is hereby enacted, by the authority aforesaid, that the returning officer shall come to the place at the time appointed by the public notice given and shall enter the names of every person presented or presenting himself as candidate, in a book or roll, leaving a fair column under each candidate's name for the names of the voters, and when a voter comes and votes the returning officer shall repeat distinctly the person or persons' names for whom the vote is given before he writes the voter's name in the fair column under the name of such candidate or candidates as shall be voted for by that person, and that no voter shall alter his voice after it be entered or vote twice at one and the same election. And that the candidate or candidates who, after the poll is closed and the votes summed up, shall be found, upon scrutiny made if demanded, to have the majority of votes shall be deemed and declared to be a member or members of the succeeding Commons House of Assembly.

IV. And be it enacted, by the authority aforesaid, that the time for taking votes at any election shall be between the hours of nine of the clock in the forenoon and six in the afternoon, and that at adjourning the poll, at convenient hours during the time of an election, the returning officer shall first sum up the votes given for each candidate and declare the same to the candidates present, and also declare the same when he has opened the poll at the ensuing meeting, and that the said election shall not continue longer than two days unless a scrutiny is demanded. Provided, nevertheless, that the returning officer is hereby empowered and required to close the poll when he or they have waited two hours after the last vote has been given, or at any time by and with the consent and desire of all the candidates then present.

V. And be it enacted, by the authority aforesaid, that every person who shall be elected and returned, as is before directed by this act, to serve as a member in the Commons House of Assembly of this province shall be qualified in the following manner, viz., that he shall be a free-born subject of Great Britain or of the dominions thereunto belonging, or a foreign person naturalized, professing the christian religion and no other, and that has arrived at the age of twenty-one years, and has been a resident in this province for twelve months before the date of the said writ, and being legally possessed in his own right in this province of a tract of land containing at least five hundred acres.

VI. And be it enacted, by the authority aforesaid, that if any member or members chosen or hereafter to be chosen to serve in this or any other Commons House of Assembly shall refuse to serve, or any member or members should die or depart this province, or shall be expelled the House, so that his or their seat or seats become vacant, then and in such case the House shall, by address to the Governor or Commander-in-Chief for the time being signify the same and desire that a new writ or writs may issue to elect a member or members to fill up the vacancy or vacancies in the House, and, in consequence of such address, a new writ or writs shall be issued to choose in that parish, district, town, or village such other member or members to serve in the place or places of such member or members whose seat or seats are become vacant, and every person so chosen and returned, as aforesaid, shall attend the Commons House of Assembly and shall be reputed, deemed, and judged a member thereof.

vii. And be it enacted, by the authority aforesaid, that if any returning officer, as aforesaid, shall admit of or take the vote of any person refusing, at the request of one of the candidates or any two persons qualified to vote, to take the following oath, "I, A.B., do swear that I am legally possessed in my own right of a freehold estate of fifty acres of land in the township or district of   , and that such estate is legally or bona fide in my own right and not made over or granted to me purposely or fraudulently to entitle me to vote at this election," or at the request of any candidate or any two freeholders shall refuse to administer the following oath to any candidate who is hereby obliged to take this oath if so required, "I, A.B., do swear that I am in my own right truly and legally possessed of five hundred acres of land within this province and that the said right is truly and bona fide within myself and not fraudulently made over or granted to me for the purpose of qualifying me to be a representative in General Assembly," or if the provost marshal shall make any fraudulent or shall influence or endeavor to influence or persuade any voter not to vote as he first designed, shall forfeit for each and every such offense the sum of fifty pounds sterling to be to his Majesty for defraying the expense of the sitting of the General Assembly and to be sued for and recovered in the general court of the province by bill, plaint, or information.

viii. And be it enacted, by the authority aforesaid, that the provost marshall, or any person properly authorized by him to manage an election, as aforesaid, shall not return himself as a member to serve in General Assembly; and if the provost marshall refuses or neglects, on a summons from the

Commons House of Assembly, to attend that House to inform them to the best of his knowledge of any matter or dispute that did arise or may have arisen about the election of the member or members by him returned to serve in Assembly, or refusing to show the poll taken, shall forfeit for every such offense fifty pounds sterling, to be applied and recovered as is herein before directed.

IX. And be it further enacted, by the authority aforesaid, that if any person or persons whatsoever shall, on any day appointed for the election of a member or members to serve in the Commons House of Assembly, as aforesaid, presume to violate the freedom of the said election by any arrest, menace, or threats, or attempts to overawe, afright, or force any person qualified to vote, against his inclination or conscience, or otherwise by bribery obtain any vote, or who shall, after the election is over, menace, despitefully use, or abuse any person because he has not voted as he or they would have had him; every such person so offending, upon due and sufficient proof made of such his violence or abuse, menacing, or threatening, before any two justices of the peace, shall be bound over to the next general sessions of the peace, himself in twenty pounds sterling money and two sureties, each in ten pounds like money, and to be of good behavior and abide the sentence of the said court where, if the offender or offenders are convicted and found guilty of such offense or offences, as aforesaid, then he or they shall each of them forfeit a sum not exceeding twenty pounds sterling money and be committed to gaol without bail or mainprize till the same be paid. Which fine so imposed shall be paid as before directed.

X. And be it further enacted, by the authority aforesaid, that no civil officer whatsoever shall execute any writ or other civil process whatsoever upon the body of any person qualified to vote for members of the Commons House of Assembly, as before in this act directed, either in his journey to or in his return from the place of such election, providing he shall not be more than forty-eight hours upon his journey either going to, returning from, or during his stay there upon that account, or within forty-eight hours after the scrutiny for such election is finished; under the penalty of a sum not exceeding twenty pounds sterling money, to be recovered of and from the officer that shall arrest or serve any process, as aforesaid, after such manner and form, and to be disposed of as herein before is directed. And all such writs or warrants executed on the body of any person going either to or being at, within the time limited by this clause, or returning from the place where such election is appointed to be managed, he being qualified to give his vote thereat, are hereby declared void and null.

XI. And be it further enacted, by the authority aforesaid, that this act or any part thereof shall not extend to debar the Commons House of Assembly of the right to judge and determine, agreeable to the directions of this act, the qualifications of any member or members of that House, or to take away from the General Assembly, or any part thereof, any power or privilege whatever that any General Assembly, or part thereof, heretofore of right had, might, could, or ought to have had in the said province, anything herein contained to the contrary in anywise notwithstanding. Provided, always, that this act or any part thereof shall not be construed to take away the power and prerogative given the Governor or Commander-in-Chief for the time being from the Crown to adjourn, prorogue, or dissolve any General Assembly of this province when and as often as he shall think fit and expedient to do so, or to take away any other power or prerogatives whatever had from the Crown.

By Order of the Commons House of Assembly
Grey Elliott,
Speaker

By Order of the Upper House
James Habersham

In the Council Chamber, the 9th day of June, 1761.
Assented to: James Wright

The text is taken from W. S. Jenkins and L. A. Hamrick, eds., *Microfilm Collection of Early State Records*, Georgia, B.2 Reel 1a, 1735–1772.

76
[The New England Confederation]

1643

*T*hese articles drawn up and approved by the four colonies of Massachusetts, Plymouth, Connecticut, and New Haven constitute the first attempt in America to join several colonies. The New England Confederation differed in two important respects from earlier documents of union in the colonies, such as the Government of Rhode Island, 1642 [37], the Fundamental Orders of Connecticut, 1639 [43], and the Fundamental Articles of New Haven, 1639 [46]. First, this confederation included settlements operating under different charters. There was no provision in any of the four colonial charters that implied the authority to erect such a union, but the "distractions in England," as these Articles term the onset of the English Civil War, combined with colonial inclinations for self-government, seemed to make the historic step seem a natural one. Second, the other agreements established federations of towns that rehearsed the federal system erected in 1787, whereas this Confederation was a rehearsal for the Articles of Confederation. It is a true confederation, properly named, and describes itself internally as "a firm and perpetual league of friendship" (Article 2) much as the Articles of Confederation describes itself internally as "a firm league of friendship" (Article 3) and "perpetual union." The New England Confederation, a confederation of federations, lasted formally until 1684, although it effectively ceased functioning in 1664, shortly after the "distractions" of the Commonwealth era came to an end.

A RTICLES OF CONFEDERATION between the plantations under the government of the Massachusetts, the plantations under the government of New Plymouth, the plantations under the government of Connecticut, and the government of New Haven with the plantations in combination therewith:
WHEREAS we all came into these parts of America with one and the same

end and aim, namely, to advance the kingdom of our Lord Jesus Christ and to enjoy the liberties of the Gospel in purity with peace; and whereas in our settling (by a wise providence of God) we are further dispersed upon the seacoasts and rivers than was at first intended, so that we cannot according to our desire with convenience communicate in one government and jurisdiction; and whereas we live encompassed with people of several nations and strange languages which hereafter may prove injurious to us or our posterity; and forasmuch as the natives have formerly committed sundry insolences and outrages upon several plantations of the English and have of late combined themselves against us; and seeing by reason of those sad distractions in England which they have heard of, and by which they know we are hindered from that humble way of seeking advice, or reaping those comfortable fruits of protection, which at other times we might well expect, we, therefore, do conceive it our bounden duty, without delay, to enter into a present consociation among ourselves, for mutual help and strength in all our future concernments.

That, as in nation and religion, so in other respects, we be and continue one according to the tenor and true meaning of the ensuing articles. Wherefore it is fully agreed and concluded by and between the parties of jurisdictions above named, and they jointly and severally do by these presents agree and conclude that they all be and henceforth be called by the name of the United Colonies of New England.

2. The said United Colonies, for themselves and their posterities, do jointly and severally hereby enter into a firm and perpetual league of friendship and amity for offense and defense, mutual advice and succor upon all just occasions, both for preserving and propogating the truth and liberties of the Gospel and for their own mutual safety and welfare.

3. It is further agreed that the plantations which at present are, or hereafter shall be, settled within the limits of the Massachusetts shall be forever under the Massachusetts, and shall have particular jurisdiction among themselves in all cases as an entire body; and that Plymouth, Connecticut, and New Haven shall each of them have like particular jurisdiction and government within their limits, and in reference to the plantations which already are settled, or shall hereafter be erected, or shall settle within their limits respectively; provided that no other jurisdiction shall hereafter be taken in as a distinct head or member of this confederation, nor shall any other plantation or jurisdiction in present being, and not already in combination or

under the jurisdiction of any of these confederates, be received by any of them; nor shall any two of the confederates join in one jurisdiction without consent of the rest, which consent to be interpreted as is expresed in the 6th article ensuing.

4. It is by these confederates agreed that the charge of all just wars, whether offensive or defensive, upon what part or member of this confederation soever they fall, shall both in men and provisions and all other disbursements be borne by all the parts of this confederation in different proportions according to their different ability in manner following, namely, that the commissioners for each jurisdiction, from time to time as there shall be occasion, bring a true account and number of all the males in every plantation or any way belonging to or under their federal jurisdictions of what quality or condition soever they be from sixteen years old to threescore being inhabitants there. And that according to the different numbers which from time to time shall be found in each jurisdiction, upon a true and just account, the service of men and all charges of the war be borne by the poll; each jurisdiction or plantation being left to their own course and custom of rating themselves and people according to their different estates with due respects to their qualities and exemptions among themselves though the confederation take no notice of any such privilege; and that according to their different charge of each jurisdiction and plantation, the whole advantage of the war (if it please God to bless their endeavors), whether it be in lands, goods, or persons, shall be proportionately divided among the said confederates.

5. It is further agreed that, if any of these jurisdictions or any plantation under or in combination with them be invaded by any enemy whatsoever, upon notice and request of any three magistrates of that jurisdiction so invaded, the rest of the confederates, without any further meeting or expostulation, shall forthwith send aid to the confederate in danger but in different proportions; namely, the Massachusetts, 100 men sufficiently armed and provided for such a service and journey, and each of the rest, 45 so armed and provided, or any less number, if less be required according to this proportion. But in any such case of sending men for present aid, whether before or after such order or alteration, it is agreed that at the meeting of the commissioners for this confederation the cause of such war or invasion be duly considered; and if it appear that the fault lay in the parties so invaded that then that jurisdiction or plantation make just satisfaction, both to the invaders whom they have injured, and bear all the charges of the war them-

selves, without requiring any allowance from the rest of the confederates toward the same. And, further, that if any jurisdiction see any danger of any invasion approaching, and there be time for a meeting, that in such case three magistrates of that jurisdiction may summon a meeting at such convenient place as themselves shall think meet, to consider and provide against the threatened danger; provided when they are met they may remove to what place they please. Only while any of these four confederates have but three magistrates in their jurisdiction, their request or summons from any two of them shall be accounted of equal force with the three mentioned in both the clauses of this article, till there be an increase of magistrates there.

6. It is also agreed that for the managing and concluding of all affairs proper and concerning the whole confederation, two commissioners shall be chosen by and out of each of these four jurisdictions; namely, two for the Massachusetts, two for Plymouth, two for Connecticut, and two for New Haven, being all in church fellowship with us, which shall bring full power from their several General Courts respectively to hear, examine, weigh, and determine all affairs of our war or peace leagues, aids, charges, and numbers of men for war, division of spoils and whatsoever is gotten by conquest, receiving of more confederates for plantations into combination with any of the confederates, and all things of like nature, which are the proper concommitants or consequents of such a confederation for amity, offense, and defense, not inter-meddling with the government of any of the jurisdictions, which by the 3rd article is preserved entirely to themselves . . . It is further agreed that these eight commissioners shall meet once every year, besides extraordinary meetings (according to the 5th article), to consider, treat, and conclude of all affairs belonging to this confederation . . .

8. It is also agreed that the commissioners for this confederation hereafter at their meetings, whether ordinary or extraordinary, as they may have commission or opportunity, do endeavor to frame and establish agreements and orders in general cases of a civil nature, wherein all the plantations are interested, for preserving peace among themselves and preventing as much as may be all occasion of war or difference with others, as about the free and speedy passage of justice in every jurisdiction, to all the confederates equally as to their own, receiving those that remove from one plantation to another without due certificates; how all the jurisidictions may carry it toward the Indians, that they neither grow insolent nor be injured without due

satisfaction, lest war break in upon the confederates through such miscarriage.

It is agreed that if any servant run away from his master into any other of these confederated jurisdictions, that in such case, upon the certificate of one magistrate in the jurisdiction out of which the said servant shall be delivered either to his master or any other that pursues and brings such certificate of proof. And that upon the escape of any prisoner whatsoever, or fugitive for any criminal cause, whether breaking prison, or getting away from the officer, or otherwise escaping, upon the certificate of two magistrates of the jurisdiction out of which the escape is made, that he was a prisoner, or such an offender at the time of the escape, the magistreates, or some of them of that jurisdiction where for the present the said prisoner or fugitive abides, shall forthwith grant such a warrant as the case will bear for the apprehending of any such person, and the delivery of him into the hands of the officer or other person who pursues him. And if there be help required for the safe returning of any such offender, then it shall be granted to him that craves the same, he paying the charges thereof.

9. And for that the justest wars may be of dangerous consequence, especially to the smaller plantations in these United Colonies, it is agreed that neither the Massachusetts, Plymouth, Connecticut, nor New Haven, nor any of the members of them, shall at any time hereafter begin, undertake, or engage themselves, or this confederation, or any part thereof in any war whatsoever (sudden exigents with the necessary consequents thereof excepted which are also to be moderated as much as the case will permit) without the consent and agreement of the forenamed eight commissioners, or at least six of them, as in the 6th article is provided; and that no charge be required of any of the confederates in case of a defensive war till the said commissioners have met and approved the justice of the war, and have agreed upon the sum of money to be levied, which sum is then to be paid by the several confederates in proportion according to the 4th article...

11. It is further agreed that if any of the confederates shall hereafter break any of these present articles, or be any other ways injurious to any one of the other jurisdictions, that both peace and this present confederation may be entirely preserved without violation.

Text taken from Thorpe, *Federal and State Constitutions,* 77–81.

77

[The Albany Plan of Union]

1754

*I*n *1754 the colonies sent representatives to a general congress to conclude a treaty with the Iroquois. Although Benjamin Franklin was much impressed by the Iroquois Confederation, neither this document nor the later Articles of Confederation bears any serious resemblance to the Iroquois system. For example, the Iroquois required unanimous approval by all tribes; tribal representation was not proportional to tribal population. Their confederation council was divided into three parts, each with a specific role in the overall decision making process: council members, assuming their good behavior, were not elected but appointed by "royal" (royaneh) families for life; the executive branch was internal to the council and functioned only when the council was in session; and constituent tribal government was organized along traditional tribal lines and not democratically. The Albany Plan of Union proposed that the democratically elected colonial legislatures elect confederation delegates for three-year terms; the executive was to be appointed by the king and function as a separate entity during and between sessions of the Grand Council; and the unicameral Council was to be based on proportional representation and use majority rule. The unicameral legislature created by the Articles of Confederation was really no closer to the Iroquois model; because its delegates were also elected to terms by the state legislatures, it used either simple or three-fourths majorities, and it used a thirteen-member (one from each state) Council of States between sessions as an executive branch. The Albany Plan and the Articles of Confederation were natural extensions of The New England Confederation, 1643 [76]. The Albany Plan was much closer to Penn's Plan of Union, 1697, and the Articles of Confederation were closer to Galloway's Plan of Union, 1774 (see Appendix), than to any reasonable interpretation of the Iroquois system. The Albany Plan of Union* *failed adoption by the colonial legislatures and did not go into effect but is included here because it was adopted by a colonial body authorized to produce a mechanism for enforcing and maintaining the treaty with the Iroquois, the essential purpose of this Plan, and because it was the immediate model for the operation of the Continental Congress and the design for the Articles of Confederation.*

It is proposed, that humble application be made for an act of Parliament of Great Britain, by virtue of which one general government may be formed in America, including all the said colonies, within and under which government each colony may retain its present constitution, except in the particulars wherein a change may be directed by the said act, as hereafter follows.

PRESIDENT-GENERAL AND GRAND COUNCIL

That the said general government be administered by a President-General, to be appointed and supported by the crown; and a Grand Council, to be chosen by the representatives of the people of the several colonies met in their respective Assemblies.

ELECTION OF MEMBERS

That within [   ] months after the passing of such act, the House of Representatives that happens to be sitting within that time, or that shall be especially for that purpose convened, may and shall choose members for the Grand Council in the following proportion—that is to say:

Massachusetts Bay	7	Pennsylvania	6
New Hampshire	2	Maryland	4
Connecticut	5	Virginia	7
Rhode Island	2	North Carolina	4
New York	4	South Carolina	4
New Jersey	3		48

PLACE OF FIRST MEETING

[   ] who shall meet for the first time at the city of Philadelphia in Pennsylvania, being called by the President-General as soon as conveniently may be after his appointment.

NEW ELECTION

That there shall be a new election of the members of the Grand Council every three years; and on the death or resignation of any member, his place should be supplied by a new choice at the next sitting of the Assembly of the colony he represented.

PROPORTION OF MEMBERS
AFTER THE FIRST THREE YEARS

That after the first three years, when the proportion of money arising out of each colony to the general treasury can be known, the number of members to be chosen for each colony shall from time to time, in all ensuing elections, be regulated by that proportion, yet so as that the number to be chosen by any one province be not more than seven, nor less than two.

MEETINGS OF THE GRAND COUNCIL, AND CALL

That the Grand Council shall meet once in every year, and oftener if occasion require, at such time and place as they shall adjourn to at the last preceding meeting, or as they shall be called to meet by the President-General on any emergency, he having first obtained in writing the consent of seven of the members to such call, and sent due and timely notice to the whole.

CONTINUANCE

That the Grand Council have power to choose their speaker and shall neither be dissolved, prorogued, nor continued sitting longer than six weeks at one time, without their own consent or the special command of the crown.

MEMBERS' ALLOWANCE

That the members of the Grand Council shall be allowed for their service ten shillings sterling per diem during their session and journey to and from the place of meeting; twenty miles to be reckoned a day's journey.

ASSENT OF PRESIDENT-GENERAL AND HIS DUTY

That the assent of the President-General be requisite to all acts of the Grand Council, and that it be his office and duty to cause them to be carried into execution.

POWER OF PRESIDENT-GENERAL AND GRAND COUNCIL; TREATIES OF PEACE AND WAR

That the President-General, with the advice of the Grand Council, hold or direct all Indian treaties in which the general interest of the colonies may be concerned; and make peace or declare war with Indian nations.

INDIAN TRADE

That they make such laws as they judge necessary for regulating all Indian trade.

INDIAN PURCHASES

That they make all purchases, from Indians for the crown, of lands not now within the bounds of particular colonies, or that shall not be within their bounds when some of them are reduced to more convenient dimensions.

NEW SETTLEMENTS

That they make new settlements on such purchases, by granting lands in the King's name, reserving a quit-rent to the crown for the use of the general treasury.

LAWS TO GOVERN THEM

That they make laws for regulating and governing such new settlements till the crown shall think fit to form them into particular governments.

RAISE SOLDIERS AND EQUIP VESSELS, &C

That they raise and pay soldiers and build forts for the defence of any of the colonies, and equip vessels of force to guard the coasts and protect the trade on the ocean, lakes, or great rivers; but they shall not impress men in any colony without the consent of the legislature.

POWER TO MAKE LAWS, LAY DUTIES, &C

That for these purposes they have power to make laws, and lay and levy such general duties, imposts, or taxes as to them shall appear most equal and just (considering the ability and other circumstances of the inhabitants in the several colonies), and such as may be collected with the least inconvenience to the people; rather discouraging luxury than loading industry with unnecessary burthens.

GENERAL TREASURER AND PARTICULAR TREASURER

That they may appoint a General Treasurer and Particular Treasurer in each government, when necessary; and from time to time may order the sums in the treasuries of each government into the general treasury, or draw on them for special payments, as they find most convenient.

MONEY, HOW TO ISSUE

Yet no money to issue but by joint orders of the President-General and Grand Council; except where sums have been appropriated to particular purposes, and the President-General is previously empowered by an act to draw such sums.

ACCOUNTS

That the general accounts shall be yearly settled and reported to the several Assemblies.

QUORUM

That a quorum of the Grand Council, empowered to act with the President-General, do consist of twenty-five members, among whom there shall be one or more from a majority of the colonies.

LAWS TO BE TRANSMITTED

That the laws made by them for the purposes aforesaid shall not be repugnant, but, as near as may be, agreeable to the laws of England, and shall be transmitted to the King in Council for approbation as soon as may be after their passing; and if not disappoved within three years after presentation, to remain in force.

DEATH OF THE PRESIDENT-GENERAL

That in case of the death of the President-General, the Speaker of the Grand Council for the time being shall succeed, and be vested with the same powers and authorities, to continue till the King's pleasure be known.

OFFICERS, HOW APPOINTED

That all military commission officers, whether for land or sea service, to act under this general constitution, shall be nominated by the President-General; but the approbation of the Grand Council is to be obtained before they receive their commissions. And all civil officers are to be nominated by the Grand Council, and to receive the President-General's approbation before they officiate.

VACANCIES, HOW SUPPLIED

But in case of vacancy by death or removal of any officer, civil or military, under this constitution, the Governor of the province in which such vacancy happens may appoint, till the pleasure of the President-General and Grand Council can be known.

Each Colony May Defend Itself On Emergency, &c. That the particular military as well as civil establishments in each colony remain in their present state, the general constitution notwithstanding; and that on sudden emergencies any colony may defend itself, and lay the accounts of expense thence arising before the President-General and General Council, who may allow and order payment of the same, as far as they judge such accounts just and reasonable.

The complete text is taken from Thorpe, *Federal and State Constitutions*, 83–86.

78

The Articles of Confederation

November 15, 1777

*T*he Articles of Confederation is a straightforward extension, and the natural culmination, of colonial theoretical and institutional development. Until its adoption, even though they had declared independence, Americans were not constitutionally postcolonial. Put another way, the Declaration of Independence and Articles of Confederation together composed the American founding compact, and as of 1781, the United States was for the first time a formal constitutional entity. The Declaration and Articles, however, overlapped in the attention of the Continental Congress, as its members fashioned our initial national compact. The version of the Declaration of Independence we read today, the one with "Unanimous" in its title, was engrossed in August of 1776, and the last signature was added in January of 1777. It then replaced the earlier version from July of 1776 that did not have "unanimous" in its title. The Articles of Confederation, finally approved by the last state legislature in 1781, was adopted by the Continental Congress November 15, 1777, after a long debate that began with the introduction of the first draft on July 12, 1776. The two parts of the first national compact were thus not separated in time but pursued simultaneously. As a substitution for only the Articles, the 1789 Constitution implicitly retained the Declaration of Independence as the first half of our second national compact, a fact that has been ratified by more than two hundred years of our celebrating the Fourth of July as our national founding. This is, then, the last piece in the colonial documentary history leading to the U.S. Constitution. Its status as a compact is revealed and underscored not only by earlier American confederations but also by a content that is in keeping with that found in the many other colonial compacts reproduced in this volume. Viewed together as a national compact, the Declaration and Articles create a people, lay out their common val-

ues and goals, create a government, and lay out the institutions for collective decision making—all of the compactual elements present from earliest colonial times. A careful reading of the text indicates that, like the Declaration, the Articles of Confederation assumes both a national people and a collection of state peoples, including the statement of dual citizenship in Article IV that was carried over, as with most of the document, into the U.S. Constitution. Federalism, a fundamental principle of American politics derived from the early colonial documents and inspired by the federal theology these colonists brought with them, is thus a consistent theme in both our national compacts.

Articles of Confederation and Perpetual Union between the states of Newhampshire, Massachusetts-bay, Rhodeisland and Providence Plantations, Connecticut, New-York, New-Jersey, Pennsylvania, Delaware, Maryland, Virginia, North-Carolina, South-Carolina and Georgia.

Article I. The Stile of this confederacy shall be "The United States of America."

Article II. Each state retains its sovereignty, freedom, and independence, and every Power, Jurisdiction and right, which is not by this confederation expressly delegated to the United States, in Congress assembled.

Article III. The said states hereby severally enter into a firm league of friendship with each other, for their common defence, the security of their Liberties, and their mutual and general welfare, binding themselves to assist each other, against all force offered to, or attacks made upon them, or any of them, on account of religion, sovereignty, trade, or any other pretence whatever.

Article IV. The better to secure and perpetuate mutual friendship and intercourse among the people of the different states in this union, the free inhabitants of each of these states, paupers, vagabonds and fugitives from justice excepted, shall be entitled to all privileges and immunities of free citizens in the several states; and the people of each state shall have free ingress and regress to and from any other state, and shall enjoy therein all the privileges of trade and commerce, subject to the same duties, impositions and restrictions as the inhabitants thereof respectively, provided that such restriction shall not extend so far as to prevent the removal of property into any state, to any other state, of which the Owner is an inhabitant; provided also that no imposition, duties or restriction shall be laid by any state, on the property of the united states, or either of them.

If any person guilty of, or charged with treason, felony, or other high misdemeanor in any state, shall flee from Justice, and be found in any of the united states, he shall, upon demand of the Governor or executive power, of the state from which he fled, be delivered up and removed to the state having jurisdiction of his offence.

Full faith and credit shall be given in each of these states to the records, acts and judicial proceedings of the courts and magistrates of every other state.

Article v. For the more convenient management of the general interests of the united states, delegates shall be annually appointed in such manner as the legislature of each state shall direct, to meet in Congress on the first Monday in November, in every year, with a power reserved to each state, to recall its delegates, or any of them, at any time within the year, and to send others in their stead, for the remainder of the Year.

No state shall be represented in Congress by less than two, nor by more than seven Members; and no person shall be capable of being a delegate for more than three years in any term of six years; nor shall any person, being a delegate, be capable of holding any office under the united states, for which he, or another for his benefit receives any salary, fees, or emolument of any kind.

Each state shall maintain its own delegates in a meeting of the states, and while they act as members of the committee of the states.

In determining questions in the united states in Congress assembled, each state shall have one vote.

Freedom of speech and debate in Congress shall not be impeached or questioned in any Court, or place out of Congress, and the members of congress shall be protected in their persons from arrests and imprisonments, during the time of their going to and from, and attendance on congress, except for treason, felony, or breach of the peace.

Article vi. No state, without the Consent of the united states in congress assembled, shall send any embassy to, or receive any embassy from, or enter into any conference, agreement, alliance or treaty with any King prince or state; nor shall any person holding any office of profit or trust under the united states, or any of them, accept any present, emolument, office or title of any kind whatsoever from any king, prince or foreign state; nor shall the united states in congress assembled, or any of them, grant any title of nobility.

No two or more states shall enter into any treaty, confederation or alliance whatever between them, without the consent of the united states in congress assembled, specifying accurately the purposes for which the same is to be entered into, and how long it shall continue.

No state shall lay any imposts or duties, which may interfere with any stipulations in treaties, entered into by the united states in congress assembled, with any king, prince or state, in pursuance of any treaties already proposed by congress, to the courts of France and Spain.

No vessels of war shall be kept up in time of peace by any state, except such number only, as shall be deemed necessary by the united states in congress assembled, for the defence of such state, or its trade; nor shall any body of forces be kept up by any state, in time of peace, except such number only, as in the judgment of the united states, in congress assembled, shall be deemed requisite to garrison the forts necessary for the defense of such state; but every state shall always keep up a well regulated and disciplined militia, sufficiently armed and accoutred, and shall provide and constantly have ready for use, in public stores, a due number of field pieces and tents, and a proper quantity of arms, ammunition and camp equipage.

No state shall engage in any war without the consent of the united states in congress assembled, unless each state be actually invaded by enemies, or shall have received certain advice of a resolution being formed by some nation of Indians to invade such state, and the danger is so imminent as not to admit of a delay till the united states in congress assembled can be consulted; nor shall any state grant commissions to any ships or vessels of war, or letters of marque or reprisal, except it be after a declaration of war by the united states in congress assembled, and then only against the kingdom or state and the subjects thereof, against which war has been declared, and under such regulations as shall be established by the united states in congress assembled, unless such state be infested by pirates, in which case vessels of war may be fitted out for that occasion, and kept so long as the danger shall continue, or until the united states in congress assembled, shall determine otherwise.

Article vii. When land-forces are raised by any state for the common defense, all officers of or under the rank of colonel, shall be appointed by the legislature of each state respectively, by whom such forces shall be raised, or in such manner as such state shall direct, and all vacancies shall be filled up by the State which first made the appointment.

Article VIII. All charges of war, and all other expences that shall be incurred for the common defence or general welfare, and allowed by the united states in congress assembled, shall be defrayed out of a common treasury, which shall be supplied by the several states in proportion to the value of all land within each state, granted to or surveyed for any person, as such land and the buildings and improvements thereon shall be estimated according to such mode as the united states in congress assembled, shall from time to time direct and appoint.

The taxes for paying that proportion shall be laid and levied by the authority and direction of the legislatures of the several states within the time agreed upon by the united states in congress assembled.

Article IX. The united states in congress assembled, shall have the sole and exclusive right and power of determining on peace and war, except in the cases mentioned in the sixth article—of sending and receiving ambassadors—entering into treaties and alliances, provided that no treaty of commerce shall be made whereby the legislative power of the respective states shall be restrained from imposing such imposts and duties on foreigners as their own people are subjected to, or from prohibiting the exportation or importation of any species of goods or commodities, whatsoever—of establishing rules for deciding in all cases, what captures on land or water shall be legal, and in what manner prizes taken by land or sea forces in the service of the united states shall be divided or appropriated—of granting letters of marque and reprisal in times of peace—appointing courts for the trial of piracies and felonies committed on the high seas and establishing courts for receiving and determining finally appeals in all cases of captures, provided that no members of congress shall be appointed a judge in any of the said courts.

The united states in congress assembled shall also be the last resort on appeal in all disputes and differences now subsisting or that hereafter may arise between two or more states concerning boundary, jurisdiction or any other cause whatever; which authority shall always be exercised in the manner following. Whenever the legislative or executive authority or lawful agent of any state in controversy with another shall present a petition to congress stating the matter in question and praying for a hearing, notice thereof shall be given by order of congress to the legislative or executive authority of the other state in controversy, and a day assigned for the appearance of the parties by their lawful agents, who shall then be directed to appoint by joint consent, commissioners or judges to constitute a court for hearing and determining the matter in question: but if they cannot agree, congress shall name three persons out of each of the united states, and from the list of such persons each party shall alternately strike out one, the petitioners beginning, until the number shall be reduced to thirteen; and from that number not less than seven, nor more than nine names as congress shall direct, shall in the presence of congress be drawn out by lot, and the persons whose names shall be so drawn or any five of them, shall be commissioners or judges, to hear and finally determine the controversy, so always as a major part of the judges who shall hear the cause shall agree in the determination: and if either party shall neglect to attend at the day appointed, without showing reasons, which congress shall judge sufficient, or being present refuse to strike, the congress shall proceed to nominate three persons out of each state, and the secretary of congress shall strike in behalf of such party absent or refusing; and the judgment and sentence of the court to be appointed, in the manner before prescribed, shall be final and conclusive; and if any of the parties shall refuse to submit to the authority of such court, or to appear or defend their claim or cause, the court shall nevertheless proceed to pronounce sentence, or judgment, which shall in like manner be final and decisive, the judgment or sentence and other proceedings being in either case transmitted to congress, and lodged among the acts of congress for the security of the parties concerned: provided that every commissioner, before he sits in judgment, shall take an oath to be administered by one of the judges of the supreme or superior court of the state, where the case will be tried, "well and truly to hear and determine the matter in question, according to the best of his judgment, without favour, affection or hope of reward": provided also, that no state shall be deprived of territory for the benefit of the united states.

All controversies concerning the private right of soil claimed under different grants of two or more states, whose jurisdictions as they may respect such lands, and the states which passed such settlement of jurisdiction, shall on the petition of either party to the congress of the united states, be finally determined as near as may be in the same manner as is before prescribed for deciding disputes respecting territorial jurisdiction between different states.

The united states in congress assembled shall also have the sole and exclusive right and power of regulating the alloy and value of coin struck by their own authority, or by that of the respective states—fixing the standard of weights and measures throughout the united states—regulating the trade and managing all affairs with the Indians, not members of any of the states, provided that the legislative right of any state within its own limits be not infringed or violated—establishing or regulating post-offices from one state to another, throughout all the united states, and exacting such postage on the papers passing through the same as may be requisite to defray the expenses of the said office—appointing all the officers of the land forces, in the service of the united states, excepting regimental officers—appointing all the officers of the naval forces, and commissioning all officers whatever in the service of the united states—making rules for the government and regulation of the said land and naval forces, and directing their operations.

The united states in congress assembled shall have authority to appoint a committee, to sit in the recess of congress, to be denominated "A Committee of the States," and to consist of one delegate from each state; and to appoint such other committees and civil officers as may be necessary for managing the general affairs of the united states under their direction—to appoint one of their number to preside, provided that no person be allowed to serve in the office of president more than one year in any term of three years; to ascertain the necessary sums of money to be raised for the service of the united states, and to appropriate and apply the same for defraying the public expences—to borrow money, or emit bills on the credit of the united states, transmitting every half year to the respective states an account of the sums of money so borrowed or emitted,—to build and equip a navy—to agree upon the number of land forces, and to make requisitions from each state for its quota, in proportion to the number of white inhabitants in such state; which requisition shall be binding, and thereupon the legislature of each state shall appoint the regimental officers, raise the men and cloath, arm and equip them in a soldier like manner, at the expence of the united states; and the officers and men so cloathed, armed and equipped shall march to the place appointed, and within the time agreed on by the united states in congress assembled: But if the united states in congress assembled shall, on consideration of circumstances judge proper that any state should not raise men, or should raise a smaller number than its quota, and that any other state should raise a greater number of men than the quota thereof, such extra men shall be raised, officered, cloathed, armed and equipped in the same manner as the quota of such state, unless the legislature of such state shall judge that such extra number cannot be safely spared out of the same, in which case they shall raise officer, cloath, arm and equip as many of such extra number as they judge can be safely spared. And the officers and men so cloathed, armed and equipped, shall march to the place appointed, and within the time agreed on by the united states in congress assembled.

The united states in congress assembled shall never engage in a war, nor grant letters of marque and reprisal in time of peace, nor enter into any treaties or alliances, nor coin money, nor regulate the value thereof, nor ascertain the sums and expences necessary for the defense and welfare of the united states, or any of them, nor emit bills, nor borrow money on the credit of the united states, nor appropriate money, nor agree upon the number of vessels of war, to be built or purchased, or the number of land or sea forces to be raised, nor appoint a commander in chief of the army or navy, unless nine states assent to the same: nor shall a question on any other point, except for adjourning from day to day be determined, unless by a majority of the united states in congress assembled.

The congress of the united states shall have power to adjourn at any time within the year, and to any place within the united states, so that no period of adjustment be for a longer duration than the space of six Months, and shall publish the Journal of their proceedings monthly, except such parts thereof relating to treaties, alliances or military operations, as in their judgment require secrecy; and the yeas and nays of the delegates of each state on any question shall be entered on the Journal, when it is desired by any delegate; and the delegates of a state, or any of them, at his or their request shall be furnished with a transcript of the said Journal, except such parts as are above excepted, to lay before the legislatures of the several states.

Article x. The committee of the states, or any nine of them, shall be authorized to execute, in the recess of congress, such of the powers of congress as the united states in congress assembled, by the consent of nine states, shall from time to time think expedient to vest them with; provided that no power be delegated to said committee, for the exercise of which, by the Articles of confederation, the voice of nine states in the congress of the united states assembled is requisite.

Article xi. Canada acceding to this confederation, and joining in the measures of the united states, shall be admitted into, and entitled to all the advantages of this union: but no other colony shall be admitted into the same, unless such admission be agreed to by nine states.

Article xii. All bills of credit emitted, monies borrowed and debts contracted by, or under the authority of congress, before the assembling of the united states, in pursuance of the present confederation, shall be deemed and considered as a charge against the united states, for payment and satisfaction whereof the said united states, and the public faith are hereby solemnly pledged.

Article xiii. Every state shall abide by the determinations of the united states in congress assembled, on all questions which by this confederation are submitted to them. And the Articles of this confederation shall be inviolably observed by every state, and the union shall be perpetual; nor shall any alteration at any time hereafter be made in any of them; unless such alteration be agreed to in a congress of the united states, and be afterwards confirmed by the legislature of every state.

And Whereas it hath pleased the Great Governor of the World to incline the hearts of the legislatures we respectively represent in congress, to approve of, and to authorize us to ratify the said articles of confederation and perpetual union. Know Ye that we the undersigned delegates, by virtue of the power and authority to us given for that purpose, do by these presents, in the name and in behalf of our respective constituents, fully and entirely ratify and confirm each and every of the said articles of confederation and perpetual union, and all and singular the matters and things therein contained: And we do further solemnly plight and engage the faith of our respective constituents, that they shall abide by the determinations of the united states in congress assembled, on all questions, which by the said confederation are submitted to them. And that the articles thereof shall be inviolably observed by the states we respectively represent, and that the union shall be perpetual. In Witness wherof we have hereunto set our hands in Congress. Done at Philadelphia in the state of Pennsylvania the ninth day of July, in the Year of our Lord one Thousand seven Hundred and Seventy-eight, and in the third year of the independence of America.

Josiah Bartlett,
John Wentworth, jun^r
August 8th, 1778,

} On the part & behalf of the State of
New Hampshire

John Hancock,
Samuel Adams,
Elbridge Gerry,   On the part and behalf of the State of
Francis Dana,   Massachusetts Bay
James Lovell,
Samuel Holten,

William Ellery,
Henry Marchant,   On the part and behalf of the State of
John Collins,   Rhode-Island and Providence Plantations

Roger Sherman,
Samuel Huntington,
Oliver Wolcott,   On the part and behalf of the State of
Titus Hosmer,   Connecticut
Andrew Adams,

Jaˢ Duane,
Fra: Lewis,   On the part and behalf of the State of
Wᵐ Duer,   New York
Gouvʳ Morris,

Jnᵒ Witherspoon,   On the Part and in Behalf of the State of
Nathˡ Scudder,   New Jersey, November 26th, 1778.

Robert Morris,
Daniel Roberdeau,
Jon. Bayard Smith,   On the part and behalf of the State of
William Clingar,   Pennsylvania
Joseph Reed,
  22d July, 1778

Thoˢ McKean
  Febʳ 22d, 1779,
John Dickinson,   On the part & behalf of the State of
  May 5th, 1779,   Delaware
Nicholas Van Dyke,

John Hanson,   On the part and behalf of the State of
  March 1, 1781,   Maryland
Daniel Carroll, do

Richard Henry Lee,
John Banister,
Thomas Adams,
Jnᵒ. Harvie,
Francis Lightfoot Lee,

} On the Part and Behalf of the State of Virginia

John Penn,
   July 21st, 1778,
Cornˢ Harnett,
Jnᵒ. Willams,

} On the part and behalf of the State of North Carolina

Henry Laurens,
William Henry Drayton,
Jnᵒ. Mathews,
Richᵈ Hutson,
Thoˢ Heyward, junʳ.

} On the part and on behalf of the State of South Carolina

Jnᵒ Walton,
   24th July, 1778,
Edwᵈ Telfair,
Edwᵈ Langworthy,

} On the part and behalf of the State of Georgia

The text reproduced here was adopted by the Continental Congress on July 9, 1778, after nine of the thirteen state legislatures had ratified the document sent to them the previous November. Except for the last paragraph and the signatures, the text is from Merrill Jensen, *The Articles of Confederation* (Madison: University of Wisconsin Press, 1966), 263–70. The final paragraph and signatures of an otherwise identical text is included because it shows who had ratified by July 9, 1778, and the dates of later state ratifications. The text is taken from Thorpe, *Federal and State Constitutions*, 9–17.

Appendix: Unadopted Colonial Plans of Union

Even though there were no successful plans for uniting the colonies prior to the Revolution, there was no shortage of proposals. Even a partial listing of proposals would have to include the Royal Commission to Governor Andros to unite all of New England, New York, and the Jerseys, 1688; William Penn's Plan of Union, 1697; D'Avenant Plan, 1698; A Viginian's Plan, in "An Essay on the Government of the English Plantations on the Continent of America," 1701; Livingston Plan, 1701; Earl of Stair's Proposal, 1721; Plan of the Lords of Trade, 1721; Daniel Cox's Plan, in "A Description of the English province of Carolina," 1722; Kennedy Plan, 1751; Albany Plan of Union, 1754; Richard Peter's Plan, 1754; Hutchinson's Plan, 1754; Plan of the Lords of Trade, 1754; Dr. Samuel Johnson's Plan, 1760; and the Galloway Plan, 1774. Two of these proposals are of particular interest and are reproduced here.

William Penn's Plan, sent unsolicited to the Board of Trade in London, was the first comprehensive proposal for unifying all the colonies. Although quite simple, and too general, Penn's Plan is surprisingly similar in intent, structure, and powers to the 1754 Albany Plan of Union.

Joseph Galloway was a Loyalist who tried to resolve the "no taxation without representation" problem by proposing a union of the colonies under a confederation parliament. If his plan had been accepted in Britain, the Revolution might well have been averted, and America would have started down a road very similar to the one used by Canada to achieve gradual independence as a federal parliamentary system. Ironically, if one ignores the crown-appointed executive, Galloway's Plan would have created a system quite similar to that made by the Articles of Confederation, which is an indication of the extent to which the Articles reflected general American preferences for a national government as well as the extent to which even most Tories agreed with this general American perspective.

Although neither proposal was adopted, and therefore neither meets the criteria for formal inclusion in this collection, William Penn's Plan of Union and Joseph Galloway's Plan of Union are reproduced to illustrate the long-standing consistency in the thinking about how to design a national government and thus place the Albany Plan of Union and Articles of Confederation in a more meaningful documentary context. All of our major political documents—from the Declaration of Independence and Articles of Confederation to the U.S. Constitution and the Bill of Rights—were rehearsed in colonial precursors with which they share form, content, and underlying political principles.

79

[William Penn's Plan of Union]

February 8, 1697

*P*enn's Plan lists only nine colonies, but these nine encompass the existing settled seaboard. As of 1697 New Hampshire is claimed by Massachusetts, (here identified idiosyncratically as "Boston"); Delaware is included as one of "the Jerseys" (so implicitly there are ten colonies); Carolina has not yet been differentiated into north and south, and Georgia is not yet chartered. The emphasis in this proposal is on resolving intercolonial disputes.

A BRIEFE AND PLAINE SCHEAM

How the English Colonies in the North parts of America Viz: Boston, Connecticut, Road Island, New York, New Jerseys, Pensilvania, Maryland, Virginia and Carolina may be made more usefull to the Crowne, and one anothers peace and safty with an universall concurrence.

1st. That the severall Collonies before mentioned, do meet once a year, and oftener if need be, dureing the Warr, and at least once in two yeares in times of Peace, by their Stated and Appointed Deputies, to Debate and Resolve if such Measures, as are most adviseable for their better understanding, and their Public Tranquility and Safety.

2dly That in Order to [effect] it two persons, well Qualified, for Sence Sobriety and Substance, be appointed by each Province, as their Representatives or Deputies; which in the whole make the Congress to Consist of Twenty persons.

3dly That the Kings Commander, for that purpose specially appointed, shall have the Chaire, and Preside in the said Congresse.

4thly That they shall meet as neer as Conveniently may be, to the most Centrall Colony for ease of the Deputies.

5thly Since that may, in all Probability, be New Yorke, both because it is neer the Center of the Collonys, and for that it is a Fronteir, and in the Kings

Nomination, the Governour of that Colony may therefore also be the Kings high Commander during the Session, after the manner of Scotland.

6thly That their businesse shall be [to] hear and Adjust all matters of Complaint or difference Between Province and Province; as 1st where Persons quit their own province and go to another, that they may avoid their Just debts. Tho' able to Pay them. 2dly where Offenders fly Justice, or Justice cannot well be had upon such offenders in the Provinces that entertaine them. 3dly to prevent or cure Injuries in point of Commerce. 4thly To consider of wayes and meanes to support the Union and safety of these Provinces against the Publick Enemies; In which Congress the Quota's of Men and Charges will be much easier, and more equally sett, then it is Possible for any Establishment made here to do: for the Provinces knowing their own Condition and one anothers, can debate that matter with more freedome and satisfaction, and better adjust and ballance their affaires in all respects for their Common safety.

7thly That in times of War the Kings high Commander shall be Genll or Cheife Commander of the severall Quota's upon service against the Common Enemy, as he shall be advised, for the good and benefitt of the whole.

The calendar in use during the seventeenth century designated February as the twelfth month of the year, so this document is often reproduced with the date as "1696." The text is reproduced from Marianne S. Wokeck et al., eds., *The Papers of William Penn: Volume Three, 1685–1700* (Philadelphia: University of Pennsylvania Press, 1986), 482–83.

80

[Joseph Galloway's Plan of Union]

1774

*E*ven *though it was never ratified by the colonial legislatures, the Albany Plan of Union, adopted by the Albany Congress in 1754, continued to influence the thinking of American nationalists. In Galloway's Plan, as in the Albany Plan of Union, the appointed executive is termed a "President General" and the legislature is termed a "Grand Council." The Grand Council is to meet at least once a year, and its members serve three-year terms. Indeed, if one excludes the provisions dealing with the President General, Galloway's Plan is more or less adopted as the core of the Articles of Confederation—often word for word. The Galloway Plan lists the colonies in the same order as do the Albany Plan of Union and the Articles of Confederation but leaves blank the number of representatives allocated to each. The Articles, however, will use the same range of representation as the Albany Plan, between two and seven representatives, and comprise the same total number of representatives—forty-eight. The pedigree of the Articles of Confederation in Galloway's Plan and Galloway's Plan in the Albany Plan of Union will be clear to any careful reader. Most interesting is that even though Tories like Galloway did not want to break with Britain, they still supported the right of Americans to their own representative bodies. Galloway's Plan would have created what he calls "a British and American legislature" by construing the American legislature as "an inferior and distinct branch of the British legislature" that would nevertheless "hold and exercise all the like rights, liberties, and privileges, as are held and exercised by and in the House of Commons of Great-Britain." This exceedingly clever structure would have thus made the American Grand Council a part of the British Parliament, inferior to the British part of Parliament in theory but in fact fully capable of making policy for the colonies. The legislature of each*

colony, in turn, would be free to make policy on matters not dele-
gated to the Grand Council. The differences between Galloway's Plan
and the Articles of Confederation served to make the latter too weak
and ineffective. In sum, Galloway's federal structure might well have
been the precise formulation that would have kept America in the
British Empire, at least for a while longer, and created a national
government strong enough to preclude the need for the Constitution
of 1787. The Continental Congress chose to largely adopt, but weaken,
Galloway's proposal. Still, his Plan stands as an important document
in the colonial background to the U.S. Constitution.

A Plan of a proposed Union between
Great Britain and the Colonies

That a British and American legislature, for regulating the administration of the general affairs of America, be proposed and established in
America, including all the said colonies; within, and under which government, each colony shall retain its present constitution, and powers of regulating and governing its own internal police, in all cases what[so]ever.

That the said government be administered by a President General, to be
appointed by the King, and a grand Council, to be chosen by the Representatives of the people of the several colonies, in their respective assemblies,
once in every three years.

That the several assemblies shall choose members for the grand council
in the following proportions, viz.

New Hampshire.	Delaware Counties.
Massachusetts-Bay.	Maryland.
Rhode Island.	Virginia.
Connecticut.	North Carolina.
New-York.	South-Carolina.
New-Jersey.	Georgia.
Pennsylvania.	

Who shall meet at the city of [   ] for the first time, being called by
the President-General, as soon as conveniently may be after his appointment.
That there shall be a new election of members for the Grand Council every

three years; and on death, removal or resignation of any member, his place shall be supplied by a new choice, at the next sitting of the Assembly of the Colony he represented.

That the Grand Council shall meet once in every year, if they shall think it necessary, and oftener, if occasions shall require, at such time and place as they shall adjourn to, at the last preceding meeting, or as they shall be called to meet at, by the President-General, on any emergency.

That the Grand Council shall have power to choose their Speaker, and shall hold and exercise all the rights, liberties and privileges, as are held and exercised by and in the House of Commons of Great-Britain.

That the President-General shall hold his office during the pleasure of the King, and his assent shall be requisite to all acts of the Grand Council, and it shall be his office and duty to cause them to be carried into execution.

That the President-General, by and with the advice and consent of the Grand-Council, hold and exercise all the legislative rights, powers, and authorities, necessary for regulating and administering all the general police and affairs of the colonies, in which Great-Britain and the colonies, or any of them, the colonies in general, or more than one colony, are in any manner concerned, as well civil and criminal as commercial.

That the said President-General and the Grand Council, be an inferior and distinct branch of the British legislature, united and incorporated with it, for the aforesaid general purposes . . .

The abbreviated text is taken from W. C. Ford et al., eds., *Journals of the Continental Congress, 1774–1789*, vol. I (Washington, D.C., 1904), 49–51.

Bibliography

Multivolume Works of Colonial Documents

Force, Peter, ed. *A Documentary History of the North American Colonies,* 9 vols. (Washington, D.C., 1837–53).

_____. *Tracts and Other Papers Relating Principally to the Origin, Settlement, and Progress of the Colonies in North America,* 4 vols. (New York, 1836–46).

Hazard, Ebenezer, ed. *Historical Collections: Consisting of State Papers and Other Documents,* 2 vols. (Philadelphia, 1792–94).

Jensen, Merrill, ed. *American Colonial Documents to 1776,* vol. 9, *English Historical Documents,* edited by David C. Douglas et al. (New York and Oxford, 1964).

Kavenaugh, W. Keith, ed. *Foundations of Colonial America: A Documentary History,* 3 vols. (New York: Chelsea House, 1973).

MacDonald, W., ed. *Documentary Sourcebook of American History, 1606–1898* (New York, 1908).

_____. *Select Charters and Other Documents Illustrative of American History, 1606–1775* (New York, 1899).

Swindler, William F., ed. *Sources and Documents of the United States Constitutions,* 10 vols. (Dobbs Ferry, N.Y., 1973–79).

Thorpe, Francis N., ed. *The Federal and State Constitutions, Colonial Charters, and Other Organic Laws of the United States,* 7 vols. (Washington, D.C.: Government Printing Office, 1907).

Multivolume Works of State Documents

Bartlett, J. R., ed. *Records of the Colony of Rhode Island and Providence Plantations in New England, 1636 to 1792,* 10 vols. (Providence: A. Crawford Greene and Brother, State Printers, 1856–65).

Bouton, N. et al., eds. *New Hampshire Provincial, Town, and State Papers,* 40 vols. (Concord and Nashua, N.H., 1867–1943).

Browne, W. H. et al., eds. *Archives of Maryland,* 65 vols. (Baltimore: Maryland Historical Society, 1883–1952).

Candler, Allen D. et al., eds. *The Colonial Records of the State of Georgia,* 26 vols. (Atlanta, 1904–16).

Chapin, H. M., ed. *Documentary History of Rhode Island,* 2 vols. (Providence, 1916–19).

Colonial Records of Pennsylvania, 1683-1790, 16 vols. (Philadelphia, 1852–53).

Delaware Archives, 5 vols. (Wilmington, Del., 1911).

Easterby, J. H., ed. *The Colonial Records of South Carolina: The Journal of the Commons House of Assembly,* 3 vols. (Columbia, S.C., 1951–53).

Hammond, Isaac W., ed. *Documents Relating to Towns in New Hampshire* (Concord, N.H.: Parsons B. Cogswell, 1882).

Hazard, Samuel et al., eds. *Pennsylvania Archives,* 9 series, 138 vols. (Philadelphia and Harrisburg, 1852–1935).

Hoadly, C. J., ed. *Records of the Colony and Plantation of New Haven, from 1638 to 1649* (Hartford, 1857).

Hutchinson, Thomas, ed. *Collection of Original Papers Relative to the History of the Colony of Massachusetts Bay,* 2 vols. (Boston, 1769; reprinted, Albany, 1865).

Journal of the Votes and Proceedings of the General Assembly of the Colony of New York, 1691–1765, 2 vols. (Albany, 1842).

McIlwaine, H. R., and John P. Kennedy, eds. *Journals of the House of Burgesses of Virginia,* 13 vols. (Richmond, 1905–15).

Mitchell, J. T., and Henry Flanders, eds. *Statutes at Large of Pennsylvania from 1682 to 1801,* 15 vols. (Harrisburg, 1896–1908).

O'Callaghan, E. B., ed. *Documentary History of the State of New York,* 4 vols. (Albany, 1849–51).

———. *Documents Relating to the Colonial History of the State of New York,* 15 vols. (Albany, 1883).

Saunders, William L., ed. *The Colonial Records of North Carolina,* 10 vols. (Raleigh, 1958).

Shurtleff, N. B., ed. *Massachusetts Colonial Records: Records of the Governor and Company of the Massachusetts Bay Colony in New England, 1628–1686,* 5 vols. (Boston, 1853–59).

Shurtleff, N. B., and David Pulsifer, eds. *Records of the Colony of New Plymouth in New England,* 12 vols. (Boston: The Press of William White, 1855– 61).

Trumbull, J. H., and C. J. Hoadly, eds. *The Public Records of the Colony of Connecticut Prior to the Union with New Haven Colony, 1636–1776,* 15 vols. (Hartford: Brown & Parsons, 1850–90).

Votes and Proceedings of the House of Representatives of the Province of Pennsylvania, 1682–1776, 6 vols. (Philadelphia: B. Franklin and D. Hall, Printers, 1752–76).

Whitehead, W. A. et al., eds. *Archives of the State of New Jersey,* 33 vols. (Newark, 1880–1928).

Wynne, T. H., and W. S. Gilman, eds. *Colonial Records of Virginia (1619–1680)* (Richmond, 1874).

*This book was set in Adobe Garamond, a typeface
adapted by Robert Slimbach from the original
design of Claude Garamond, who, in the mid-sixteenth
century, established what is thought to be the first
type foundry. After his death in 1561 his types were
dispersed and his designs were widely adapted.
The beauty and legibility of Garamond's designs
have inspired contemporary type designers to
use them as models.*

Book design by Berry Binns
Typography by Brad Walrod, High Text Graphics
Printed and bound by Thomson-Shore, Dexter, Michigan